THE
OAK PARK
STUDIO OF
FRANK LLOYD
WRIGHT

LISA D. SCHRENK

THE OAK PARK STUDIO OF FRANK LLOYD WRIGHT

The University of Chicago Press   Chicago and London

This book is supported by a grant from the National Endowment of the Humanities and by funding from Norwich University and the University of Arizona.

The University of Chicago Press, Chicago 60637
The University of Chicago Press, Ltd., London

Published 2021
Printed in the United States of America

30 29 28 27 26 25 24 23 22 21   1 2 3 4 5

ISBN-13: 978-0-226-31894-3 (cloth)
ISBN-13: 978-0-226-31913-1 (e-book)
DOI: https://doi.org/10.7208/chicago/9780226319131.001.0001

Library of Congress Cataloging-in-Publication Data

Names: Schrenk, Lisa Diane, author.
Title: The Oak Park studio of Frank Lloyd Wright / Lisa D. Schrenk.
Description: Chicago : The University of Chicago Press, 2021. | Includes
    bibliographical references and index.
Identifiers: LCCN 2020026482 | ISBN 9780226318943 (cloth) |
    ISBN 9780226319131 (e-book)
Subjects: LCSH: Wright, Frank Lloyd, 1867–1959—Homes and haunts—
    Illinois—Oak Park. | Frank Lloyd Wright Studio (Oak Park, Ill.) |
    Architecture—Illinois—Oak Park.
Classification: LCC NA737.W7 S294 2020 | DDC 720.9773/11—dc23
LC record available at https://lccn.loc.gov/2020026482

♾ This paper meets the requirements of ANSI/NISO Z39.48-1992
(Permanence of Paper).

To John Thorpe, Don Kalec, and the rest of the early volunteers of the Frank Lloyd Wright Home and Studio Foundation who contributed countless hours to the restoration of Wright's Oak Park home and studio, preserving it for future generations.

Recognizing that architecture possesses two distinctive sides and that its highest development depends upon properly combining its artistic and commercial elements, Mr. Frank Lloyd Wright of Chicago has adopted to this end a rather unique plan. Mr. Wright has his business office at 1119 The Rookery, and has erected an architectural workshop containing draughting rooms, studio, architectural and private libraries, at the corner of Forest and Chicago avenues, in the pretty suburb of Oak Park. The perspective of the studio as one passes on the electric cars, presents an original and interesting study and reflects strongly the personality of its author, as is characteristic of all of Mr. Wright's work. A neat circular of announcement of this change contains a photogravure of the studio and also presents the motive of the architect in a salient comment to the effect that the practice of architecture as a profession has fine art as well as commercial elements; that these should be combined to their mutual benefit, not mixed to their detriment.

CONSTRUCTION NEWS, 9 FEBRUARY 1898

CONTENTS

P.1 Early rendering of the front of the Oak Park studio with diamond-paned windows, sculpture in the second-floor niches, wood fence, and broad entrance stair. John Lloyd Wright Collection. 1974.004.00005, Avery Architectural & Fine Arts Library, Columbia University, New York.

P.2 Oak Park studio drafting room interior showing the door to the reception hall with panels of the Heller house frieze on the fireplace, a rendering of a residential design for Aline Devin on the drawing board, and copies of classical sculptures, including a bust of Michelangelo's *Dying Slave* and *Venus de Milo*. The art glass window behind Venus also appears on page 64 of Robert C. Spencer Jr.'s 1900 *Architectural Review* article on Wright's work, ca. 1898–99. Photographer unknown. *House Beautiful*, December 1899. TAL 9506.0020, Avery Architectural & Fine Arts Library, Columbia University, New York. © 2020 Frank Lloyd Wright Foundation, Scottsdale, AZ. All rights reserved.

PREFACE

Standing in the doorway under the large triangular gable of his home a young boy with long curly hair clung tightly to his mother's hand. He wondered why she was in tears when his father in front of them was smiling as he waved goodbye. It was years later that the boy, Frank Lloyd Wright's youngest son Robert Llewellyn, understood what had taken place during the only "small child memory" he had of his father. The architect was turning his back on his Oak Park home and studio, a site where he had previously found tremendous fertile growth in both his personal and professional lives.

In happier times, Frank Lloyd Wright's suburban studio, connected to the boy's quaint, shingle style home by an unheated corridor, served as one of the most important sites in the development of modern architecture in the United States. The unusual-looking brick and shingle structure, at the intersection of a major artery into Chicago and one of Oak Park's most desirable residential streets, included a large two-story drafting room attached to an octagonal-shaped library by a reception hall with a business office in the rear. Wright decorated the interior spaces with native plants and other inspirational elements, from reproductions of classical sculptures to Japanese prints to his own furnishings and drawings. Within the walls of this unconventional workplace the architect incorporated exploratory practices introduced to him as a youth and lessons learned in the offices of early employers and from progressive colleagues into a personal design ideology appropriate to the rapidly changing cultural and societal conditions of an industrializing world. It was during the years he operated his Oak Park studio (between 1898 and 1909) that Wright achieved broad recognition as a leading American architect.

As a young designer sensitive to his environment, Wright strove to place himself in a setting that allowed him to continue the type of firsthand explorations of the world he had experienced as a child among the rolling hills of south central Wisconsin. This desire contributed to his flight from a series of professional settings early in his adult life—from the classrooms at the University of Wisconsin, from the architectural offices of his early employers and Steinway Hall colleagues in Chicago, and even from the peaceful tranquility of his own suburban home studio—eventually to return to Spring Green, Wisconsin, and the rural, familial landscape of his childhood.

The unusual office Wright built immediately north of his Oak Park home in 1897–98 formed the most significant stop on this developmental peregrination. The domestic environment of the home studio and its suburban surroundings offered a more integrated, organic setting for the production of his predominantly residential projects than would a downtown architectural office. It additionally presented a more feminized environment, making the studio a comfortable place for women, both as employees and as clients, in an era of a growing public female voice in the United States.[1] The presence of strong women and the close proximity to the architect's home and family played major roles in shaping the office.

Free of institutional constraints, Wright produced a personal work environment that served as a central site in the rise of a new modern form of architecture and in the furthering of design principles that came to define his work throughout a long and productive career. This advancement took place within a carefully conceived yet continually evolving setting. While design education in the United States was moving away from the tradition of training through apprenticeship to structured educational programs at universities, colleges, and technical schools, Wright fashioned his studio more like a French atelier or an English Arts and Crafts workshop, allowing for hands-on educational experiences.[2] Particularly during the early years, spirited dialogues and debates filled the office as it presented a vibrant learning environment for not only Wright but also the small community of designers working for him. The deep personal significance of the Oak Park home studio for the architect is, in part, reflected in the fact that he designed changes for the property even after his departure, including a major alteration of the studio in 1911, less dramatic modifications in the later 1910s and 1920s, and additional remodelings as late as 1956, just three years before his death.[3]

The Home and Studio Building

Only eighteen years after his last design changes for the building, the architect's suburban home and studio complex was deemed "architecturally confusing having lost the thrust of Wright's original inspiration."[4] Divided into six separate apartments, the building had deteriorated significantly and was filled with "green shag carpets, water-damaged walls, and uneven floors."[5] One note from the 1960s read, "There were layers of paint on the beautiful woods, the window frames in his former drafting room were painted

a garish red, some of the walls had flowered wallpaper on them."[6] Wright's son Lloyd was greatly dismayed that "so little of his childhood home remained visible through its various 'modernizations.'"[7]

Rumors of the building's imminent dismantling emerged, some of which speculated that its art glass windows were going to a museum in France and the home's magnificent playroom to a sheik.[8] At the time these stories seemed plausible, as a not very different fate had just befallen the Deephaven, Minnesota, residence Wright designed for Francis Little: its living room shipped off to the Metropolitan Museum of Art in New York City, a hallway to the Minneapolis Institute of Arts, and the library to the Allentown Art Museum in Pennsylvania.[9] The reports of the demise of Wright's home and studio galvanized community leaders to save the building. After two years of negotiations, a consortium of local banks under the name of the Oak Park Development Corporation bought the property in May 1974.[10] In the same year, the Frank Lloyd Wright Home and Studio Foundation was established to acquire, restore, and open the site for public tours.[11] The foundation transferred ownership of the property to the National Trust for Historic Preservation under an innovative co-stewardship arrangement with the trust leasing the site to the foundation, which was tasked with restoring and operating the building as a museum.[12]

P.3 Former Oak Park studio office before restoration, showing water-damaged walls and Nooker-era office furniture, light fixture, geometric wall treatment, and shag carpeting, as well as the post-1909 Roman brick fireplace and wood banding, ca. 1979. Photographer unknown. BL133-2, Frank Lloyd Wright Trust.

At the time, the site's historical significance was evident in the fact that in 1972 it became one of the first properties to meet all criteria for listing on the National Register of Historic Places: (1) it was associated with "events that have made a significant contribution to the broad patterns of our history" (the rise of a new form of modern American architecture known as the prairie house); (2) it was associated with "an event that significantly contributed to American history" (the early career of Frank Lloyd Wright); (3) it embodied "the distinctive characteristics of a type, period, or method of construction" or represented the work of a master or possessed high artistic values (both the residence and studio were important projects in Wright's oeuvre); and (4) it yielded "information important in history" (the complex provides great insight into Wright's early career).[13] In 1975 the building became a National Historic Landmark, and the foundation launched a meticulous, volunteer-led restoration.

Their aim was to bring the building back to its physical state in 1909, the last year Wright resided there.

I was hired as education director for the foundation near the end of the building's restoration phase to help make both the museum and the knowledge uncovered during the process more accessible to the public. Unfortunately, the physical restoration does not reveal the tremendous interactions between Wright and his employees and clients or other experiences and events relating to the studio, including the creation of some of the most remarkable works of modern American architecture. Neither does it fully address the relationship of Wright's home and family next door to his work environment. Furthermore, it does not disclose the dramatic evolution of the building over time, not only in the years that Wright worked and lived there but throughout its life. This book offers insight into these formidable stories.

I.1 Early photograph of the Oak Park studio exterior showing the original fence, planters, and stairs leading to the entrance, and a single level of diamond-paned balcony windows on the drafting room. The plaque identifying the building as Frank Lloyd Wright's is located below the east (left) Boulder sculpture. Photo taken after the ninety-degree rotation of that figure. Photographer unknown. *House Beautiful*, December 1899.

INTRODUCTION

The architect should place himself in an environment that conspires to develop the best there is in him. The first requisite is a place fitted and adapted to be protected and set aside from the distractions of the busy city. The worker is enabled on this basis to secure the quiet concentration of effort essential to the fullest success of a building project.

FRANK LLOYD WRIGHT (1898)

Frank Lloyd Wright's early residential studio in suburban Oak Park served as the nontraditional setting for the maturing of his architectural ideology, including the development of the prairie house. Unlike the more traditional, businesslike downtown offices of colleagues, the studio, located in a peaceful, bucolic community, had an informal homelike quality. Situated on the narrow strip of land between his existing home and Chicago Avenue, the building was originally separated from the street by a wood fence made of vertical spindles spaced by small wooden balls that encircled the lot.[1] Wright chose shingles and wood trim with a base of common brick, "the whole stained in quiet bronze tones," for the studio's exterior. It was a sensible choice that not only responded to the area's harsh winters but also helped to harmonize the structure with the shingle-style residence he had built as a home for his new wife, Catherine Lee "Kitty" Tobin Wright, next door in 1889.[2] When completed, the studio's formal design, contextually distinct from the other buildings in the community, served as an important advertisement for the architect, as it heralded that this was no ordinary business.

The unusual design of the studio reflected Wright's desire to make a clear stylistic break from the past. The majority of middle- and upper-class residences built during this era in the United States derived from the highly decorative Victorian styles, such as the Queen Anne, the Italianate, and the Colonial Revival. Repeated across the rapidly developing heartland in numerous variations, the facades of these houses typically consist of complex compositions of applied decorative elements and materials. Many emphasize verticality, with little regard to their surrounding context. Interiors tend not to reflect the intricacies of the exteriors but instead have simple arrangements of box-shaped rooms typically cluttered with commercially produced furnishings and objects. Wright referred to these ornate houses as "monogoria," a term he coined out of disgust.[3] In sharp contrast, the prairie houses developed in his studio characteristically exhibit a close relationship to their site by featuring a strong horizontal emphasis due to the fact that "every detail of elevation becomes exaggerated" in the flat landscape of the Midwest.[4]

Wright's Oak Park–era residences were not initially referred to as *prairie houses*. Early terms used to describe these works, as well as the architect and his peers, include *Chicago School* and *Chicago Group*. Wright used "Prairie" as early as 1901 in his article "Home in a Prairie Town." Horticulturist Wilhelm Miller coined the term *prairie style* around 1914 in reference to a midwestern school in landscape gardening. Like its architectural counterpart, the style reflected the open, horizontal spaces of the prairie. The term "Prairie School," used by Wright in a 1936 article, began to be applied by scholars in the 1950s to help distinguish between the commercial architecture of Louis Sullivan and his contemporaries, labeled *Chicago School*, and the predominantly residential architecture of Wright and his colleagues. This distinction was solidified in 1964 when Wilbert Hasbrouck began

I.2 Page of sketches by Frank Lloyd Wright showing an elaborate Victorian house on the upper left and a simpler shingle-style house vaguely reminiscent of his Oak Park home on the lower right, along with sketches of women and notations, including the price of beer, ca. late 1880s. Frank Lloyd Wright Trust.

publishing the quarterly *Prairie School Review* and further popularized by H. Allen Brooks with his seminal book *The Prairie School: Frank Lloyd Wright and His Midwest Contemporaries* (1972).[5]

Wright's mature prairie houses incorporate a limited number of decorative features, reflecting the perceived practical character of the region. Each element of the design serves as an integral part of the whole, with decoration not dependent on applied ornament but on the expressive characteristics of the building materials. One notable exception is the art glass windows that often include geometric representations of midwestern and garden varieties of plants, such as hollyhocks, purple asters, sumacs, and tulips.[6] Unlike more traditional Victorian houses, Wright's prairie house interiors typically contain a central hearth with rooms radiating outward, often in highly sophisticated spatial arrangements.[7]

Early in his career, Wright displayed a deep desire to be a leader in his field. By moving his studio to Oak Park, he progressed from a position as an equal in a

lively community of colleagues to the leader and focus of his own architectural workshop. At the time it was not unusual for solo architects to work out of their residences, as Wright himself had done during his early days in Oak Park. It was, however, rather uncommon for an in-home architecture office to be large enough to support more than one or two employees. At times, Wright had as many as seven and possibly more.

Within the walls of his studio's aesthetically pleasing two-story drafting room, the architect and his employees created over 175 building designs between 1898 and 1909, including notable prairie houses, such as the Susan Lawrence Dana residence in Springfield, Illinois, and the Frederick Robie house in Chicago, as well as an administrative headquarters for the Larkin Soap Company of Buffalo, New York, and Unity Temple, a church for his own congregation in Oak Park (for a list of projects, see appendix A).

A strong believer in lifelong learning, Wright continued his education by making numerous physical modifications to his property in addition to carrying

I.3 Rendering from the Wasmuth portfolio of the Willits residence, one of Frank Lloyd Wright's first fully-developed prairie house designs. Plate XXV, *Ausgeführte Bauten und Entwürfe von Frank Lloyd Wright* (Berlin: Verlegt bei Ernst Wasmuth A. G., 1910). Special Collections, J. Willard Marriott Library, University of Utah.

out drawing-board exercises and making exploratory forays into the countryside. The collaborative environment in the office, especially during the early years of its operations, significantly contributed to its educational character. Alterations and investigations resulted in a dynamic, ever-changing work environment. While some of the remodeling projects were largely functional or decorative, others were more experimental. Occasionally they led to changes integral to Wright's architecture and reappeared in later projects, such as the use of decorative wood banding and the incorporation of geometric abstractions of nature in designs for leaded glass windows.

The building's life as a studio can be divided into

I.4 Portrait of Frank Lloyd Wright with architectural model. Photographer unknown. H275, Frank Lloyd Wright Trust.

three major phases defined by Wright's own architectural development, office procedures, and relationships with associates. From 1898 to 1902 he was trying to establish himself as an independent architect as he moved away from the historical experimentations that characterized his work in the mid-1890s and more fully adapted exploratory processes he was exposed to as a youth to building design. Facets of these fundamental practices, which focused largely on nature and geometry, were also present in Wright's Oak Park home as they were incorporated into his children's educational activities there. Several of the academically trained architects working in the studio then who were close to Wright in age were gifted in their own right— among them Walter Burley Griffin and Marion Mahony. Wright had continuous fertile interactions with his talented employees, as well as with colleagues outside of the office. Major studio commissions in these years include residences for Frank Thomas, Ward Willits, Susan Lawrence Dana, and Arthur Heurtley. The studio building provided Wright with an additional design project not constrained by client tastes or desires. Most of the alterations he made to the building during this period, however, were relatively minor refinements.

The second phase, between 1903 and mid-1905, was an extremely hectic time for Wright as he developed into an established designer while overseeing his active office. In addition to continuing to produce prairie

I.5 Studio drafting room with added wood banding on the balcony. Copies of *Venus de Milo* and other sculptures, plants, and a banner with a Rudyard Kipling quote, in addition to books and architectural drawings, decorate the room, ca. 1900. Photographer unknown. TAL 9505.014, Avery Architectural & Fine Arts Library, Columbia University, New York.

houses for clients in the Chicago area, the studio carried out several large projects connected to Buffalo businessman Darwin Martin. The most significant involved the design of the Larkin Company Administration Building. To meet the increased workload, Wright hired additional employees with various levels of training and experience, resulting in a growing division of office labor. He also augmented his staff with part-time and temporary hires. During these years he continued his personal explorations of nature and ge-

ometry and urged his employees to do the same. He also encouraged the studio staff to experience other sources of inspiration, including the 1904 St. Louis World's Fair. However, within the walls of the studio lively dialogues began to ebb in these years as the architect focused more on his own continuing development and left much of the educating of his newer employees to other experienced designers. Even with major project deadlines looming, Wright undertook significant renovations to the office in 1903 and again in 1904, such as installing a new floor as he explored the qualities of magnesite (a form of magnesium carbonate) as a concrete binder for use in the Larkin building and other projects. His three-month absence while on a trip to Japan in early 1905 derailed office momentum, contributing to growing tensions between the architect and several of his more advanced employees, in particular Griffin, who had been entrusted with running the studio in his absence.

The last major phase of the studio began after Wright returned from the Orient and was marked by Griffin's departure in early 1906. The edifying conversations that filled the studio in earlier years further dwindled as the architect began to hire primarily younger and less experienced male designers. This made it easier for him to mold his employees to meet the specific needs of his own design procedures and ideas. Except for a few commissions Wright found particularly interesting or challenging, such as Unity Temple, the architect became less engaged in studio operations, often delegating significant design responsibilities, particularly on more mundane residential projects. While Wright continued to make some alterations to his Oak Park property, the changes tie less clearly to his architectural development. In many ways, Unity Temple, just a couple blocks from the studio, took over as the main setting for his design explorations. During this period, Wright increasingly grew restless with both his private and professional lives. Closing the studio in 1909, he left his family and suburban community and headed to Europe to reflect upon his early career as he prepared a major retrospective portfolio of the work produced in the Oak Park studio.

Sources of Information

The numerous changes Wright made to the studio building and the activities that took place there are documented by physical evidence, historic drawings and photographs, and written sources, including letters by studio member Charles White. In November 1903, for example, White wrote that Wright "is certainly the most impractical man—is way behind in his work, but calmly takes seven weeks to alter his office

and lets the work wait."[8] The following May, White wrote, "The studio is again torn up by the annual repairs and alterations. Twice a year, Mr. W. rearranges and changes the different rooms. He says he has gotten more education in experimenting on his own premises, than in any other way."[9] Wright also continually changed how the studio appeared in renderings. Over time he presented the building as lower and longer in proportion, making it more reflective of the horizontal lines of the midwestern prairie. He also manipulated dimensions in some of the interior renderings, such as a section of the drafting room published in June 1900, in which the balcony railing as represented would be just two feet high.[10]

Attempting to create a clear picture of life in the Oak Park studio and the evolution of its design presents a challenge. Secondary sources often contain inaccuracies, and important office documents have been lost.[11] Numerous alterations are known only through fragmentary evidence such as architectural drawings, historic photographs, contemporary articles, physical markings, and recorded memories of Wright, members of his family, and those who worked in or visited the studio. These recollections, however, are often murky and, in some cases, include deliberate errors. Marion Mahony, Barry Byrne, William Gray Purcell, and John Lloyd Wright, among others, wrote private and public accounts, sometimes decades later, that contain questionable details. In 1947 Purcell wrote to a colleague that he had just run across a forgotten diary and reported being "chagrined to find, in my own words, accounts which differed very much from my vivid memory of those events."[12] On several occasions, different firsthand references to the studio directly conflict. For example, in a 1963 article, Byrne claimed that "the apprentices rarely saw architectural publications" in it.[13] In contrast, Wright's son Lloyd remembered, "Copies of the English arts and crafts magazine, *The Studio*, were to be found in the office and drafting studio. This publication was later joined by American arts and crafts magazines—*The House Beautiful* and, after 1901, by Gustav Stickley's *The Craftsman*."[14] His brother David, meanwhile, recalled that the library always had current magazines, such as "*Atlantic Monthly, Harpers*, etc."[15]

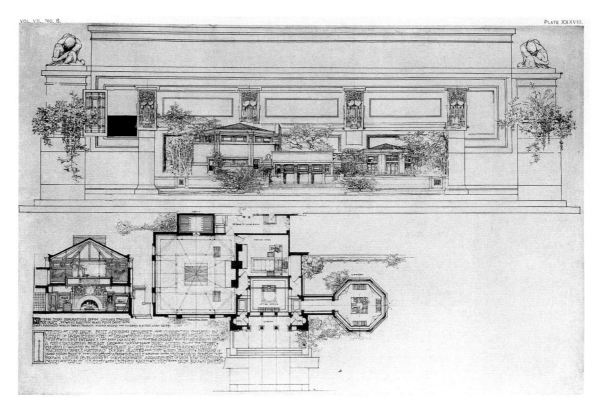

I.6 Plate of the Oak Park studio published in *Architectural Review* showing mirrored Boulder sculptures in elevation and unrealistically low balcony walls in the section of the drafting room. The plan includes the original angled walls in the reception hall shown in figure 2.8. "Studio of Frank Lloyd Wright, Oak Park, IL." Plate XXXVIII, Robert C. Spencer Jr., "The Work of Frank Lloyd Wright," *Architectural Review*, June 1900.

A master raconteur, Wright later claimed he deliberately chose honest arrogance over hypocritical humility and became an expert in self-mythologizing, especially in recounting his early life and career.[16] Several years after he died, daughter Catherine observed that her father "seemed to prefer to ignore or improvise if fancy suited the occasion better than fact."[17]

The basic details of Wright's early career evolved even in his own accounts. Barry Byrne warned early Prairie School scholar Mark Peisch that he should avoid taking the "master's" (Wright's) statements as being factual.[18] Byrne later wrote that "there is so much in it [Wright's autobiography] with which I am in entire disagreement that I can only think of the lesser parts as one does of the less good qualities in a valued friend."[19] His architectural partner, George Elmslie, was not so generous, declaring Wright "an unprincipled egotist, a liar and a cheat," referencing the lack of truthfulness in the 1932 edition of *An Autobiography*.[20]

Wright was also reported to have altered documents. One of the Taliesin apprentices witnessed him "rubbing out dates on certain drawings and substituting others," while historian Grant Manson recalled watching the architect "with swift strokes of a soft pencil" redraw a facade detail on a drawing of his unrealized American Luxfer Prism building, "obliterating a forty-four-year-old record."[21] I myself spent much of a day in the Frank Lloyd Wright Archives at Taliesin West correcting dates on photographs of the Oak Park home and studio, some that appeared intentionally misdated.

While a complete picture of life in Frank Lloyd Wright's suburban studio cannot be achieved, through exploring what information does survive, we can better understand what the place meant to its owner and others who lived, worked, and visited the building. In doing so, we can assess more clearly the historical significance of the site in the development of Wright's career.

1
ROOTS OF THE OAK PARK STUDIO

Education and Exploration

If I were making a plea for the kindergarten idea in education, I could adduce no better living example of its value as a factor in the development of the artistic faculties than by referring to [Wright].

ROBERT C. SPENCER JR. (1900)

More significant than any other facet of the environment in Wright's Oak Park studio was an emphasis on personal development through self-exploration. Among the company of like-minded architects both within and beyond the studio, Wright strove to develop a modern form of architecture reflective of the social, political, and technological changes taking place around him. Like other forward-looking designers, by the time his suburban office opened in 1898 Wright had largely rejected the use of historic building forms, especially neoclassicism, which had experienced a wave of popularity after the 1893 World's Columbian Exposition. Instead he looked more specifically for design inspiration in nature, geometry, and music, areas of study introduced to him in his youth and reinforced in the years prior to the opening of the studio. This included during his time at Adler and Sullivan and, after beginning his own practice, while working in shared offices downtown with other young progressive colleagues and in the small, second-floor workroom in his own suburban residence. While Wright's independent projects of the mid-1890s suggest a growing interest in nature and geometry for the basis of his architecture, it was within the walls of his new studio that they informed a fully realized vein of modern architecture most clearly revealed in the prairie house. While Wright's core design influences and early career have been addressed in numerous writings, this chapter specifically explores major roots of the architect's early independent career in relation to the creation and working conditions of the Oak Park studio and the building designs produced there.

Wisconsin: Music and Nature

Born into a large family of educators and freethinkers in rural Wisconsin, Wright was taught early the benefits of learning from personal experiences, in particular from explorations of the natural world, but also from various facets of culture, including music and the arts. Both of Wright's parents shaped his core views. Although his father, William Carey Wright, a circuit-riding minister and music teacher, left his family in 1884, Frank shared his father's strong sense of self-assurance and an ability to carry out a variety of tasks with relative ease. Both men also possessed restless souls and often found themselves in nontraditional situations and precarious financial circumstances.[1] That restlessness contributed to Wright moving his architectural office to Oak Park from Chicago and later his need to depart his suburban situation.

One of the most significant gifts William Wright passed on to his son was a love of Beethoven and Bach. As William played the piano far into the night, Frank learned pieces by heart, the musical structures echoing in his mind. He wrote that his father taught him "to see a symphony as an edifice—of sound."[2] Later, Wright attempted to incorporate the structure and ornament of music into the architectural designs he produced in Oak Park. He declared that he often heard classical music in his head when working and thought Beethoven's compositions formed "a delightful, inspiring school," observing that the composer's "rhythms are integral to those of Nature!"[3] When the architect needed inspiration for a particularly difficult design

1.1 Frank Lloyd Wright in a bathrobe playing piano in his Oak Park home living room, with a copy of *Venus de Milo* to the left and a bust of Beethoven and other decorative objects on top of the piano and on a heavy arts-and-crafts–style table to the right. Photographer unknown. H230, Gift of Elizabeth Ingraham. Frank Lloyd Wright Trust.

problem he was working on in his drafting room, he would slip off to his home next door to play the piano.

Wright later wrote that education was his mother's passion and that his maternal family was "imbued with the idea of education as salvation."[4] Anna Lloyd Wright stressed to her son the value of hands-on explorations of nature, reinforcing this belief during his Oak Park days when she lived in her own house next door. The family closely read the words of John Ruskin, the leading English art critic of the era, following his belief that one should study nature and turn to it for inspiration.[5] Wright recalled that he learned to display flowers as he did at his Oak Park property from his mother, who would "take the stems long, or the branches, and would arrange them not, as was the mode, in variegated bunches, but freely and separately—never too many together" in a glass vase that showed the stems and water.[6]

Wright himself came to address nature with a capital *N* to signify that it was there where he found his God. "Nature," he explained near the end of his life, "is all the body of God we mortals will ever see."[7] He

spent most summers during his formative years roaming among the trees, brooks, and stones around Spring Green, learning to "know the ground-plan of the region in every line and feature."[8] As a teenager carrying out agricultural chores, Wright began "to *experience* what he heard, touched or saw" in nature, becoming particularly fascinated with the varied structural and formal qualities of plants.[9] He soon began linking the organic patterns found in nature to musical rhythms, which became engrained within his body during outdoor physical labor and later through the use of geometric forms, which became more sophisticatedly integrated in his architectural designs during his Oak Park years.

Froebel: Geometry and Nature

Wright's mother and schoolteacher aunts also shaped his early understanding of the world by exposing him to the educational ideas of the eminent nineteenth-century German educator Friedrich Froebel, the originator of kindergarten.[10] Anna Wright first exposed

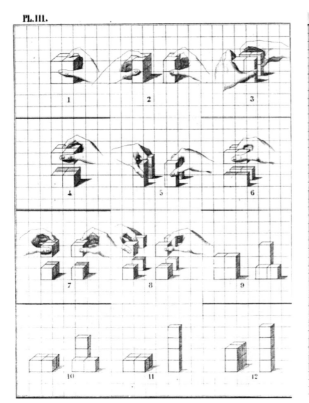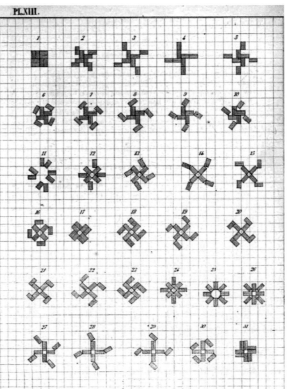

1.2 Illustrations of Froebel exercises showing the manipulation of the blocks, including the resulting "pinwheeling" forms that influenced some of Wright's designs. Plates 3 and 13, *J.-F. Jacobs, Manuel Pratique des Jardins D'Enfants* (Brussels: F. Claassen, 1859).

1.3 View of the Oak Park home playroom toward the *Fisherman and the Genie* mural with prints, including of the cathedral complex at Pisa and the Colosseum, and copies of classical sculpture, toy sailboats, and bowling pins on the shelf. A large circle and other barely visible lines mark the floor for Froebel kindergarten group activities, ca. late 1890s. Photographer unknown. Walter Willcox Papers, box 6, folder PH110, Special Collections and University Archives, University of Oregon Libraries, Eugene, Oregon.

her son to the Froebel system after she observed a demonstration of it at the 1876 Centennial Exposition in Philadelphia.[11] At the time Wright was nine, significantly older than the typical child being introduced to the materials. Like members of the Lloyd Jones clan, Froebel believed that understanding nature through firsthand explorations was a quintessential aspect of a child's education.[12]

Froebel's educational program reflects his belief in a direct relationship between the geometric handiwork of God and the development of healthy children and societies. Designed to strengthen a child's natural inclinations and enrich his or her environment, the Froebel method allows children to self-discover elements of color, texture, pattern, and form through a systematic exploration of abstract design activities. Structured interactions with materials referred to as *gifts* and *occupations* are intended to cultivate a child's ability to observe, reason, express, and create.[13] Froebel designed most of the gifts to be assembled and then reassembled on a grid in a variety of two-and three-dimensional compositions that usually exhibit strict forms of symmetry.[14] The occupations, meanwhile, incorporate materials, such as paper, sticks, peas, and clay, that are irreversibly transformed through craft-like activities, such as folding, weaving, cutting, and modeling. The gift and occupation experiences often lead to group activities, such as songs, stories, circle games, or plays. Actual gardening and observing plants form other important components of the curriculum.

Reflecting his early work organizing crystals at the Mineralogical Museum of the University of Berlin, Froebel promoted the idea that organic and inorganic processes alike developed "outwards from within, while striving to maintain balance between inner and outer forces" and that there should be a harmonious sense of unity between the parts and the whole. On a more spiritual level, the idea of interconnectedness involves the child developing a sense of unity with "God" as manifested in nature. Froebel's ideas strongly shaped Wright's view of the world and his architecture. He admitted that he "became susceptible to constructive patterns evolving in everything I saw. I learned to 'see' this way and when I did, I did not care to draw casual incidentals of Nature, I wanted to design."[15]

This exploratory approach to learning strongly reverberated within the walls of Wright's Oak Park property. As early as 1892, Wright's wife Catherine ran a small Froebel kindergarten with neighbor Kate Gerts in the family's home attended by the Wrights' three oldest children.[16] The presence of this kindergarten had a major impact on the architect, who carried out his own Froebel explorations at the time. For example, son John remembered his father buying colored gas balloons by the dozen and then arranging and rearranging them for hours.[17]

The Office of Joseph Lyman Silsbee

Wright never graduated from high school and completed only two terms at the University of Wisconsin.[18] By early 1887, at the age of nineteen, he had departed for Chicago, where his informal design education continued in apprenticeships first with Joseph Lyman Silsbee and later in the prestigious office of Adler and Sullivan.

Wright claimed in his autobiography that he was hired as an unknown entity by Silsbee, but it is highly likely that Wright moved to Chicago specifically to work for him.[19] The Lloyd Jones family had previously commissioned building designs from Silsbee, including a new church for his uncle Jenkin in Chicago and a chapel in Spring Green. Nevertheless, Wright's description of what specifically attracted him to that office provides clues to aspects of his own suburban workplace. These include the physical work environment and the musical and artistic interests and backgrounds of colleagues. He reported that he "liked the atmosphere" at Silsbee's better than those of other offices, taking particular note of Silsbee's sketches on the wall. He also perceived "artist-musician" Cecil Corwin, a fellow employee, as a kindred spirit.[20]

While Silsbee's architecture tended to follow popular tastes, his use of simplified forms echoed in residential designs later produced in Wright's studio. Also significant during his time at Silsbee's was the immense talent of other young progressive architects there. In addition to Corwin were George Washington Maher and George Grant Elmslie, both of whom became prominent Prairie School architects. These enthusiastic young designers learned from each other as well as from their employer, much as Wright's employees did in Oak Park a decade later. An additional important element of his time with Silsbee was his exposure to Japanese art, of which Silsbee was an important collector.[21]

Adler and Sullivan

Ever restless, Wright soon began searching for a more challenging and exciting position. He found this in the office of Adler and Sullivan, which he entered early in 1888. At the time the prominent office was busy preparing drawings for the Auditorium Building, a massive multifunctional structure that included a hotel, a four-thousand-seat theater, and offices and shops. Upon its completion in 1889 the firm moved into the sixteenth and seventeenth floors of the building's tower. Wright had done well enough during his first years with the firm to warrant the position of head draftsman and was given a glassed-off work space facing Lake Michigan at the end of a large two-story rectangular draft-ing room with balcony.[22] While few records remain documenting the daily interactions within the firm's drafting room, more is known about Wright's close relationship with his *Lieber Meister,* Louis Sullivan.

Building upon the ideas of American Transcen-dentalists and architectural theorists including John Ruskin and Eugène Emmanuel Viollet-le-Duc, Louis Sullivan, like Wright a few years later, rejected his-torical European precedents in favor of nature and functional needs to achieve more appropriate design solutions for the United States in the industrial age. Sullivan too had spent much of his childhood explor-ing nature and integrated Froebel's ideas in his archi-tecture. In 1887 he proclaimed believing in an "expan-sive and rhythmic growth, in a building, of a single, germinal impulse or idea, which shall permeate the mass and its every detail with the same spirit, to such an extent, indeed, that it would be difficult to deter-mine … which is the more important."[23] This Froebel-like progression of manipulated forms is particularly visible in his plant-based ornamentation.

According to Wright, Sullivan often gave him infor-mal lectures late into the night on topics that included nature, music, and literature as well as building de-sign, from which the young architect found "encour-agement" for his "already forming" ideas.[24] In a 1900 speech, Sullivan expressed his distaste for formal archi-tectural education, directing young designers to avoid books and strive to form their own judgment, looking to nature for inspiration.[25] His words were taken to heart not only by Wright but also by at least one of the eventual architects in Wright's studio who was in at-tendance. Walter Burley Griffin, in fact, recalled that Sullivan's words "completely changed his life."[26] Of the relationship between nature and education in archi-tecture, Sullivan subsequently wrote: "Kindergarten has brought bloom to the mind of many a child.… But there is alas! no *architectural kindergarten*—a garden of the heart wherein the simple, obvious truths, the truths that any child might consent to, are brought fresh to the faculties and are held to be good because they are true and real."[27]

An architectural "kindergarten," where truths are not only passed on from "master" to disciples but also achieved through independent childlike explorations of nature and geometry, underlay the communal ex-ploratory atmosphere that Wright strove to achieve in his lively suburban studio. His first workplace in Oak Park, a second-story room under the large gable of the shingle-style residence he built in 1889 while still in the office of Adler and Sullivan, however, was just for himself.

The Oak Park Home

Wright's decision to move to Oak Park from his uncle's neighborhood on the South Side of Chicago mirrored the movement of millions of people in industrializing countries in the late nineteenth century.[28] Recounting the dirt and the din of the city the architect later wrote: "Chicago! Immense gridiron of noisy streets. Dirty.… Heavy traffic crossing both ways at once, managing somehow: torrential noise. A stupid thing, that grid-iron: cross-currents of horses, trucks, street cars grind-ing on hard rails mingling with streams of human be-ings in seeming confusion and clamor.… The gray, soiled river with its mist of steam and smoke, was the only beauty. And that smelled to heaven."[29]

Rudyard Kipling, whom Wright celebrated by dis-playing a quote from one of the author's writings in large letters on a face of the studio balcony, had a sim-ilar impression of Chicago in 1889, writing: "This place is the first American city I have encountered. It holds rather more than a million of people with bodies, and stands on the same sort of soil as Calcutta. Having seen it, I urgently desire never to see it again. It is inhabited by savages. Its water is the water of the Hooghly, and its air is dirt."[30]

Some, like Wright, chose to flee the congestion, poor sanitation conditions, and high noise and crime levels for developing parklike suburbs linked to the central business district by regional transportation sys-tems. Nine miles west of the Chicago Loop, Oak Park, with its fresh air, trees, and open stretches of prairie, was becoming a fashionable middle-class community. By 1909, the village offered paved roads, streetlights, a water and sewage disposal system, telephones, police

1.4 View north on Oak Park Avenue from Lake Street in Oak Park showing paved streets and sidewalks, 1912. Philander Barclay Collection, Special Collections, Oak Park Public Library Special Collections.

and fire protection, good schools, a library, an opera house, and even an innovative district hot water heating system.[31] Oak Park's suburban lifestyle, which for many included living in homes on large residential lots and participating in community-focused events and organizations, was typical of other Chicago suburbs for which Wright went on to design residences.

Wright's mother, Anna, likely encouraged her son to settle in Oak Park after his wedding to Catherine Tobin in 1889.[32] To be closer to her son and other members of the Lloyd-Jones family, Anna herself had moved to the Oak Park home of family friend Augusta Jane Chapin, Universalist minister of the suburb's

Unity Church.[33] The newlyweds joined her in Chapin's red-brick residence on Forest Avenue to "see if Oak Park was really the place" they wanted to call home.[34] At the time the village was flourishing, with around four thousand residents.[35] The tranquil community offered an ideal setting for Wright and his new bride to build a house and start a family. The architect found the neighborhood particularly desirable due to its ancient oaks and maturing landscapes and its convenient rail line to downtown. It also presented a continual supply of potential clients.

Wright acquired a plot of land marked by "a tangle of oaks and wild vines" on the corner of Forest and

1.5 Members of Wright's family on the porch of the Oak Park home, ca. 1890. From left to right: Jenkin Lloyd Jones, his wife Susan, Wright's sister Jane, Catherine Wright holding son Lloyd, Wright's mother Anna Lloyd Wright, Wright's sister Maginel, Frank Lloyd Wright, and Jenkin's daughter Mary. Photographer unknown. H92, Frank Lloyd Wright Trust.

Chicago Avenues from Scottish landscape gardener John Blair.[36] The grounds featured beautiful trees, including black walnuts, catalpas, syringas (lilacs), giant clubs, and tulip and ginkgo trees, along with native shrubs, such as viburnums, hawthorns, sumac, barberry, and bridal wreath.[37] Wright's mother bought Blair's Eastlake-style house immediately to the east. While Forest Avenue was one of the first streets paved in Oak Park, Chicago Avenue at the time was still a dirt road. An open expanse of flat prairie extended to the north. Wright situated his new residence close to the southern border of the lot, leaving room for a future office along the east–west street.[38]

When Wright moved to Oak Park in 1889, he was still employed by Adler and Sullivan. With funds borrowed from Sullivan, he constructed a small "honeymoon" cottage, going $1,800 over his $5,000 budget.[39] Wright was to repay the loan plus 6 percent interest over the next five years.[40] The front facade with its large triangular gable above canted bays on the first floor recalled Bruce Price's large gabled, shingle-style Chandler and Kent cottages built in Tuxedo Park, New York, several years earlier. Wright likely became familiar with the designs through their inclusion in George William Sheldon's lavish, taste-defining, two-volume *Artistic Country-Seats: Types of Recent American Villa*

1.6 Frank Lloyd Wright reading on the front veranda of the Oak Park home, ca. 1889. Photographer unknown. TAL 8901.0035, Avery Architectural & Fine Arts Library, Columbia University, New York.

1.7 Open prairie near the Wrights' home in the Fair Oaks District of Oak Park, ca. 1896. *Oak Park, 1896.* Oak Park River Forest Historical Society.

1.8 Oak Park home with the original "saddlebag" window formation in the pediment, ca. 1889. Photographer unknown. H158, from scrapbook of John Lloyd Wright. Gift of Elizabeth Ingraham. Frank Lloyd Wright Trust.

and Cottage Architecture with Instances of Country Club-Houses (1886).[41] While originally Wright's second floor had a rather awkward "saddle-bag" composition, with windows framing a section of shingled wall under a central arched pane, the architect soon altered this into a more cohesive Palladianesque form.

Inside, large openings unified the main public rooms. The entrance hall featured an overly grand staircase that cascaded to a series of broad lower stairs designed to impress and lead potential clients upwards to Wright's second-floor home office. A band of plaster panels copied from the frieze of the Hellenistic Altar of Zeus at Pergamon and topped by dentils around the upper part of the walls (see figure E.10) not only provided decoration but also signaled to visitors a level of aesthetic taste.[42]

An inglenook in the living room, soon marked by the family's motto, "Truth is Life," and a related quote

carved over the hearth served as both the physical and spiritual center of the residence.[43] Wright located the dining room to the north of the inglenook and the kitchen to the south. In addition to his home office across the front of the house, the second floor consisted of a bedroom, a bathroom, and a nursery. Wright initially furnished his dwelling with popular Victorian fittings, such as a bearskin rug, ferns, and a plethora of decorative objects. As his aesthetic senses matured, he replaced many of the furnishings with Oriental objects and simple arts-and-crafts-styled furniture, including pieces of his own design. Son John remembered "scattered vases filled with leaves and wild flowers, massive fireplaces seemed to be everywhere. Here and there a Yourdes [Ghiordes rug] of rare beauty covered a floor. A Persian lantern, samovars, windows which met and tuned the corners.... [T]hese made the house that was our home."[44]

1.9 Oak Park home living room. View toward the central inglenook and into the original dining room, which was later used as a study. The photograph was taken after Frank Lloyd Wright replaced the bearskin rug in the living room with Oriental and Turkish carpets and eliminated some of the more ornate decorations. Photographer unknown. TAL 8901.0022, Avery Architectural & Fine Arts Library, Columbia University, New York.

1.10 View from the master bedroom into the front room of the Oak Park home that Wright used as his early studio, ca. late 1890s. The bust in the front room appears in later photographs of the playroom and studio drafting room (see figures 1.3 and 4.6). Photographer unknown. TAL 8901.0012, Avery Architectural & Fine Arts Library, Columbia University, New York.

Wright's Early Architectural Offices

In the second-floor home office, between 1891 and 1893, while still employed by Adler and Sullivan, Wright designed approximately ten residences on his own time later known as the "bootleg houses." While completing this work, he began realizing the benefits of working at home. He could squeeze in a few extra hours while still being available for his family. The arrangement also allowed him to work within the setting for which he was primarily designing.

In 1893, Wright established his own practice, design-ing primarily suburban dwellings. While he carried out work at home, he also opened a studio downtown with his friend Cecil Corwin in the Schiller Building, an Adler and Sullivan commission that Wright later claimed to have had a large hand in designing.[45] The office environment provides clues to his early notions about working conditions that he later incorporated into the design of his suburban studio. Wright and Corwin each had their own drafting room and shared a business office. The central room, which held a large square table with chests of drawers for legs, was decorated with objects, both artistic and natural. Fresh-cut

1.11 Nathan Moore residence with neighborhood children playing on the balustrade. Photographer unknown. William Gray Purcell Papers, Northwest Architectural Archives, University of Minnesota.

flowers usually filled a glass globe on the table, preferably arranged in the naturalistic manner Wright learned from his mother.

The Schiller Building office, like the architect's later Oak Park studio, featured skylights and figurative sculpture. According to Wright, the plain-walled vestibule had a glass ceiling providing indirect lighting and large oak chests topped with Indian statuettes by noted artist Herman MacNeil. Stylish plate-glass doors at the entrance and between the vestibule and the shared room created a sense of transparency.[46] Wright met with clients and worked on some of his earliest independent commissions in the Schiller office, including the William Winslow house with its classically symmetrical front facade and Sullivanesque details; the Dutch Colonial Frederick Bagley house, the French Chateauesque Chauncey L. Williams house, the Tudor-styled Nathan Moore house, and likely the playroom addition for his own home.

Although Wright had previously published several of his "bootleg" designs under Corwin's name, including the Blossom, McArthur, and Harlan houses, his officemate probably did not directly contribute to their design or to any other project of his.[47] Wright stated later that he and Corwin were not partners per se but that they did often discuss design ideas.[48] This resulted in great similarities in their architecture at the time, such as between Wright's Bagley house and Corwin's H. G. Mitchell house in Racine, Wisconsin, which include similar gambrel roofs, dormers, and entries located on a long facade. Corwin's design also included a corner octagonal bay like those Wright incorporated in the McArthur residence and a round entrance porch with Ionic columns reminiscent of the Blossom house.[49]

On occasion Wright employed other people while in the Schiller Building. German-born Louis Guenzel, who had previously worked for Adler and Sullivan,

1.12 Portrait of Marion Mahony. Photographer unknown. Marion Mahony Griffin, "The Magic of America," ca. 1937–49, IV.11.251. © New-York Historical Society.

ists, Mahony had much in common with her employer. She became the first designer to work for Wright long term, including much of the time the Oak Park studio was in operation.[54]

Wright initially paid Mahony a low ten dollars a week to work on drawings for the Francis Apartments. She later wrote that he consoled her by giving her the meaningless title of "superintendent of the office force," of which she was likely the only real member.[55] Still, she was able to contribute to all stages of design production. While Mahony went on to produce spectacular renderings for projects in the suburban studio, Wright relied upon other designers and artists, including Paul Lautrup, Ernest Albert, Hugh Garden, Charles Corwin, and Robert C. Spencer Jr., to produce presentation drawings of his projects in these years.[56]

Steinway Hall and Other Later Downtown Business Offices

In 1897 Wright moved his downtown office to a much more vibrant environment that had a direct impact on the design aesthetic of the Oak Park studio. Dwight Perkins, who had transferred his own practice to the top floor of his new Steinway Music Hall, invited Wright and architects Robert C. Spencer Jr. and Myron Hunt to share its spacious loft.[57]

Similar in age, the four designers all had experience in prominent American architectural firms and shared relatively similar views on the direction of modern building design.[58] Additional like-minded architects also joined in.[59] While some, like the brothers Irving and Allen Pond, worked in their own quarters, many "officed co-operatively" in the big loft, which Perkins subdivided with wood and paper partitions.[60] Steinway Hall developed into a lively place that permitted informal discussions and debates over design ideologies and concepts. Latecomer Roy Lippincott recalled: "We were all good friends, in and out of each other's offices, as though they were our own. We all knew about the work the others were doing, worked for each other from time to time as pressures necessitated."[61]

Most of the designers, including Wright, sought to realize architectural solutions for the modern era. They found inspiration in the English Arts and Crafts Movement and the writings of A. W. N. Pugin, John

may have worked for him early on.[50] At some point between 1894 and 1895 George Kikutaro Shimoda, an architect trained in Tokyo under Josiah Conder and an early link to Japanese design and culture for Wright, entered the office.[51] Shimoda's time there, however, was brief. Wright said that he ended up firing the Japanese architect for "speaking obliquely of a lady who got into the habit of leaving flowers in the glass globe on the big office table."[52]

In addition to his willingness to hire foreigners, Wright also employed female designers at a time when most of his colleagues would not. Around 1895 he hired Anna Cordelia Hicks, although it is not clear if her responsibilities were architectural or clerical. She departed for Boston in 1896 where, likely on office colleague Marion Lucy Mahony's encouragement, she studied architecture and mathematics at the Massachusetts Institute of Technology.[53] Mahony had also joined the office in 1895, shortly after her graduation from the architectural program at MIT. Raised by teachers and surrounded by progressive educators, intellectuals, religious reformers, feminists, and art-

STEINWAY HALL, VAN BUREN STREET, CHICAGO.
Dwight & Perkins, Architect; Prof. Lewis J. Johnson, Designer of Steel Work.

1.13 Steinway Hall. *Engineering News* 34 (17 October 1895): 251.

Ruskin, William Morris, and other aestheticians who were reacting against the social evils of factory work and the shoddy quality of mass-produced machine goods while romantically calling for a return to good "moralistic" values and the working conditions of the preindustrial medieval guilds.[62] They tended to prefer simple, handcrafted designs that celebrated the concept of the House Beautiful.[63] A number of English practitioners, including Walter Crane, Charles Ashbee, and Joseph Twyman, brought the ideas of the movement to Chicago in the 1890s through lectures or exhibitions.

Many of the Steinway Hall colleagues were members of the "Eighteen," a group of progressive architects who met occasionally to discuss architecture and other topics.[64] Like Wright's architecture, their work reflected a unity in design aesthetics, as well as a strong preference for simplified linear forms that celebrated

the innate beauty of natural materials. This favoring of purer, cleaner forms became a hallmark of the prairie style (what Wright called "the New School of the Middle West"), which arose from this milieu.[65]

Like London, Chicago was a major industrial city that became a prominent center for the Arts and Crafts Movement as Wright and his colleagues found meaning in its ideas.[66] Most of the architects in Steinway Hall became members of the Chicago Arts and Crafts Society. Founded in 1897 at Hull House, one of the first social settlement houses in the United States, the society promoted quality workmanship through various activities.[67] As part of a program of social reform that used educational and artistic activities to uplift the poor and working class of the city, Hull House itself offered classes in literature, history, art, and domestic activities, as well as free concerts and lectures on current issues. Many of these activities were made possible through the work of volunteers, including Catherine Wright.[68]

Members of the Chicago Arts and Crafts Society—more than 125 educators, businessmen, lawyers, artists, and architects, including Wright—considered "the present state of factories and the workmen therein, and to devise lines of development which shall retain the machine in so far as it relieves the workman from drudgery, and tends to perfect the product."[69] In response, Wright delivered his essay "The Art and Craft of the Machine" to a small audience at Hull House in 1901.[70] While people like Ruskin and Morris wrote of the evils of machines, Wright and his colleagues believed that, with properly trained operators and as long as they did not dominate the workman, machines could become integral to the development of good modern design.

A number of the designers at Steinway Hall also held prominent positions in the Chicago Architectural Club, which promoted professional development through discussions, debates, competitions, and annual exhibitions.[71] While Wright never became an official member of the organization, he used it to network, publicize his projects, and promote his ideas even after he moved his studio to Oak Park.[72] His growing standing was reflected in the fact that the club's 1901 annual catalog prominently featured his "Art and Craft of the Machine" essay. At the exhibition the following year, organizers gave Wright his own gallery, which featured sixty-five items highlighting architectural and decorative designs produced in the Oak Park studio, including drawings, photographs, models, copper and bronze vases filled with native grasses and weeds, leaded glass, furniture, and a marble font.[73] Wright also received a fourteen-page section in the related catalog that highlighted the Oak Park studio and a number of his earlier designs.[74]

Wright's Early Architectural Development

The period prior to the construction of Wright's suburban studio provided a time of great exploration for the developing architect. Throughout much of the 1890s he borrowed from his early employers' design vocabularies, while experimenting with a variety of popular historic idioms before finally rejecting the overt use of traditional elements.[75] His earliest independent designs produced in the front room of his Oak Park home, even those exhibiting strong historical tendencies, clearly reflected his interest in nature and basic geometric forms. During these years Wright began integrating elements that later came to define his prairie houses, such as Roman brick and horizontal groupings of windows.[76] In addition, wood banding displayed across wall surfaces, which he explored as early as 1895 in his home, was later used to help visually "break the box" of the standard-shaped Victorian-era room.

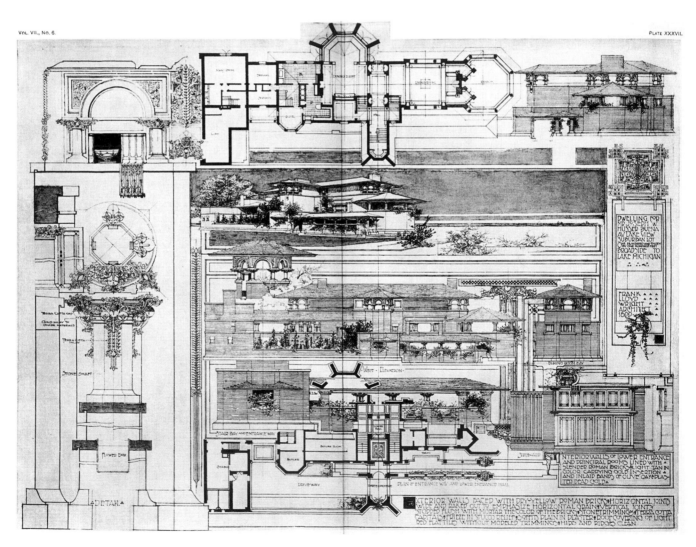

1.14 Husser house with elongated rooms projecting from the basic massing of the residence. Plate XXXVII, Robert C. Spencer Jr., "The Work of Frank Lloyd Wright," *Architectural Review*, June 1900.

1.15 Rear view of the Winslow residence showing projecting elements, including the octagonal stair tower and semicircular break-fast bay, ca. 1903. Photographer unknown. Walter Willcox Papers, box 6, folder PH110, Special Collections and University Archives, University of Oregon Libraries, Eugene, Oregon.

In these years Wright developed a process akin to the Froebelian practice of producing designs from the inside out, starting with a plan and then deriving the elevations and exterior form from it. Wright's early compact designs, like his Oak Park home and the George Blossom and Allison W. Harlan houses of the early 1890s, were superseded later in the decade by plans arranged with rooms protruding from a basic massing, as in the Joseph Husser residence and in an unrealized project for A. K. McAfee. The Winslow residence (1893–94) served as a transition between the two design concepts; it features a compact, classically

composed front elevation (see figure 3.20), while the rear facade consists of an asymmetrical composition of projecting elements, including a semicircular dining room bay and a tall octagonal stair tower.

Wright consistently incorporated basic geometric shapes into the designs of his early residential projects as he explored possible relationships between elementary forms as if they were Froebel exercises. In the late 1890s, when he was in the process of designing his Oak Park studio, Wright became particularly fascinated with the octagon, which he favored for libraries, projecting bays of dining rooms, and stair halls, as in the

1.16 Boulder sculpture and octagonal piers on the roof of the hallway connecting the studio reception hall with the library. Photographer: Gerald McManus.

Winslow house. He also used the octagonal form for various details, such as corner supports, railings, and piers between windows, as at the Heller and Winslow houses. In addition to his octagonal-shaped studio library and balcony of the drafting room, Wright installed four short octagonal columns on the roof of the hallway leading from the reception hall to the library, which support horizontal elements that help unify the library with the rest of the building while visually screening the house behind. The process of exploration, in which Wright honed his understanding of the potential of specific design details by experimenting with them again and again, often over the course of a series of commissions, became a common practice in his Oak Park studio. Prior to the construction of the suburban office, many of his initial experimentations took place in his residence.

Alterations to the Oak Park Home

Wright expanded his understanding of architecture at home by experimenting almost immediately with its physical structure. As his son John later recalled, his father "conceived something new in the building of his time. And he started with the building of his own house—a continuously mortgaged and periodically remodeled experimental laboratory of design and finance!"[77] The evolution of the property mirrored Wright's professional development. In addition to major additions, he moved walls and ceilings, altered windows, installed new floors and skylights, and replaced furnishings and decorations. He also repainted interior spaces numerous times.[78] The property soon became a showcase of his ideas for clients. In addition, the growing number of houses of his design in the surrounding neighborhood served as a three-dimensional portfolio of his work.

He made many of the changes for functional or aesthetical reasons, while others served as exploratory exercises. The earliest major alteration involved remodeling the second-floor windows on the front of the home from the "saddlebag" arrangement to a purer, more visually pleasing Palladian composition.[79] Wright regularly spent Saturdays attending auctions "toiling home in the evening with a roll of rugs over his shoulder, or a bowl or vase held tenderly in his hands."[80] Sunday activities included cleaning and rearranging the furniture in the living room, often discarding old items to make room for the new treasures. Wright continued this practice throughout his life, gaining a reputation among family and former clients for making design "improvements" to their living spaces by repositioning freestanding furnishings and other moveable objects. Wright's third wife, Olgivanna, wrote that the furniture was changed so many times at their Taliesin homes that no one could remember how it was from year to year.[81] The architect often made alterations without consent. As an adult, Llewellyn Wright woke one morning to the sound of sawing; his father was cutting the back legs off a chair he had designed and given to his son twenty years earlier.[82] Wright continually rearranged the Darwin Martin house furnishings on visits to Buffalo, "always attempting to make his arrangement closer to his artistic idea, which was in a perpetual state of development."[83]

In 1895, Wright made substantial alterations to his home to accommodate his growing family, including adding a wing to the east and an octagonal bay to the south.[84] The wing consisted of a kitchen and a maid's room on the first floor and the children's playroom on the second level. The original kitchen, with the addition of a southern bay, became the dining room and the previous dining room a study. Wright's children completed their schoolwork there and remembered the space filled with books and magazines.[85] His son John later exclaimed, "The library was *books*! Long thick, big, little books. Covers without books, books without covers; colored, patterned, and textured papers in large folios, all piled up and pushed on wide

ledges on either side of a long window."[86] Wright likely used the space as a home office prior the completion of the studio, after his original second-floor workspace was transformed to bedrooms for his children.

The new dining room became Wright's first example of a *Gesamtkunstwerk*, or comprehensive interior design scheme, a practice common to architects at the time with ties to the Arts and Crafts Movement and the Art Nouveau in Europe. Not only did Wright decide where to locate the walls; he also designed the furniture, light fixtures, art glass, and cabinetry, and selected the tile for the floor and artist canvas for the walls. For some clients, including the Boyntons and the Coonleys, he also designed table linens. He even designed dresses for his wife Catherine, as well as Susan Lawrence Dana, Queene Coonley, and Laura Robie.[87]

Wright did not achieve the final composition for his dining room all at once but made numerous modifications to the space over time. The design initially included a plain floor and double-level windows above projecting wooden cabinetry in three facets of the bay. Tall built-in cabinets held ornamental objects on each side. Slender wood piers running along each side of the cabinets to the ceiling and a piece of projecting molding at the top framed the bowls, vases, and other items.[88] Wright raised the floor level within the bay over a foot, making a stagelike platform, probably with the idea of creating a tiny conservatory for ferns and other plants to take advantage of the room's southern exposure.[89]

Shortly after the addition of the dining room bay, the house to the south was torn down and the lot divided. In 1897 a new house was erected just a few feet from Wright's property. To maintain a modicum of privacy, he filled in the lower windows of the bay and took out the side cabinets. In their place, radiators, hidden by built-in cabinetry, were installed. To make up for light lost, Wright added double levels of panes above the radiators to each side. Around the same time he placed shelving below the bay windows and removed the raised platform, providing more dining space for his growing family.

One of the most innovative features of the new dining room was the indirect lighting in the ceiling—

1.17 View of the Oak Park home from the south before the house next door was built, ca. 1896. The photograph shows the window on the west facade after Wright transformed it from a "saddlebag" into a Palladian composition. Also visible are the 1895 dining room bay and second-floor playroom additions on the south. The original playroom windows are visible in the rectangular bay. The small child is probably Frank Lloyd Wright's son John. Photographer unknown. Walter Willcox Papers, box 6, folder PH110, Special Collections and University Archives, University of Oregon Libraries, Eugene, Oregon.

1.18 Oak Park home dining room shortly after the original kitchen was transformed into the new dining room. Photograph shows the original window formation and raised platform of the new bay, as well as the dining room chairs with their original twisted spindles, ca. 1895. Photographer unknown. H654, Gift of Eric Lloyd Wright, Frank Lloyd Wright Trust.

1.19 Son Robert Llewellyn with Catherine Wright in a dress designed by Frank Lloyd Wright, ca. 1907. Photographer unknown. Gift of Llewellyn Wright, Frank Lloyd Wright Trust.

1.20 Oak Park home dining room after window modifications and removal of the platform, ca. 1897–98. *Ladies Home Journal*, January 1903.

possibly the first use of this illumination method in the United States. Artificial light filtered through rice paper within the voids of an elaborate fret-sawed wooden grille. During the day, it gave the appearance of a skylight, while at night the large rectangular fixture above the dining table, along with tall back chairs the architect designed, created an intimate eating area within the larger room.

Wright sometimes experimented further with ideas used in his clients' buildings by incorporating them into alterations of his own property. For example, the initial design of the dining room chairs, topped by balls similar to the spheres in the original fence around the property, included thin twisted spindles and straight legs. After Wright designed chairs with squared vertical slats for the Husser house (1899), he replaced the slats in his own chairs with similar elements and flared the bottom of the legs by cutting the front and adding a piece of wood to the back. Often variations of successful design forms appeared in a number of Wright's commissions. For example, he created dining room chairs of similar design for many

of his prairie houses, including residences for Ward Willits, Susan Lawrence Dana, Darwin Martin, Frederick Robie, and Isabel Roberts.[90] Other innovative elements in the Oak Park dining room—including the built-in wooden radiator cabinets, the cloth wall and ceiling coverings, the wood banding, and the art glass windows—all appeared in later projects produced in the adjacent studio.

Wright also significantly altered the nursery, later referred to as Catherine's dayroom, in the 1895 remodeling as he further explored the manipulation of the traditional box-shaped room. He extended the south bay upward from the dining room, ending just shy of the ceiling height in the dayroom. Later, likely after his 1905 trip to Japan, Wright inserted a clerestory window of translucent buff-colored art glass above the bay in a configuration recalling that found in the Japanese print *The Hobby Horse Dancer* by Utagawa Toyoharu, a copy of which Wright owned.[91] The added footage of the bay replaced space lost when he moved the interior wall of the original nursery several feet to the south to create a central hallway to the playroom

1.21 Catherine in the nursery/dayroom of the Oak Park home located above the dining room with sons Lloyd and John, and daughter Catherine in the crib, ca. 1895. Photographer unknown. H432, Frank Lloyd Wright Trust.

addition. The remodeling of the room also reflects developments in Wright's aesthetic taste, as he covered over earlier Sullivanesque stenciling around the top of the walls with fabric and plain wood banding. Strips of wood, like those elsewhere in the house, ran around the room well below the ceiling, recalling Japanese *uchinori nageshi* beams, which helped to visually dissolve the junctions between the walls and ceiling. Other bands of wood on the ceiling added to the effect. Wright incorporated similar banding into many of his prairie house designs and later in a much more sophisticated manner at Unity Temple. The architect also experimented with the visual experience of space when he turned his second-floor office into two bedrooms. He divided the tall vaulted volume down the center with a partition wall approximately seven and a half feet high, well short of the ceiling. This permitted privacy but helped to retain a sense of spaciousness in the small rooms.[92]

Wright additionally experimented with window designs in his home. Almost immediately, he replaced original single-pane windows with traditional Colonial Revival–style diamond panes that contained a simple border of thin rectangles. Setting each individual piece of glass at a slightly different angle creates a prismatic effect, making it difficult to see into the house. In the dining room bay of 1895, Wright included windows in a lotus pattern. He had used a similar composition two years earlier for the second-floor windows of the Winslow house.[93] Wright made several design changes to the glass in the playroom. Most likely after his return from Japan, he added pairs of small windows at the base of the barrel vault to either side of the room's low, rectangular side bays and above the Roman brick walls. Around the same time, he replaced Victorian wall sconces with fixtures of a geometric water lily (or lotus) motif. Prior to this, he changed the glass in the bays from windows with thin, rectangular central panes surrounded by grids of tiny squares and narrow rows of glass around the center pane and along the outer edges like those in the cabinets he added on either side of the fireplace. (The original playroom windows appear in the rectangular second-floor bay in figure 1.17.)[94] The new bay

1.22 Japanese print once owned by Frank Lloyd Wright showing wood banding and clerestory openings. "Interior of Shoin Style Architecture with Dancers Performing Horse Dance or Festivities in a Mansion on the First Rat Day of the Year," ca. 1770, from *Perspective Views of Japan* by Utagawa Toyoharu. Full-color woodcut (*nishiki-e*). Purchased from the Frank Lloyd Wright collection. Grunwald Center for the Graphic Arts, Hammer Museum, UCLA.

1.23 Catherine's day room after restoration, 1986. Photographer: Jon Miller. BL83, Frank Lloyd Wright Trust.

1.24 View from balcony of the Oak Park home playroom after the restoration. Photographer: James Caulfield.

fenestration contains rows of geometricized tulips reflecting his design concept for art glass, that led to geometric representations of familiar plants in the windows of some of his most prominent prairie houses, most notably sumac (and butterfly) motifs at the Dana residence and later a wheat theme at the Robie house.[95]

Once his new office opened next door, Wright carried out design experimentations to it as well. His studio explorations resulted in new furniture and art

glass window designs, as well as further development of other decorative elements, such as wood banding. He also investigated various materials, like magnesite and metallic paint, and experimented with innovative forms of horizontal and vertical elements that helped define and provide greater interest to the spaces.

Wright's early design explorations, which built upon lessons in geometry and nature he experienced as a youth, as well as influences from his time in the architectural offices of noted Chicago designers and with colleagues in shared offices, resulted in aesthetically pleasing compositions for some projects and rather awkward assemblages for others, such as the houses he designed for George and Rollin Furbeck around the time the Oak Park studio opened. Wright was still in an early stage of a lifelong learning process, and the first years of the studio's operation were some of the most fertile as his ideas and formal design vocabulary achieved high levels of synthesis—developments made possible in part by the workshop-like environment of his suburban home studio.

2
OPENING OF THE OAK PARK STUDIO (1898)

Establishment and Ownership

2.1 Early drawing of the Oak Park studio (left) along with a sketch of the *Fisherman and the Genie* playroom mural. TAL 9512.001, Avery Architectural & Fine Arts Library, Columbia University, New York. © 2020 Frank Lloyd Wright Foundation, Scottsdale, AZ. All rights reserved.

The place had always a sort of magic. It was too cold in the winter. You had to depend on the fireplace and the heat in the fireplace smoked. The floor had no basement under it and therefore was cold. All this was nothing. There was delight.

BARRY BYRNE

After Wright transformed his upstairs home office into bedrooms for his many offspring, he needed a new place to work. He began contemplating the construction of a large office addition. A conceptual sketch of the studio exterior appears on a drawing of a mural he designed for the end wall of the playroom addition, but the building was not to come right away.[1] Wright stated that he could afford to realize his vision only after receiving a consulting engineering contract in mid-1897 to design prismatic glass from the Luxfer Prism Company.[2] Construction appears to have been completed by early February of the following year when an announcement of its opening appeared in *Construction News*.[3] Wright also began to use letterhead that month announcing his availability between the hours of 8:00 and 11:00 a.m. and 7:00 and 9:00 p.m. in the "Draughting Rooms and Studio at the Corner of Forest and Chicago Avenues Oak Park Illinois."[4]

The Suburban Studio

Wright's decision to move the core of his growing practice to a suburban location countered the prevailing fashion, as most progressive architects who lived in the Chicago suburbs at the time worked in the Loop.[5] While Wright had wanted to eliminate his commute downtown, he initially continued to make the trip on a regular, if not daily, basis.[6] The studio announcement notes that he could be reached "from twelve to two, P.M." for "purely business purposes, consultation and matters in connection with superintendence," in his downtown office.[7]

Wright moved his Chicago office several times in the years he operated the Oak Park studio. During the winter of 1897–98, he relocated to Burnham and Root's fashionable Rookery Building, within space rented by the American Luxfer Prism Company. Two of the glass-block firm's directors, Edward C. Waller and William H. Winslow, were friends and important early clients. It was probably those connections that led to the architect producing designs for Luxfer prism blocks, panels, and a canopy.[8] Wright may have received the office space as partial payment for this work or as a courtesy from one of the company officers. Listings in city directories suggest he moved his office several times within the Rookery Building before returning to Steinway Hall.[9] After a short-lived business venture with architect Henry Webster Tomlinson, which had dissolved by early 1902, he took over Tomlinson's Steinway Hall office.[10] Wright may have continued to work in the building until 1907, but it appears that he did not officially keep an office there.[11] In 1908 he briefly rented Room 1020 of the Fine Arts Building on Michigan Avenue.[12] Maintaining an office in the Loop made it possible for Wright to stay connected to the architectural community in Chicago. Having his own office space allowed for a quiet workplace and privacy when meeting with clients, yet at Steinway Hall

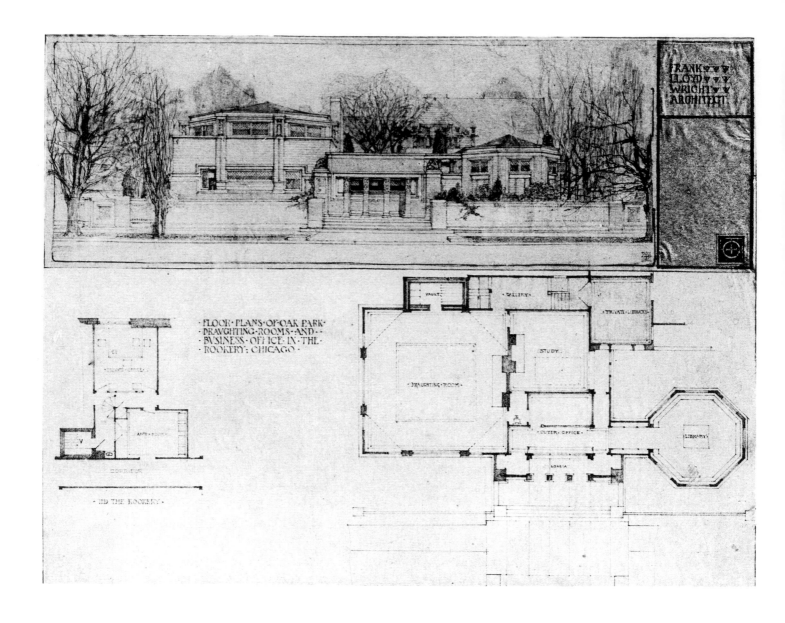

2.2 Rendering and plan of the Oak Park studio and plan of Wright's downtown office in the Rookery Building from the opening announcement of the suburban studio, ca. 1898. John Lloyd Wright Collection, Oak Park Public Library Special Collections.

he could contribute to and benefit from the intellectually stimulating environment and innovative ideas of colleagues.

The announcement of his Oak Park studio offers clues to factors that contributed to Wright's decision to open the suburban office. He began the notice by stating, "The practice of architecture as a profession has fine art as well as commercial elements" and that "these should be combined to their mutual benefit, and not mixed to their detriment." To best accomplish this, he argued, the architect should "place himself in an environment that conspires to develop the best there is in him" and that in doing so one needs a place that is "fitted and adapted to the work performed and set outside distractions of the busy city." This should allow the worker "the basis to secure the quiet concentration of effort essential to the full success of a building project."[13] In short, Wright yearned for a more tranquil, artistic setting.[14] By creating a home studio akin to a craft workshop, Wright could also better maintain artistic control of his architectural production and avoid having design time eaten up by the obligatory managerial activities of a prominent commercial architectural firm.[15] It additionally offered a more nurturing, welcoming environment—particularly for his independent-minded female clients.[16] It also made it easier for the architect to keep an eye on local projects underway.

Wright was not alone in desiring an aesthetic work environment like those of the English Arts and Crafts Movement. By the mid-1890s cooperative craft environments began appearing in the Chicago area that allowed for rich interactions among like-minded artists and architects. One of the earliest cooperative artistic complexes was the Tree Studio Building constructed by Judge Lambert Tree and his wife Anne in 1894 to help persuade European artists who had come to Chicago to work on the World's Columbian Exposition to remain in the city. The picturesque brick structure, which contained small shops on the ground level that helped to subsidize the brightly lit studios above, soon became a lively center of artistic life. Another workshop that focused on interior designs, the Crafters, was established in Steinway Hall by two graduates of the Art Institute and Lawrence Buck, a member of the

Eighteen group of progressive architects.[17] One of the most prominent area workshops was the Kalo Arts and Crafts Community House and Shop. Founded by Clara Barck Welles and five other young women who had studied at the Art Institute in 1900, it served as a training site for silversmiths, leading to Chicago becoming a major center for hand-wrought silver and jewelry.[18] In 1905, the Kalo Shop moved to the fresh air and country sunlight of suburban Park Ridge. In meeting his own desire to escape the grime and congestion of the city, Wright found inspiration in two sources in addition to the two-story balcony drafting room at Adler and Sullivan, the successful home office of Henry Hobson Richardson and a student thesis project of one of his early employees.[19]

The Studio of Henry Hobson Richardson

After closing his New York office in 1878, Richardson, one of the most prominent American architects during the building boom that followed the Civil War, began using his Brookline residence outside of Boston as his main studio.[20] Wright likely became aware of Richardson's home office sometime between 1888 and 1893 while working for Sullivan, who owned a copy of Mariana Griswold Van Rensselaer's book *Henry Hobson Richardson and His Works*.[21] This major monograph on Richardson's architecture includes a detailed description of the Brookline studio.[22] Wright later wrote of Richardson and his influence on Sullivan in *An Autobiography*, noting "Outside the initial impetus of John Edelman, in his early days, H. H. Richardson, the great emotional revivalist of Romanesque, was one whose influence the Master [Sullivan] felt" and that "Richardson at the time had a decided effect upon Sullivan's work as may be seen in the outside of the Auditorium Building itself, the Walter Wholesale, and others."[23]

Prominent firsthand examples of Richardson's work in Chicago at the time include the massive Marshall Field and Company Wholesale Store and the fashionable Glessner house. Wright's familiarity with Richardson's work is reflected in several renderings he produced while at Adler and Sullivan, including one for the Victor Falkenau row houses in 1888. Wright

2.3 Interior view of H. H. Richardson's drafting room in Brookline, Massachusetts. RSID 158935, Courtesy of Historic New England.

likely gained further knowledge about Richardson's studio through Dwight Perkins and others in Chicago with links to that Boston office.[24]

Richardson's architectural studio connected directly to his house through French doors leading off of his home library. The office, which projected from the residence at an angle, exhibited a simple, utilitarian exterior. The interior, meanwhile, consisted of several large workrooms added as the need for office space grew.[25] Simply decorated, they included a "liberal display of photographs and drawings from Richardson's portfolios."[26] At the rear of the addition, the architect located his well-appointed study or "library" that

contained fireproof storage for drawings and documents.[27]

According to Van Rensselaer, Richardson's library housed a vast array of interesting objects, each bearing "witness to the strong personal tastes and the actual material or professional needs of the owner."[28] Her description of the library, with its "harmonious and restful" atmosphere, could have applied just as easily to the library Wright went on to design for his own studio. Both rooms contained a variety of small decorative objects and arrangements of dried flowers and weeds. It was probably no coincidence that plaster copies of a frieze panel titled *Boys Singing from a Book* by the

Renaissance artist Luca della Robbia and portieres of William Morris's stylized floral-patterned *Campion* woven in woolen fabric appeared in each studio.[29]

Not only did Wright's home office include some of the same objects as Richardson's, but much of what Van Rensselaer wrote about daily life in Richardson's studio might have easily been written by Wright to describe activities in his Oak Park office during its peak period of operation.[30] The author depicted the Brookline studio as filled with workers of wide-ranging ages and experiences, "all loyally devoted to their chief, all laboring together on work which had a single inspiration and a common accent, and each feeling a personal pride in results which the world knew as the master's only."[31] Richardson supported the continual professional development of his workers, a practice that Wright later embraced in Oak Park. They also shared the occasional intrusion of family members, which helped to reinforce basic requirements of good residential design in distinctly personal ways.[32]

2.4 Interior view of H. H. Richardson's library in Brookline, Massachusetts, with a large framed print of the interior of Hagia Sophia, plaster copies of sculpture, including Luca della Robbia's *Boys Singing from a Book* in the center rear next to an image of the Hellenistic sculpture *Winged Victory of Samothrace*, and portieres of William Morris's floral pattern *Campion*. RSID 808, Courtesy of Historic New England.

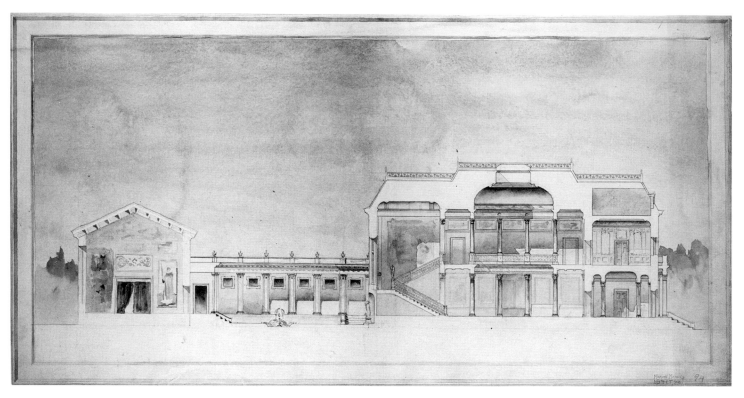

2.5 Section drawing of Marion Mahony's MIT thesis project, "House and Studio of a Painter," 1894. MIT Museum.

Mahony's House and Studio Thesis as Model

Marion Mahony, who entered Wright's employment in 1895 around the time he was feeling growing pressure to turn over his home workspace to his children, had particular insight into the design of a home studio, having chosen the topic for her MIT thesis the year before. Her Beaux Arts–style renderings of "The House and Studio of a Painter" feature a large courtyard house in an eclectic French Second Empire style with a corridor connecting it to a well-lit three-room studio.[33] This project undoubtedly influenced Wright's residential office. The two architects likely discussed the concept of a home studio while completing drawings in Steinway Hall for projects such as the Francisco Terrace apartments and the Heller house. While the style and scale of Wright's complex differ from his employee's, both present binuclear designs that share a number of common elements: fireplaces, balconies, piered loggias decorated with bas-reliefs, and linking passageways that separate work space from home life. Mahony wrote an essay describing her design and, as with Van Rensselaer's description of Richardson's office, one can hear in her words a prefiguring of Wright's later design.:

[T]he studios ... are thus separated from the dwelling in order to give opportunity for quiet and seclusion.... On one side of the vestibule is the library ... separated from the salon by porticos.... This salon is lit by a very large group of windows opening onto a balcony ... making a little reception room immediately off the vestibule ... using piers instead of columns.... This entrance is for the use of clients, and from it one turns either to the reception room or directly to the studios.... I have made it possible to enter each without passing through either of the others.[34]

While Wright borrowed ideas from both Richardson's actual architectural home office and Mahony's conceptual one, the Oak Park studio presented a design clearly reflective of its owner's own ideas of a residential office.

2.6 Oak Park studio entrance with both boulder figures facing forward, ca. 1898. Photographer unknown. TAL 9506.019, Avery Architectural & Fine Arts Library, Columbia University, New York.

The Design of the Oak Park Studio

An 1899 description of Wright's studio by Chicago architect Alfred Granger and period photographs, many likely taken by the architect himself, provide insight into its initial design.[35] One early photograph shows pairs of large urns framing steps leading to an open loggia with entrances hidden to each side. A low sidewall to the right of the stair initially enclosed an existing tree.[36] To the left, a large stone plaque announcing "Frank Lloyd Wright, Architect" included his early logo—a cross within a circle within a square.[37] The loggia contained four piers with decorative "stork" capitals, cast from a design possibly rendered by Mahony and then transformed into bas-relief panels by artist Richard Bock.[38] The capitals feature a tree of life, an open book (interpreted as representing a book of knowledge or a book of architectural specifications),

and two birds (often referred to as storks or secretary birds) flanking an architectural plan.[39] The plan illustrates a rectangular space with apses at each of the short ends and a loggia to one side. Connected to the rectangular space by a short hallway is an octagonal space framed in semicircular niches. The plan appears to be not of a specific building but vaguely suggestive of the studio itself.[40]

Sculptures of crouching figures facing outward above each side of the entrance greeted early visitors.[41] According to Robert Spencer, the figures represent the "struggle of the oppressed and shackled soul to break its bonds and find self expression."[42] Richard Bock recalled that he "versified" the "boulder figures" with the line "Old and strong, depressed and dreaming of an epoch past and gone."[43] While the niches on the exterior of the drafting room's second story remained empty throughout the life of the studio, early render-

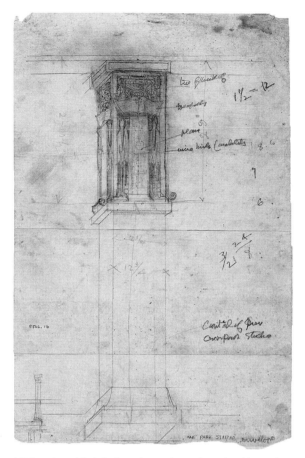

2.7 Drawing of Oak Park studio stork panels, realized by sculptor Richard Bock. TAL 9506.016, Avery Architectural & Fine Arts Library, Columbia University, New York.

ings show indistinct sculptural forms in the alcoves, suggesting plans for additional, initially unrealized, decorative elements. The boulder figures and stork panels represent the first major decorative elements on a Wright building that illustrate a clear move away from the leafy organic Sullivanesque ornamentation of his earlier commissions, such as at the Winslow and Heller houses, and hinted at future commissions Bock would carry out for the architect.

Wright constructed the studio building on a tight budget.[44] Although not as well built as the home next door, it presented a vision of his evolving design sensibility for a suburban workplace.[45] As Alfred Granger wrote of it, "[The drafting room] has the air of a charming living room. The fireplace is large, and at once makes you feel at home, while wherever you look is some interesting bit of plaster or some quaint motto, or a jar of wild flowers."[46] When visiting the studio,

potential clients would first enter the shallow reception hall, which originally contained a built-in desk with railings blocking off each side. Doors in angled walls led to other spaces. An interior row of "stork" capitals separated a series of windows with elaborate art glass borders of colored rectangles. Below, the architect set several large chairs, believed to be of his own design. As a nod to his *Lieber Meister*, a picture of the "Golden Portal," the main arched entrance of Sullivan's Transportation Building from the 1893 World's Columbian Exposition, hung on a side wall.

Granger noted, "[T]he walls of the [reception] room are a deep, rich red, while the woodwork throughout is of oak, filled enough to give it the rich, golden tone which Mr. Wright seems especially to love."[47] A plate of the studio plan, published the following year, identifies the trim as a "soft wood stained," and restoration architects found basswood, not oak, throughout the studio.[48] Granger, possibly working from photographs, may have assumed or was informed that the architect used the same wood in the studio as in the house.

Wright designed his new drafting room as a twenty-seven-by-twenty-seven-foot two-story workspace off the reception hall. The octagonal balcony on the second level surrounds a thirteen-foot-square central opening to the first floor. An exposed octagon-shaped chain tension ring located just below the roof beams helps hold together the exterior walls by resisting the outward thrust of the pitched roof (visible in figure E.14). Wright anchored the balcony to the exterior walls, while chains from the roof beams end in metal balls on the low parapet walls along the opening. Rods attached to the balls run through the walls to the underside of beams at the edge of the balcony.[49] The larger square footprint of the drafting room rises five feet above the floor level of the octagonal balcony, leaving four triangular-shaped storage closets half the height of the balcony.[50] Above, clerestory windows wrap around all eight sides of the room. A drawing at the Wisconsin Historical Society suggests that Wright experimented with several options for the roof design before settling on a single eight-sided shallow form.

Granger described the sand-finished plaster walls of the drafting room as painted a "dull quiet red" on the first story and a "tawny yellow" above.[51] As in many of Wright's later designs, flat wood banding added

2.8 Oak Park reception hall looking east into the drafting room with stork panels on the left, a rendering of the "Golden Portal" entrance to Louis Sullivan's Transportation Building at the 1893 World's Columbian Exposition on the back wall, and the original reception desk to the right, ca. 1898. Photographer unknown. *House Beautiful*, December 1899. TAL 8901.0026, Avery Architectural & Fine Arts Library, Columbia University, New York.

2.9 Early view of the Oak Park studio drafting room showing diamond-pane windows and various sculptures, including a copy of the *Winged Victory of Samothrace* on the balcony, the Rudyard Kipling quote on the face of balcony, and drafting equipment and architectural drawings, including renderings of the Husser and Heller houses. Photographer unknown. *House Beautiful*, December 1899.

2.10 (*facing*) Drawings of the studio drafting room exterior illustrating alternate roof designs. John Howe Collection, PH Mss 842, folder D6, Wisconsin Historical Society.

shortly after the studio opened decorated the ceiling below the balcony, providing interest to the wall surfaces. On the floor, he almost immediately covered the original tongue and groove pine floor with dark brown linoleum.[52] Photographs show adjustable drafting tables and stools along the perimeter of the room. Wright noted the presence of a "big detail table" in the center of the room when Barry Byrne arrived in 1902.[53] On the north and east exterior walls, tall vertical cabinets framed long horizontal windows with shelving below. Smaller vertical diamond-paned casements to the outside of the cabinets helped with air circulation during the warmer months.[54] The relatively high placement of the windows allows for light to enter while hiding potentially distracting views of outside activity. To augment the natural light, Wright hung large globe fixtures from the balcony on chains. Additional hanging lamps above the workspaces, shaded with green glass, supplied task lighting.[55] Like Richardson, Wright expressed great concern about fire, as most of his product was combustible. To protect his work, Wright installed a large fireproof vault on the south wall under the stair leading to the balcony.[56]

A large fireplace with a Romanesque-style arch of Chicago common brick formed the focal point for the drafting room (see figure P.2). Wright decorated the front of the fireplace with four large identical panels of a frieze design Richard Bock had created for the Heller house in 1896; these plaster panels of young maidens surrounded by a leafy Sullivanesque design, stained a "deep wood-brown," may have been samples or extra copies.[57] Other sculpture filled the office, including plaster versions of notable classical and Renaissance works. The architect placed a small bust of Michelangelo's *Dying Slave* on a fireplace cap, while casts of the *Winged Victory of Samothrace*, *Venus de Milo*, *Psyche of Naples*, and other figures, along with plants and weed arrangements, decorated the rest of the drafting room.[58] On the east face of the balcony Wright hung the hand-lettered quotation from Rudyard Kipling's *McAndrew's Hymn*: "Ye've left a glimmer still to cheer the man—the artifex that holds in spite o'knocks and scale o'friction waste an' slip. An' by that light—now mark my word we'll build the perfect ship."[59]

To the right of the reception hall opposite the drafting room, Wright located a short hallway leading to the small library and lined it with cabinets in which he most likely stored building material samples. Woven portieres of William Morris's *Campion* pattern divided the hallway from the reception hall.[60] As with the drafting room, natural light entered the library through diamond-paned clerestory windows that encircled the space. At each corner, round globes on octagonal posts, reminiscent of Wright's design for a tall, slender weed holder that appears in many of the early photographs of the room, provided artificial light. Period photographs show double-door cabinets on the angled walls and a horizontal cabinet below a thin pull-down panel on the west wall that hid access to an innovative storage area for drawings. The thin flap, located above a larger drop-down panel also hinged at the bottom, opened to allow access to a contraption consisting of pairs of rods with ring clips to hold drawings. The rings could be manipulated between the rods, placing a desired drawing at a small gap between them for easy access when the larger panel was open.[61] Physical evidence suggests the library included similar cabinetry on the north and south walls. Wright displayed prints, fabrics, and other decorative objects above on shelves that wrapped around the room. Furnishings included a square table and large cube chairs like those in the reception hall.

Granger described the library as "the most beautiful room in this series which forms his studio," with walls painted a "rich olive green."[62] In a studio plan published in 1900, Wright labeled the space as a "free circulating fine art library"; however, there is no evidence of it ever having that function.[63] The library in essence served as a *kunstkammer*, or cabinet of curiosities, where the architect could show off his design work as well as objects that reflected his ideas of beauty and good taste. Wright and the other studio architects probably used the space most frequently as a place to meet clients.

Wright located his private office behind the reception hall. A shallow fireplace on the east wall shared a chimney with the drafting room hearth. Three windows on the western wall, and possibly a skylight on the ceiling, featured art glass that echoed the design of the reception hall windows.[64] Like the other spaces in the studio, office décor included prints and an assortment of interesting objects, such as the large plaster cast of Luca della Robbia's *Boys Singing from a Book*

2.11 Studio reception hall looking toward the library showing stork panels, a sculpture, and portieres of William Morris's *Campion* pattern, ca. 1898. Photographer: Henry Fuermann. *House Beautiful*, December 1899. Digital file 80764, Ryerson and Burnham Archives, AIC.

and an image of Beethoven's life mask.[65] Textiles hung on the backs of large cube chairs and on the long, simple desk for additional decorative effects. The textiles, casts, and other decorative objects that filled the studio provided inspiration for not only Wright but also the other designers.

Life in the Studio: Architects and Artists

Five men, two women. They wore flowing ties and smocks suitable to the realm. The men wore their hair like Papa, except Albert, he didn't have enough hair.

JOHN LLOYD WRIGHT (1946)

The studio served as an atelier for many young designers. The architects and artists, often drawn to Wright by his designs, philosophy, and growing reputation, came and went with no official record of their names, contributions, or lengths of stay.[66] While several worked in the studio for well over a decade, most left within a few years to open their own offices, or to find regular if not better-paying employment elsewhere.[67] Unlike at Adler and Sullivan, Wright allowed designers to leave and return or to work on outside commissions.[68]

Wright typically employed five to seven people. Initially, however, the staff was not that large. Around the time he opened his suburban office he hired George Willis as head draftsman. Talented and known for his quick wit, Willis became one of Wright's "best beloved draftsmen."[69] Marion Mahony continued to work for Wright as needed. They, and possibly an additional draftsman or two, comprised the original staff. Wright's former coworker at Adler and Sullivan George Grant Elmslie helped out on occasional evenings when the architect was "pressed for help."[70] Little evidence survives about any employees' specific contributions to the work produced during the studio's first couple of years.[71] But Wright did develop his design ideology on projects like the Husser residence in the company of well-trained architects.

While the architects primarily worked on the main floor of the drafting room, artists, eventually including Richard Bock, Albert Van den Berghen, George Niedecken, and a sculptor known only as DuBuois, worked on the balcony where messier design activities could take place out of the view of visitors.[72] Other artists, such as Orlando Giannini, Blanche Ostertag, Burch Burdette Long, and Niedecken in later years, most likely carried out work for Wright in their own studios.[73] Marion Mahony and eventually Isabel Roberts and Wright's younger sister Maginel (Margaret Ellen) worked on art glass designs on the balcony.[74] Maginel, an illustrator of children's books, also pursued her own projects at an easel there.[75] The Coonley house living room fireplace mural of birch trees and ferns by Niedecken (ca. 1909), which exhibits similarities to an illustration for a children's book by Maginel, offers just one example of the cross-fertilization of ideas and forms among the artists.[76] The upper level of the drafting room also served as a place for Wright's hobbies. In later years, he used the space to organize and edit his growing collection of Japanese prints and kept his large-format view camera and other photographic equipment there as well.[77] Both sons John and David recalled their father's darkroom in the studio where "he developed the plates, sensitized Japanese paper and printed from his photographs."[78]

Partnerships

In addition to hiring people, Wright entered into at least two professional relationships with other architects outside of the studio staff during the early years.[79]

2.12 *(facing, top)* Original interior design of the studio library with octagonal light posts, a large square table, cube chairs, and an assortment of objects, including a large round urn and a weed holder in the form of a winged boy, both of Wright's own design, and a large blue and white Asian dragon plate. An art glass pane similar in design to those in the studio office leans on one of the original diamond-paned windows to the right, ca. 1898. *House Beautiful*, December 1899.

2.13 *(facing, bottom)* Studio office with cube chairs, as well as a large round urn and a tall slender weed holder designed by Wright, decorate the room, as do early examples of his decorative art glass windows, his copy of della Robbia's *Boys Singing from a Book*, and on a back wall a Japanese scroll and an image of Beethoven's life mask ca. 1898. *House Beautiful*, December 1899.

2.14 Rendering of the Frank Thomas house by Birch Burdette Long. The artist's monogram appears in the grass on the left side of the drawing. TAL 0106.001, Avery Architectural & Fine Arts Library, Columbia University, New York. © 2020 Frank Lloyd Wright Foundation, Scottsdale, AZ. All rights reserved.

It does not appear that either colleague ever worked in the Oak Park office or that the associations resulted in any significant long-term collaboration. Prior to the opening of the studio, Wright joined with Dwight Perkins to produce a design for the Abraham Lincoln Center for Wright's uncle Reverend Jenkin Lloyd Jones on the South Side of Chicago—the sole documented project of a seven-year relationship. Wright was involved in the design during the early years of the Oak Park studio, but after clashes between the architects and client, Perkins finished the project alone.[80]

Wright entered a more formal "copartnership" with Steinway Hall colleague Webster Tomlinson[81] sometime prior to January 1901. It ended before July 1902, possibly several months earlier.[82] *Construction News* reported in February 1901 that the partnership designed "a two-story frame house to be built at River Forest for E. Arthur Davenport to cost $3,000."[83] Other published projects include the F. B. Henderson house in Elmhurst, Illinois; the William G. Fricke and Frank Thomas houses in Oak Park; and the unrealized Victor Metzger house for Sault Ste. Marie, Michigan.[84] Tomlinson primarily handled the business affairs and supervised construction from their downtown office.

Wright completed the design work "and directed the draftsmen" in Oak Park.[85] While Tomlinson gave the design credit entirely to Wright, he later stated that he took charge of "finishing up" several of the projects.[86]

At the time Wright opened his Oak Park studio, he was in the midst of one of the most experimental phases of his career as he moved away from Sullivanesque and historic architectural forms and focused his attention more fully on explorations of nature and geometry. The studio building reflects this shift, particularly in the play of octagonal forms, such as those found in the library and drafting room, as well as in

smaller elements, such as the decorative roof columns. Wright also began using less intricate but more symbolic ornamentation like the Studio's stork panels and boulder figures.

While the lack of office documents from when the studio first opened has resulted in large voids in the historical understanding of the initial design activities in the Oak Park studio, including the individual roles of employees, information on the projects and activities for the next few years is slightly more plentiful, allowing for greater insights into Wright's vibrant work environment.

3
EARLY YEARS OF THE OAK PARK STUDIO (1898–1902)

Dialogue and Growth

The Architectural Review.

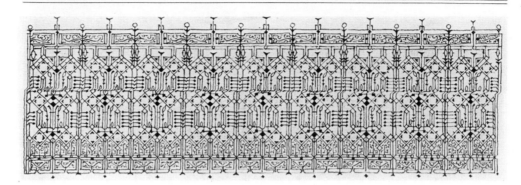

The Work of Frank Lloyd Wright.

By Robert C. Spencer, Jr.

THE last year of the century finds the majority of our prominent and successful architects still busily engaged in the transplanting of exotics. From every fashionable foreign source the outward forms of the various styles and periods are being "adapted," plagiarized or caricatured according to the calibre and taste of the individual designer.

From New York to San Francisco the photographer and the

have made architecture pay and can well afford to ride. Others, full of the strength of youth, still affecting the beard and the slang of the ateliers, do not yet realize that they are riding. On the contrary, some of them imagine that they are marching in architectural seven-league boots. A younger man who has scorned this easy and popular route, swinging easily along amid the beauties of the forests and flower-sown prairies of his own country, has shown a more intelligent grasp of what architecture means

publisher have placed the "historic styles" at the disposal of the humblest draughtsmen, who may, by the exercise of due care and patience in their use, very fairly reproduce them, *ad libitum, ad nauseum.* In the midst of a nervous, hurried, commerce-driven community, which hurries and drives him in turn, the architect finds, by way of his well filled library, a short line to practical results which seem, for the time being at least, to satisfy the public. This short line is rather uninteresting and monotonous, and the architect who continually travels thereon grows feeble and rheumatic in his legs for lack of good healthy exercise; but he meets so many well dressed, scholarly men travelling that way, that he becomes loth to try other routes and less keen for results above and beyond the present public demand. Some of his fellow travellers may never walk again without crutches, but they

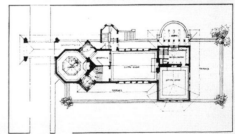

Note.— A list of the illustrations in the text of this article is given at the end, on page 72.

3.1 Front page of Robert C. Spencer Jr., "The Work of Frank Lloyd Wright," *Architectural Review*, June 1900, showing Wright's design for the McAfee house.

All the buildings I have built—large and small—are fabricated upon a unit system—as the pile of a rug is stitched into the warp. Thus each structure is an ordered fabric;—Rhythm and consistent scale of parts and economy of construction are greatly facilitated by this simple expedient:—a mechanical one, absorbed in a final result to which it has given more consistent texture, a more tenuous quality as a whole.

FRANK LLOYD WRIGHT (1925)

The first few years of the Oak Park studio's operation saw tremendous professional growth for Wright. He began to take on a greater leadership role in the Chicago architectural scene including in the development of the prairie house, which arose out of the work of the dynamic group of architects later identified as the Prairie School. While much of the initial formation of the underlying ideas of the Prairie School took place in the upper floors of Steinway Hall, Wright's suburban studio quickly emerged as a pivotal location in its development.[1] There, assisted by designers including Marion Mahony, Walter Burley Griffin, and William Drummond, Wright created a rich, aesthetic environment that allowed for fertile explorations and interactions, resulting in one of the greatest periods of architectural development of his career. Lessons from various experiences merged into a cohesive personal mode of architecture designed to meet the rapidly changing conditions of an industrializing nation. This resulted in the creation of fully developed prairie houses in these years, such as residences for Frank Thomas, Ward Willits, Arthur Heurtley, and prominent socialite Susan Lawrence Dana.

The Work of Frank Lloyd Wright

The first major article on Wright's professional work, the June 1900 *Architectural Review* piece by Robert C. Spencer Jr., featured discussions on his design principles and projects, including the new suburban of-fice. The article served as an important introduction of Wright beyond the Chicago area and strengthened his prominent position in the local architectural community. It showcased over twenty of his pre-prairie houses, including designs for Harrison P. Young, Nathan Moore, and Stephen A. Foster, and several larger projects—an early version of the Abraham Lincoln Center and a recreational complex for Cheltenham Beach on the south shore of Chicago. Elaborate plates illustrate his Winslow, Heller, and Husser house designs. Spencer highlighted Wright's new suburban studio with a series of photographs and a plate of renderings. These images, along with those published in the 1899 *House Beautiful* article, clearly reveal the rapid development of Wright's architecture at the time.

Spencer, undoubtedly with strong input from Wright, introduced readers to the architect's core influences: nature, music, the ideas of Froebel and Sullivan, and "the Orientals and the Japanese."[2] He described how Wright expressed "certain ideals of home and of quiet, simple home life" through his design of nontraditional middle-class dwellings, including the Winslow and Moore houses, as well as the Oak Park studio. Crucial to the future success of the studio, Spencer's article brought important attention to Wright through beautifully illustrating his previous work and articulating the basic roots of his design ideology, concepts the architect explored further in alterations he made to his own property and in his initial prairie house designs.

3.2 Arthur Heurtley residence. Photographer unknown. Courtesy of Helen Berkeley and Allen Heurtley.

Development of the Prairie Houses

Two of Wright's earliest fully formed prairie houses, the Ward Willits and Arthur Heurtley houses of 1902, reflect architectural developments that took place during the initial years of the Oak Park studio. These include greater sophistication in room arrangements and in choices of materials, furnishings, and ornamentation. He also began applying a "unit-system" of design for an underlying sense of cohesion. Some of the advancements build upon explorations Wright had made to his own property.

The main public rooms of the Willits house, in Highland Park north of Chicago, for example, project from a central hearth, forming a full cruciform shape that had been hinted at in earlier designs, including

for his own home. The perpendicular arrangement of the living and dining rooms, recalling that in Wright's residence, is also almost identical to a plan the architect published in *Ladies' Home Journal* in July 1901. His choice of stucco as the main exterior material and articulation of the facades with vertical wood banding for the Willits house vaguely evokes both the half-timbering of an English Tudor manor and the modular wood divisions found in traditional Japanese architecture. Banding on the house's interior recalls wood strips that appeared in his work as early as Catherine's dayroom after the 1895 remodeling of his home. He also experimented with it in the early days of his drafting room with the addition of banding along the edge of the balcony shortly after the studio was built.[3]

Wright went on to further develop his use of wood banding in a much more sophisticated way at Unity Temple after his trip to Japan. Another important development illustrated at the Willits house is the prominent use of ribbon windows running across the front of the facade that developed out of his use of horizontal series of windows, such as on the breakfast bay of the Winslow house and in several places at his own property, including in the Palladian composition on the front facade of the house, in the dining room bay, and in the arrangement of the clerestories on both the studio's drafting room and library.

The Heurtley residence, down the street from Wright's own home on Forest Avenue, contains many of the basic characteristics of the architect's mature prairie houses. However, unlike the Willits design, the house presents a compact rectangular box set on the flat suburban "prairie" with only subtle pinwheel projections. In this design, as with most of his prairie houses, Wright eliminated the basement and attic and located the main public rooms on the second floor. Incorporating vaulted ceilings into the main living spaces like he had on the second floor of his own residence permitted a vertical expansion of the rooms. In raising the public areas above ground level similar to the Thomas house he had designed (also on Forest Avenue) the year before, Wright gave the Heurtleys a greater sense of privacy and a better view of the surrounding landscape. The massive entrance arch, broad overhanging eaves, tented ceiling, and protecting inglenook helped reinforce the primitive sense of shelter found in most prairie houses. As at the Willits house, space projects outward from a central hearth, traveling to the exterior through ribbons of art glass windows on the west, a porch to the south, and openings toward other interior vistas on the north.

Contributing to the creation of these designs was a growing group of well-educated architects, and in 1902, an inexperienced but eager to learn office boy.

Studio Employees

By architectural tradition, building designs are typically attributed exclusively to the principals of a firm, with the contributions of others often lost to history.

This is much the case with the Oak Park studio. Few substantive records document the work of Wright's employees. What does survive suggests that in its early years the gifted designers with whom the architect surrounded himself made significant contributions to the practice. Each brought different talents and educational backgrounds. Marion Mahony, with her Beaux Arts–style schooling and artistic talent for rendering, likely reminded Wright of the type of training he had eschewed.[4] New hires William Drummond and Walter Burley Griffin, meanwhile, introduced to the studio the type of practical architectural preparation provided by Nathan Ricker's curriculum at the University of Illinois, which emphasized structure and materials over style.[5]

The first known major hire Wright made in the suburban office was Drummond, who joined Willis and Mahony. The dashing, dark haired draftsman arrived in late 1899 after encountering Wright's residential work while on walks from his home in neighboring Austin.[6] Introduced to the building trades by his father, Drummond briefly attended architectural classes at the University of Illinois and worked for several months in the offices of Adler and Sullivan before starting at Wright's. In his early days, Drummond carried out fairly basic tasks but soon was turning preliminary sketches into working drawings for commissions such as the Larkin building and the Edwin and Martha "Mamah" Cheney residence.[7] His tenure was not continuous or always full time. Desiring more financially secure employment, he worked as chief draftsman for Richard E. Schmidt from 1901 to 1902 and, after returning to Wright's studio part time around 1903, in the office of D. H. Burnham. By 1905 he had resumed full-time employment in Oak Park.[8]

As Wright's reputation grew, an increasing number of commissions, primarily for residential projects in the Chicago suburbs, began entering the office, and as a result the staff expanded. The "usually agreeable" redhead Walter Burley Griffin most likely arrived sometime between July 1901 and early September of that year, when the working drawings for the Thomas house were under way.[9] As an architecture student at the University of Illinois, Griffin had furthered an interest in landscape design with courses in horticulture

3.3 Richard Bock, William Drummond, and Walter Burley Griffin with two women and a child, probably Bock's daughter Dorathi, at tea. Photographer unknown. Eric Milton Nicholls Collection, National Library of Australia.

and forestry. Like Mahony, after graduation he found employment with Dwight Perkins and later other Steinway Hall architects, including Webster Tomlinson around the time of his partnership with Wright.[10] Possibly lured by the promise of some form of partnership or profit sharing with Wright, as well as a shorter commute from his residence in the western suburb of Elmhurst, Griffin served as a job superintendent and later as the general office manager of the Oak Park studio.[11] His duties included writing specifications and supervising local construction.[12] Because of his compassionate personality, he also often found himself in the thankless role of mediator, calming upset clients.[13]

Griffin's interest in landscape design inspired greater attention to both the siting and the surrounding conditions of residential projects. Evidence includes detailed planting plans he produced for the

Ward Willits, Darwin Martin, and Francis Little (I) residences.[14] Griffin also worked on several independent commissions, including a landscape design for Eastern Illinois State Normal School and his first major building project, a house for his friend William H. Emery Jr. in Elmhurst (1902).[15]

Wright also hired Isabel Roberts a few months after Griffin's arrival, in late 1901 or possibly early 1902.[16] Often identified as a secretary or bookkeeper, she also worked as a draftsman. Roberts had completed three years of formal architectural education in New York City under French designer Emmanuel Louis Masqueray and his American colleague Walter B. Chambers.[17] Her training focused on interior decoration and encompassed instruction in both furniture and glass design. While Roberts primarily assisted Griffin in his office duties, she contributed to the production

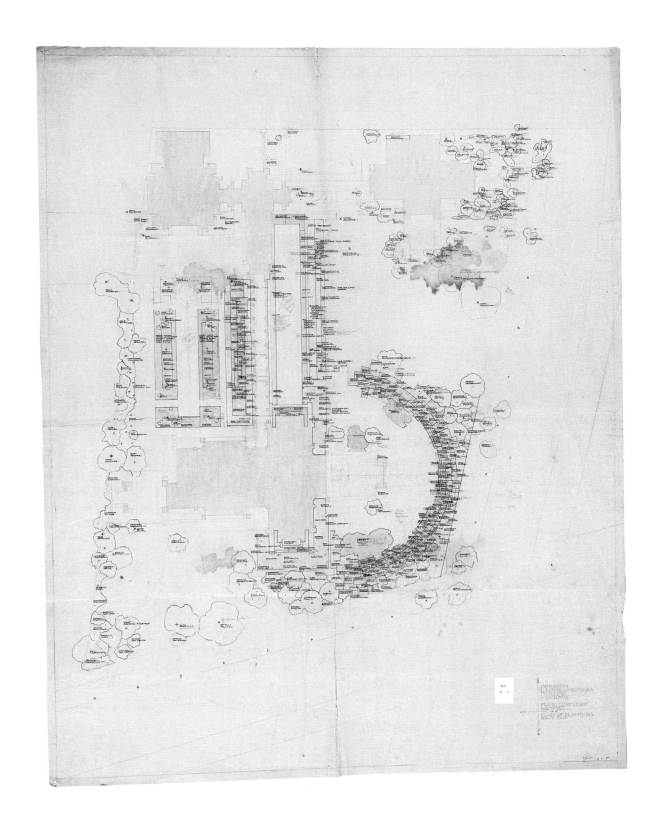

3.4 Darwin Martin property planting plan, drawn by Walter Burley Griffin. Courtesy University Archives, University at Buffalo, State University of New York. © 2020 Frank Lloyd Wright Foundation, Scottsdale, AZ. All rights reserved.

3.5 W. H. Emery house, Elmhurst, Illinois, 1903, designed by Walter Burley Griffin. Eric Milton Nicholls Collection, National Library of Australia.

of architectural designs, helping out with drafting and other tasks, including the design of art glass.[18]

Barry Byrne recalled that when he entered the studio in June 1902, there were five people working for Wright: Griffin, Roberts, Willis, "Cecil Barnes" (most likely Cecil Bryan), and Andrew Willatzen.[19] Mahony had temporarily departed to focus on her first major independent commission, the All Souls Unitarian Church in Evanston, Illinois, supplementing her income by working as a teacher.[20] Drummond meanwhile had left for Richard Schmidt's office. New hires Bryan and Willatzen both had previous construction experience and primarily helped in the production of working drawings. Bryan had trained as a builder with his father and then took classes in engineering at the Lewis Institute in Chicago. Willatzen, meanwhile, had

worked with his own father, a cabinetmaker, and attended a trade school in Europe before immigrating to Illinois in 1901. He briefly worked as a carpenter in Moline and then as a mechanic in Rock Island.[21] Willatzen stumbled upon some of Wright's published designs while in Rock Island, and when he expressed an interest in the work, his employer encouraged him to seek a position with the architect.[22] Willatzen visited the Oak Park studio sometime shortly before spring 1902 and Wright, needing help, immediately hired him.[23] Wright also hired architect Charles Erwin Barglebaugh around this time and possibly artist and architect Clarence Shepard, who later went on to practice in Kansas City.[24]

Byrne, a teenager with no previous training, sought employment with Wright after seeing the architect's

3.6 Photograph of Barry Byrne, ca. 1913. Vincent L. Michael / Byrne Family Collection.

work in the spring 1902 annual Chicago Architectural Club show.[25] Romantically recalling his interview, Byrne wrote (shifting his point of view as he went):

He had presented himself at the studio door in Oak Park promptly on time, and after repeated ringings, had been admitted by a charming red-haired, smiling lady, with children clinging to her skirts. It was Sunday morning and the wait for his promised interview was a long one. . . . It was an enthralling place, however, and the pleasure I had in being there was deepened by my throbbing longing to be allowed to come and work in it. Like everything of this architect's design, the quality of the room enveloped your being and gave a sense of becoming part of a thing of rare distinction. It was as if you were caught up in a rhythm in which you moved in grave delight. My pleasure in it and my great desire to be taken on as a working pupil by Frank Lloyd Wright had an almost painful intensity.[26]

Wright, who recalled he didn't really need the "short, quiet youth," initially hired Byrne as an office boy.[27] Projects on the boards at the time included the Dana, Heurtley, Little, and William Martin residences

and a new building for the Hillside Home School. After several years of hands-on training, the bright young apprentice with a dry sense of humor became a full-fledged member of the practice. He prepared scale designs from preliminary sketches, occasionally assisting with renderings, and eventually served as a project manager.[28] In 1906 he executed drawings for a "complete remodeling" of the Edward Hills house and for the design of the Peter Beachy residence, both on Forest Avenue, as well as for nearby Unity Temple. Two years later, he worked on the Boynton house for Rochester, New York.[29]

Together, Byrne and the other designers formed a cooperative informal educational environment echoing that of Steinway Hall, which encouraged lively exchanges of ideas, although in Oak Park Wright assumed a solitary leadership position.

Studio Interactions

When working out new concepts, Wright typically initiated discussions with the other architects, especially Mahony and Griffin. Often everyone would join in.[30] Mahony, who worked on a corner table in the drafting room, served as a particularly valuable sounding board for Wright, matching him in argument and often critiquing his lectures.[31] Byrne recalled her kindness and mordant humor: "Her dialogs with Frank Lloyd Wright, who, as we all know, is no indifferent opponent in repartee, made such days particularly notable."[32] After her return to the studio in late 1902, Mahony, who had occasionally worked on designs for ornamental elements as early as 1897–98, spent most of her efforts on designing decorative components, such as furniture, sculpture, lighting fixtures, and glass mosaics. She often produced designs with limited input or in some cases only final approval from Wright.[33]

One of the most talented members of the Oak Park staff, Griffin contributed the most to Wright's developing design ideology, particularly regarding landscape and other contextual aspects.[34] Byrne remembered him serving as a "lens through which his employer could reexamine his own ideas" and the two men carrying out an almost continuous dialogue during the design process in these years.[35] Office debates, particu-

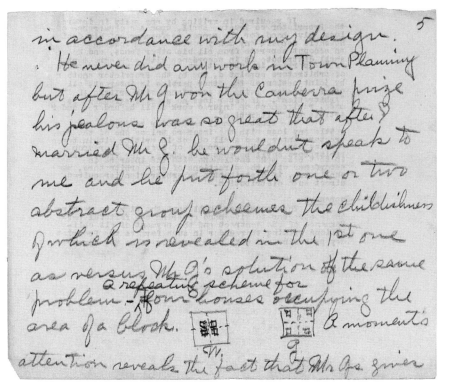

3.7 Note by Marion Mahony with sketches illustrating office debate between Frank Lloyd Wright and Walter Burley Griffin over site layout of four houses. Eric Milton Nicholls Collection (MS 9957, file 17, box 3), National Library of Australia.

larly between Wright and Mahony and Griffin, spurred innovation, while also serving as a release valve for tensions. Bock noted that Wright could be particularly sarcastic, using biting and caustic irony while attempting to rattle his opponent before "shoot[ing] his adversary's argument full of holes."[36] His debating style perhaps stemmed from an underlying sense of competitiveness with Griffin and Mahony.[37] While he repeatedly discounted the value of formal education, Wright likely harbored jealousy over the fact that several of his employees held professional degrees from top architectural programs. Furthermore, Mahony, Griffin, and Drummond had demonstrated their architectural proficiencies by passing the grueling three-day Illinois licensing exam, with Mahony in 1898 and Griffin in 1901 receiving the third-highest and highest scores in their years, respectively.[38]

Beyond introducing greater sensitivity to a building's relationship to its site, the specific influences Griffin exerted on his employer's designs were well "assimilated" and difficult to ascertain.[39] However, years later, both Mahony and William Purcell wrote

of Wright "borrowing" from his employees, particularly Griffin. While principals of firms often take full credit for design projects, a jaded Mahony later complained that her employer did not acknowledge her or Griffin for any of their contributions, acrimoniously branding him a "cancer sore … who originated very little but spent most of his time claiming everything and swiping everything."[40] Purcell recalled Griffin making "very extensive and basic contributions to many of Wright's projects" yet receiving "no acknowledgement!" Wright was unwilling, Purcell wrote, "to give any credit whatsoever to the contributions of others to his projects" and rarely, if ever, mentioned Griffin or Mahony.[41] Byrne remembered the "sharp reprimands which any reference to 'Miss Mahony's design' would elicit" from Wright.[42]

Evidence suggests that informal design competitions took place between Wright and Griffin. Mahony recalled an incident in which each architect produced a layout of a block that consisted of four houses. Illustrating the results with a diagram, she reported that Wright placed his houses next to each other in the center of the block, while Griffin spaced his apart with lawn surrounding each residence.[43] Discussions that took place during this competition may have contributed to the quadruple-block layout in Wright's first *Ladies' Home Journal* article.[44] While this layout appeared in print several months prior to Griffin entering Wright's employment, the design's sophisticated planning and landscape suggest his influence.[45] One can imagine the two men conversing about the design in Webster Tomlinson's Steinway Hall office at the time of Griffin's employment and Wright's partnership with the architect.

Purcell reported another contest between Wright and Griffin in 1901 that centered upon the design for the Frank Thomas house (see figure 2.14): "Walter B. Griffin who was virtually an unacknowledged partner of Wright's at that time--'We'll have a little contest.

You do one [a sketch], I'll do one--see which is best.' Griffin solved the project with so unique a solution that Wright had to acknowledge it in toto--and the house was carried to completion under Griffin's direction."[46] Purcell's description closely echoes one of Mahony's, who claimed that Griffin's "revolutionizing" of the work in Wright's office was first expressed in this residence.[47] She remembered her employer initially situating the structure in the center of the deep, narrow lot, set well back from the street "as if shrinking from an ugly thing of which it was afraid."[48] Purcell had reported that Wright clearly ignored the specific conditions of the site, which he should have known well, as it, too, was on Forest Avenue. The location included a series of red-brick row houses only ten feet from the sidewalk to the south, houses with setbacks ranging

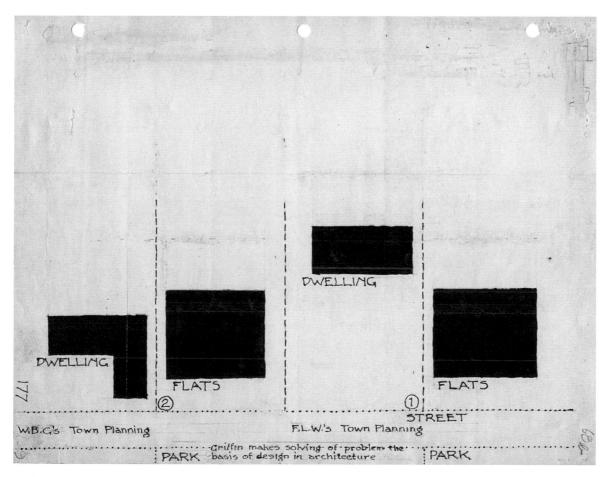

3.8 Diagrams comparing Walter Burley Griffin's and Frank Lloyd Wright's site plans for the Frank Thomas house authored by Mahony. Marion Mahony Griffin, "The Magic of America," ca. 1937–49, III.10.177. © New-York Historical Society.

3.9 Preliminary sketch of the Larkin building with an unrealized central entrance drawn by Walter Burley Griffin. Eric Milton Nicholls Collection, National Library of Australia.

from twenty-five to thirty-five feet to the north, as well as the "charming woods" of Austin Gardens, a five-acre park across the street to the southwest.[49] The architect's initial site plan allowed little privacy from the row houses and removed the clients from "the delightful view" of the park.[50]

When Wright revealed his sketches, Griffin offered constructive criticism, stating that "some useful part of this Thomas house should come forward to line with the flats, providing some afternoon sun and a look down the street--but keeping the main mass back."[51] To maintain a sense of privacy and to take advantage of the views across the street, he informed Wright, the obvious solution would be to elevate the main floor eight feet, above the eyes of passersby.[52] The

plan should be L-shaped instead of rectangular, with the whole building brought forward so that it acted as a "screen" from the flats next door and providing views to the "beautiful virgin forest" across the street and the "better class dwellings" to the north.[53] Mahony later wrote that the L-shaped plan "established a new type" in Wright's office.[54]

How much of the Thomas house design can be directly attributed to Griffin, or any other member of the studio staff, is difficult to ascertain, considering the continual banter that took place in the office and the practice of having multiple employees work on a single drawing. Additionally, Wright had already begun using an L-shaped plan prior to the Thomas commission. He had also raised the main living spaces in earlier residential designs for Aline Devin and Joseph Husser, suggesting the concepts predate Griffin joining the studio.

Another possible contribution by Griffin to the studio are the prominent corner piers that appear in works such as the Larkin building. He in fact authored an early sketch of the building showing the piers.[55] Corner piers emerged in studio work after Griffin entered the office, and they soon would be found in designs for the Willits, Dana, Little, and Heurtley houses, as well as an unrealized summer house for Edward Waller and Wright's second building for the Hillside Home School. One of the earliest examples of corner piers, however, appears on the Thomas Edward Wilder stables in Elmhurst, Illinois. While a plan for the complex dated 1901 includes a title block stating "Frank Lloyd Wright, Architect, Oak Park, Illinois," scholars identify the design as Griffin's.[56] Both the Wilder stables and Griffin's independent Emery house feature roofs with gabled ends and flared eaves as well as heavy corner piers––characteristics common in some of Griffin's other prairie-era designs. In contrast, most residences designed in the studio prior to his arrival include hipped roofs.

Armed with an architectural education that privileged structure over style, Griffin contributed to the significant shift in how Wright approached building design around the time the young architect entered the studio, including the full adoption of a "unit system" process. Byrne, who noted this shift, reported that Griffin had a "flair for systems" and "made an effort to systematize design."[57] Mahony also later recalled that, whereas she and Wright made picturesque compositions in the early years, Griffin emphasized structure, conceiving buildings not as facades but as three-dimensional compositions. She stressed that her colleague tended to think "in terms of construction … inventing and solving problems."[58] While Mahony, who did not hide her disgust for Wright at the time, may be giving too much credit to Griffin, Wright's architecture does become more systematized after Griffin's arrival in the studio.

If Griffin did bring with him the concept of designing from within using a module, Wright was definitely prepared to adopt it. Froebel's core design methods, including the application of a basic unit and the celebration of relationships between the parts to the whole, had already been on his mind. Robert Spencer reflected upon this in his 1900 article, stating that Wright's work "organically related" from the "smallest detail to the building as a whole," noting that "a repetition of a simple unit is only interesting and effective when there is a progressive rhythm horizontally or vertically between terminals in sympathy with structure."[59] In 1904, Charles White noted that the basic unit varied in size and number according to the need of each building project, though it was typically based on the width of a casement window.[60]

An additional contribution Griffin likely made to the Oak Park studio involved the manipulation of space vertically through the use of half-floor levels. Throughout his career, he displayed much more interest than Wright in "breaking the box" vertically through the incorporation of "split-floors." Even Griffin's early Emery residence consisted of five different floor levels within the three-story house, providing a sense of interconnectedness between the main rooms.[61]

Wright incorporated half-story areas in several of his Oak Park–era designs, although he usually limited their use to stair landings that offered views into public spaces, often screened by wood posts or grilles. Examples include the small mezzanine sitting area off the stair in the Rollin Furbeck house and in the front stair hall at the Dana house. Later, in the sanctuary of Unity Temple he more fully incorporated a split floor by raising the central main floor level halfway between surrounding lower "cloister" areas and balconies above. The changing views into other spaces are consonant with the architect's practices of breaking the form of the traditional box-shaped room and manipulating sequential spaces to achieve a specific effect.

Hiring gifted designers significantly contributed to Wright being able to build upon the momentum he had generated during the early years of his independent practice. The large drafting room in Oak Park gave him the space to expand his office from two or three workers to at least six in 1902. Contributing to

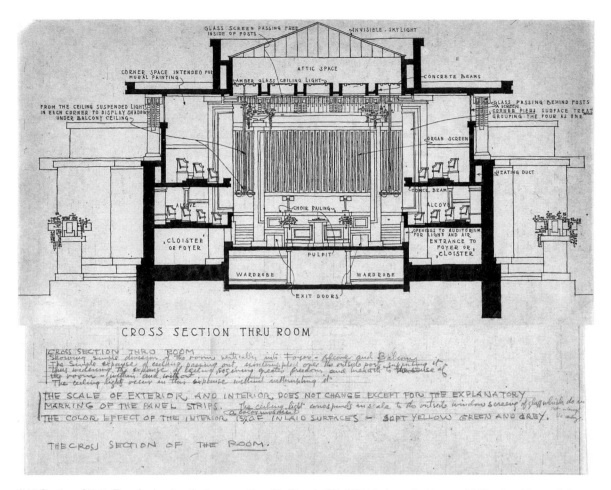

CROSS SECTION THRU ROOM

3.10 Section of Unity Temple showing the incorporation of half levels. TAL 0611.111, Avery Architectural & Fine Arts Library, Columbia University, New York. © 2020 Frank Lloyd Wright Foundation, Scottsdale, AZ. All rights reserved.

the chaotic drafting room atmosphere were the presence of artists, the regular intrusions of family members, and the occasional visits of out-of-town guests.

Artists, Family Members, and Other Visitors

The young husband found his work cut out for him now. The young wife found hers cut out for her. Architecture was my profession. Motherhood hers. Fair enough, but it was division. The willow tree grew in the corridor between my establishment—the studio—and hers, the home.

FRANK LLOYD WRIGHT (1943)

By 1902, with work under way on the Dana house, artists in residence included George Niedecken and Albert Van den Berghen. Bock wrote that Wright allowed Van den Berghen, who had long hair and a full beard trimmed in the style of Jesus Christ, to work in the drafting room, making "the studio somewhat confusing with conversations being carried all around."[62] Van den Berghen's one known work for Wright was an early version of a statue to represent Lord Alfred Tennyson's poem "Flower in the Crannied Wall" for the Dana residence. Not satisfied with the result, Wright asked Bock to redo the commission.[63] Attempting to capture Wright's conceptual but far from worked-out vision led to a long and tedious effort for Bock, whose version the architect eventually installed.

Wright's son John, not yet a teen, witnessed Bock's artistic struggle. He recalled,

Papa kept a naked woman on his drafting room balcony. I saw her through the high windows [from the playroom] opening over the flat gravel roof. She was pretty and had freckles. I tore across the street to get my playmate Cliff McHugh.[64] Dickie Bock, the sculptor, squinted his eyes in her direction, and then pressed clay into curves like those of which she was made. Papa came to the balcony and scrutinized Dickie's work. All of a sudden he ripped it apart. Dickie watched him with big tears streaming down his cheeks then proceeded to do the parts over to suit Dad. Papa spied us and chased us off the roof, brought us in and sat us down next to Dickie. Here we could get the artistic viewpoint.[65]

It was not until Wright was called out of town on business that Bock finally finished the sculpture.

John remembered a steady stream of other interesting people stopping by the property. While most callers confined their visits to the studio, others joined the family for dinner in the home; some even stayed overnight. The guest who stood out most in the Wright children's minds was the Canadian activist Honoré Jackson (also known as Jaxson), who claimed Métis blood and told the children wild yarns.[66] The mysterious long-haired and bearded Rabindranath Tagore from India, who went on to receive the 1913 Nobel Prize in Literature, came in swooshing robes.[67] Other only a bit less exotic visitors included English architect Charles Ashbee; American "Anarkist" artist and writer Elbert Hubbard; American architecture critic Russell Sturgis, German *Jugendstil* architect and urban planner Bruno Möhring; and Kuno Francke, a Harvard professor from Germany.[68] Charles White, who met Sturgis during his visit, observed that Wright did not think that the aging critic understood the work of the studio.[69] Sturgis's published critique of the Larkin building a few years later supports this belief. Wright's son John recalled Hubbard as being "almost

3.11 Albert Van den Berghen on the drafting room balcony next to one of the original diamond-paned clerestory windows with his version of the *Flower in the Crannied Wall* sculpture for the Dana residence. Courtesy of Mary Jane Hamilton.

3.12 Passageway between the Oak Park home and studio looking east toward the tree and drafting room balcony staircase with a door to the studio on the left. Photographer unknown. TAL 8901.0031, Avery Architectural & Fine Arts Library, Columbia University, New York.

as picturesque as Father" and that "they talked arts, crafts and philosophy by the hour."[70] Lloyd had fond memories of Ashbee and his wife teaching the Wright family "Morris songs and dances and old English rounds" and his father talking to the British architect about Scotsman Charles Rennie Mackintosh's "original and fresh approach to architecture."[71]

The proximity of Wright's home had a major impact on life in the architectural office even though Wright tried to maintain division between the environments.[72] While he regularly traversed the corridor between them to join his family for lunch, his employees did not.[73] Yet his professional and personal lives inevitably overlapped, offering a constant reminder for the studio architects about the basic needs of a suburban family. In 1900, Wright's first five children ranged in age from two to ten.[74] While the architect typically did not allow the youngsters in the studio, they occasionally ventured into the drafting room, creating havoc until banished.[75] Wright recalled that "[t]he connecting door to the studio would open cautiously, when some rather important client would be in to go over the plans. And I would see curly heads and mischievous eyes challenging mine knowing I could do nothing about it in the circumstances."[76] Barry Byrne remembered that even during his initial interview with Wright, "a couple of small children came to peep over the balcony rail and eye the boy with giggles and friendly derision and then fled with loud shouts of joy."[77]

The spirits of the children seeped into the studio. John eavesdropped on his father's conversations on an extension phone and at other times quietly threw things over the balcony railing onto the drafting tables and heads of the drafting men.[78] The children often raced around the studio encouraged by their father, who would pursue them. One day someone asked, "'What would you do if you caught one of them?' 'Well,' he said, 'I really don't know. I'm very careful not to.'"[79]

Wright's sister Maginel also remembered the children's love of running around the balcony of the drafting room and watching their father talk business. She recalled a young Catherine, chewing gum and with a dirty face and one stocking sagging down to her shoe, entering the studio and telling Papa that her mama wanted a dime. "We're busy little one," Wright replied, about to show Aline Devin plans for her new home.[80] He then escorted the girl firmly from the room and closed the door behind her. Not deterred, Catherine climbed up to the balcony, leaned over the rail, and hollered, "Papa, Mama wants a dime!" Wright had to admit to both his daughter and his client that he did not have one.[81] While the incident highly amused Devin, a "fashionable, fastidious client" on her first visit to the studio, she never constructed the house the architect designed for her.[82]

The studio also served as a place where Wright entertained groups of friends. Clambakes, tea parties, and cotillions were held in the drafting room, with blazing logs that snapped and crackled in the big fireplace in which Wright baked clams.[83] Bock recalled one wintery day when Wright received a barrel of fresh oysters from a client and a party quickly ensued. He wrote "tressel [sic] tables were put up in the studio, and it was fun to watch the jubilant children roasting the oysters in the fireplace and serving them to the guests."[84]

The weddings of Wright's sisters Jane and Maginel also took place in the studio.[85] For Jane's wedding to Andrew Taylor Porter on 28 June 1900, the couple entered under a canopy of daisies into a room profusely decorated with black-eyed Susans and more daisies.[86] Even with the drafting tables and other furnishing moved out of the way, the studio must have felt quite crowded for the two hundred guests.[87] In October 1904 the studio served as the site for Maginel's wedding to Walter J. "Pat" Enright, a fellow artist whom she met while working as a commercial illustrator.[88]

After hours, the studio served as a refuge where Wright could free himself from clients and contractors as well as other business and family responsibilities. In place of natural light, warm illumination emanated from the green task lamps and ten-inch prismatic globes and from indirect lighting through decorative ceiling panels in the other spaces, creating peaceful settings for inspirational contemplation. Wright often continued his architectural explorations well into the night. Son Lloyd remembered his father regularly heading to bed totally exhausted at two or

3.13 The Oak Park home playroom looking west toward the balcony showing sons Lloyd and John at the chalkboard before the installation of the piano. Lloyd maintained that the chest in the photograph came from the same shop where his father bought Oriental rugs. It was returned to the home during the restoration. Photographer unknown. TAL 9307.0003, Avery Architectural & Fine Arts Library, Columbia University, New York.

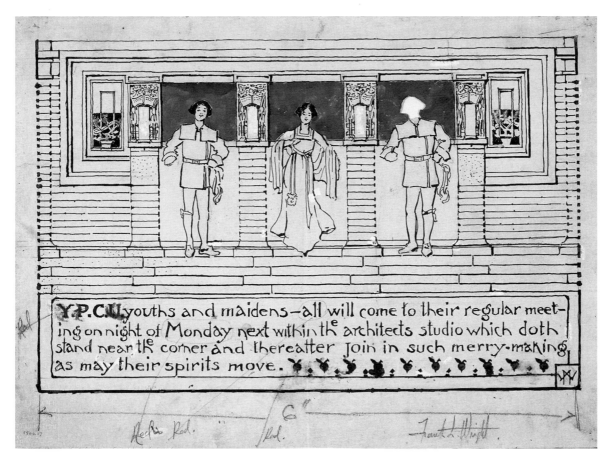

3.14 Unfinished invitation showing the studio entrance by Maginel Wright. TAL 9506.017, Avery Architectural & Fine Arts Library, Columbia University, New York.

three o'clock in the morning after working on a difficult design problem.[89] And if unable to sleep because of one idea or another, he would "get up, go down stairs to the 'studio' by the way of the connecting corridor, and work."[90]

Some evenings the studio presented a less peaceful environment, as when Wright and his employees worked around the clock when necessary to complete projects. The architect recalled that sometimes they even slept on the drafting boards.[91] He himself did not have his own specific workspace in the drafting room but labored on whatever desk available.[92] Barry Byrne recalled that frequently he would sit at an employee's drafting table and spend hours on a minor detail.[93] One could imagine, as Wright took a break from the work at hand, ideas developing in his mind of innovative ways to improve the design of his workplace.

Early Alterations to the Studio

During his initial visit to the studio in 1902, Barry Byrne found the diamond-paned casement windows in the drafting room "swung wide and the odors of an early June day drifted in from a garden filled with an overgrowth of the luxuriant foliage, with which the prairie country welcomes the summer."[94] By this time Wright had already undertaken a series of renovations. As with the house next door, the studio served as an ever-changing exploratory design setting. While some alterations were extremely minimal, such as the introduction of a new decorative object, others involved major construction activity that significantly affected office production.

The earliest changes primarily consisted of minor refinements to accommodate the functional needs of

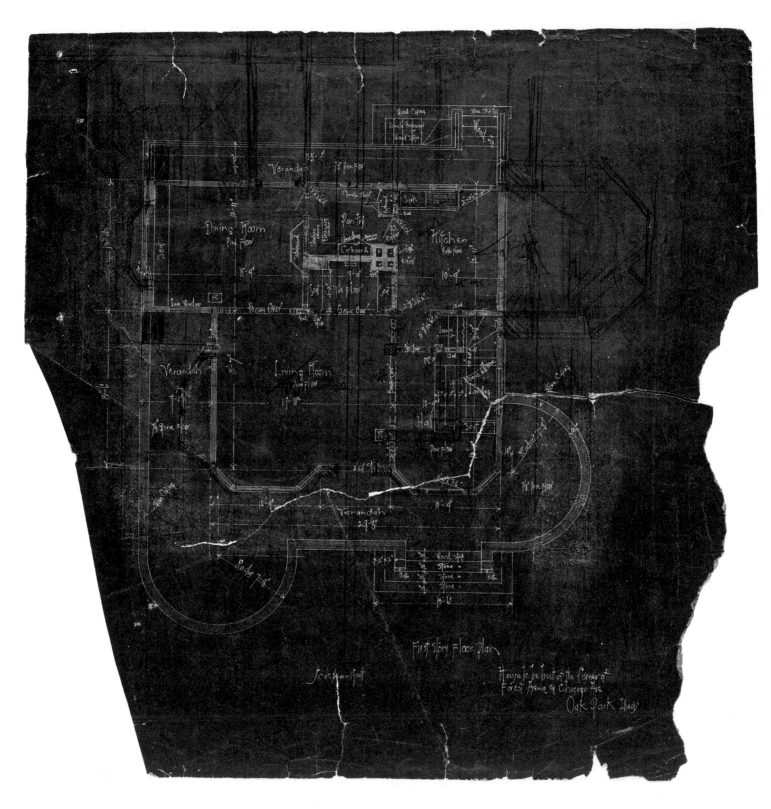

3.15 First floor plan of the Oak Park home revealing the start of Wright's "pinwheel" rotation of spaces, ca. 1889. TAL 8901.002, © 2020 Frank Lloyd Wright Foundation, Scottsdale, AZ. All rights reserved.

the studio. One, however, was purely aesthetic. Within months of the opening of the office, Wright rotated the eastern boulder figure at the entrance ninety degrees so that the crouching man faced west (compare the east boulder in figure I.1 with figure 2.6).[95] Although it might appear insignificant, by rotating the sculpture Wright achieved a greater sense of balance to the composition while at the same time making the sculptures appear as two unique works.[96] The practice of rotating elements, common to many Froebel exercises, became central to Wright's "pinwheel" design forms, beginning in the subtle arrangement of rooms around a central hearth in house plans, as in his own residence in 1889 and the Quadruple Block Plan design of 1901 and later much more prominently in many of his skyscraper plans, including his one realized tall building, the Price Tower in Bartlesville, Oklahoma.

A much more substantial alteration to the front of the studio, likely carried out just after 1902, offers an example of the architect's explorations of what scholars have labeled his *paths of discovery*, an attribute that involved the creation of a carefully crafted processional route that typically begins at the street curb, transverses the main entrance of a building, and continues inside toward a central hearth. Wright built a wall of Chicago common brick that spans most of the original broad staircase leading up to the studio loggia. He then added new stairs to the outside of each of the large piers that held urns, creating two carefully crafted zigzagging pathways that led from the street to the doors tucked into the sides of the raised entrance porch, moving visitors off and then back onto the original entrance axis, subtly encouraging them to slow their pace and experience the building from specific vantage points. The new wall also helped to make the entrance less visually accessible to passersby and to protect the reception hall from the increasing clamor of Chicago Avenue, as the street had developed from a

3.16 The Oak Park studio with two levels of diamond-paned windows on the drafting-room balcony to the left, but only one level of windows on the library on the right. Also visible are the new planters and brick wall across the front that created a more elaborate entrance pathway from the street, ca. 1906. TAL 9506.0025, Avery Architectural & Fine Arts Library, Columbia University, New York. © 2020 Frank Lloyd Wright Foundation, Scottsdale, AZ. All rights reserved.

dirt road to a paved thoroughfare with a streetcar line. At the same time he built the wall, Wright also added additional piers to the outer sides of the new stairs and moved the original two round urns to the front of the house. In their place he installed four larger, more elaborate planters on the piers that form three-dimensional versions of his early logo—the cross within a circle within a square.[97]

Wright went on to create more complex paths of discovery for most of his designs after 1902, providing a sense of pilgrimage for visitors. For example, in the house he designed for his neighbor Arthur Heurtley, he placed the main approach to the residence off axis from the front door (see figure 3.2). This created a deliberately long entry route that begins at the edge of the property and continues after several turns through a heavy arched front door. Inside, the pathway continues through additional changes of direction before traversing a flight of stairs and several more turns to finally reach the central main hearth in the living room.[98]

Clients

Clients like Heurtley who commissioned prairie houses from Wright were, according to the architect, "businessmen with unspoiled instincts and untainted ideas," although they often shared many of his progressive views.[99] Male clients primarily consisted of self-made managers of small- or medium-sized companies in the Chicago Loop concerned with the mechanical side of production. They tended to be Republicans who, like the architect, enjoyed music and practiced liberal religions like Unitarianism and Christian Science to various degrees.[100] A number of Wright's female clients, including Mrs. Frank (Susan) Thomas and Mrs. William (Winifred) Martin, supported the women's suffrage movement.[101] Like Catherine and Anna Wright, several were deeply interested in childhood education.[102] Both Winifred Martin and Queene Coonley became central in the establishment of kindergartens in Oak Park and Riverside, respectively.

Arthur Heurtley served as secretary of the Northern Trust Company when he commissioned his residential design from Wright.[103] If the two men had

3.17 Portrait of Arthur Heurtley. Moffett Studio. Courtesy of Allen Heurtley.

not previously met through Oak Park or River Forest community activities, they may have met either on the train into the Loop or at the Rookery sometime during 1898 or 1899, as both the trust and Wright kept offices there at the time.[104] Heurtley actively participated in many social organizations, including the Cliff Dwellers Club, the Chicago Golf Club of Wheaton, and the River Forest Tennis Club.[105] Like Wright, music played a large role in Heurtley's life, and in addition to being a member of the Chicago Orchestral Association, he served as president of the Oak Park Chamber Music Association.[106]

Throughout his long career, Wright's charisma and self-marketing ability helped to attract clients like the Heurtleys. Early patrons, however, often risked public ridicule due to their unusual-looking residences.[107] According to Wright himself, fellow rail commuters derided William Winslow on his way to work in the Loop, leading the businessman to avoid the popular morning and evening express trains in order to escape the constant bantering about his Wright-designed home in River Forest.[108] Buffalo client Darwin Martin reported in 1903 that people had labeled Wright's residential designs as "'freak' houses" and that he himself thought one of them, owned by a banker (probably Heurtley), resembled "an automobile barn with a second story dancing pavilion."[109] During its construction the Heurtley house's unusual form attracted great attention. The client reported to his eleven-year-old son Richard, out of town at the time, that as the construction of their house neared completion the boy would laugh if he saw "the procession of people that stream in, around, and out of the house, especially on Saturdays and Sundays."[110] In 1910, even after a whole series of prairie houses materialized in Oak Park, the *Chicago Tribune* referred to the "bizarre style" of Wright's architecture.[111]

The architect's ability to charm clients, both while meeting them in the studio and in correspondence, resulted in many homeowners overlooking huge cost overruns on their new dwellings in addition to public ridicule.[112] In some cases, the final cost came in at three or more times the original budget. As Wright scholar Grant Manson observed, "Wright's genius was never at home in the realm of the merely economical."[113] While his underlying design process provided a straightforward procedure for the creation of new works of architecture, numerous design modifications and delays for various reasons, including for studio remodeling projects, often amplified budget overruns. Despite this fact, several clients, including Thomas and Laura Gale, Avery and Queene Coonley, and Francis and Mary Little, returned to the studio and commissioned additional designs.

Design Process

No man ever built a building worthy the name of architecture who fashioned it in perspective sketch to his taste and then fudged the plan to suit.

FRANK LLOYD WRIGHT (1908)

Wright's design process reflected his conception of an organic architecture in which structure, materials, and construction methods come together to respond to specific functional needs and settings, as well as to the larger context of a rapidly industrializing America. In 1904 studio draftsman Charles White wrote, "Most men outline the strictly utilitarian requirements, choose their style, and then mold the design along those lines, whereas Wright develops his unit first, then fits his design to the requirements as much as possible, or rather, fits the requirements to the design."[114] Wright noted how his early employer, the gifted renderer Joseph Lyman Silsbee, "made his pretty sketch, getting some charming picturesque effect he had in his mind. Then the sketch would come out into the draughting room to be fixed up into a building, keeping the floor-plan near the sketch if possible."[115] In explaining his alternative process, Wright expounded: "The 'architecture' is not 'thrown up' as an artistic exercise, a matter of elevation from a preconceived ground plan. The schemes are conceived in three dimensions as organic entities, let the picturesque perspective fall how it will.... I have great faith that if the thing is rightly put together in true organic sense with proportions actually right the perspectives will take care of themselves."[116] The usual first step for Wright in designing one of his prairie houses involved the development of the floor plan based on a specific unit. Wright later wrote, "[A] good plan is the beginning and the end, because every good plan is organic.... There is more beauty in a fine ground plan than in almost any of its ultimate consequences. In itself it will have the rhythms, masses and proportions of a good decoration if it is the organic plan for an organic building with individual style—consistent with materials."[117] Generating the exterior form of the house from the plan, he preached, would result in a strong sense of overall unity. Wright also applied these principles to nonresidential Oak Park–era designs, such as the Larkin building and Unity Temple.

White believed that his employer's "greatest contribution to Architecture" was the "unit system of design."[118] Wright, who viewed the unit as a way to order space and to simplify the technical difficulties of construction as early as 1900, had, possibly with the input from Griffin, fully adopted his unit-based system by 1902 when he produced cottages for George and Mary Gerts and their son Walter in Whitehall, Michigan.[119]

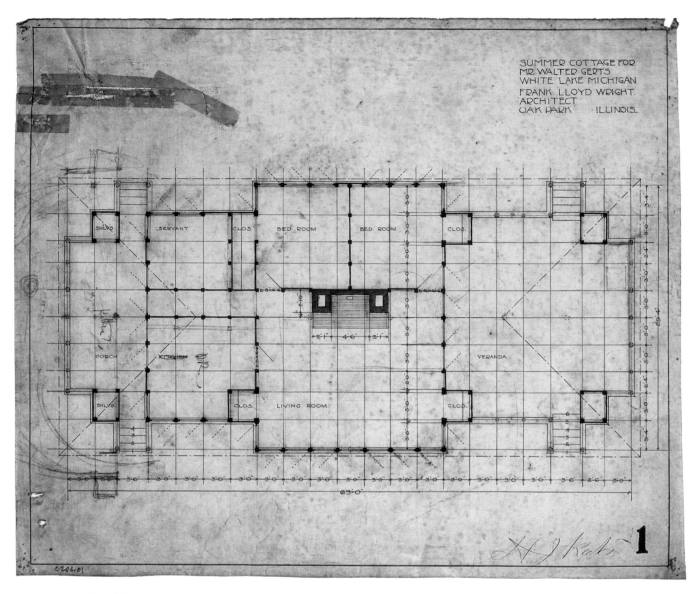

SUMMER COTTAGE FOR
MR. WALTER GERTS
WHITE LAKE MICHIGAN
FRANK LLOYD WRIGHT
ARCHITECT
OAK PARK   ILLINOIS.

3.18 Plan of the Walter Gerts summer cottage, Whitehall, Michigan, that includes an underlying grid, 1902. TAL 0203.001, Avery Architectural & Fine Arts Library, Columbia University, New York. © 2020 Frank Lloyd Wright Foundation, Scottsdale, AZ. All rights reserved.

The grids are clearly visible on these plans. The architect's reliance upon grids was undoubtedly reinforced by the presence of such activities in the Froebel kindergarten next door run by Catherine and George's daughter Kate. This unit approach became central to Wright's creative process.[120] The result offered a strong sense of unity between the plan and the other features of the building, including furniture, art glass windows, and other decorative details.

In 1908, Wright reported that the use of such an or-dering system was "expedient to simplify the technical difficulties of execution."[121] The process, however, was often not so effortless and straightforward. He often would work on an architectural idea over and over again until he felt it was relatively complete. This frequently involved revising an idea throughout the course of a number of commissions. Byrne remembered, "[S]ometimes there was a struggle, one scheme superseding another, to achieve a high degree of expressive unity between such an initial plan, and the

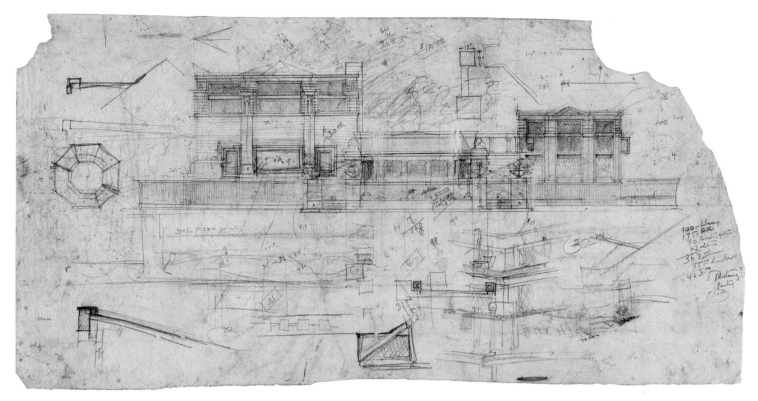

3.19 Studio elevation from the 1906 remodeling, with various added comments and sketches, that shows the addition of a second row of clerestory windows on both the drafting room balcony and the library, ca. 1906. TAL 9506.002, Avery Architectural & Fine Arts Library, Columbia University, New York. © 2020 Frank Lloyd Wright Foundation, Scottsdale, AZ. All rights reserved.

expression of it in mass and detail."[122] This can be seen in the numerous drawings produced for individual commissions. For the Beachy house, for example, approximately seventy-five developmental, presentation, detail, and working drawings survive.[123]

The many documents produced in the Oak Park office that exhibit later additions of sketches, modifications, side comments, and financial notations illustrate that the design process did not end with the production of working drawings. Examples of this include a second-floor plan of the Willits house showing several small sketches labeled with dimensions and the residue of pencil lines from what appears to be the designer working out the roof structure.[124] Section drawings for the Dana house, meanwhile, exhibit lightly penciled additions that suggest later refinements of roof, window, foundation, and flue details.[125] Most of the drawings for Wright's Oak Park property clearly reflect this practice.

Early Renderings

While Wright rejected using perspectives as a starting point in his design process, they did play a prominent role in publicizing his architecture. Even from the start of his independent career Wright typically hired others to produce presentation drawings of his work, often after the project was built. In fact, renderers even based some of their drawings on traced photographs of completed buildings.[126]

Many artists and architects involved in the Oak Park studio, including Birch Burdette Long, Louis Rasmussen, George Niedecken, Marion Mahony, George Willis, William Drummond, Barry Byrne, and Harry Robinson, produced presentation renderings.[127] George Grant Elmslie wrote that he completed the lettering and some of the drawings for plates of Wright's work published in the June 1900 issue of *Architectural Review*.[128] In most cases, however, the early drawings that

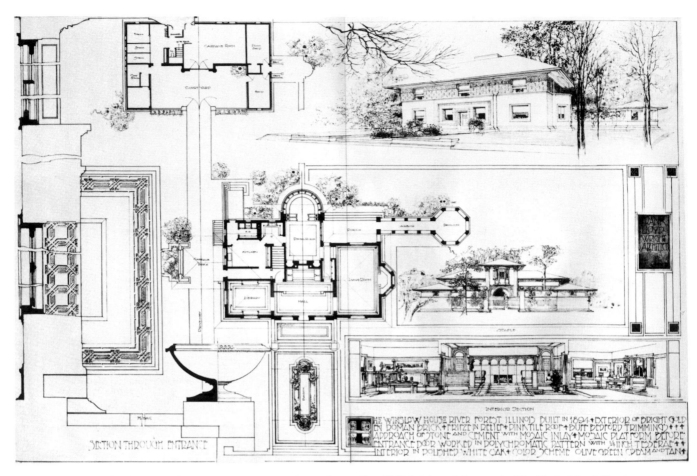

3.20 Winslow house rendering incorporating an analytique layout. Plate XXXVI, Robert C. Spencer Jr., "The Work of Frank Lloyd Wright," *Architectural Review*, June 1900.

have survived are unsigned. To complicate matters of identification, at times several draftsmen worked on the same rendering, and in other instances a number of versions of the same drawing exist, including reworked copies made for *Ausgeführte Bauten und Entwürfe von Frank Lloyd Wright*, an elaborate portfolio of Wright's Oak Park work published in 1910 by the Berlin publishing house Ernst Wasmuth Verlag, often referred to as the Wasmuth Portfolio.[129]

While George Elmslie may have contributed to the *Architectural Review* plates, the perspectives and overall compositions appear to be in Wright's own hand. The delicately rendered trees and foliage in the drawings of the Oak Park studio and the Winslow and Husser houses recall the lightness of pen lines in sketches of plants the architect produced as a teenager.[130] The contrasting crispness of the buildings help to draw the viewer's focus to the architecture framed by the pleas-

ant natural surroundings. The intricate compositions of the plates recall the Beaux Arts *analytique* tradition popular at the time in which other related architectural drawings surround a rendering. The *Architectural Review* article pages also exhibit aesthetically composed assemblages of photographs, perspectives, details, and, in some cases, plans, suggesting Wright worked closely with author Robert Spencer on its layout.

This collage style of rendering largely disappeared from the Oak Park office by 1901 in favor of less intricate drawings.[131] Birch Burdette Long produced a number of these perspectives, but not necessarily in the studio. An active member of the Chicago Architectural Club, Long developed a reputation for his exceptional drawing ability and style of pen-and-ink renderings that reflected his interest in Japanese art. Wright, not one to bestow praise on other designers freely, later identified him as a "young and talented 'renderer.'"[132]

commonplace of our life, those simple, normal feelings which the people of this day will be helpless otherwise to express. And here you have the key with which individually you may unlock in time the portal of your art."

Into these small things it is always possible for the architect to put something of his higher self, something which will give grace, meaning and beauty to the simplest combination of humble material, just as the tiny flower expresses in exquisite and organic form and detail the life-principle and life-purpose of the humblest weed.

The illustrations in their diversity and completeness tell the story of each individual work according to its importance and pictorial value from the standpoint of the series of set here, where of light and which a parallel fail to exhibit, however, that we should clearly apprehend the significance of these refreshingly unhackneyed types, so thoughtfully and ingeniously presented.

Diverse in form, purpose and expression, there is a quality of style in each of Mr. Wright's works which, even to the unschooled eye of the layman, stamps it as his, and which relates each to all the others. This is true even in the case of the Moore House, where a plain, practical American citizen, who insisted upon

workman, and no categorical descriptions seems called for a few straight lines or a patch of shade convey to the mind ideas graph of mere words might easpress. It is of importance,

and for which no English prece-has been managed in composi-as in its minor details, in a new way. The amputated "lean-to" gable end, or the weak, hipped terminal so common in the finest of our mod-houses, giving to the porch the appearance of an unrelated excrescence or an applied make-shift, did not satisfy Mr. Wright, and he worked over the problem until he succeeded in making his timber porch a part of his brick and half-timbered house. Organically related in general scheme and smallest detail to the building as a whole, this porch is evidently the work of an architectural free-thinker. A careful study of his work as represented upon these pages will show that while Mr. Wright has an evident love

having an English half-timbered house, was saved from himself in a large measure by the stubborn selfhood of his architect. Yet a better example of the spirit, if not the letter of the half-timbered, gabled house at its best, it would be hard to find, although, confessedly, in its affectation of exposed and ornamented sturdy timber construction, but a clever bit of architectural scene painting. But with these forced tributes to tradition, which have in themselves a certain undeniable charm, there is not only an admirable directness and simplicity of plan shown here, but a breadth and symmetry of massing and composition as well. The main gable is beautifully proportioned. The large porch or loggia on the garden side, the bane of the designer, dent exists, tion, as well and individual roof or half-terminal so ern country

3.21 Page of the 1900 Spencer article with an *analytique*-influenced layout of images. Robert C. Spencer Jr., "The Work of Frank Lloyd Wright," *Architectural Review*, June 1900, 63.

3.22 Worm's-eye rendering of the E. H. Pitkin cottage on Sapper Island, Ontario (1900). Birch Burdette Long's logo appears in the lower left of the drawing. TAL 0005.001, Avery Architectural & Fine Arts Library, Columbia University, New York. © 2020 Frank Lloyd Wright Foundation, Scottsdale, AZ. All rights reserved.

The studio drawings attributed to Long, including a 1902 watercolor of a summer cottage design for E. H. Pitkin identified by his logo, demonstrate his use of powerful compositions, dramatic contrasts of light and shade, and decorative foliage reminiscent of Japanese prints (see figure 3.22).[133] Landscaping frames and highlights the architecture in a fashion similar to Wright's, but Long's treatment of vegetation is stylistically heavier and more pattern-like. Renderings of the Hillside Home School and the Victor Metzger house, later reworked for the Wasmuth Portfolio, also appear to be in Long's hand.[134] The drawing of the school presents a high bird's-eye perspective, while the Metzger residence, like that of the Pitkin cottage, places the viewer below, giving the house a dramatic presentation.[135] Long's monogram additionally iden-

tifies him as the author of an ink drawing of Wright's Thomas house (see figure 2.14), which also features color washes, angled trees, and flattened, abstract foliage. After winning the 1903 Chicago Architectural Club Travelling Scholarship, Long left the Midwest for Europe. Eventually Marion Mahony took over the role of main studio renderer, building upon Long's stylistic technique to produce the characteristic perspective drawings of the studio's later years.[136] Immediately after Long's departure, however, she continued to focus on producing drawings for decorative elements for commissions such as the residence of socialite Susan Lawrence Dana in Springfield, Illinois, as Wright turned to artist George Niedecken to produce color renderings of its spectacular interiors.

Dana House

One of Wright's largest and most significant residential commissions in this period, the extravagant Susan Lawrence Dana house, offers insights into the elaborate choreography of designers, draftsmen, artists, and others in the early years of the studio. The substantial project arrived at a critical time. Despite having had several noteworthy projects, in January 1902, Wright wrote to Charles Ashbee that the previous year had proved to be "neither feast nor famine, but a very modest mean." He went on: "I don't feel that I have grown much either,—in fact I am truly blue."[137] The rapid pace of his architectural development during the previous few years had begun to slow. Soon, however, the Dana house presented him with a stimulating design exercise that demanded much of him and the studio staff.

Dana initially hired Wright to update and transform her family's Italianate mansion on Aristocratic Hill located only a few blocks from the state capitol into "a gathering place for the artistic activities of the community."[138] Despite keeping a close eye on expenses, she essentially handed the architect a blank check, resulting in a 12,600-square-foot, thirty-five-room home.[139] Resolving the design of the new residence, in particular the relationship of its central core with the remains of the earlier home, presented a major challenge. An awkward preliminary plan includes an "ugly island of obstructions" in the central reception hall that contained fireplaces, a safety vault, a powder room, and a coatroom.[140] Wright and the other studio architects successfully solved this and many other design issues, creating a sophisticated, sprawling composition that engulfs the original house. The defining relationship of the gallery (studio) wing to the rest of the residence likely stemmed from input provided by Mahony, as the basic layout of the wing with its long corridor strongly recalls her MIT thesis project.[141]

The exterior of the completed residence consists of an elaborate composition of vertical and horizontal elements. Wright had the mortar on the horizontal brick joints of the exterior walls raked to give the appearance of horizontal bands. As in several of his earlier designs, including the Winslow and Heller houses, an elaborate frieze surrounded the upper level of the facades.[142] The design, more angular than the leafy, Sullivanesque forms of Wright's earlier friezes, reflects the architect's growing interest in geometric abstractions of nature.

Visitors stroll down an uncharacteristically straight walkway from the street to the arched entrance portal. Bock's seductive *Flower in the Crannied Wall* sculpture draws guests forward through a low, barrel-vaulted entrance vestibule lit by the golden arches of butterfly-patterned leaded glass and an arched, art glass laylight.[143] Inside, visitors find themselves standing with the statue in a tall but compact entrance hall. Here, Wright produced an interior "path of discovery" significantly more complex than that at his studio.

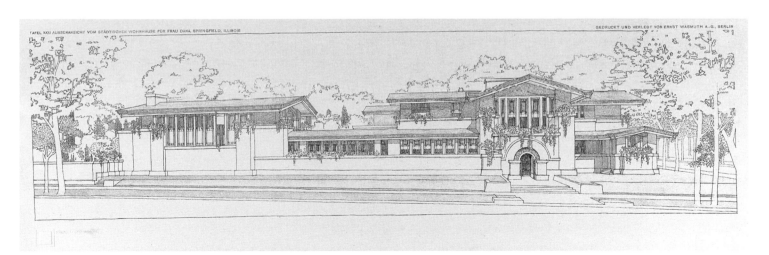

3.23 Dana house. Plate XXXI, *Ausgeführte Bauten und Entwürfe von Frank Lloyd Wright*, 1910. Special Collections, J. Willard Marriott Library, University of Utah.

3.24 Dana house reception hall as restored, showing multiple floor levels and location of Bock's *Flower in the Crannied Wall* sculpture, 1996. Photographer: Doug Carr.

He wove layers of light and space around the hall by surrounding it with a staircase that leads to a reception hall and to other major spaces on different floor levels. Warm light shines through leaded glass windows during the day and from wall sconces at night. The resulting sensual, visual experience presented ever-changing glimpses into the spaces beyond, a quality Wright carried out elsewhere in the house. Griffin, who was exploring the potential of split levels in dwellings around this time in his own work, likely had a hand in the vertical complexity of the residence, which includes three main and sixteen secondary floor levels.

Wright also used varying ceiling heights, creating compressed hallways that open up to spacious, vaulted rooms. This echoed the inclusion in his own home of the narrow hallway leading to the second-floor playroom, as well as the dark passageway to the studio library. He made public rooms at the Dana house feel even larger during the day through the careful placement of windows that help to visually extend the rooms. Art glass light screens—both between interior spaces and between major rooms and the outside— help to control vistas. During the evening, the golden light from dozens of leaded-glass light fixtures recalls the hues of late autumn on the midwestern prairie.

The Springfield residence featured three major spaces designed for entertaining large numbers of guests: a drawing room and a dining room, both located off of a reception hall, and the gallery, separated from the rest of the house by the connecting corridor. Two of these rooms included curved ceilings. The dining room with its musician's loft illustrates Wright building upon a previously used design concept, in this case the barrel-vaulted playroom with balcony in his own home, a space that the Wrights often used for entertaining in the evenings. Even more reminiscent of the playroom was the gallery, which includes similar wood banding to draw one's eyes toward the vaulted ceiling. The Dana house rooms resulted in some of the last barrel-vaulted spaces in Wright's oeuvre, as he soon perceived the form as inappropriate for modern architecture, particularly in buildings that incorporate steel. He shared this view with his studio employees, for in 1904 Charles White informed his friend architect Walter Willcox that "in this day of steel, he [Wright]

uses the arch very rarely and recognizes the lintel construction, by strong horizontal lines throughout the building. He is so adverse to the arch, that in a barrel vault [sic] room, he usually tries to eradicate the effect of the sloping lines of the tympanum, by horizontal architectural lines in the decoration, or trim. He enjoys the soffit of the vault, but dislikes the tympanum."[144] In the Dana dining room, Wright hid the tympanum behind a pair of columns topped by a lintel that supported portieres used to block off the balcony area.

Dana's wealth allowed for the most elaborate decorative program of Wright's early career, resulting in an impressive *Gesamtkunstwerk* far more complex than in his Oak Park dining room or studio library. Here it consisted of one hundred pieces of furniture and approximately 450 art glass windows, as well as skylights, door panels, sconces, and other light fixtures. As in Oak Park, additional decorative works also encompassed large murals and both bas-relief and freestanding sculpture. A number of studio designers and artists participated in the creation of these elements, including Mahony, Griffin, Bock, and Niedecken, demonstrating the active collaborations in the studio and the unity between the architectural and artistic elements in Wright's designs. The two major sculptures created for the Dana house resulted from joint efforts. In addition to Bock's *Flower in the Crannied Wall* sculpture, *Moon Children*, a bas-relief that serves as the backdrop for a fountain in the reception hall just above the main staircase, was drawn by Mahony, sculpted by Bock, and then approved by Wright, reflecting a common practice in the studio.[145] Griffin's contribution included the design of a rectangular, double-bracket light sconce that could operate on both gas and electricity, used throughout the house as well as in his own Emery house design.[146]

Niedecken produced much of the interior decoration for the Dana house.[147] In a May 1904 letter, White told Willcox that "Niedecken, the artist, has returned for a few days a week. . . . He certainly has great individual talent as a decorative painter. . . . He is to make a few perspectives."[148] Wright must have respected Niedecken's abilities, as he displayed one of the artist's striking interior renderings of the Dana dining room on a cork display door in the studio library. (The

3.25 Rendering of the Dana house dining room by George Niedecken that appears pinned up in historic photographs of the Oak Park studio library (see figures 4.14 and 5.12). NYDA 1969.001.00001, Avery Architectural & Fine Arts Library, Columbia University, New York.

drawing appears in figures 4.14 and 5.12.) His use of delicate color washes recalls a number of the exterior perspectives of Wright's earlier work, including those produced by Birch Burdette Long. The rendering shows a mural of sumac, goldenrod, and purple aster in autumn tones that Niedecken created for the wall below the dining room's barrel vault.[149] As in Wright's studio, plants, small vases, a copy of the *Venus de Milo*, and other decorative elements completed the room.

The remarkable design of the Dana residence presents a magnificent example of what Wright could achieve with a willing client and a vibrant office environment that included the contributions of gifted designers with a range of talents, interests, and abilities. The residences produced in the suburban studio in its early years, even those nowhere near as grand as the Dana house, stood out from the numerous other dwellings that were quickly sprouting up in Oak Park and other communities in the heartland of America. The national publicity Wright received for his archi-

tectural ideas and early projects exposed his work to the larger design community and to potential clients in expanding suburbs and towns throughout the Midwest and beyond.

As Wright's reputation grew his studio became busier, with a dozen or so design projects each year. Soon new faces began appearing in the drafting room as the architect began hiring additional employees. A large percentage of the increase in business after 1902 was due to the arrival of the most important client of Wright's early independent career—Darwin D. Martin of Buffalo, New York. Martin-related commissions brought a sense of stability to the studio during its middle years. They also provided financial resources that allowed for major renovations to be made to the office as, despite the growing workload, Wright patiently took time to continue his own design education, which included constantly reassessing and reenvisioning the physical condition of his suburban work environment.

4
MIDDLE YEARS OF THE OAK PARK STUDIO (1903–1905)

Opportunity and Diversity

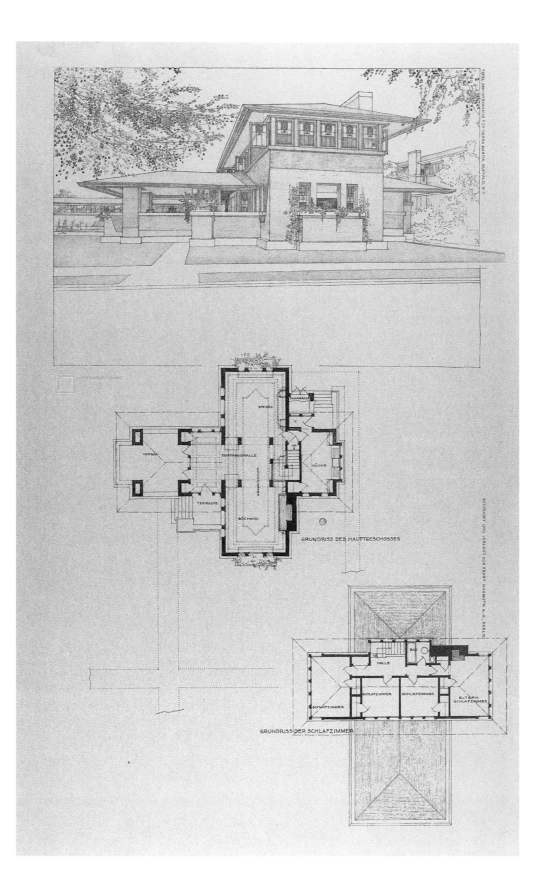

GRUNDRISS DES HAUPTGESCHOSSES

GRUNDRISS DER SCHLAFZIMMER

GEDRUCKT UND VERLEGT VON ERNST WASMUTH A.-G., BERLIN.

The character as well as the opportunity for beauty of our own age were both coming clear to me at that time. In fact I saw then as now that they are all one. I saw our own great chance in this sense still going to waste on every side. Rebellious and protestant as I was myself when the Larkin Building came from me, I was conscious also that the only way to succeed as either rebel or protestant was to make architecture [a] genuine and constructive affirmation of the new Order of the Machine Age.

FRANK LLOYD WRIGHT (1932)

By the start of 1903 Wright had successfully completed one major prairie house after another, including the Frank Thomas house down the block from his own home and the Francis Little residence further afield in Peoria, Illinois. As he entered what became one of the most productive eras of his suburban office, he had several noteworthy projects in progress. Construction was under way on the new building for his aunts' Hillside Home School and on the large residence for Susan Lawrence Dana. Other work included a relatively secluded house for Edwin and Mamah Cheney in Oak Park and a modest dwelling for Delta and George Barton in Buffalo, New York, one in a series of major commissions in that city connected to Darwin Martin. The most significant of the Martin-related projects—the new administration building for his employer, the Larkin Soap Company—was moving forward. Despite an abundance of work that included regular trips to Buffalo, Wright disregarded the demands of clients and contractors and unhurriedly carried out significant alterations to his studio. He also left work sitting or in the hands of employees while undertaking pleasure trips to St. Louis and Japan. Not entirely frivolous activities, the alterations and excursions offered new experiences that both contributed to and reconfirmed

for Wright his design ideology and architecture in significant ways. The experiences also influenced others working in the Oak Park office.

Studio Employees

Evidence suggests that the studio staff was at its largest during 1903 and 1904 when drawings for the Larkin building were on the boards. The number of major residential jobs in the office at this time fueled the need for additional assistance.[1] In a letter to architect Walter Willcox in November 1903, Charles White wrote, "Wright is very busy—has seven draftsmen."[2] The office staff probably consisted at the time of Cecil Bryan, Barry Byrne, Marion Chamberlain, Walter Burley Griffin, Marion Mahony, Isabel Roberts, and Andrew Willatzen.[3] George Willis had moved to California to work with former Steinway Hall architect Myron Hunt.[4] Drummond, likely away in late 1903, eventually returned as head draftsman.

The employment of Chamberlain and White, along with Byrne the previous year, demonstrates Wright's willingness to hire designers with various backgrounds, particularly if they showed up on his doorstep expressing admiration for his work or were re-

---

4.1 (*facing*) Barton house. Plate XXVI, *Ausgeführte Bauten und Entwürfe von Frank Lloyd Wright*, 1910. Special Collections, J. Willard Marriott Library, University of Utah.

ferred by colleagues. Chamberlain likely arrived on a recommendation from Marion Mahony. She had entered the architecture program at MIT in 1892, in the class right behind her namesake. The two Marions greatly enjoyed each other's intellect, discussing "the philosophies of the Western peoples, Kant's 'Critique of Pure Reason' and so on" to the point that once they forgot to attend their classes.[5] Chamberlain fully expected to make her mark on the male-dominated field of architecture. Instead, after receiving her degree in 1896, she found employment in the Boston Public Library.[6] She married her MIT classmate architect Herbert Chamberlain, who had won a fellowship to study architecture at the American School in Rome. While they were visiting Siena in May 1899, Herbert contracted acute peritonitis and died.[7] A few years later, Mahony's continuing friendship and the willingness of "Chicago men" to "welcome women into the profession" drew the young widow to Oak Park.[8] Yet she did not stay long.

What specific contributions Chamberlain made to Wright's architectural practice during her short stay are unknown. While unwanted personal interactions with the architect may have factored into her departure, as she later expressed great distaste for Wright, labeling him a womanizer, she apparently did not have the design abilities of Griffin or the artistic talents of Mahony.[9] After her departure, Charles White wrote that "she seemed to have so little ability along architectural lines, that Mr. Wright frankly advised her to give up, and try and get back into Librarianism."[10] She did.

Less is clear about Charles White's architectural education. In 1894, at the age of eighteen, he began working in the office of Boston architect Samuel J. Brown, quickly rising to the rank of chief draftsman.[11] Between 1897 and when he entered the Oak Park studio in late 1903, White worked as a designer at a number of businesses, in Boston; Rockford, Illinois; Steubenville, Ohio; and Burlington, Vermont. In 1901 White married Alice Roberts of Oak Park. Undoubtedly, her father, early Wright client and friend Charles E. Roberts, recommended that the architect take on his son-in-law.[12] William Purcell remembered White as "an awful nice fellow—just charming, honest, sincere, capable and a <u>very</u> deft, agile, imaginative planner."[13]

4.2 Marion Chamberlain, 1906. Photographer: Francis Watts Lee. Francis Watts Lee collection, DLC/PP-2015:052.243, Library of Congress.

CHARLES E. WHITE JR.,
President of Oak Park's New Fine Arts
Society.

4.3 Charles White. William Gray Purcell Papers, Northwest Architectural Archives, University of Minnesota.

Wright also attempted to hire Purcell, his neighbor's son, after the young man returned to Oak Park with a freshly minted degree in architecture from Cornell University in 1903. However, tensions were already building between Wright and others in the community that later contributed to his departure from Oak Park. While Purcell perceived the offer as attractive, his father vehemently objected. William recalled that his "father hated Wright worse than poison" due to the architect's growing dishonorable reputation that stemmed more from his fiscal irresponsibility and arrogance than wandering eye. Purcell declined the offer.[14]

During this peak period, Griffin's responsibility managing the office grew, particularly during Wright's many absences. Byrne and Willatzen continued training under Griffin and then, after his return, Drummond. Willatzen primarily worked with Drummond on the drawings for the Larkin building, claiming authorship of the surrounding fence, and on the ornament for Wright's remodeling of the Rookery Building lobby and the interiors of the Willits, Dana, and Darwin Martin houses.[15] Byrne and Bryan also kept busy completing drawings for the Larkin building, while White concentrated almost all of his energy on the related Buffalo residences.[16] Isabel Roberts and often an artist or two creating decorative works on the drafting room balcony added to the hectic studio environment.[17]

With much of the design activity for the Buffalo buildings beginning to wind down in mid-1904 and fewer projects entering the studio, Willatzen, Chamberlain, and Bryan departed.[18] Around the start of 1905, Drummond returned full time, taking over hours from White, who, having come to the realization that he would "rather do bum architecture" in his own way than "fine architecture" under someone else, had dropped to half time in order to set up his own practice.[19] The chaotic conditions in the studio, including disruptions due to various office remodelings, may have contributed to White's desire to strike out on his own. Client William Martin, informing his brother Darwin about a major round of renovations in May 1904, exasperatedly exclaimed that the studio "has been torn up from stem to stern for the last two weeks."[20]

Alterations to the Studio

The Martins had a right to be frustrated with their architect. Wright's numerous alterations to the studio undoubtedly contributed to a lack of the timely completion of promised designs in Buffalo. Charles White reported to Walter Willcox that the spring 1904 renovations included his employer "putting down a monolith floor, throughout, consisting of wood pulp and a cement imported from Greece. Has also torn out some partitions, cut in ceiling lights etc.," creating an unsettled environment.[21] The new concrete floor consisted of magnesite, a product composed of a powdered magnesium carbonate compound, mixed with cement, wood pulp, and water. Marketed as offering better sound absorption and greater resilience than plain concrete, the material can also take on the warm appearance of worn leather when pigment is added. Wright specified magnesite for the floors, stairs, windowsills, coping, and capitals, as well as the tops and sides of desks and cabinets of the Larkin building.[22] Installing the magnesite floor in the studio in May 1904 offered a way to test the functionality, durability, and aesthetic qualities of the material prior to its more prominent use in the large office building. The resulting durable yet attractive floors at the studio, which only needed touching up "with floor wax about once a week in the places subjected to wear," led Wright to specify the material for other commissions, including the Darwin Martin house, a bank in Dwight, Illinois, and Unity Temple.[23]

The partitions that White mentioned probably included the original angled walls in the reception hall. Wright replaced these with narrow glass French doors and sidelights that acoustically divided the reception and drafting rooms. He also removed the business desk, replacing it with a more functional plan desk below the row of exterior windows.[24] A less obvious change at this time consisted of shifting the location of the reception hall windows to just inside the stork columns. While doing so, he replaced earlier panes that included a wide, geometric-patterned border framing a central area of clear glass with a simpler design that consisted primarily of clear glass and wide cames running along the edges, allowing greater illumination.

4.4 Office area of the Larkin Company Administration Building with magnesite flooring. Photographer unknown. Frank Lloyd Wright, *Ausgeführte Bauten* (Berlin: Ernst Wasmuth A.-G., 1911), 134.

Additional light directly above the plan desk radiated through the new ceiling glass. Each of the three long, narrow laylights of an intricate geometric design consists of hundreds of small squares and rectangles of art glass in creams, yellows, oranges, and greens forming one of the most complex window designs of the architect's career and built upon the elaborate windows designed for the Dana house.[25] Laylights of related color schemes soon appeared in houses for both William and Darwin Martin. Similarly colored glass panes may have been added over the Oak Park studio office desk around this time.[26] Other changes to the reception hall involved numerous repaintings as the architect explored new color schemes, eventually arriving

at a dull gold that complimented the dark stained basswood trim, the warm tones of the magnesite floor, and the autumn colors of the art glass.

Wright made significant additional changes to the drafting room on several occasions during these busy years. In July 1904 the local newspaper the *Oak Leaves* announced, "Frank Loyd [*sic*] Wright of Chicago avenue is again remodeling his house."[27] The notice was likely referring to extensive alterations he made to the drafting room shortly after installing the magnesite floor. As in the reception hall, Wright strove to improve both natural and artificial illumination of his main workspace. He replaced the original smooth hanging round light fixtures with state-of-the-art prismatic

4.5 Studio reception hall with the new plan desk and elaborate art glass laylights. The view into the drafting room reveals the new storage piers, ca. 1904. Photographer unknown. Frank Lloyd Wright, *Ausgeführte Bauten* (Berlin: Ernst Wasmuth A.-G., 1911), 99.

4.6 Studio drafting room with new storage piers, suspended shelving, and light fixtures, as well as a second level of diamond-paned clerestory windows. A model of the Larkin building appears on the shelving, as does the bust that appears in photographs of Wright's early home office and playroom (see figures 1.3 and 1.10). Photographer unknown. H309, Frank Lloyd Wright Trust.

Holophane glass globes that emitted more uniform light.[28] At some point, soon after he replaced the windows in the reception hall, Wright added a second tier of diamond pane windows on the drafting room balcony to raise the natural light level. As illustrated by a sketch on an elevation drawing of the studio, instead of undergoing the effort and expense of raising the whole roof to acquire the wall area needed for the new band of windows, Wright lifted only the edges.[29] This strategy illustrates his keen ability to achieve creative solutions while meeting functional needs.

During the major 1904 remodeling, Wright extended shelving below the central horizontal windows directly in front of the casements and added suspended shelves running across the drafting room below and just beyond each edge of the balcony.[30] He also installed four tall wooden storage cabinets underneath the intersections of the shelving that served as visual piers similar in spirit to those he later incorporated into the design of the Darwin Martin house

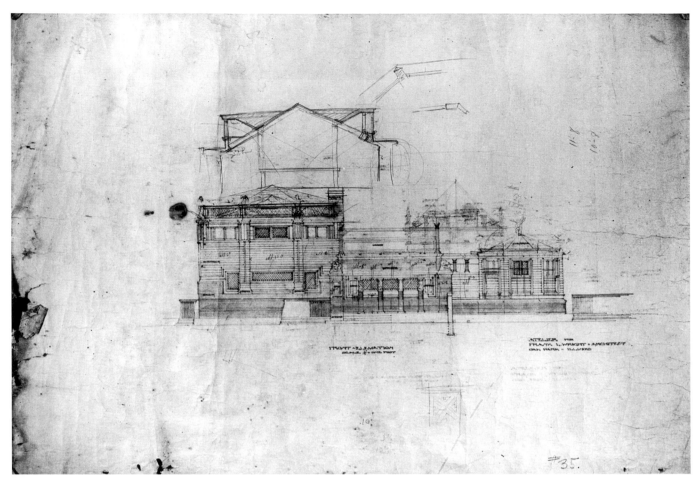

4.7 Studio elevation with addition of second-story windows on the drafting room and a sketch illustrating how to modify the roof to provide adequate space for the new windows. John Lloyd Wright Collection, 1969.001.00010, Avery Architectural & Fine Arts Library, Columbia University, New York.

to help define individual spaces. The new horizontal members and the cabinets formed three-dimensional extensions of the flat wood banding the architect had earlier added to his home, affixed to the faces of the studio balconies, and specified for many of his prairie designs. Plants and architectural models were displayed on top of the shelving and cabinets. It was also likely around this time when custom drafting stools replaced commercially available seating such as the stool that appears near the back wall in figure I.5.

Little information exists on changes Wright made to the studio office and library in these years beyond replacing the floor. The plan published in the 1899 *House Beautiful* article shows doorways leading to the office on either side of the desk in the reception hall, yet it is not clear if he actually built the entry near the west wall. The only known significant alterations to the office prior to 1909 was the addition of a staircase in the western bay. The flight led from the reception hall down to the basement of the house to toilet facilities and possibly a cloakroom for staff and visitors.[31] While the octagonal library became the architect's favorite room for design experimentation, undergoing more alterations than any other studio space prior to 1911, most of the known changes took place in later years.

Education in the Studio

In addition to exploring new design concepts and materials, Wright began to contemplate more consciously other educational activities that influenced his own architectural thinking, as well as that of his employees. He later wrote that he had to take time to train the draftsmen (downplaying the fact that most arrived

4.8 Two of Wright's tall vases framing a cube chair on which stands a winged boy weed holder sculpted by Richard Bock for which young John Lloyd Wright modeled. Photograph probably taken in the studio office. Photographer unknown. TAL 9506.0015, Avery Architectural & Fine Arts Library, Columbia University, New York.

with architectural degrees or some experience), when in reality he spent little time doing so. In fact, he expressed disdain for academic teaching and avoided presenting formal lessons. Novice studio architects had to acquire knowledge from their employer as he felt he himself best learned, primarily through observation and hands-on experience. Barry Byrne recalled, "As for teaching, in the ordinarily accepted sense of the word, there was none. It was a true atelier where one learned, if one had the capacity, by working on

the buildings that Mr Wright designed."[32] Byrne felt indebted to Drummond and Griffin for the assistance they gave him, particularly Drummond's "encouragement and solicitude."[33] Wright, he added, "gave me no attention, condescending or of any kind."[34] John Van Bergen later acknowledged Griffin's abilities, writing that his mentor "was not only a skillfully trained architect but also a great teacher for me. He had no end of patience for a very poor draftsman.... Walter took great pains in explaining things to me—pains that no other architect ever took."[35] Byrne and others believed that "the value of training under Wright lay in the matter of seeing top grade talent (or shall I say genius) function."[36]

This indirect form of instruction was not limited to architecture and its allied arts. Nature and music loomed large in the studio members' informal continuing education. The wide range of objects that Wright displayed in the studio offered inspiration and lessons in design, including items brought back from trips to secondhand stores in Chicago and the woods along the nearby Des Plaines River. Echoing the sentiment of English art critic John Ruskin, who wrote, "An architect should live as little in cities as a painter. Send him to our hills, and let him study there what nature understands," Wright shared his strong belief in the importance of nature to architecture with his associates.[37] Occasionally studio members would set out on expeditions during the work day to gather interesting grasses, leafy branches, and dried or fresh wild flowers to decorate the studio along with the Japanese prints, casts of classical sculpture, vases, and bowls of apples and nuts. In the 1890s Wright designed several containers for displaying collected branches and weeds. The first, a large, round, hand-hammered copper and galvanized tin urn decorated with concentric linear geometric forms vaguely reminiscent of his early logo; the second, a slender, tapered vase almost thirty inches tall specifically designed for exhibiting grasses (the vases appear in figure 2.13, as well as in many of the historic photographs of the studio library).[38] Another weed holder, realized by artist Richard Bock, included the figure of a young boy with butterfly wings for which the architect's four-year-old son John involuntarily modeled.[39] That the vases appear in historic photographs of the Oak Park studio and other Wright designs, suggests their importance to the architect.

In late 1903 White informed his colleague back east, "W. tells me to stop reading books for a while, and do nothing but study nature and sketch. He says to continually and eternally sketch the forms of trees—'a man who can sketch from memory the different trees, with their characteristics faithfully portrayed, will be a good architect'!"[40] White apparently took Wright's advice. In a later letter, he mentioned, "We of the sketch club

have particularly noticed the ever-changing forms of the trees and shrubs."[41]

Music also continued to play an important role in Wright's life. He attempted to pass his passion for music on to his children by encouraging them to play instruments, and the harmonious sounds of cello, violin, flute, guitar, and mandolin as well as voice and piano could be heard originating from the home.[42] Explaining music's close relationship to architectural design, he wrote that "music may be for the architect ever and always a sympathetic friend whose counsels, precepts and patterns even are available to him and from which he need not fear to draw."[43] Son Lloyd recalled music serving as a "source of refreshment" from his father's "labours at the drawing board," as he played the grand piano in the playroom.[44] To save floor space, Wright placed the piano under the balcony and hung the back of the instrument from the ceiling of the rear stair hall with a large hook.[45] Doing this had the additional benefit of exposing only the front of the piano, making the instrument less susceptible to damage from his high-spirited children. For fuller sound, he turned the landing of the balcony stair located directly above the piano into a trapdoor so that when opened sound could more directly fill the room.[46] If the windows were open in the playroom and on the balcony of the drafting room, the music would waft into the studio. Wright shared with his employees his love of music and its structural links to architecture. Byrne remembered his employer encouraging Griffin to take up piano, which he did with little success.[47]

By 1904 Wright had acquired a Cecilian player piano.[48] Designed to be placed in front of a regular piano, it made the instrument "self playing" through the use of an air pump and perforated scrolls. The operator or *pianolist* controlled the tempo and provided their own emphasis to the music through hand-operated levers and foot pumps. The musical novelty provided great enjoyment for the studio employees, as well as for Wright's family. In May 1904 White wrote, "We are still enjoying Wright's 'Cecilian.' Scarcely a day goes by that we do not go up and 'hit' it. It is truly wonderful how much individual experience can be obtained from a mechanical piano player. Sometimes three or four of us play the same composition, one after the

4.9 View of the restored Oak Park home playroom toward the balcony with a grand piano and a Cecilian player piano. Wright kept scrolls for the Cecilian in the vertical cabinet to the right of the piano. Photographer: Lisa D. Schrenk.

other, and it is astounding how varied is the interpretation."[49]

Throughout his career, Wright often played the piano late into the night, letting the geometries of his architecture formulate as his mind filled with the structures of the music.[50] Maginel, living next door with her mother, remembered lying awake hearing "the rolling cadences and thundering majestic chords of Bach or Beethoven issuing across the garden" until two or three o'clock in the morning.[51] Like his father before him, Lloyd found comfort in falling asleep listening to soft melodious strains of the piano, recalling his father

playing "like his heart would break," the structure of the music subconsciously informing his architecture as he played.[52]

The explorations of nature and music that took place within the walls of the suburban studio and in the developing suburban landscape nearby offered lessons in form, function, and structure for Wright and his employees not easily replicated in Steinway Hall or elsewhere in the Loop. Other educational experiences beyond the western suburbs of Chicago also influenced the architects and the work they produced in the Oak Park studio.

4.10 Palace of Varied Industries at the 1904 St. Louis Exposition, where artist Orlando Giannini exhibited his work. Robert A. Reid, *The Greatest of the Expositions Completely Illustrated Official Views of the Louisiana Purchase Exposition* (St. Louis: Louisiana Purchase Exposition Co., 1904), 20.

St. Louis

In the spring of 1904 Wright visited the Louisiana Purchase Exposition in St. Louis and upon his return encouraged his employees to attend, as it could provide them with a "liberal education."[53] The works of two artists connected with the studio could be found at the fair. Richard Bock created a traditional sculptural group for the Missouri State Building, which included a festooned female figure representing abundance framed by a farmer below on one side and a horticulturist on the other.[54] After his return from a weeklong visit to the exposition in mid-May, Bock shared his own description of the event with those in the studio.[55] Orlando Giannini, who exhibited art glass lamp shades, Teco pottery, and "Indian-style" baskets of his own design in the fair's Palace of Varied Industries, may have also been an early source of information on the exposition.[56] Studio designers, including Byrne, White, and Griffin, took Wright's advice and attended the fair.[57]

While large neoclassical buildings dominated the fairgrounds, the event featured exhibits highlighting the work of progressive European designers. It offered the studio architects the first opportunity to study the work of their central European counterparts beyond the pages of architectural publications. Exhibits of particular interest included those of the German *Jugenstil* and the Austrian Secessionists, groups they had known little about. In at least a couple of cases, however, it appears that the European architects already were familiar with the work emanating from the Oak Park studio.[58] Bruno Möhring, the designer of the Deutsches Haus, which represented Germany at the fair, was unbeknownst to Wright a fan of his work.[59]

The Austrian Pavilion was a major highlight for the architects. An official view book described the building, created in the "so-called secession style," as a "perfect exponent of the modern movement in art."[60] Ornate works from *Kunstgewerbe* schools and art societies of Austria, Poland, and Bohemia filled many of the rooms with a different architect designing each

4.11 Replica of the reading room at the State Library, Düsseldorf, designed by Peter Behrens, at the 1904 St. Louis Exposition. Leo Nachtlicht, *Deutsches Kunstgewerbe* (St. Louis: Ernst Wasmuth, 1904), 76.

space.[61] Joseph Maria Olbrich displayed the elegant fountain courtyard of his *Sommerstiz eines Kunstfreundes*.[62] The Dutch architect Henrik Petrus Berlage, who later revealed that he had studied the article on Wright in the June 1900 issue of *Architectural Review*, was represented at the fair by a series of drawings and photographs of his designs, including his recently completed Amsterdam Bourse.[63] Berlin modernist Peter Behrens exhibited a reconstruction of his reading room for the State Library in Düsseldorf featuring rigid, boxlike decorative forms reminiscent of the pure geometrical shapes in Wright's work (see figure 4.11).

Wright and the other designers who visited pavilions like the Palace of Varied Industries and the Palace of Fine Arts beheld additional architectural designs and decorative elements from Europe as well as examples from the East.[64] Exhibits from Japan could be found in ten other pavilions, while a prominent Japanese garden featuring a traditional teahouse proved to be one of the most popular attractions.[65]

Japan

Captivated by the Asian displays at St. Louis, Wright brought back Japanese prints and other objects to Oak Park as souvenirs.[66] According to David Wright, the excursion to St. Louis prompted his father to visit Japan the following year.[67] That trip provided a much-needed break after the grueling work of the Larkin building and Martin commissions.[68] The Buffalo projects, which dominated studio activities for several tremendously busy years, entailed a continual barrage of letters from Darwin Martin, in addition to frequent train trips to New York.

By mid-December 1904 an exhausted Wright, who had not taken a proper vacation in several years, was battling tonsillitis, which had spread to his whole family.[69] Charles White reported around this time that it was almost impossible for the studio architects to receive any attention from their employer. Wright himself admitted to having "no appetite for work."[70] With the fluctuation of staff, the camaraderie between coworkers that had initially permeated the studio began to dissipate. White mercilessly recorded this in 1905:

There is no one at the Studio who appeals to me in the least, with the exception of young Byrne, and he is only a child. The rest of the bunch are interested strictly in their own affairs. The one thing they need above all else there is the French "esprit de corps," instead of each one pulling in an opposite direction. Of course they are all exceedingly friendly, but you feel it comes from the lips instead of from the heart.... Artists and architects are a crumby lot of men anyhow, with their petty jealousies, and their "professional etiquette" that allows them to do anything but help their fellow practitioners![71]

Things were no better in the architect's home. Wright's relationship with Catherine was faltering. He felt abandoned by her as she focused less attention on him and more on the increasing demands of their children. The fact that he had begun looking elsewhere for female adoration and intellectual stimulation did not help the situation. Catherine must have believed that the trip to Japan would rekindle their deteriorating relationship, possibly viewing it as a romantic second honeymoon, to have left the children behind, including Llewellyn, barely fifteen months old.[72] The couple departed on or around Valentine's Day in 1905, along with former clients Ward and Cecelia Willits, for a visit to Asia expected to last four months.[73] Burned out and experiencing a lull in his practice, Wright hoped the trip would provide experiences and insights that would reinvigorate his architecture and possibly bring new vitality to his personal life.[74]

Wright's interest in Japanese art likely began during his early days with Joseph Lyman Silsbee and exposure to his collection of "Orientalia."[75] In 1893, with the construction of the Hōōden (Ho-o-den), the Japanese pavilion at the World's Columbian Exposition, modeled after the eleventh-century Byodoin Buddhist temple in Uji, Japan, Wright and other Chicagoans could experience traditional Japanese architecture firsthand. Even though he later denied it, he likely visited the pavilion, which was filled with Japanese porcelain and prints, numerous times.[76] He also may have acquired several of the objects on exhibit after the exposition closed, including a large blue and white dragon plate.[77]

Other studio architects also expressed great inter-

4.12 Interior of the Hōōden at the World's Columbian Exposition, 1893. *Official Views of the World's Columbian Exposition, Issued by the Department of Photography* (Chicago: Photo-Gravure, ca. 1893).

est in the Japanese displays at the exposition. Mahony recalled that the exhibits profoundly affected all of the early members of the "Chicago School" and noted that some, like Wright, soon began collecting Japanese prints.[78] Enthralled by the Hōōden, Griffin later designed a cottage for the Elmhurst Electric and Power Company that featured simplified *onigawara* at the ridge ends of what came to be his characteristic gable roof form.[79]

Wright expanded his knowledge of Japanese art and culture through his association with George Ki-

kutaro Shimoda, the Japanese designer who ran in the same architectural circles and who briefly worked for Wright in the mid-1890s, as well as through Japanese scholar Arthur Wesley Dow. Dow gave at least two lectures at Hull House and at the Art Institute of Chicago, which in March 1901 also hosted an exhibition of his work.

Heavily influenced by Japanese prints, Dow's ideas reinforced those fermenting in Wright's mind. For example, he promoted the view that instead of attempting to just copy nature, artists should look to elements

4.13 The Sutra Library, Chion-in Temple, Kyoto. From Frank Lloyd Wright's 1905 Japan trip photo album. Gift of David Lloyd Wright, Frank Lloyd Wright Trust.

of composition, such as line, mass, and color, to create "visual music" designs highlighted by a sense of harmony.[80] Like Froebel and others before him, Dow discussed the importance of a clear relationship between the part and the whole. His description of their mutual interdependence could have easily been penned by Wright, when he wrote: "[E]very part of a work of art has something to say. If one part is made so prominent that the others have no reason for being there, the art is gone. So in this case; if one line asserts itself to the detriment of the others, there is discord. There may be many or few lines, but each must have its part in the whole. In a word, wholeness is essential to beauty; it distinguishes Music from Noise."[81] Wright's success in developing this type of unity in his Oak Park–era residential designs was expounded upon in an article on his work in *Architectural Record* shortly after his return from Japan. The writer observed that "every mass, surface, shadow, and detail [in Wright's buildings] contributed to one consistent and spectacular effect."[82]

Wright increased his understanding of Japanese art and culture on his 1905 visit to the Orient, exploring temples and other historic sites in places like Kyoto and Nikkō.[83] In addition to examining prints, he ex-

perienced various other aspects of Japanese culture. In fact, Cecelia Willits became quite upset after Wright took her husband to a traditional bathhouse staffed by young women. The two couples parted ways shortly thereafter.[84] It is not clear how Catherine occupied her time during her husband's many escapades exploring the country on his own in native dress.[85] On one of these outings in Takamatsu, on the island of Shikoku, Wright visited an art school and observed the students studying and drawing wildflowers as inspiration for their craft designs—an exercise similar to one he had been taught as a youngster and that he encouraged his studio employees to practice.[86]

While in Japan, Wright purchased a large number of block prints. He saw in the images an "elimination of the insignificant and a process of simplification" that meshed with Dow's observations as well as his own design tendencies, writing, "Hiroshige did, with a sense of space, very much what we have been doing with it in our architecture."[87] Wright felt that Japanese art and architecture were "organic," "nearer the earth" and "more indigenous product[s] of native conditions of life and work," which therefore made them closer to "modern" than those of any European civilization

4.14 The remodeled studio library showing single panel-hinged corkboards (hinges for the second set of panels are visible), as well as slender hanging vertical elements behind the light fixtures and piers that visually, but not physically, support the triangular shelving in the corners. A second set of triangular shelves that appear below the windows in figure 5.12 are absent, possible removed because they visually encroached into the small space. Grilles have been added to cover the upper level of windows. Wright replaced the large square table with two print tables of his design (the table to the right holds the left panel of the diptych *Gentlemen Entertained by Courtesans and Geisha at a Teahouse in Shinagawa*, 1783 by Torii Kiyonaga, today in the collection of the Metropolitan Museum of Art, New York), ca. 1906–8. Photographer: Henry Fuermann and Sons. Photograph purchase: Herman G. Pundt Gift and Edward Pearce Casey Fund. 1981.1005.17, Metropolitan Museum of Art, New York.

alive or dead. He also found the Japanese house with its tatami mats to be a "perfect example of modern standardization" and analogous to the concept of unit-system design used in the studio.[88]

Seduced by Japanese art and culture, the Wrights brought back to Oak Park trunks of traditional clothing, lacquerware, ceramics, books, and paper cutouts in addition to stacks of prints. Many of these objects decorated their home and the studio. For example,

patchwork brocades in golden tones, originally Buddhist priests' robes, were displayed in the home as table scarves. Son David recalled using some of the items in his and his siblings' education as well as in their daily play. They employed paper fabric stencils in their artistic projects and even cut up a number of prints to create paper dolls.[89] It is not clear if Wright was aware of his children's defacement of what today would be priceless Japanese prints.

Design Process

With so many commissions on the boards and having
to travel often to Buffalo, Wright found it difficult to
supervise fully both his children's activities and the
studio endeavors taking place at the other end of the
connecting corridor.[90] Fortunately, within the chaotic
atmosphere of the office he still had a strong workforce capable of effectively carrying out projects. In
these years, most of the studio architects contributed
to the production of working drawings typically derived from sketches by Wright. For the less advanced
designers, delineating working drawings became a
major facet of their architectural training. Byrne recalled the more experienced Drummond studying
work in freehand perspectives while preparing scaled
designs. Wright, he noted, did not need this type of
"crutch."[91] Drummond also initiated designs but imitated his employer's other work and manners.[92] Byrne
remembered, "Wright always hovered over Drummond when he was working on designs and, if Drummond added anything, it was likely to be modified by
F.L.W."[93] Meanwhile, Griffin, not known for his rendering abilities, kept busy working on landscape plans,
writing specifications, meeting with clients, and supervising construction.[94]

While Paul Mueller, Wright's "able engineer," supervised the office's more complicated construction
projects including those in Buffalo, studio draftsmen
typically oversaw the realization of the more routine
Chicago-area residential jobs.[95] Drummond served
as project manager for a number of them, including
the Cheney residence in Oak Park and later the Isabel Roberts house in River Forest.[96] Reflecting the in-
tricacy of studio operations, correspondence between
Darwin Martin and the office staff include letters from
Wright as well as Griffin, Drummond, Roberts, and
Wright's brother-in-law Arthur Tobin. One typed
letter to Martin ended with a forged "Frank Lloyd
Wright" signature clearly in Griffin's hand.[97]

Griffin made several trips east to check on the progress of Darwin Martin's house and other Buffalo commissions while Wright was in Japan.[98] With the Barton
residence close to completion in fall 1904, Griffin created a landscaping diagram for the entire Martin prop-

erty, working on it during his trip to attend the St. Louis
exposition in early October.[99] The following year, while
running the office, Griffin completed a planting plan
designed to visually unite the two houses. The major
landscape elements––a large, elaborate *floricycle* that
surrounded the east terrace, with semicircular planting beds composed of a variety of shrubs, perennials,
biennials, and bulbs selected to produce a sequential
series of blooms from March through late fall––could
be enjoyed from both houses.[100]

After completion of the *Flower in the Crannied Wall*
figure for the Dana residence, Wright kept Richard
Bock engaged creating sculptural elements for both
the Larkin building and the Darwin Martin house.[101]
Byrne recalled that if Mahony worked on the Larkin commission it was only a minor contribution, as
she was primarily occupied with designing art glass
and furniture.[102] In May 1904 White recalled Mahony "modelling for a fountain for the Dana house at
Springfield" (almost certainly the bas-relief *Moon Children* fountain for the reception hall) and Isabel Roberts spending most of her time working on ornamental
glass.[103]

Soon Mahony was filling Birch Burdette Long's role
as the main producer of presentation drawings. Byrne identified her as executor of most of the perspective drawings for the studio between 1902 and 1907.[104]
White maintained she was one of the finest renderers in the country.[105] In contrast to Wright "hovering"
over Drummond, White remembered that there was
"stimulation, approval, and supplemental accord" but
not what one could call "close direction" of Mahony in
these years. Byrne remembered Wright occasionally
sitting down at her drawing board and working on her
drawings. On one occasion when he ruined the rendering, Willatzen loudly proclaimed Mahony Wright's
superior as a draftsman. The architect uncharacteristically "took the statement of her superiority equally."[106]

Mahony began to further develop Long's rendering
style. Exposure to the work of midwestern designer
Harvey Ellis, who had succumbed to the "spell of Japanese art" several decades earlier, also likely contributed
to the studio's iconic drawing style.[107] Wright encouraged studio architects to study Ellis's rendering techniques, which used delicately drawn foliage to frame

glass,-it is needed.
        Follow the detail for leaded glass in all
respects except the particular prism shaped
piece you refer to and make that yellow-green.
        "This glass should not go in the house be-
fore plastering unless you protect it with
muslin inside and this would be foolish as your
house will dry out quicker with muslin doubled
in the windows, without the glass, and could
be kept sufficiently warm.
        The front door panel may be of wood and no
detail is necessary, simply build it up with
veneers on a compound core. Branch veneers, if
possible, matched at center and directed outward
on center line to develop flower in the grain."
        The kitchen windows may remain plain if you
will be good and put in the right kind elsewhere,
though, if Mrs.Barton does her own work, there
would be a certain dignity in having things Queen
Anne front and Queen Anne (not Mary Ann) behind.
        "The coat room door should simply stop at the
seat level or at the level of the windowsill with
door and trim to match other side."
        Plain radiators are the best but they are all
covered with Jay ornament and there is small choice.
Use the plainest you can find.
        It seems to me the change made in Bath Room
on plan is a good one but if yours works out, all
right.
        Will make all the sketches for the house de-
sired and will bring something with me.
        I am hustling to get ready for Buffalo but just
when I will arrive I can't say. I have the
"Superintendent" working on the details here so
that he can familiarize himself thoroughly with the
construction. We wish to send you a complete outfit
for figures at the earliest possible moment.
                        Yours truly,

Mr.D.D.Martin,   *Frank Lloyd Wright*
Buffalo, New York.

January 18, 1904.

4.15 Letter from "Frank Lloyd Wright" to Darwin D. Martin dated 18 January 1904 with Wright's signature in Griffin handwriting. Courtesy University Archives, University at Buffalo, State University of New York © 2020 Frank Lloyd Wright Foundation, Scottsdale, AZ. All rights reserved.

buildings.[108] Not all studio renderings present such artistic beauty. For example, the perspective of the Larkin building believed to be in Griffin's hand exhibits a less developed drawing style. The rendering was one of several hundred drawings produced by the studio staff for the series of major projects Wright secured from clients in Buffalo in these years.[109]

Buffalo

Studio commissions tied to William and Darwin Martin provide insights into Wright's interactions with clients and how the office functioned during these busy middle years. The architect clearly understood the significance of the Buffalo projects, as Darwin became the most important client of his Oak Park studio years.[110] He presented Wright with crucial opportunities that allowed him to realize innovative architectural ideas and further establish his suburban practice. In addition to offering interesting design exercises and helping to fund major alterations to the studio, the commissions expanded the geographical reach of the practice five hundred miles to the east, and the Larkin building gave him his first prominent, large-scale commercial work. Like Susan Lawrence Dana, Darwin Martin proved to be a client with deep pockets. He also had a willingness to financially back Wright and his distinctive vision of American architecture. Martin, who began working for the Larkin Soap Company at the tender age of twelve, craved personal interactions and approval, which he found at Larkin as he quickly moved up the corporate ladder. He also received it from Wright, at least as long as Martin provided commissions and financial support.[111]

Wright's relationship with the Martin brothers began in the fall of 1902 with their visit to the Oak Park

4.16 Darwin Martin, April 1908. Photographer: Howard Dwight Beach. Darwin D. Martin Photograph Collection, MS_22.5_414. Courtesy University Archives, University at Buffalo, State University of New York.

studio. In mid-September Darwin visited his older brother William, who lived in Chicago. Darwin was looking for an architect to design his residence and a new administration building for his employer. At the same time, William was in the market for a new home of his own. He likely had some familiarity with Wright's work, which had received notice in the local press. Additionally, two multifamily housing projects the architect had designed in the mid-1890s, the Francisco Terrace and Waller apartments, were just a few blocks from the original location of the Martin brothers' polish factory on Chicago's West Side.[112] William had initially contemplated building north of the city but may have been encouraged to consider Wright's office and a location in Oak Park by his brother, who possibly learned about the architect from coworker William Heath.

Trained as a lawyer in Illinois, Heath had moved to Buffalo in 1899 after his brother-in-law, John D.

Larkin, convinced him to join the Larkin Soap Company. Heath married Mary Elizabeth Hubbard, whose brother Elbert founded the Roycroft, the arts and crafts community in rural East Aurora, New York. At the Larkin Company, Heath and Darwin Martin worked closely together overseeing the mail-order retail business.[113] Like Martin, the Heaths were also contemplating building a new home in Buffalo and looking to Wright to design it.[114] Another of William Heath's brothers-in-law, Elmer Andrews, served as an additional link between Wright and the Buffalo businessmen. Andrews, an Oak Park contractor, carried out work for the architect including on the Joseph Jacob Walser Jr. house in the Chicago neighborhood of Austin just east of Oak Park.[115]

Darwin described his and his brother's initial visit to the Oak Park studio in a letter to Elbert Hubbard informing him that they met with "Mr. Wright's Red One" (undoubtedly the redheaded Griffin), as Wright was away. Martin wrote that to his "uncultivated mind Mr. Wright's houses, of which there are many examples in Oak Park and vicinity, seem very fancy" and that the studio was "very Roycroftie." He then suggested adding an example of the architect's work to the Roycroft community.[116] Martin did not mention which buildings they visited, but Griffin could have directed them toward the recent Fricke, Thomas, Heurtley, and Davenport houses. In addition, the stately Tudoresque Moore residence was just down the street from the studio. Other possibilities include the Williams and Winslow houses in River Forest and the George and Rollin Furbeck houses in Oak Park.

William Martin met Wright after Darwin had returned to Buffalo. The architect's charming personality impressed the businessman, who described him to his brother as "one of nature's noblemen." William expressed surprise that the architect was "not a fraud––nor a 'crank,'" but "highly educated & polished." He predicted that his brother would immediately fall in love with Wright and that the architect would build him the finest and most sensible house in Buffalo.[117]

William continued, writing: "[F]urther he is the man––to build your office = he has had large experience in large office buildings with Adler & Sullivan[,] was educated as a Civil Engineer[,] was head man in

4.17 Walser house, Chicago. Note similarity to Wright's Barton house design (figure 4.1). William Storrer Collection, Oak Park Public Library Special Collections.

A & S & stood next to Mr. S[ullivan]. = he says it is strange that he is only known as a residence architect––when his best & largest experience was in large buildings."[118] In the following months, Wright told Darwin Martin much the same thing as he courted the Larkin commission.[119] In reality a significant amount of the architect's time at Adler and Sullivan was spent on residential commissions, such as the James Charnley house. Wright was not above exaggerating his credentials when courting a patron.

Darwin invited Wright to come to Buffalo for a consultation. The architect arrived for a two-day visit in mid-November. The trip, the first of approximately thirty Wright made between 1902 and 1906, was deemed a success by both parties.[120] Soon the studio architects busied themselves producing residential designs for William Martin in Oak Park and for Darwin

Martin and William Heath in Buffalo as well as preliminary sketches for the Larkin building.

In January 1903, William Martin received a design from Wright and sent it to his brother for review. It is surprising that Darwin continued to strongly support Wright, for in reply he and his wife berated the architect's poorly thought-out design. Isabelle Martin exclaimed that the plan greatly discouraged her. "I am afraid Wright is impracticable," she declared. "[T]he plan does not show care and appreciation of the needs of a home."[121] Darwin, meanwhile, believed the exterior good but complained about the size and location of rooms, the heating, the art glass, and the lack of a veranda, a maid's room, and a second staircase. Sardonically he wrote, "The fireplace in the playroom is a dangerous thing. In this one city of Buffalo alone there is just about one little girl per month burned up. You

4.18 The William and Winifred Martin house, Oak Park. Wright, who was reported to have admitted that this house was his least successful residential design, hid the dwelling behind trees while featuring the garden and pergola in the foreground in the smaller Wasmuth publication. Photographer unknown. Frank Lloyd Wright, *Ausgeführte Bauten* (Berlin: Ernst Wasmuth A.-G., 1911), 69.

only have two girls. You need a dozen to start with if you are going to have a fireplace in the play room." He finishes the letter exclaiming, "Wright's plan of having the dining room where you propose to have the library is positively inhuman to a maid who would have to travel 30' or more from range to dining table; nobody but a wife would keep such a job."[122] Even with later alterations, including additions of a maid's room and a veranda, Wright later admitted that it was the worst house he ever designed.[123] As he did repeatedly during his Oak Park years and throughout his career, he had prioritized formal design experimentation over the functional desires of his clients.

Darwin returned to Oak Park in March with his wife. This time he spent a full day interviewing Wright in the studio, including discussing an early design of the Larkin building. The architect suggested the use of magnesite, showing him samples, and they discussed the inclusion of a great open court. Wright waylaid Martin's concerns about potential drafts and problems heating such a large open space by suggesting its similarities to the two large courts of D. H. Burnham and Company's Marshall Field's State Street building in Chicago. Martin visited the store for himself, later informing Larkin that the departments on the ground floor of the court were the "pleasantest in the building."[124] During his visit he also saw a preliminary sketch for the Heath residence and toured five of Wright's houses. He reported that he talked to the owners of four of them and had "never witnessed such enthusiasm. Not one will admit a fault in their house." They were, however, willing "to admit faults in others of Wright's houses."[125] The Martins visited the Heurtley and Fricke residences (thinking the Fricke entrance awful) and the exterior of the Davenport.[126]

William was right in his prediction. Darwin apparently did fall in love with the architect, admitting to Larkin upon his return that he might appear "to have been made intoxicated" by his contact with Wright. He went on to explain, "That, Mr. Wright says is because he studies his client and builds the house to fit him, so his different houses do not fit his clients who live in other houses."[127] One wonders if Darwin really believed Wright or was just passing the remark along to help convince his boss to hire the architect. If the architect had truly studied William's needs, would so many faults exist in the design of his brother's house?

Darwin initially hired Wright to design a residence for his sister Delta Barton as a test run before the Larkin Company formally contracted with him (see figure 4.1).[128] That design offers an example of Wright bending his principles during his Oak Park years when the realization of a commission was at stake. Despite claiming to fit each project to the specific client, here he reused the design for the Walser house in Chicago, which Martin had selected while visiting the studio.[129] The only significant changes made were a different art glass pattern for the windows, a more elaborate plumbing system, and a different form of foundation.[130] The desire for a prompt start on construction of the Barton house undoubtedly contributed to his decision to use an already completed design.

The chosen design reflects a development in how Wright thought about space in these years. In his early prairie houses such as the Willits residence, the architect explored the use of the central hearth to help define different areas in residential buildings. Here, as with the new piers and beams in the Oak Park drafting room, additional vertical masses helped delineate separate functional areas. Most prominently, a series of piers set off the central hall from the living room to one side and the dining room to the other. Beams that crossed the space at the thresholds further defined the areas. Mahony later claimed that the idea of placing a void instead of a fireplace at the crossing was hers.[131] The play of vertical and horizontal forms at the Bar-

ton house additionally informed the design of the Larkin building. Most prominently, the four large corner vertical piers helped to define the building's exterior massing and housed stairs and ductwork for the heating and air-purifying systems. The early sketch of the structure in Griffin's hand suggests that he played a role in the design (see figure 3.9).[132]

Building on earlier spatial explorations in the Oak Park studio and the Barton house, Wright designed an elaborate composition of different-sized piers and beams for the Darwin Martin residence that helped to define the exterior and separate functional areas inside. Each of four major cluster piers inside consists of four smaller ones linked by low bookcases with art glass panes above, creating small uninhabitable spaces that held lights and parts of the heating system. These piers, as well as shorter, freestanding nonstructural elements, and low walls, a major fireplace mass, and built-in furniture, contributed a new layer of spatial complexity to Wright's residential interiors.

In addition to serving as an early exploration of space-defining piers, the Barton house offers a good illustration of the architect's lack of regard for the fiscal considerations of his clients. Darwin had requested a modest house that would cost around $4,500.[133] By August 1903 he realized that that the design could not be built for under $9,000.[134] Wright largely ignored his client's numerous suggestions and requests for ways "to cheapen the house" and instead advocated changes that would increase its overall cost. For example, in January 1904 he recommended replacing the glass and lead specified for the windows with "crystal plate glass" and "metal bar," which, he informed his client, "would be worth the difference in cost, whatever it may be."[135] Total construction cost topped $12,000.[136] Darwin's own house, with an original budget of $35,000 came in around $74,000. The client ended up spending a total of $173,000 on the entire Martin complex: the main house, the Barton house, a long pergola and conservatory, a carriage house with stables and an apartment, and a gardener's cottage.[137]

Due in part to the unusual nature of Wright's studio projects, the design process and construction did not always go smoothly. Charles White wrote in 1904 that

4.19 Darwin Martin house rendering with a drain spout detail, likely drawn by Walter Burley Griffin. TAL 0405.027, Avery Architectural & Fine Arts Library, Columbia University, New York. © 2020 Frank Lloyd Wright Foundation, Scottsdale, AZ. All rights reserved.

his employer never allowed any of the "petty wants of his clients to interfere with the architectural expression of his design" and that clients attempting to assert their desires or needs often encountered his contempt and indignation. White explained that clients' wishes were taken care of by "a sort of absorption and repression within the scope of the plan as a whole" and were never allowed to interfere with "the system, or skeleton of the house."[138]

William Martin found this out the hard way in 1905, when constructing a factory building that he and his brother had commissioned from Wright for their E-Z Polish Company in Chicago. William had confronted the architect after discovering, with excavations well underway, that the basement was to have a height of just seven and a half feet, not the eight feet he had seen labeled on a drawing in the studio.[139] This made the space too low for the workroom he envisioned. William, who had unsuccessfully asked Wright numerous times for copies of the plans and specifications so that he could carefully go over them, believed that

he would have noticed the height discrepancy prior to groundbreaking. He was particularly irritated that Wright wanted $465 in additional fees for his contractor Paul Mueller to make the required changes. In an attempt to force Martin to pay, Wright sent one of the office staff (likely Griffin) to the site to call off work on the building temporarily.[140] Both Martin and Wright then posted letters to Darwin in Buffalo complaining about each other's stubbornness. With great aversion to discord, Darwin reminded them that "there isn't any justification for vituperation and recrimination among men" and hoped that their "vaudeville stunts" would not continue. He then encouraged them to remember each other's good qualities.[141] Yet William's opinion of Wright had significantly shifted from the warm, gushing review he had written a couple of years earlier. He informed his brother that Wright had served him "a dirty, mean trick," striking him "below the solar-plexis [sic]," and he warned his brother to be "very careful in your dealings with him––if he is sane––he is dangerous."[142]

4.20 Martin brothers' E-Z Polish Factory building on the west side of Chicago. Gilman Lane Collection, Oak Park Public Library Special Collections.

Such contentions plagued many of the Oak Park studio projects, as client and architect often had different goals: the client, a well-functioning building; the architect, an aesthetic realization of his innovative ideas. Incidents caused by Wright's less-than-professional behavior occurred regularly. Correspondence between the Martin brothers was filled with comments such as: "If you discover any way in your dealings with him, whereby you are able to keep tabs on him, I would like to know how you do it.... Certainly, if Wright's plans appear to be 'queer,' his business methods are more so.... [W]hile I thoroughly appreciate his plans and ideas, I would not give two cents for his superintendence of a job."[143]

In addition to disregarding budgets, Wright showed little regard for schedules and justifiably received a reputation for not delivering work when promised. William Martin kept an eye on the Buffalo commissions for his brother, as Wright was not always forthcoming in progress reports. Many of the numerous letters from Darwin to Wright went unanswered.[144] On 20 May 1904, with major alterations under way in the studio, William informed his brother that one of the draftsmen told him that upon the architect's return from his recent trip to Buffalo, "he threw the plans into one corner of the office" and said nothing about any requested changes until several days later when he inquired if they had been made. Only then did the staff

4.21 Interior of studio drafting room with drawings and drafting equipment and a model of the Abraham Lincoln Center sitting on top of one of the four storage piers. Photographer unknown. TAL 9506.0005, Avery Architectural & Fine Arts Library, Columbia University, New York.

get "busy and, by working all day and part of the night," managed to complete the plans when promised.[145]

Hearing such accounts, Darwin had concerns about Wright not giving his commissions top priority. His worries were founded, as the architect already exhibited signs of fatigue and distraction, which increased over the course of the year. In July 1904 Darwin wrote to his brother, "Since Wright was here last I have written him a dozen letters and asked him forty questions. He has written me two letters, both of them ignoring all my questions and confined entirely to his finances."[146] Martin then started pressing Wright harder for results. He sent William to the studio again in August to check on the status of the Larkin building design. His brother reported that he "found the trestle boards in the drafting room covered with drawings and sketches of your plant. Whether this had been specially arranged for my benefit or not I am unable to say, as I telephoned Mr. Wright on my return home last evening that I would be down after dinner. However, the lay-out did not look as though it had been specially arranged, but did have the ear marks of having been earnestly worked upon." Wright must have inflicted some of his charm on William, who warned Darwin that he was beginning to "rush the job too fast" and that if he continued "to push and crowd Mr. Wright," not only would it potentially increase costs, but it would prevent the architect from giving his best."[147]

William and Darwin eventually received their buildings. And, despite the many headaches, Darwin hired Wright to produce other designs, including Graycliff, a summer home for his family, and an unrealized mausoleum in the 1920s. When Martin passed away in 1935, Wright was reputed to exclaim, "Today my best friend has died."[148] Martin was not only a friend but also a longtime financial backer. Wright owed Darwin many thousands of dollars at the time of his death for loans that, among other things, helped finance the 1911 remodeling of his Oak Park home and studio and the construction of Taliesin. In fact the Martin family held deeds of trust to Wright's suburban property for many years after the studio closed (for more see the epilogue).

During this incredibly busy era, Wright and his employees "endeavored" to give their clients the best architecture possible, despite cost overruns and delays. Yet by early 1905, having invested considerable energy into his architecture and educational explorations (with the latter sometimes impeding progress on the former) and experiencing growing paternal pressure from six rambunctious children, Wright felt drained and overworked. His trip to Japan allowed him to escape the intensity of the studio and helped to validate many of his core underlying ideas on architecture. In addition, the trip brought him closer to Catherine, at least briefly. His sense of professional and personal rejuvenation, however, did not last. Within a few years, Wright again felt burned out and confined by his professional and personal conditions. For a second time, he tried to escape through foreign travel, but with dramatically different results.

5

LAST YEARS OF THE OAK PARK STUDIO (1906–1909)

Consistency and Change

5.1 "Fireproof House for $5000." Plate XIV, *Ausgeführte Bauten und Entwürfe von Frank Lloyd Wright*, 1910. Special Collections, J. Willard Marriott Library, University of Utah.

I have endeavored in this work to establish a harmonious relationship between ground plan and elevation of these buildings, considering the one as a solution and the other in expression of the conditions of a problem of which the whole is a project. I have tried to establish an organic integrity to begin with, forming the basis for the subsequent working out of a significant grammatical expression and making the whole, as nearly as I could, consistent.

FRANK LLOYD WRIGHT (1908)

Three days after returning from Japan reenergized, Wright informed Darwin Martin that he was "much improved in health and spirits—can lick my weight in wild-cats."[1] Plunging into his work, the architect boarded an eastbound train less than a week later to check up on the Buffalo commissions. Wright's sense of renewal, however, soon came up against the realities of his tattered personal and professional lives. His absence from the office resulted in a significant drop in new revenue-generating work beyond a recent local church commission. Ten months after his return, Charles White reported that there had "not been much other work of importance at Wright[']s.... [H]e has had a few houses of [the] Five Thousand Dollar size, and always loses money on such, it cannot be said that his affairs have been particularly prosperous lately. If it hadn't been for the Buffalo [Larkin] building, he would have been in straits long ago. He made a great mistake in going abroad just when he did."[2] Wright himself also commented on the dire situation at the end of 1905 and the lack of profit he saw on residential works, even large projects like the Darwin Martin house, noting that "Unity Church is the only thing immediate and that will serve only to hold the forceover [sic] for a couple of months."[3]

Nevertheless, articles highlighting Wright's architectural ideas, including a series in *House Beautiful* during the summer of 1906, led to a small stream of residential commissions entering the Oak Park studio.

Almost all were of the "Five Thousand Dollar" variety. These included variations of a compact design recalling an American foursquare published in the April 1907 issue of *Ladies' Home Journal* as his concrete "Fireproof House for $5000." While the commissions kept the studio staff busy, they did not provide stimulating enough design exercises to warrant much of Wright's attention. A few larger projects offered more interesting architectural explorations; the most remarkable was not, as Wright had hoped, another prominent commercial structure for a site elsewhere in the country but rather one that came from his neighborhood congregation. The architect, however, fully capitalized on the commission for a new, low-cost home for the local Universalist and Unitarian community, turning it into his most inspirational realized design of his post-Japan Oak Park years. Commissioned in December 1905, the modern, concrete church most visibly reveals the early impact of his trip to the Orient on his design development. The influence of that trip, however, emerged in other ways at the Oak Park studio and elsewhere.

Japanese Influences

While Wright exhibited some of the woodblock prints he and Catherine brought back from Japan in their Oak Park home, he stored most of the prints in his office's fireproof vault and would sort through them on the drafting room balcony, choosing favorites to

5.2 Frank Lloyd Wright's Hiroshige print exhibition at the Art Institute of Chicago, 1906. TAL 0600.0002, Avery Architectural & Fine Arts Library, Columbia University, New York. © 2020 Frank Lloyd Wright Foundation, Scottsdale, AZ.

display in the studio library on print tables similar to ones he had designed for the Dana house gallery.[4] Modifications to the home's playroom around 1906 suggest influence from the trip, including the replacement of Victorian wall sconces with the floating water lily or lotus motif fixtures. Cantilevering lights were also incorporated into the design of the nearby Beachy house. The Oriental feel of that home's dining room would have been even greater had a mural designed for the space consisting of a pair of Kano Sanraku screens been installed.[5]

The Wrights shared their Japanese experiences with others in a variety of venues. They educated the local community through a series of events around the time of Wright's first major public exhibit of Japanese prints. Held at the Art Institute of Chicago from 29 March to 18 April 1906, *Hiroshige: An Exploration of Colour Prints from the Collection of Frank Lloyd Wright* included more than two hundred woodblock prints by the early nineteenth-century master.[6] The month before the exhibit opened, Wright read a paper titled "The Art of Japan" to the River Forest Women's Club, and a few weeks later the Wrights hosted a "Japanese social" in their home for the local Unity Club "com-

plete with lantern slides, prints, curios, music, and tea served by young ladies from the club in Japanese costume."[7] Catherine also lectured on her own to Oak Park's Nineteenth Century Women's Club.

Wright's employees' interest in the country and its culture increased correspondingly. Beginning in 1906, Mahony began to imbue in her renderings an even more pronounced Japanese feel, particularly displaying an affinity to the block prints of Hiroshige.[8] Around this time, she began following Long's practice of signing renderings with a personal monogram. Hence perspectives, such as those of the K.C. DeRhodes house in South Bend, Indiana, and the "Fireproof House for $5000" project, with their exquisite landscapes, can clearly be attributed to her. Charles White reported that the Unity Temple renderings were Mahony's as well.[9]

The DeRhodes house drawing is one of her finest. Its elegant composition consists of luscious plantings surrounding the residence. Wright later inscribed it, "Drawn by Mahony after FLLW and Hiroshige." A more correct statement would be "Drawn by Mahony after FLLW, Long, Ellis, and Hiroshige." The delicate flat, abstract-patterned foliage strongly evokes renderings

5.3 DeRhodes house rendering by Marion Mahony with a bird and flower in the foreground reminiscent of a Hiroshige print. Wright's comment on authorship appears on the right. TAL 0602.001, Avery Architectural & Fine Arts Library, Columbia University, New York. © 2020 Frank Lloyd Wright Foundation, Scottsdale, AZ. All rights reserved.

5.4 *Bluebird and Wild Rose*, woodblock print (*nishiki-e*) by Utagawa Hiroshige (1797–1858). William S. and John T. Spaulding Collection, 21.9729. Photograph © 2020. Boston Museum of Fine Arts.

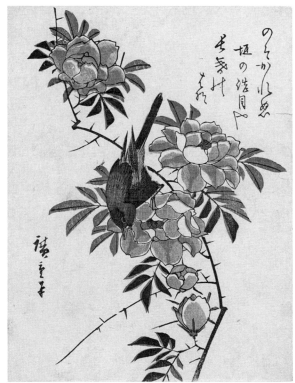

Long had produced for Wright, as well as drawings by Harvey Ellis. After 1906 Mahony and others in the studio began employing this style, including for the Wasmuth Portfolio. In addition to continuing the practice of using nature to aesthetically frame buildings, Mahony borrowed from Utagawa Hiroshige the practice of placing plantings in the foreground that help draw the viewer into the composition. The bowing bird and flower blossom in the DeRhodes rendering are a direct homage to Hiroshige's bird and flower prints, such as *Bluebird and Wild Rose*.[10]

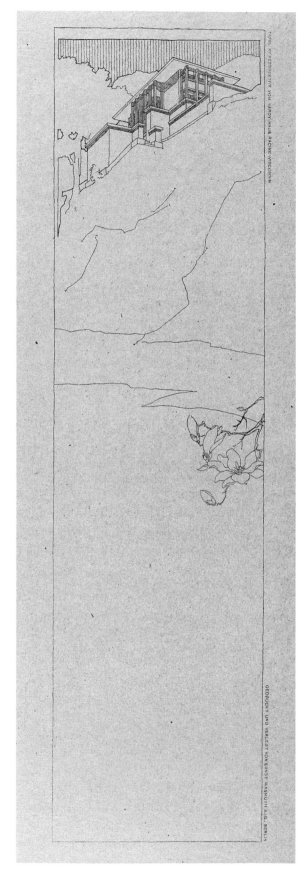

A vertically composed representation of the Hardy house in Racine, Wisconsin, is one of the most stunning renderings produced in the office attributed to Mahony. Recalling the elegance of a *kakejiku* (a Japanese scroll painting), it depicts a dramatically composed lakeside view of the house perched high above on a cliff. While the low vantage point recalls some of the studio renderings by Long, the trees that surround the dwelling have been reduced to mere outlines. Mahony left the lower four-fifths of the page almost untouched apart from a few light lines suggesting the cliff and shoreline. Except for areas of light blue representing the sky and the waters of Lake Michigan and a bit of white highlighting the east-facing walls of the house, the ocher-colored paper shows through. As often in Asian works of art, the negative or blank spaces are just as important to the composition as the ink lines of the house and landscaping, an idea similar in concept to Wright's recent realization that architecture involves the careful formation of the space between the walls. The inclusion of a couple of magnolia blossoms in the foreground, in place of colored shadings in a later version that appears in the Wasmuth Portfolio, gives the composition a structure even more strongly reminiscent of a Hiroshige print.

In addition to Mahony, Drummond, Byrne, and (after spring 1906) Harry Robinson all produced eye-catching presentation drawings evoking Japanese prints. Like Long, Drummond attempted to create realistic patterns of sunlight and shadow in his renderings and often made use of bird's-eye views.[11] A gifted renderer, Robinson worked on many presentation drawings in the last years of the studio, most likely including one of the Glasner house that appeared in the August 1906 issue of *House Beautiful*. The rendering, like the house itself, illustrates the Zen practice of "hide-and-reveal," where the design is never fully disclosed to the viewer.[12] In the case of the rendering, two tree trunks in the center deliberately conceal part of the house. Byrne, meanwhile, so closely adopted Mahony's "Japanese" style that years later he claimed he could not distinguish his own drawings from hers.[13]

5.5 Hardy house rendering redrawn with magnolias for the Wasmuth portfolio. Plate XV, *Ausgeführte Bauten und Entwürfe von Frank Lloyd Wright*, 1910. Special Collections, J. Willard Marriott Library, University of Utah.

5.6 Glasner house. Plate XLIII, *Ausgeführte Bauten und Entwürfe von Frank Lloyd Wright*, 1910. Special Collections, J. Willard Marriott Library, University of Utah.

Studio Employees

Following his return from Japan, Wright experienced significant turnover in his office staff. Younger, less-experienced designers like Robinson replaced departing associates after "serious rifts" developed between the architect and some of the more senior designers in the studio by late 1906, due to Wright's "cantankerous behavior"; his developing extramarital relationship with the attractive, well-educated client Mamah Cheney; and his "continual neglect in paying his employees on time."[14] Wright's penchant for spending beyond his means often led to a lack of resources for paying bills. His disinterest in bookkeeping and his system of partial payment, with the balance to be paid at some unspecified date (or in some cases with Japa-

nese prints) only exacerbated the problem.[15] It is not clear if his growing relationship with Cheney was a contributing factor, but records indicate he stopped hiring women to work in the studio after 1904, although Roberts and Mahony (intermittently) continued to work for him.

The first major fissure in these years involved Walter Burley Griffin. Upon leaving for Japan, Wright placed his office manager in charge of the commissions still underway. Misunderstandings ensued. Wright particularly expressed dismay with Griffin's treatment of the unrealized Herbert J. Ullman residence for a nearby lot for which he developed a landscape plan. Tension had arisen between Griffin and the Ullman family, and when Wright returned he felt that his employee had "tarried a bit on that commission in a way that he

5.7 Charles E. White's Oak Park office, ca. 1906. Oak Park River Forest Historical Society.

should not."[16] Wright also accused Griffin of using the studio staff to work on a personal project for a Chicago Architectural Club exhibition.[17]

According to Barry Byrne, Griffin and Wright's major dispute centered on money the architect owed his employee. If this was the case, it may have involved a loan Griffin made to Wright to help fund his trip to Japan and to settle various debts before his departure, or possibly it arose out of missing back wages or revenue from a profit-sharing agreement between them.[18] Wright eventually made a partial payment of his debt using Japanese prints. Weary of studio conditions, Griffin left in early 1906 (most likely in mid- to late January), returning to Steinway Hall to open his own practice.[19] The departure had a major impact on the studio. Not only did Wright lose an in-house colleague whom he could bounce new ideas off, but attention to landscape waned as no other employee could fully fill the resulting void.[20]

Wright, wanting Griffin to continue to produce landscape work for him, wrote to his "dear Walter" in a passive-aggressive manner requesting "the offi-

cial record of my private affairs" back and exclaiming, "Judging from your present conduct I feel that you consider your connection with this office of no further consequence to you."[21] The messiness of Griffin's departure and Wright's disregard of financial matters was reflected in a second letter in March when Wright wrote: "My dear Walter, I have been so busy with the [Japanese] print exhibition that the check given you for payment March 30 would better be held until the Monday or Tuesday following. I hope you will not find it inconvenient. Yours as life, Frank Lloyd Wright."[22]

One former studio architect who managed to keep on good terms with Wright during these years was Charles White, who had departed the office around the time his former employer left for Japan. The fact that White was no longer working in the studio and therefore did not have to worry about receiving pay likely helped their relationship. A great admirer of Wright, White continually sought out advice from him, especially on how to run a small practice, as he had opened his own architectural office a few blocks from the Oak Park studio. The two regularly conversed about cur-

5.8 Frank Lloyd Wright and family on the porch of the Oak Park home, ca. 1904. From left to right: Wright, Catherine's mother Flora Tobin holding Llewellyn, John, daughter Catherine, Frances, Maginel Wright, David, Catherine (Kitty), and Lloyd. Gift of John Lloyd Wright. Oak Park Public Library Special Collections.

rent projects and collaborated in 1906 with local architect Vernon S. Watson on the design of the River Forest Tennis Club.[23]

In contrast, Wright battled with Drummond around this time. Unlike "placid and sweet natured" Griffin, Drummond could be difficult and seemed "assertive and somewhat resentful" of his employer.[24] White recalled that he could be deceitful and had some "very nasty streaks in his makeup."[25] Wright apparently wanted to let Drummond go in early 1906 but found him a good worker and needed his experience in the office after Griffin's departure. Drummond continued to work in the studio until around early 1909, finally departing after a dispute, not surprisingly over pay.[26]

Wright began hiring younger, more malleable replacements. Unlike those who "defected" from the studio, Wright wrote in 1908, "these young people have found their way to me through natural sympathy with the work, and have become loyal assistants."[27] Byrne's "unspoiled" enthusiasm when he had entered the studio several years earlier led Wright to favor hiring novices over more experienced architects. In keeping with his own early bond with Louis Sullivan, master-student relationships soon replaced the more equal affiliation between colleagues of similar age and stature that marked the environment of Steinway Hall and, to

a larger extent than Wright would ever admit, the early years of the Oak Park studio.

During the latter years of the studio, Wright began to view his two oldest sons as potential future members of his office staff. For Lloyd and John, their father's drafting room evolved from an enchanting but off-limits playground into an architectural training ground. Having the boys in the studio allowed their father to have some connection with them, as the divide between home and studio continued to grow. Lloyd recalled becoming a "junior member" of the staff around the age of seven or eight, designing art glass before even being able to climb up on a drafting stool easily by himself.[28] At the age of nine he began to delineate his first architectural drawings.[29] He remembered carefully watching, listening, and talking with the architects while helping out. In early 1903, when he and his brother were twelve and ten years old, respectively, samples of their drawings circulated "through the Illinois Public and Normal schools as exhibitions of what children of their age can do."[30] As teenagers the two boys became valuable contributors to the studio. Lloyd's interest in landscape architecture developed out of conversations he had with Griffin there. By the time he went to college in 1907, the young man had become an accomplished draftsman and delineator.

By mid-1906, Robert Hardin, Harry Robinson, and

Wright's brother-in-law, Arthur Tobin, had joined the studio staff, which still included Byrne, Roberts, and Drummond, as well as Mahony on occasion. The three new men replaced Griffin, White, and Willatzen (the last having departed the studio for a second time just prior to March 1906 to work for Robert Spencer).[31] Tobin, Catherine Wright's younger brother, had been working at the Armour and Company meatpacking enterprise. He was a good businessman but had no previous experience in architecture. Wright hired him primarily to fill the vacancy of office manager and placed him in charge of specifications. Tobin also worked with contractors as needed.[32] He did not stay long. By the end of the year, he had accepted a position with the General Fireproofing Company of Youngstown, Ohio.[33]

Robinson attended the University of Illinois and during his senior year served as president of the school's architectural club. In this capacity he invited Wright to come to the university and speak at a club meeting on his design philosophy. Following the presentation, Wright invited Robinson to work in his Oak Park office. Soon after graduating with a degree in architectural engineering in June 1906, the young man entered the studio.[34]

Hardin also attended the University of Illinois, although it is not clear how well he had known Robinson there. He attended for less than a year, and official records indicate that he was not formally registered in the architecture program.[35] What design training Hardin had when he entered the studio was minimal at best.

Office turnover continued. By 1907, "feeling ready for a holiday from drafting" Mahony left the Chicago area for her brother's idyllic farmhouse in Elkhart, Indiana, where she stayed for about a year before returning to the studio.[36] Around this time she illustrated at least one advertisement for Marshall Field and Company and, with her cousin Dwight Perkins's wife Lucy, produced a series of illustrations for a couple of children's primers.[37] The foliage in many of the drawings is clearly reminiscent of renderings Mahony drew in the Oak Park studio.

Wright hired Albert McArthur and Taylor Woolley prior to Byrne's departure in August 1908. McArthur, the son of Warren McArthur, an early client of

5.9 Harry Robinson, ca. 1910. Photographer unknown. Courtesy of James Robinson.

Wright's, nicknamed "the Goat" because of his beard, had a reputation for laziness.[38] Isabel Roberts often needed to telephone him to come to work.[39] Whether Wright fired him or he quit, McArthur was gone by the end of the year. Woolley, a Mormon from Utah, proved more reliable. Wright's son Lloyd remembered him as "a sensitive draftsman … though lame, was active, helpful and a hard worker."[40]

The last known draftsman hired by Wright for his suburban studio was John Van Bergen. A 1905 graduate of Oak Park High School, he had some previous building and office experience, first working for Griffin and then with Oak Park architect E. E. Roberts. In October 1908, around the time he entered Roberts's office, Van Bergen began attending architecture classes at Chicago Technical College. Three months later, he entered Wright's office, replacing Robinson, who had left to become Griffin's chief draftsman at a time when things were "looking quite bleak" at Wright's.[41] Van Bergen assisted with both drafting and supervising construction projects, working alongside Mahony, Drummond, McArthur, Woolley, and Roberts.[42] Mahony (again) and Drummond departed soon afterward. When Wright left for Europe in late September, only Van Bergen and Roberts remained. Despite a shifting employee roster and growing debt in these years, Wright continued to further his architectural development on select commissions and also on his Oak Park property.

More Alterations to the Studio

Unlike the significant changes Wright made to the drafting room in 1903–4, he made few alterations to his main workspace after returning from Japan. Darwin Martin admonished Wright in December 1905 for "felicitating" himself on having acquired additional property adjoining his Oak Park home so soon after an "expensive vacation trip and large investments in art" while miscalculating his means and obligations

to creditors.[43] Comments like this may have made Wright more cognizant of how detrimental tearing up his drafting room was to the completion of clients' work and thus receiving payments from them.

Wright did make one major change to his drafting room during this period: installing new windows sometime just prior to 1907. Panes of a similar simple art glass design appear as early as in the studio plate for the 1900 *Architectural Review* article (see figure I.6). It is not clear why he waited so long to replace the windows. The new panes featured wide cames similar to those replaced earlier in the reception hall. Wright gave some of the original diamond-pane windows to Richard Bock, possibly as payment for sculptural ornament produced for one of the Buffalo commissions. The artist installed the windows in his own home and studio in River Forest.[44]

Minimizing disruption to office operations, Wright focused most of his later studio alterations on the library. These included the installation of a second level of clerestory windows sometime after the addition of the second level in the drafting room but before fall

5.10 Studio drafting room window showing new art glass panes with wide cames. Photographer unknown. H89.2, Frank Lloyd Wright Trust.

5.11 Studio of artist Richard Bock with diamond-pane windows from Wright's studio drafting room. Photographer: Richard W. Bock. Courtesy of Richard W. Bock Sculpture Museum, Greenville University, Greenville, Illinois.

1907.[45] To diffuse the extra light, Wright installed decorative wood grilles over the new windows (see figures 4.14 and 5.12).[46] Curtains that could close off at least the lower windows hung behind the grilles.

Diagrams and notes surrounding a drawing of the studio elevation showing double clerestories on both main rooms illustrate how Wright planned to raise the library roof and how much it would cost (see figure 4.7).[47] A sketch suggests how part of the interior of the library would look with the added windows.[48] The drawing provides evidence that the lower area of the library received a major update only after Wright added the second level of clerestories as an original octagonal light post with a spherical globe removed during the remodeling appears below the new arrangement of windows. Changes to the lower section of the library included replacing the cabinet doors that lined the room with laminated ones devoid of projecting

hardware and adding double-hinged panels covered in cork for displaying drawings and prints. Wright also exchanged the original solid pull-down doors on alternating wall sections with ones that contain panes of art glass, creating protective spaces to show off books or decorative objects. His innovative storage areas for drawings below each display case remained. Other changes made shortly after Wright installed the new clerestories include the addition of two piers that stopped short of the shelves in each corner in place of the octagonal light posts. That they visually but not physically support the horizontal planes recalls the tall storage piers in the drafting room, as well as the nonfunctioning piers that projected upward on either side of the reception hall plan desk. Wright also explored this concept in client projects, including the Darwin Martin house.

Two photographs of the studio library taken not

long after the addition of the upper clerestories and removal of the octagonal light posts present the room in
slightly different configurations. One shows triangular shelving running from center point to center point
of the walls, forming an octagon shifted 22.5 degrees
from the eight-sided floor plan (see figure 5.12). Additional thinner, triangular shelves run from corner
to corner in the center of the first triangular shelves,
providing the manifestation of a Froebel exercise, as
the octagon appears to rotate as one looks upward.
The double sets of cork display panels also appear in
the photograph. In the second image (see figure 4.14),
possibly taken at a slightly later date, the thin shelves
have disappeared and square vertical posts hang from
the grille in the corners of the room. Only a single
layer of cork panels remains, but the hardware for the
missing second layer is present. These subtle changes

reveal the important role of the studio, and the library
in particular, as a place of architectural experimentation, although, even for Wright, sometimes designs
did not work out as planned.

In 1931 Wright told students, "The physician can
bury his mistakes—but the Architect can only advise
his client to plant vines."[49] He, however, managed to
"bury" one of his mistakes at the studio. While the
upper clerestory windows added natural light to the
library, the resulting increase in the height of the walls
made the interior of the small, central-plan room feel
like a silo. This led Wright to curve the ceiling down-
ward, completely covering the new windows. At the
same time, he added shingles on the exterior, effectively hiding the existence of the windows until restoration workers discovered their framing decades
later.[50]

5.12 Studio library showing slight variations from figure 4.14, including a second layer of hinged corkboard panels and an additional
set of triangular shelves centered under the clerestory windows, but without the slender hanging vertical elements in the corners,
ca. 1906–8. Photographer unknown. Frank Lloyd Wright, *Ausgeführte Bauten* (Berlin: Ernst Wasmuth A.-G., 1911), 106.

5.13 Studio library as restored showing fireplace, concave edge of the ceiling, and laylight. Photographer: James Caulfield. Frank Lloyd Wright Trust.

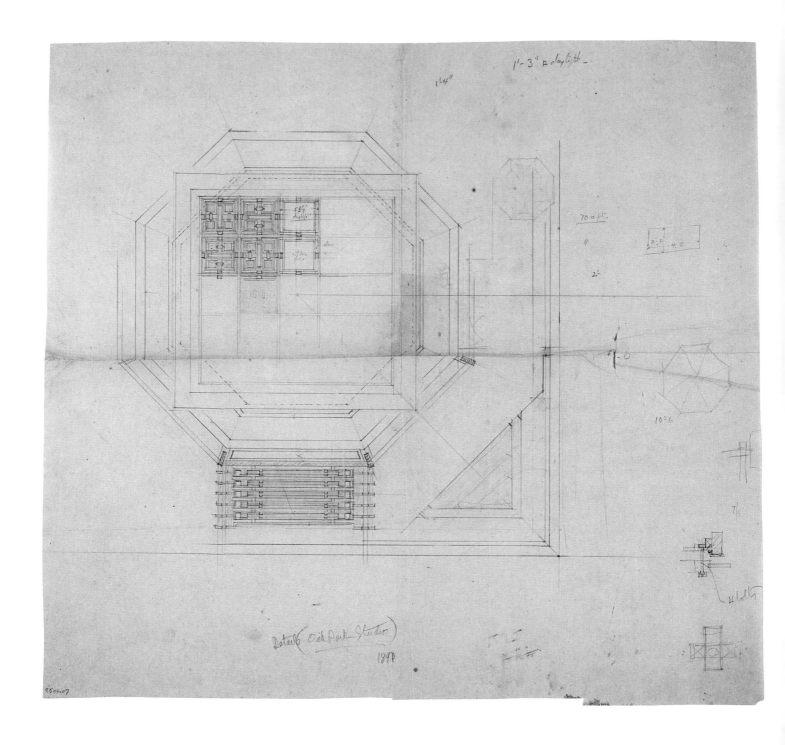

5.14 Reflective ceiling drawing of the studio library illustrating a design for the glass laylight (probably never realized) and grilles. TAL 9506.007, Avery Architectural & Fine Arts Library, Columbia University, New York. © 2020 Frank Lloyd Wright Foundation, Scottsdale, AZ. All rights reserved.

Curving the ceiling lessened the claustrophobic nature of the library by reducing the perception of the room's height and improving its proportions. At the same time Wright replaced the lower diamond panes with a simple art glass design similar to those in the drafting room and installed a skylight to compensate for the reduction in natural lighting.[51] A drawing in the Frank Lloyd Wright Archives identified as the library shows the design for a large square art glass laylight composed of a five-by-five matrix of smaller squares, which also appears on the post-1911 first-floor plan in a sales brochure for the property.[52] Each square consists of a cross pattern vaguely reminiscent of Wright's later concrete block designs but rotated ninety degrees from adjacent squares. The restoration architects, found no evidence of this skylight. Instead, they believe Wright installed a laylight of sandblasted glass discovered during the restoration but, according to physical evidence, only after he added a fireplace to the south side of the room.

Conflicting evidence makes it unclear if the fireplace was added before or after Wright's time in Europe. Neither the fireplace nor its chimney show in photographs until after 1911. While they do appear in the Wasmuth drawings of the studio, those renderings do not always reflect what was actually built. At some point in the building's later history, the brick facing of the fireplace had been stacked in the firebox and the opening walled over. Restoration workers uncovering this area decades later found a 1908 newspaper suggesting construction at or shortly after that date.[53] The use of common brick for the facing that matches the original drafting room fireplace also suggests an earlier date, as Wright fronted the other fireplaces in the studio in Roman brick in 1911; however, two of Wright's children claimed the library did not have a fireplace prior to the 1911 remodeling.[54] While the studio, in particular the library, still functioned as a personal design laboratory, Wright concentrated much of his architectural explorations in the later studio years on Unity Temple and a few select residential projects, such as the Coonley and Robie houses, while leaving the completion of smaller residential projects largely to his staff.

Design Process

Echoing the ideas of Froebel and others, Wright wrote in 1908 that democracy is "the highest possible expression of the individual as a unit not inconsistent with a harmonious whole."[55] Yet his views on the proper way to run an architectural office conjure more of a dictatorship than a democracy. He claimed that the principal architect secured sole authorship of the design work by maintaining complete control of the design process. This, he wrote, ensured the creation of a work of art, declaring, "Only when one individual forms the concept of the various projects and also determines the character of every detail in the sum total, even to the size and shape of the pieces of glass in the windows, the arrangement and profile of the most insignificant of the architectural members, will that unity be secure which is the soul of the individual work of art." He went on, "With no more propriety can an architect leave the details touching the form of his concept to assistants, no matter how sympathetic and capable they may be, than can a painter entrust the painting in of the details to a pupil."[56] Nonetheless, he turned over significant design responsibility on many projects to his staff.

Byrne recalled, "We all (Drummond particularly) initiated designs . . . but we followed Wright's other work and manner in doing so."[57] In later years, Wright would often leave his ideas in sketch form, with just the plan established and the main theme of the exterior design clearly defined in elevation. The development of all "implied but not delineated portions of the project then became the problem of the student draftsman," although, he admitted, this was usually "subject to the master's approval and often to his correction."[58] As in earlier years, significant revisions continued to occur late in the design process; Byrne lamented that erasing and redoing working drawings of the buildings entrusted to his care was a common and often wearisome procedure.[59] William Martin viewed such reworked drawings on one visit to the office, telling his brother that "unless he [Wright] gets it right he keeps on trying. . . . His tracing cloth shows the results of his labors, as it is ragged in many places where changes have been made repeatedly."[60]

5.15 Tan-y-deri, the home of Jane and Andrew Porter, Spring Green, Wisconsin. William Storrer Collection, Oak Park Public Library Special Collections.

Byrne created details and working drawings for the Beachy, Tomek, and Coonley houses, overseeing construction of the latter two. He additionally executed the working drawings for the Hills and Boynton residences, as well as Unity Temple. For most of these projects, he also wrote specifications and supervised construction, including interacting directly with the clients.[61] In addition to initiating designs, Drummond served as project manager on many local projects, including the Robie house. Robinson, meanwhile, produced drawings for several of the major commissions, including designs for the Coonley house windows in addition to presentation renderings.[62] Little evidence remains of Hardin's contributions (although his informal duties apparently included babysitting Wright's children on occasion).[63]

When Wright returned from Japan, he was several years older than Louis Sullivan had been at the time Wright had worked for him. Having entered middle age with a solid record of architectural accomplishments but growing disillusionment with architectural education and the profession in general in the United States, Wright began looking back at his own training and more deliberately contemplated the role he could play as a *Lieber Meister* himself. This interest in education, however, did not receive much of his energy at the time: Wright's rapidly unraveling personal life resulting from his growing restlessness and blossoming illicit relationship with Mamah Cheney kept him occupied. He did state, however, that he had begun assigning individual employees a project that he himself had "carefully conceived," allowing the worker to follow "its subsequent development through all its phases in drawing room and field, meeting with the client himself on occasion, gaining an all-round development impossible otherwise, and insuring an enthusiasm and a grasp of detail decidedly to the best interest of the client."[64] While Wright reported that the experiment proved moderately successful among his "boys" and had "every prospect of being continued as a settled policy in [the] future," he did not fully buy into it, as it discounted his own expressed desire for complete design control of his studio.[65]

It is not exactly clear to whom or to which projects Wright was referring. The term "boys" likely referred to Byrne, Robinson, and Hardin, all in their mid-twenties. Undoubtedly the architect assigned them smaller, relatively straightforward designs, most likely those based on the "Fireproof House for $5000" project or simple cruciform plans. The Stephen Hunt residence, a variation of the Fireproof House design, may have been one of them.[66] Another was likely Tany-deri, the residence designed for Wright's sister Jane and her husband in Spring Green. While an early version of the house featured Griffinesque elements, such as prominent gables and heavy piers not unlike the Beachy house (on which Byrne had worked), the final design consisted of a shingled version of the "Fireproof House for $5000." Years later, Jane wrote to Byrne asking if he remembered the house he built for her.[67]

Education had always been a facet of life in the studio. Wright was beginning to think more purposefully about his role as a mentor and educator, roles that would eventually come to fruition in his establishment of the Taliesin Fellowship in 1932.

Late Studio Projects

Most of the later residential projects in the Oak Park studio incorporated the aesthetic vocabulary Wright had developed at the start of the decade. Both the Avery and Queene Coonley residences and an unbuilt design for Harold F. McCormick (son of the inventor of the mechanical reaper) for a 260-acre site dramatically overlooking Lake Michigan north of Chicago, however, were extensively larger than most of his previous domestic commissions. To handle the increase in scale of these 1907 designs, Wright expanded the arms of his basic crucifix plan into wings that project out over large, spacious lots.[68] Instead of incorporating one ceremonial hearth in the center of the home, the Coonley residence accommodates a series of prominent core rooms that Wright treated as separate entities, each with its own center and subservient wings. This, he said, allowed the major public spaces to have "light and air on three sides" yet still contribute to a "harmonious whole."[69]

Wright repeated the basic elements of his residential architecture over and over in carefully worked-out variations, as he refined his designs concepts. Byrne recalled: "Failing adequate development in his initial use of a given scheme he [Wright] would sometimes do as he did in the Robie House, repeat the architectural scheme of another house, in this case the one built for Mr. Tomek, but with the new design highly developed."[70] Wright reworked the earlier Tomek house design, commissioned for a site in suburban Riverside, to fit a narrow urban corner lot in the south Chicago neighborhood of Hyde Park for the Robies.[71] He sliced the long rectangular mass of the Tomek house horizontally and slid the southern half approximately forty feet to the west. This provided Robie, an early automotive enthusiast, with space for a large garage and drive on the east end of the house. To the west the shift provided space for a more elaborate exterior path of discovery than at the Tomek house. The walkway slides along the north side of the building via a carefully crafted processional sequence that evokes the concept of "hide-and-reveal" before reaching a dark recessed entrance well protected from the street.[72] The rectangular mass of the house, with its long, horizontal side balcony on the south facade and tall central core containing a large chimney stack, as well as the low hip roof that cantilevers over a raised terrace on the west end, gives the house an appearance that lives up to Wright's nickname for it: "the *Dampfer*," meaning steamship in German.[73]

In addition to the few large residential commissions, the studio carried out a series of smaller cross-axial schemes that presented variations of an unrealized domestic design created for William Norman Guthrie in 1908. Like the Walser and Barton houses,

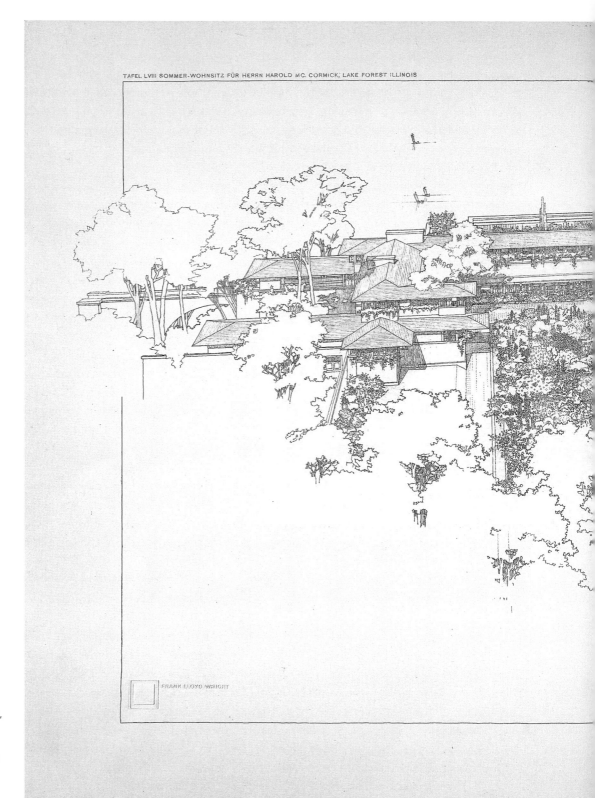

FRANK LLOYD WRIGHT

5.16 Harold McCormick residence, aerial perspective showing its sprawling wings. Plate LIX, *Ausgeführte Bauten und Entwürfe von Frank Lloyd Wright*, 1910. Special Collections, J. Willard Marriott Library, University of Utah.

GEDRUCKT UND VERLEGT VON ERNST WASMUTH A.-G., BERLIN

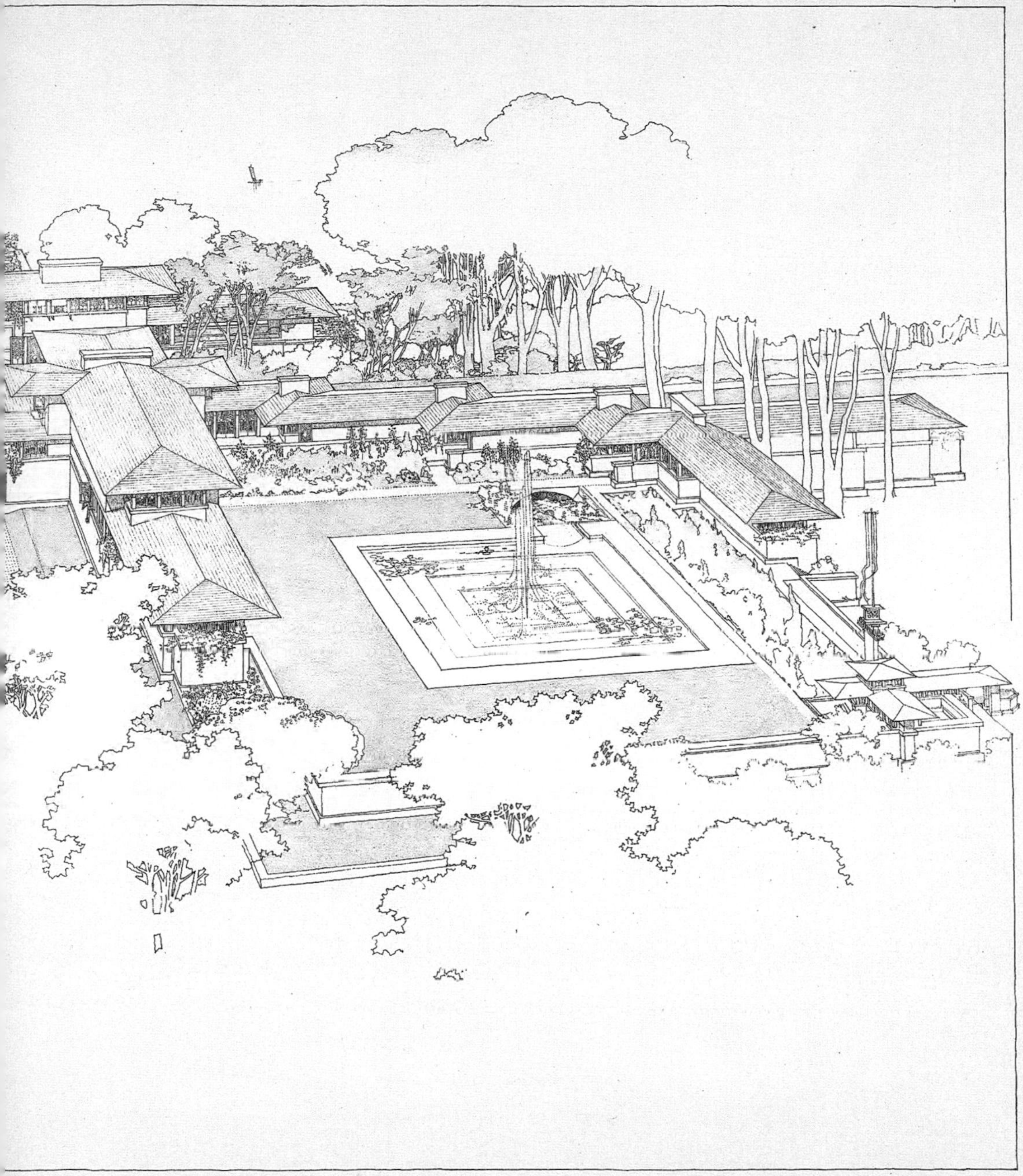

5.17 Robie house exterior. Photographer: Lisa D. Schrenk.

5.18 Robie house plans illustrating shift in north half of house footprint with recessed entrance at upper left of ground-floor plan. Plate XXXVII, *Ausgeführte Bauten und Entwürfe von Frank Lloyd Wright*, 1910. Special Collections, J. Willard Marriott Library, University of Utah.

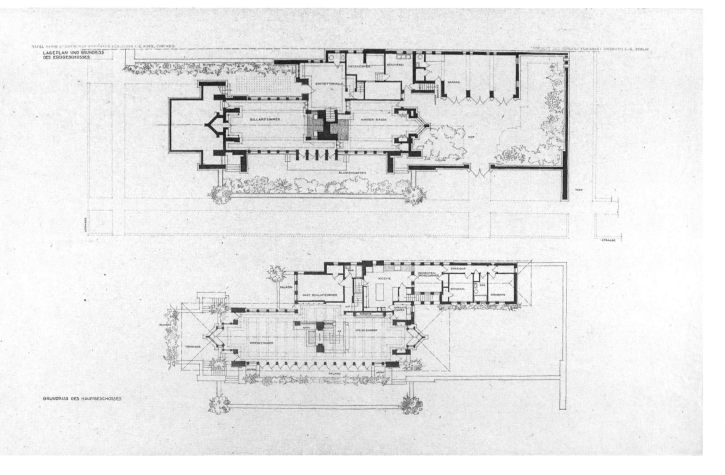

5.19 Isabel and Mary Roberts house, River Forest. Photographer: Lisa D. Schrenk.

these projects largely negated the second proposition for organic architecture laid out in the architect's 1908 "In the Cause of Architecture" essay published in *Architectural Record*: "[T]here should be as many kinds (styles) of houses as there are kinds (styles) of people."[74] Each of the designs consists of a central hearth with projecting wings and a two-story living room. In several, a second-story interior balcony overlooks the main living area. The office produced variations of the design for Frank T. Baker, Walter V. Davidson, Joshua Melson (unbuilt), Oscar Steffens, and George C. Stewart, as well as for Isabel Roberts and her mother Mary.[75] The studio staff carried out most of the work

on these projects, while Wright attempted to focus his efforts on more complex or interesting commissions.[76]

Explorations of a house for Harvey and Eliza Sutton of McCook, Nebraska, and the new church for local Universalists and Unitarians in Oak Park reveal differences in studio design processes and finished products between the small "cookie-cutter" residential commission that often exhibited little in design advancements, carried out with only minimal input from the architect, and a major project that received the bulk of Wright's attention in these years, exhibiting new architectural developments and the impact of his trip to Japan.

5.20 Postcard of the Sutton house showing the cantilever over the entrance, 1908. Grant Manson Collection, Oak Park Public Library Special Collections.

The Sutton House

A rare surviving, but incomplete, series of letters between the office staff and the Suttons between 1905 and 1908 offers a glimpse into the office choreography during the production of a rudimentary prairie house.[77] This correspondence presents a story quite different than Wright's professed ideal of an individual architect carrying out all facets of a design. The letters also illustrate that while Wright may have wanted to give his approval on all work leaving the studio, this did not actually happen, especially during periods when he was away from the office. In the case of the Sutton commission, at least six people in the office participated in the production of the residence.[78]

Like a number of Wright's earlier clients, Harvey and Eliza Sutton were heavily involved in community and musical activities. Born in New York, Harvey opened a jewelry shop in the rural railroad town of McCook, Nebraska, and became the conductor of the Chicago, Burlington and Quincy Concert Band. When

the Suttons decided to enlarge their home, they turned to Eliza's friends, Mary S. Morlan and Rose Barnes, who introduced the couple to Wright's work. Morlan had grown up in Richland Center, Wisconsin, Wright's birthplace, located about twenty-five miles northwest of Spring Green, and personally knew the architect. Rose and her husband Charles had previously commissioned an unrealized design from Wright for a lot across the street from the Suttons, after coming across Wright's first two *Ladies' Home Journal* articles.[79]

In the earliest surviving correspondence between the studio staff and the Suttons, the future clients inform Wright that they inspected the design the architect produced for their friends and were "favorably impressed." They then described the extensive remodeling they wanted to have carried out on their home for a modest cost.[80] Griffin responded on 8 February 1905, alluding to an earlier request by the Suttons for a new house, informing them that projecting costs for a remodeling was more difficult than for a completely new house.[81] Griffin, as office manager, took care of such

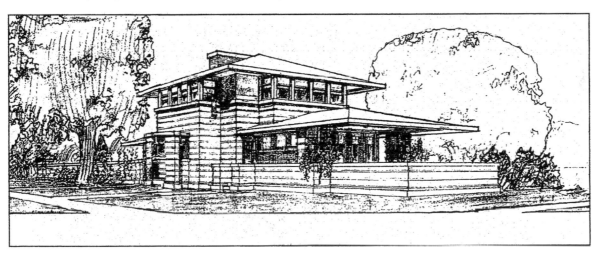

requests under normal working conditions. And with Wright's time undoubtedly consumed by preparations for his imminent trip to Japan, it is even less surprising that Griffin and not Wright responded.

In late March, after receiving at least one more correspondence (now lost) from the Suttons, Griffin wrote back indicating that sketches of a "more radical" extensive remodeling were mailed to Nebraska the day before.[82] The Suttons quickly rejected the design, which recalled Wright's 1901 *Ladies' Home Journal* cruciform composition but with Griffinesque rooflines, suggesting his authorship.[83] On April 18, while Wright was somewhere between Kyoto and Tokyo, Drum-

mond sent a reply to the Suttons signed "Yours Truly. Frank Lloyd Wright per W. E. D.," indicating an alternate, two-story scheme was in the mail that "suited requirements which the Suttons desired more fully."[84] Drummond appears to be the author of this design, as not only does the rendering appear to be in his hand, but the version shares many characteristics with his early independent work, including his own home in River Forest of 1907.

Believing they were dealing directly with Wright, Eliza wrote to the architect that she was "very unhappy" that the new plans were not what she wanted at all—too much wasted space and lacking the bedrooms and closets that she had repeatedly requested. In mid-July, two months after Wright's return from Japan, Griffin wrote to the Suttons describing a simpler, less formal design. Still not satisfied, Eliza responded, "Again I come with the same old story, not what I want yet," and presented a list of issues with the latest version. She ended her note with "trusting you will not lose all patience with me."[85] With all of the effort that Eliza had exerted up to this point, it is quite surprising that she had not lost patience with Wright and the studio staff. Once again Griffin's natural amiability undoubtedly helped smooth rough patches in client relationships.

The studio architects must have produced and sent out another design that more closely took into consideration the Suttons' wishes, as the next known letter from the clients identifies just a few minor issues, such as the location of the coal and wood room, and includes a request for a couple of sketches of the finished house. The date of this letter is hard to pinpoint; the next known response from Oak Park was not until May 28 of the following year.[86] By this time Griffin was gone and Arthur Tobin had taken over as office manager. Tobin wrote the Suttons that a set of plans had been sent and that additional sets and specifications, as well as a "mill schedule," would be mailed in a few days. Tobin composed a second letter in mid-June addressing some of the clients' latest concerns. He also referred to Eliza's trip to the studio, when Wright took her around Oak Park to see several of his houses and then hosted a lunch for her with his family.[87]

It was only after Eliza had met Wright in person that she received his personal attention. Most of their correspondence, however, involved damage control or requests for payment. For example, in two letters mailed in July 1906, Wright responded to some of Eliza's concerns and gave approximate costs of various building materials. Construction began the following winter, but by January the Suttons were "disgusted" and "discouraged" by "an unsightly hole" at their front door created by the builders while the final design was still being worked on. Attempting to make sure that their desired design changes were made, the Suttons withheld a payment. On 9 April 1907, Wright pleaded with them to "consider the architect a little"

who "really needs money badly" and requested the overdue $300.[88] The Suttons must have sent the remittance, as the topic was dropped.

With construction well underway other members of the office staff began responding to the Suttons' correspondence. Barry Byrne wrote letters on 25 September and 23 October 1907 that addressed a wall that had previously been removed from the design and details regarding art glass and plasterwork. Between May and July 1908, as construction was finishing up, Isabel Roberts wrote to the Suttons responding to additional issues with the plasterwork, including cracks. It appears that none of the office staff ever traveled to McCook. Instead Eliza Sutton took on the role of general contractor, hiring two local builders to construct the house.[89]

The basic cross-axial plan of the residence as completed in the summer of 1908 was strongly reminiscent of the Willits house but featured a dramatically cantilevered hipped roof over the veranda that predates other better-known cantilevers in his work.[90] Even with several cost-cutting changes, when construction ended the Suttons had spent close to $10,000, five times their initial budget.[91] Their "intimate friends" made fun of the design and thought Eliza was "off in her head"; still, the couple enjoyed living in the house and remained there until their deaths in the early 1950s.[92]

Another project in these years, which, in contrast to the Sutton commission, received Wright's full attention was Unity Temple. Today the church is viewed as one of the architect's masterpieces, and was one of eight buildings designed by Wright named to the UNESCO World Heritage List in 2019.[93] In the years immediately after its construction, however, the building received almost no recognition beyond Wright's own publicity efforts.[94] This most certainly contributed to his growing frustration with the direction of his professional career.

Unity Temple

Unity Temple presented an exciting exploratory exercise for the architect. Like the design process for the Sutton house project, examining that for the church offers valuable insights into studio operations. The

5.23 Rendering of Unity Temple by Marion Mahony. TAL 0611.003, Avery Architectural & Fine Arts Library, Columbia University, New York. © 2020 Frank Lloyd Wright Foundation, Scottsdale, AZ. All rights reserved.

commission allowed Wright to experiment with new materials, spatial forms, and sensory experiences. While his ability to manipulate space and forms on a more sophisticated level following his return from Japan is not readily apparent in changes made to the studio or in his minor residential projects in these years, it is clearly evident here. Near the end of his life he would write, "Unity Temple is where I thought I had it, this idea that the reality of a building does not consist in the walls and roof but in the space within."[95]

The design and construction of Unity Temple almost directly coincides with the time between Wright's first two trips abroad. On 24 May 1905, ten days after he returned from Japan, the members of Unity Church voted to build a new home.[96] Eleven days later lightning struck the current church's steeple, setting fire to the building and making construction a necessity.[97] The dedication of the new church took place on 26 September 1909, three days after Wright's departure from Oak Park for Europe.

After interviewing nine architects, the church com-

mittee selected Wright to design a building "dignified and devotional in aspect and also suited to the working needs of a modern church."[98] Wright spent most of his time in the studio during the fall of 1905 developing the initial design. In December, Unity Temple's building committee formally accepted his plans, which they published the following June in a twenty-page pamphlet describing the design.[99] As with his earlier Oak Park projects, he wrote of working from the inside out: "The first idea was to keep a noble ROOM for worship in mind, and let the room shape the whole edifice, let the room inside be the architecture outside."[100] Wright wrote that he revised the design over and over as classical music played in the background and a fire burned in the drafting room hearth late into the evening. "Night labor at the draughting board," he claimed, "is best for intense creation. It may continue uninterrupted."[101]

Years later Wright recorded some of the numerous thoughts and concerns that he recalled had passed through his mind as he was working:

[D]esign is abstraction of nature-elements in purely geometric terms'—that is what we ought to call pure design? ... This cube—this square—proportion. But—nature-pattern and nature-texture in materials themselves often approach conventionalization, or the abstract, to such a degree as to be superlative means ready to the designer's hand to qualify, simulate, and enrich his own efforts.... What texture this concrete mass? Why not its own gravel? How to bring the gravel clean on the surface? ... I knew. Here was reality.... Keep the straight lines clean and keep all significant of the idea—the flat plane expressive and always clean cut. But let texture come into them to qualify them in sunlight.... [A]fter all you will see that the pattern of reality *is* supergeometric, casting a spell or charm over any geometry, and is such a spell in itself. Yes, so it seems to me as I draw with T-square, triangle and scale. That is what it means to be an artist—to seize this essence brooding everywhere in everything, just behind aspect. These questions arising each with its own train of thought by the way, as the architect sits at his work. Suddenly it is morning. To bed for a while.[102]

Faced with a limited budget, a small, narrow, noisy site, and the rejection of traditional Christian iconography such as the steeple, Wright struggled to flesh out a solution that exhibited a strong unity between mass and detail and responded to its less-than-desirable site by turning in on itself, much like his design for the Larkin building and the main rooms of his studio. While the plan remained relatively unchanged, the basic form of the sanctuary slowly developed through thirty-four studies, from, according to Barry Byrne, an early "saucer-shaped dome" to a cube.[103] The cladding, meanwhile, evolved from brick to crushed red granite to finally (in part due to budget) exposed concrete.[104] Wright wrote of his process, "The ideal of organic architecture is severe discipline for the imagination. I came to know that full well.... How many schemes I have thrown away because some minor feature would not come true to form!"[105] Even as construction was well under way he made significant changes, such as altering the decorative design of the piers in the sanctuary.

For Wright, Unity Temple served as a personal Froebelian exercise and an evolution of the design he had created for his home studio eight years earlier with its binuclear layout.[106] The two buildings sit on long, narrow sites and feature central entrances with main spaces to either side. In both cases, instead of relying upon one big form, Wright created an assemblage of elements that express the fact that each was designed to house a different activity. In the case of the studio, the large drafting room to the left of the entrance balances the smaller library to the right. At Unity Temple, the larger, more significant, central-plan sanctuary offsets the lower, narrower, but broader social hall, referred to as Unity House. The studio layout proved successful, offering a central reception hall that divided the busy drafting room from the quieter, more intimate library. The separation meant that noise emanating from one room would not disturb work or thoughtful contemplation going on in the other. In the design for Unity Temple, the vestibule serves a similar function, dividing the sacred sanctuary for honoring God and the social hall for carrying out the work of mankind, two core tenets articulated by the quotation located over the main entrances: "For the Worship of God and the Service of Man."[107]

Some scholars have suggested that Wright borrowed the basic plan for Unity Temple from Tōshō-gū in Nikkō, Japan, an early seventeenth-century mausoleum that he had visited earlier in the year. Even if so, the two buildings exhibit important differences, including the location of their main entrances and how they are experienced. The overall layout of the mausoleum complex, which includes a walkway with a series of ninety-degree turns, probably had a greater influence on Wright, through reinforcing his "path of discovery" concept.

While the basic layout of the church exhibits similarities to the Oak Park studio, aspects of its design show that the experiential qualities of Wright's architecture were becoming richer and more complex in projects that received his full attention. Unity Temple's processional route presents a clear example of this. After Japan, Wright began to think more profoundly about the body's movement through a building and

5.24 Unity Temple model showing entrance. Photographer: Lisa D. Schrenk.

its site, including the Zen practice of not revealing all from a single vantage point. Wright designed an intricate path of discovery for Unity Temple by closely integrating the processional route with the form and function of the building. Unlike most traditional churches, the entrance is not prominently located on the front facade; instead, it is tucked away, hidden from the street. The main approach begins at the sidewalk on Lake Street, at the corner of Kenilworth Avenue.[108] It then heads south, sliding alongside the large, concrete mass of the sanctuary on a pathway separated from the sidewalk by a strip of greenery. Visitors then reach a half flight of stairs, concealed from the side street by a large square urn that marks the front edge of a walled entrance terrace.[109] Like a Tokugawa-era castle, it presents a *masugata*, an enclosed protective space with the entrance situated at a right angle.[110] Wright did not design it this way to place those entering the building in a position vulnerable to attack nor to keep evil spirits away, as was the case in Japan, but rather to serve as a transitional space between the noise and

mayhem of the secular world outside and the tranquil, sacred place within. A row of art glass doors, topped by the entrance quote, provides access to the foyer. Its low ceiling recalls the processional pattern of compression followed by release that Wright had explored earlier at his own property, in the dark, narrow barrel-vaulted hallway that leads to the spacious playroom in the home and the low reception hall that precedes the two-story drafting room on one end and the library on the other in the studio.[111]

A right-angle turn to the north from the lobby of Unity Temple reveals a plain gray wall decorated with simple wood banding, camouflaging doorways not intended for public entry. Wright stated that the "audience" instead was to enter "at the rear of the auditorium, by means of depressed passages on either side."[112] These "cloister corridors," a half level below the main floor, frame each side of the worship hall and lead to the rear corner stair towers. The cloisters offer floor-level glimpses into the sanctuary before fully entering the space.[113] Natural light emanating from the towers

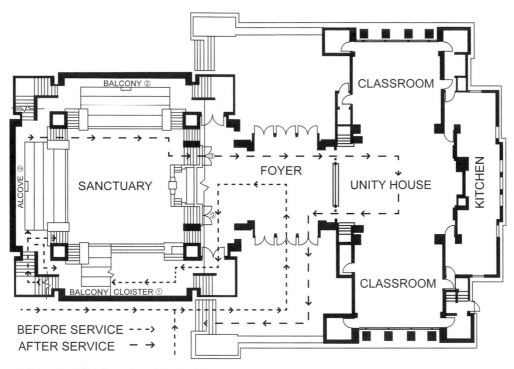

1. Cloister is a half level below the main floor level of sanctuary.
2. Lower balcony and alcove areas are a half level above the main floor level of sanctuary.
3. Exit doors between foyer and sanctuary are closed before services, blending in with the wall surface.

PROCESSIONAL PATHWAY OF UNITY TEMPLE

5.25 Plan of Unity Temple identifying its processional pathway. Lisa D. Schrenk. Rendered by Juliana Seymour.

draws parishioners upward. To arrive at the main floor level a half flight of stairs must be climbed. The staircases then continue up to two levels of balconies surrounding the sanctuary on three sides (see figures 3.10 and 5.27).[114] Wright designed the square auditorium much like a New England meetinghouse with none of the four hundred seats more than forty-five feet away from the lectern.

Because Wright located the pulpit along the side of the sanctuary closest to the entrance hall, unlike in a traditional church, after services parishioners could exit the space by heading toward instead of away from the officiator.[115] A half flight of stairs leads to the unmarked doors in the plain gray wall that open to reveal the lobby.[116] Like the view from the drafting room entrance across the reception hall to the library at the Oak Park studio, a view into the brightly lit social hall directly across the low, dark vestibule beckons people forward to Unity House for postservice coffee and

community socializing—an important part of Universalist and Unitarian services.

In the sanctuary design Wright furthered his exploration of breaking the box form of traditionally shaped rooms. After his time in Japan, he began to think of architecture in new ways, not just as enclosures of volumes, as he had done in his initial designs for his Oak Park home and studio but as dialogues between two- and three-dimensional elements.[117] In working on the design of Unity Temple, Wright was in essence overlaying a two-dimensional Froebel paper activity onto a three-dimensional block exercise to achieve an animated composition.

For the three months Wright had been away from the studio, he lived among traditional Japanese buildings consisting of compositions of planes, observing that the thin shoji screen walls were "protected by vertical wooden slats in so many cleaver geometric patterns."[118] The screens could slide open or shut,

5.26 Exit doors from sanctuary into the foyer for use after services at Unity Temple (location of the photograph is identified in figure 5.25 by the upper number 3.). Photographer: James Caulfield.

5.27 Unity Temple sanctuary. Exit doors are located a half flight below the main floor level immediately to each side of the lectern. Wood banding outlines rectangular forms that appear to be slipping around the balconies and piers. Photographer: James Caulfield.

providing flexibility and movement to spaces. Like the exterior pathway alongside Unity Temple, parts of the building seem to slip or shift within the sanctuary. Instead of outlining elements, as he had done at his own property and in many of his earlier prairie houses, Wright wrapped two sides of three-dimensional details, such as the balconies and corner piers, with wood banding, creating the impression that the rectangular forms are in the process of slipping around the elements. Wright went on to do this on several other late Oak Park–era projects. While his earlier "Fireproof House for $5000" designs include rectangular-shaped banding on the facades of the corner piers, such as at the Fuller and Hunt residences, for later dwellings, including the Evans, Hoyt, and Stockman houses, the banding slides horizontally so it wraps around the outside corners of the piers as on the interior of Unity Temple. Wright also incorporated similar banding on the 1906 remodel of the Edward Hills residence and on the Laura Gale house, both located nearby the studio.

By situating the cloisters a half level below the main floor area, Wright also managed to break the bottom plane of the box-shaped sanctuary, giving the central floor the appearance of a floating plane (see figure 3.10). The result was a significantly greater sense of plasticity and movement in his definition of the space than he had achieved three years earlier with the addition of the four static storage piers and shelving to the studio drafting room.

One can easily envision, as historian Grant Manson suggested, that the design of the church, with its plain, concrete walls, stair towers, and hollyhock columns, formed the solution to a Froebel block exploration. The parts in the composition clearly unite to present a sense of "harmony to the whole."[119] But, like the Form of Beauty compositions carried out by Wright's children in the playroom of the Oak Park home where four elements are moved at one time to produce a new design, the corner stair towers have been pulled from the main central block. As at the Larkin building they break from the underlying, rigid grid that provides structure to Froebel exercises.

The exterior of Unity Temple also reflects what Wright learned from Hiroshige and other Japanese print masters about the elimination of the insignif-

icant. He discarded the prominent pitched roof and the steeple pointing to heaven from the congregation's previous home. The simple, flat roof and monochromatic, monolithic walls conveyed to passersby that Unity Temple was quite different from the other traditional suburban houses of worship in the community dubbed "Saints' Rest."

Wright's choice of concrete as the primary material for Unity Temple arose in part out of his growing interest in it, at a time when other architects like Anatole de Baudot and Auguste Perret in France were beginning to explore its expressive potential. Previously he had produced a series of unrealized concrete projects, including designs for a monolithic bank and a concrete home and studio for Richard Bock.[120] Realized explorations include the use of a concrete frame for the Martin brothers' brick E-Z Polish Factory building, under construction at the time, and the installation of magnesite at the Oak Park studio, the Larkin building, and several residential commissions.[121] His success with magnesite led Wright to specify the material for the floors of Unity Temple.[122]

With construction under way in 1907, the process of reusing the formwork for the concrete presented a massive three-dimensional Froebel Form of Beauty exercise on the corner of Lake Street and Kenilworth Avenue. The structure rose in a spiraling pattern as construction workers repositioned sections of the wood formwork from one side of the building to another, leaving behind visual evidence of the separate concrete pours on the facades (see figure C.2).[123] The five-by-five-foot matrix of laylights in the auditorium ceiling presented Wright with another Froebelesque exercise, resulting in a geometric design where the individual art glass panels rotate ninety degrees from one square to the next.

The architect had previously explored the effects of natural and artificial lighting entering a room from above in the atrium of the Larkin building and even earlier with the incorporation of a variety of laylights and fixtures in his Oak Park home and studio. The matrix of laylights at Unity Temple likely developed out of the similar design of five-by-five openings in the early laylight design for the Oak Park studio library that also exhibited a pattern of rotations. For evenings

5.28 Unity Temple under construction, 1908. Photographer unknown. Frank Lloyd Wright, *Ausgeführte Bauten* (Berlin: Ernst Wasmuth A.-G., 1911), 4.

at the church, Wright incorporated additional artificial light in the sanctuary using fixtures that hung from the ceiling above the corners of the central floor area. The clean geometrical forms of the chandeliers, which consisted of a sphere framed by two cantilevered cubes surrounded by linear banding, recalled both the Fresnel globes that hung in the drafting room and the cube-shaped "water lily" fixtures he recently designed for the playroom in his home.

Few studio records remain documenting the design process of Unity Temple, but those that do indicate that the romantic picture Wright portrayed in his autobiography of the lone genius architect, slaving away at his drawing board at night, was not the complete story. Although the design of the building may have been largely his own, the entire office staff contributed to its realization. In March 1906 White,

who was no longer working at the studio, wrote, "The chief thing at Wright's is of course Unity Church, the sketches of which are at last accepted, after endless fighting. We have all pleaded and argued with the committee, until we are well nigh worn out. All hands are working on the working drawings."[124] Wright placed Byrne, now one of his more experienced employees, in charge of the production of those drawings.[125] An elevation produced by Wright served as a guide for some of them.[126] Mahony, meanwhile, created presentation renderings, including two exquisite illustrations reworked as line drawings for publication in the 24 February 1906 edition of the *Oak Leaves*. Paul Mueller served as contractor on the project, while Wright appointed Drummond as job superintendent. Arthur Tobin, handling the studio's business affairs, oversaw some of the scheduling for the project, and Isabel

5.29 Unity Temple sanctuary skylight. Note rotation of glass design. Photographer: James Caulfield.

Roberts managed correspondence between the studio and the church's building committee. Artist Richard Bock contributed as well, producing a model for the building's ornamental columns.

When Unity Temple held its first service on 25 October 1908, the project was far from completion and well over budget, eventually forcing Mueller into bankruptcy.[127] Wright was nervous about how the parishioners were going to receive the building and avoided the church that cool, damp fall day. But after he began receiving congratulatory phone calls, he took his eleven-year-old daughter Frances outside their Oak Park home and tossed the young girl into the sky in celebration.[128] This joyous feeling, however, would be fleeting. Within a year, Wright had abandoned his work, his family, and his community in an attempt to stave off a growing sense of restlessness that he felt within the physical and social confines of his Oak Park home and studio.

The reality of transforming Wright's vision for Unity Temple into a functioning home for the congregation, like almost all major works of modern architecture, was one of collaboration, with each player performing as one cog in a larger production machine. Sometimes the machine processes are simple affairs and other times complex. At times, when well oiled, they produce magnificent structures; other times, they break down. In the case of Wright's office, by the time construction on the church neared completion, the machine exhibited significant wear and tear, largely due to neglect. Soon it would cease to function altogether. The reinvigoration Wright felt after his return from Japan had dissipated. The composition of his office staff had shifted from well-trained employees to a less-experienced workforce that often required but at times did not receive needed guidance from him. Large, commercial commissions Wright expected to follow the Larkin building never materialized, nor did widespread acceptance of his architectural ideas. Money issues increased, as did the architect's negative personal reputation as he continued to carry on his iniquitous relationship with Mamah Cheney and to dodge his creditors. By late 1908 Wright's discontent with his personal and professional lives had grown to the point of suffocation. An undertone of his restless-

ness and frustration permeated his "In the Cause of Architecture" article published in March of that year, in which Wright addressed his views on Japanese prints, as well as various aspects of his early career. It formed the first of seventeen articles he wrote for *Architectural Record* between 1908 and 1952.

Reception of Studio Designs: "In the Cause"

Architectural Record's agenda for printing Wright's initial "In the Cause" article was to present a discussion on the significant role of nature in establishing "a vital architecture in the United States."[129] Much as Robert Spencer's 1900 article on Wright provided an early opportunity for the architect to publicize his progressive architectural ideas, this article afforded him the first of two early prominent opportunities to assess his Oak Park–era work in print (the second opportunity being the introductory essay to his Wasmuth Portfolio two years later). More than fifty pages of photographs and drawings illustrating Wright's work, including the Willits, Dana, Martin, Robie, and Coonley residences; the Larkin building and Unity Temple; as well as his Oak Park studio followed the ten-page essay.

Wright emphasized the established principles of his architecture. These included looking to the fertile role of nature as a generator of ideas in an organic design process and repeatedly stressing the importance of harmony, where all of the parts relate to a unifying theme. In addition to laying out his architectural propositions that defined the prairie house, Wright addressed his preferred forms, from windows (both in type of window and in the use of art glass) to roof shapes (three types: low-pitched hip roofs, low roofs with simple pediments, and simple slabs). He also expressed his belief that "the machine" was here to stay and needed to be employed to its best advantage through the application of "clean cut, straight-line forms that the machine can render far better."[130]

What was new in the article was Wright's projection of bitterness and defiance that often permeated his writings throughout the rest of his career as he fought for his organically derived architecture against the traditional academic practice of "adhering slavishly to dead formula" and "seeking inspiration in books."[131] He referred to himself as the "recognized enemy of the established industrial order."[132] Much of Wright's frustration stemmed from not having his architecture widely accepted, despite developing pockets of strong admirers.

For the masses, however, his architecture continued to seem peculiar. At midcareer, Wright still felt he had to continually "sell" and validate what he felt were universal and true ideas, not only to potential clients and their bankers but also to members of his own profession. Public criticism of the Larkin building particularly stung. Even Larkin executives expressed concern about the reception of it and asked Wright to author a series of articles rationalizing the design and costs to the company's consumers and employees. Sharp criticism began the following June when poet and art critic Harriet Monroe, reviewing Wright's entries in the 1907 Chicago Architectural Club Show, panned the architect's nonresidential designs as experimental, "unusual, at times even bizarre," and asserted that his limitations were "obvious enough." She thought his "more ambitious buildings," including the Larkin building and Unity Temple (under construction at the time), all "look too much like fantastic blockhouses … without grace or ease or monumental beauty." She went on: "Manifestly his imagination halts here; it labors and does not yet achieve beautiful and expressive buildings for public worship and business."[133] Three months later Charles Illsley, in Chicago's *Inland Architect and News Record*, described the disjuncture between the Larkin building's interior and exterior designs and the lack of any "attempt at grace of form or decoration."[134] The following year saw a stinging review of the building in *Architectural Record* by Russel Sturgis a month after Wright's own "In the Cause" essay appeared. The seventy-one-year-old architect and critic, who had visited the Oak Park studio in May 1904, referred to the structure as "extremely ugly" and a "monster of awk-

wardness," informing readers, "We are left, then, with our sympathies enlisted in Mr. Wright's behalf, to consider what else might have been done, had the architect felt that he could not bear to turn out a building quite so ungainly, so awkward in grouping, so clumsy in its parts and in its main mass."[135]

While Wright's "In the Cause" article provided him a platform for defending his architectural ideas, it also offers additional early evidence of his proclivity for bending the truth to fit his needs. After a brief mention of the design processes in his Oak Park office, he presented a partial list of past and current employees of his "little university," recording his perceptions of what those who had departed had taken from their experiences. Then, ignoring the architectural training of some of his employees, he erroneously stated that "the few draughtsmen so far associated with this work have been taken into the draughting room, in every case almost wholly unformed, many of them with no particular previous training and patiently nursed for years in the atmosphere of the work itself until saturated by intimate association."[136]

White reported that Wright always felt "the height of everyone's ambition should be to trail along under his guidance for the rest of their natural lives."[137] Wright belittled those who had departed the studio, condemning designers who followed too closely in his footsteps as well as those who rejected his ideas. Only those who walked the fine line in between, accepting the propositions laid out in the essay while avoiding slavish copying, were spared. Wright wrote, "It is urged against the most loyal that they are sacrificing their individuality to that which has dominated this work; but it is too soon to impeach a single understudy on this basis."[138] He would wait to do that in his second "In the Cause of Architecture" essay, published in 1914, several years after the Oak Park studio closed its doors.

6
CLOSING THE STUDIO (1909–1911)

Escape and Retrospection

6.1 Como Orchard Summer Colony Clubhouse. Grant Manson identifies the drawing as rendered by Mahony. TAL 1002.001, Avery Architectural & Fine Arts Library, Columbia University, New York. © 2020 Frank Lloyd Wright Foundation, Scottsdale, AZ. All rights reserved.

Weary, I was losing grip on my work and even my interest in it. Every day of every week and far into the night of nearly every day, Sunday included, I had "added tired to tired" and added it again and yet again as I had been trained to do by Uncle James on the farm as a boy. Continuously thrilled by the effort but now it seemed to leave me up against a dead wall. I could see no way out. Because I did not know what I wanted I wanted to go away.

FRANK LLOYD WRIGHT (1943)

In 1908, as major construction work on Unity Temple was ending, Wright experienced another lull in his Oak Park practice. He had envisioned that projects like the Larkin building and Unity Temple would lead to other prominent, nonresidential commissions, particularly after the publication of his first "In the Cause" essay and its photographic retrospective. Cities throughout the United States had witnessed the creation of new civic and cultural organizations in recent years, and Wright had hoped to produce works of organic architecture for such institutions. These commissions, however, tended to end up in the hands of larger, more conservative and better-connected firms like McKim, Mead and White on the East Coast and D. H. Burnham and Company in Chicago, which more often than not produced designs that recalled the classical architecture of Rome. The financial panic that hit in October 1907, which significantly affected the building industry, and Russell Sturgis's scathing article on the design of the Larkin building did not help Wright's situation.[1] Even new religious and major commercial commissions closer in function to his most prominent nonresidential projects to date, failed to materialize. In January 1909 Wright reported to Charles Ashbee that the previous year had been "a lean one."[2] While Wright had no new prominent corporate or religious commissions that would provide an opportunity for further innovative design explorations, conditions were not as dire as portrayed. By the time Ashbee received the

letter in England, Wright had several large residences, a number of small commercial spaces, and soon two planned communities for Montana on the boards.

Montana

In January 1909, Chicago developer W. I. Moody and his associate Frederick Nichols approached Wright to become the official designer for the Bitter Root Valley Irrigation Company, an entity set up to turn the Bitterroot Valley in Montana into a major apple-growing center. Wright made a three-day trip to the valley in mid-February. His first project for the company was a master plan for University Heights, the initial subdivision of the sixteen-hundred-acre Como Orchard Summer Colony development near Darby, Montana.[3] He completed the overall design the following April, which consisted of fifty-one "simple wooden cabins" in variations of three basic designs, a small land office, and a 213-foot-long central clubhouse "where all go for meals, and where transients may also be accommodated with rooms."[4] John Van Bergen later reported that William Drummond carried out most of the design work, while Marion Mahony produced the perspective renderings.[5] A second, more elaborate commission involved the design of Bitter Root, a new town for a thousand residents in the midst of fifteen thousand acres of apple orchards outside of Stevensville, Montana. Wright and his employees worked on the design between April and October 1909.[6] The housing featured board and batten siding, low hipped roofs with wide overhanging eaves, ribbon windows, central fireplaces, and often cruciform plans, all elements that characterized Wright's earlier prairie houses.

Construction of University Heights began in May 1909, and by the following March the clubhouse, the land-office cabin, and approximately a dozen residential structures were built. For the second project, it appears that developers only realized the Bitter Root Inn. Because of both sites' relatively remote location, construction suffered from a lack of direct supervision from Wright or one of his his employees. While Mahony and Drummond oversaw the realization of the clubhouse, it is doubtful that either actually traveled to Montana.[7] The absence of guidance likely contributed to significant differences between the drawings and the structures as built by local contractors. Most notable, revisions to the clubhouse design included the elimination of ribbon windows on the second floor along with large decorative planting boxes and corner piers, while "guillotine" sash windows, which Wright so abhorred, replaced the casements specified for the cabins.[8] Unfortunately, the Bitter Root ventures were short lived. A blight in 1913 that wiped out much of the local apple crop significantly contributed to the demise of the developments and eventually the company.[9]

Despite the new work, Wright felt his life spiraling out of control. At the end of the previous year, he wrote to Darwin Martin, "In my own life there is much that is complex, at least. Life is not the simple thing it should be if within myself I could find the harmony that you have found. It is difficult for me to square my life with myself, and I cannot rest until it is done or I am dead."[10]

Downfall

After twenty years of marriage and sixteen years of independent practice, Wright faced a midlife crisis. In his early forties, an age when many architects enter the prime of their professional lives, he found himself mentally and physically exhausted and growing increasingly discouraged about his career. Believing he had done all that he could with the prairie house, he was at a developmental standstill. He began to perceive the creative period of his career waning, possibly fearing he was following the footsteps of his *Lieber Meister*, who had not had a major commission in years except for a small bank in rural Minnesota.

Wright's frustration with his architecture and turmoil in his personal life began influencing the Oak Park office. Barry Byrne recalled that after having fallen ill and missing three months of work in 1908, he returned to the studio to find Wright rarely there.[11] One of Van Bergen's strongest memories of his last days in the office in 1909 involved Wright's inability to maintain his customary self-confident manner during a visit by an important client, most likely Childe Harold Wills, an executive at the Ford Motor Company.[12] Hermann von Holst, who eventually took over the work in the Oak Park office, also observed Wright's lack of attention to studio operations in the months leading up to its closure, which likely contributed to the loss of several important commissions, such as the Wills residence.[13] Most painful was not realizing his largest domestic project to date, a stately home for industrialist Harold McCormick. McCormick's wife, Edith, the youngest daughter of John D. Rockefeller, rejected the modern, reinforced-concrete design in favor of a more conventional Italianate "palazzo" by the noted landscape architect and writer Charles A. Platt.[14] The failed commission signaled the loss of a salient opportunity to break into the lucrative realm of building for America's elite and to garner additional credibility and prominence as an architect.

Wright also felt growing dissatisfaction in his personal life. The invisible barrier between the home and the studio became evident. Wright later reflected on the division, writing, "Architecture was my profession. Motherhood became hers. Fair enough, but it was division…. [T]he children were their mother's children."[15] With her hands full raising six spirited youngsters, ages five to nineteen, Catherine rarely showed any interest in studio operations. Wright, by his own admission, neglected his fatherly duties as he found himself unable or unwilling to support his family fully, financially or emotionally. He admitted to knowing only a few of the neighbors' names, while Catherine knew only a few of his clients. His budding extramarital relationship

6.2 Portraits of the Wrights' children, 1909. From left to right, top: Lloyd, John, Catherine; bottom: David, Frances, Robert Llewellyn. Photographer: William F. Arnold. Frank Lloyd Wright Trust.

with the well-educated, intellectual Mamah Cheney further clarified for him the shortcomings he perceived in his relationship with Catherine.

Cheney and her husband, for whom the architect had designed a low, hipped-roof prairie house several blocks from his own home in 1903, traveled in the same local social circle as the Wrights. Catherine and Mamah, in fact, were both active members of Oak Park's Nineteenth Century Women's Club.[16] At some point, Frank and Mamah's architect-client relationship evolved into a friendship and eventually into a love affair—a well-known "secret" in the community.[17] The architect's behavior led to tensions in the studio and contributed to at least one employee's departure.[18]

Wright recalled in his autobiography that "everything, personal or otherwise bore heavily down upon me. Domesticity most of all. What I wanted I did not know. I loved my children. I loved my home. A true home is the finest ideal of man, and yet––well, to gain freedom I asked for a divorce." Catherine refused.[19] Wright searched for other ways to free himself. He believed that time away from Oak Park might help him

reassess both his architectural ideas and personal situation.

In December 1908, Charles Ashbee returned to Chicago while on a lecture tour. He and his wife Janet stayed with the Wright family. Although the time together was enjoyable, the Wrights were unable to hide their marital troubles from their guests. While sitting in the playroom, Ashbee wrote in his journal that he had found Wright "full of fire and belief" during his 1900 visit to Chicago, but on this trip discovered his friend had "grown 'bitter' and 'drawn up upon himself.'"[20] Meanwhile, Janet noted of Catherine, "Every tone of her voice rings of fearless honesty.... I am certain I hear too beginnings of a different kind of sadness—a battling with what will be an increasing gloom and nervousness (spite of success) in her husband. If her children do not comfort her, she will be hard pressed."[21]

Realizing his friend and colleague needed time away from his studio and wishing to reciprocate the Wrights' hospitality, Ashbee invited his hosts to Europe. He suggested an itinerary that included visits Sicily to see

6.3 Cheney house. Plate XXX(a), *Ausgeführte Bauten und Entwürfe von Frank Lloyd Wright*, 1910. Special Collections, J. Willard Marriott Library, University of Utah.

his Villa San Giorgio under way at Taormina (today known as the Ashbee Hotel) and then Italy and Germany before heading to England to visit his home.[22] While he found the offer tempting, Wright informed Ashbee that he had some "German business" to attend to (undoubtedly related to the Wasmuth Portfolio, for which Ashbee went on to author the preface) and would have to postpone any trip to Europe for at least a year. Work had also unexpectedly piled up. Along with "a number of fine residences in different parts of the country," he had "on the boards" two bank buildings, a hotel, and some residential work in Mason City, the Lexington, all of which "needed continuous attention." Wright particularly wanted to "make hay while the sun shines."[23] At the time he was in fact fashioning plans to visit Europe and realized the income from these projects would be essential to a costly exploit. His eventual departure affected not only his friends and clients, many of whom were caught off guard, but also colleagues and family members left behind.

Europe

The opportunity for Wright to escape appeared in the form of an offer to create a retrospective folio of his early work by Ernst Wasmuth Verlag, a German publishing house. Wright traveled to Europe to work on *Frank Lloyd Wright: Ausgeführte Bauten*, a special issue of plans and photographs of his Oak Park–era designs for Wasmuth's *Sonderheft der Architektur des XX. Jahrhunderts* series, as well as *Ausgeführte Bauten und Entwürfe von Frank Lloyd Wright*, the larger, more elaborate portfolio he persuaded the publisher to also produce.[24] The venture allowed him to remove himself from both his professional and personal responsibilities and offered the opportunity for experiencing new environments that might help to reinvigorate his career, as had his trip to Japan four years earlier.

Although Wright later portrayed his decision to leave the "idyllic" suburban lifestyle of Oak Park for

Europe as one made in haste, in reality he had mulled it over for at least eight months.[25] By the end of the summer of 1909 he had finalized his decision. Within weeks of his departure, the architect wrote matter-of-factly to his loyal friend and client Darwin Martin, "I am leaving the office to its own devices, deserting my wife and the children for one year, in search of a spiritual adventure, hoping it will be no worse."[26] Wright departed on his "spiritual hegira" on 23 September 1909.[27] Cheney had already left her husband in late June, taking their children to Boulder, Colorado.[28] After contacting her husband to come pick up the children, she traveled east, meeting up with Wright in New York City, where, according to the architect, they boarded a ship to Europe on 3 October 1909.[29]

Wright's departure from Oak Park greatly affected his children. Daughter Catherine later wrote of the permanent "sorrow and emotional impact."[30] Thirty-five years after Wright's flight, son John still harbored guilt that his father left because of his and his sibling's behavior. In a 1945 letter to his papa, in which he noted Wright's "magnificent ego and sweet sentimentality," John encouraged his father to read his new book, *My Father Who Is On Earth,* in which he recalled various childhood mishaps while growing up in Oak Park.[31] These included falling into a barrel of brown creosote (used to stain the studio building), prying the wood balls from the property's fence, poking a hole through the paper of one of the fret-sawed ceiling grilles, ruining his father's good top hat by placing it on a water sprinkler and then sitting on it, and ruffling his dad's "immaculate pompadour." "[S]omething like this was going on all the time," he wrote. "Multiply this by six, double it for the things I've omitted, and it is to wonder he [his father] left home.... He left at the peak.... I often wonder now why he did not leave sooner."[32]

Closing the Studio

Prior to leaving, Wright arranged for the completion of work already under way in the studio and for the handling of any new commissions.[33] Van Bergen and Isabel Roberts finished projects close to fruition, such as the Stohr Arcade and the J. Kibben Ingalls and the Laura Gale residences, with Drummond supervising

construction of the City National Bank and Hotel in Mason City.[34] For recently acquired projects that included extensive design work, Wright appealed to several former members of his staff. Having witnessed the fallout after Walter Burley Griffin took over the studio during Wright's trip to Japan, Mahony and Byrne both foresaw potential difficulties and declined the offer.[35] Wright then took the train to Minneapolis and met with William Purcell in the Milwaukee Road station, asking if he and George Elmslie would take over the studio. Purcell recalled the event in 1941:

Wright gave me a list of the incomplete commissions on his boards, and the remaining fee due in each instance. These I was to collect as a capital amount. I was to go to Oak Park, take over the office, while G.G.E. [George Grant Elmslie] ran our business in my absence, with whatever mutual cooperation back and forth in Chicago and Minneapolis G.G.E. and I cared to work out for the best interests of all concerned. When I demurred at the loss of momentum in our own business he held out the definite prospect of some sort of collaboration continuum when he returned.

Knowing Wright[']s characteristics in human relations as I had from boyhood, and Mr. Elmslie having worked beside him for a decade, and with the dishonorable circumstances of his break with the Sullivan office in 1894 [sic] well in mind, we agreed that this would be a risky undertaking and might easily wreck our own rapidly expanding business, so we turned him down.[36]

After Wright left for Europe, Isabel Roberts wrote to inform Purcell that Wright understood his reasons for declining the offer and that Hermann von Holst had been hired to take over the studio.[37] Not a member of the Prairie School, von Holst was known for his knowledge of the classical orders, his talent in producing academic watercolor renderings, and his sensitivity in relating architectural designs to the landscape.[38] At first glance he appears to be an odd, desperate choice, but von Holst was well trained and sympathetic to much of Wright's ideology. Wright later stated that he had only met von Holst immediately prior to asking him to run the office; however, this was probably not the case.[39] Mahony, who had known von Holst since

6.4 Laura (Mrs. Thomas) Gale house rendering showing the later addition of an incorrect date. TAL 0905.001, Avery Architectural & Fine Arts Library, Columbia University, New York.

her days at MIT, most likely served as the connection between the two architects.[40]

On 22 September 1909 von Holst signed a five-page contract with Wright entitling him to take possession of the design work under way in the Oak Park studio. An appendix listed projects in process.[41] The contract favored Wright in payment for existing and new work. However, it provided von Holst with the use of the studio rent free so long as he paid "all expenses in heating, lighting and caring for the building" and stipulated that Wright would provide for part of Isabel Robert's salary and all of Taylor Woolley's, so long as Woolley was completing work relating to the Wasmuth Portfolio. In addition, Wright spelled out steps for arbitration in case a dispute arose.[42]

It is doubtful that von Holst used the Oak Park studio. He had his own architectural office in Steinway Hall, and it was there that he oversaw the work, giving Catherine Wright and her younger children privacy. Around Christmastime 1909, Wright's son David wrote a short letter on the office typewriter using studio stationary informing his father that the Oak Park office "is very cold and looks very lonesome. Miss Roberts does her work in the library because it is so cold" (suggesting that Wright had installed the fireplace in the room by this time).[43] Van Bergen recalled that upon completion of the "outstanding projects" he and Roberts worked on, the studio was closed.[44]

Realizing his lack of familiarity with Wright's unfinished work, von Holst hired Mahony to help complete the projects.[45] She agreed to do the work provided she was placed in charge, later admitting she "had great

6.5 Adolph Mueller house, designed by Marion Mahony while working for Hermann von Holst. Photographer: Rick McNees.

fun" designing.[46] Mahony's assistants included Roy Lippincott; former studio draftsman Albert McArthur; and another female designer, Arselia Bessie Martin.[47] They began work on the projects almost immediately after Wright's departure without any further input from him, as, according to Mahony, he never bothered "to answer anything that was sent over to him" in Europe.[48] Von Holst recalled that although the E. P. Irving house in Decatur was built under Wright's name, "all drawings were made by Miss Mahoney [*sic*] or under her direction."[49] He also noted that she entirely oversaw the David Amberg house and built the Adolph Mueller house under his supervision.[50] Despite his falling out with Wright and probably as a favor to Mahony, Griffin produced landscaping designs for the Irving and Mueller projects.[51] George Niedecken, meanwhile, helped with the design and production of decorative elements and furnishings.

As predicted by Purcell and others, problems arose with the arrangements made between Wright and von Holst. Wright had told Purcell that there was $25,000

cash in the bank available for current expenses and payroll, and another $30,000 or $40,000 was due and collectable from clients.[52] However, no sooner had von Holst accepted the work than he found out that Wright had already collected fees for the commissions.[53] Von Holst had to borrow money in order to finish the projects. Many involved previously completed structural work that was poorly carried out or unsolved design problems that reflected the degraded conditions of Wright and his office. There were also understandably irate clients. William Purcell recalled, "There was bad engineering to be patched up on buildings under construction, half studied new ideas that could be made to work only by major operations on the jobs, and a swarm of angry clients who had been sold on 'having a Wright house' and did not want von Holst, however sincere and capable."[54] P. C. Stohr, who had commissioned a small commercial building at an "el" stop in Chicago, went "wild when the Wright scandal broke in the newspapers."[55]

Wright returned from Europe in the fall of 1910.

Just as after his trip to Japan, he became unhappy with the handling of the commissions he had left behind. He felt betrayed by von Holst and the former studio employees.[56] As anticipated, the two architects went into arbitration. An itemized list of von Holst's work and expenses reveals that he had completed projects for clients not turned over to Wright as specified in the contract. On 7 July 1911, von Holst received the order to pay Wright $108.29 for his share of the architectural commissions.[57]

Wright in Europe

On 7 November 1909, a correspondent for the *Chicago Tribune* reported discovering "Frank Lloyd Wright and wife" had been registered at the celebrated Hotel Adlon in Berlin but had departed four days earlier. Journalists quickly uncovered the fact that the real Mrs. Wright was in Illinois. A reporter snooping through Wright's incoming mail at the hotel discovered a postcard of Unity Temple from Catherine that read: "My Dear: We think of you often and hope you are well and enjoying life, as you have so longed to. From the children and your wife. Catherine L. Wright."[58] Scandal ensued. Catherine, who may not have fully comprehended until now her husband's personal motive for the trip, had to fend off the press, which was having a field day. The children also confronted great adversity. William Purcell, whose parents had lived at the other end of the block, recalled Wright's children playing with their pony MerryLegs while "the scandalized neighbors of Forest Avenue sat upon their porches and scandaled."[59] Both John and young Catherine were shunned by their classmates. Catherine particularly faced difficulties, including apparently being ejected from her school when news of her father's affair broke.[60] The heartbreaking letters the children wrote to their father clearly reflect the abandonment they felt. Younger daughter Frances's notes contain numerous requests for her father to come home and express how lonesome she felt without him. In one letter in 1911 she exclaimed, "We never hear a word or see you anymore so please write even if you don't write to me." After signing the letter "Your ever loving, Daughter Frances Barbara Wright" she placed the family's address as if maybe her father had forgotten who she was and where his family lived. She then added, "*Please* write *please*," underlining both "pleases" for emphasis.[61]

Unmindful of the pain his actions caused his wife and children, Wright justified to his mother (and also himself) continuing his relationship with Cheney in order to avoid abandoning her to "whatever fate may hold for her––probably a hard lonely struggle in the face of a world that writes her as an outcast to be shunned, … [w]hile I return to my dear wife and children, who all along 'knew I would' and welcomed by my friends with open rejoicing and secret contempt."[62] A devoted Catherine, attempting to protect her husband and their relationship, informed the press that her heart was with him now:

He will come back as soon as he can. I have a faith in Frank Lloyd Wright that passeth understanding, perhaps, but I know him as no one else knows him. In this instance, he is as innocent of wrongdoing as I am…. He is honest in everything he does. A moment's insincerity tortures him more than anything in this world. Frank Wright never had deceived me in all of his life…. I stand by my husband right at this moment. I am his wife. He loves his children tenderly and has the greatest anxiety for their welfare…. I feel certain that he will come back when he has reached a certain decision with himself. When he comes back, all will be as it has been.[63]

She later told the *Chicago Tribune* that her husband was going to return after he "completed a course of study of the architectural world abroad … and is coming home to square himself with the public, his creditors and his family."[64] The press, however, was relentless, portraying him as a "shameful oddity."[65]

Wright's sojourn offered him the opportunity to travel for pleasure. After arriving in Europe in October 1909, he likely spent time in the company of Cheney in various locales in northern Europe, possibly including the artist colony at Darmstadt, Germany, and picturesque sites along the Rhine.[66] By early November the couple had arrived in Berlin so Wright could meet with publishers at Ernst Wasmuth. He signed a contract with the firm on November 24.[67]

And yet Wright and Cheney spent much of their year in Europe apart, pursuing their own activities––Frank, the Wasmuth publications, and Mamah, teaching and studying the writings of Swedish feminist Ellen Key. In late January Wright visited Paris, and Cheney joined him for at least part of his time in France, but then she traveled alone to Germany.[68] She spent the next few months teaching languages at the University of Leipzig.[69] Wright recalled being miserable and lonely in a café along the Boulevard St. Michel late at night at the end of a rainy day. Away from the mayhem of his family life and the continuous responsibilities of his practice, he had, maybe for the first time, allowed the ramifications of his scandalous actions to sink in. He also may have begun to reflect upon the successes and setbacks of his Oak Park studio. Wright did not dwell in the gloomy weather of Paris long, however, but departed for Florence, just missing the massive deluge and flooding of the Crue de la Seine in 1910.[70]

Although he wrote little about specific buildings in Italy, Wright noted in his introductory essay for the Wasmuth publications that he had studied the works of the great Renaissance artists in Florence, which he found "splendid." However, he sharply criticized the replication of the classical forms from that era by later generations. Particularly, he took issue with the academic architecture of Europe that, having risen out of the Greek, Byzantine, and Gothic, "flickered feebly for a time" in the Renaissance, only to have been smoldered in the "sensuality and extravagance" of later periods before finally being "extinguished in banal architecture like the Rococo or in nondescript structures as the Louvre." Instead, he strongly favored the more organic, vernacular buildings he found in Italy and elsewhere that "seemed to be born, like the flowers by the roadside" and whose designs were "intimately interrelated with the environment and with the habits of life of the people."[71] Architecture analogous to his own. As in Japan, Wright's travels in Europe helped reinforce his core architectural beliefs.

In Florence Wright began to reassess and redraw his Oak Park–era projects while living in the Villa Fonte della Ginevra, overlooking the Arno River just below Piazzale Michelangelo. His son Lloyd, who had been studying engineering and agronomy at the Uni-

6.6 Taylor Woolley at Villino Belvedere in Fiesole, Italy, 1910. Photographer unknown. Taylor Woolley Photograph Collection, Special Collections, J. Willard Marriott Library, University of Utah.

versity of Wisconsin, and studio draftsman Taylor Woolley joined him there. The Russian painter Alexander "Sasha" von Heiroth; his wife, Maria Sophie "Mascha"; and their small son lived on the other side of the inner courtyard. Mascha recalled several enjoyable gatherings with Wright.[72] One can imagine the architect reveling in the artistic beauties of the city and in the type of intellectual dialogues he found missing in recent years within the walls of his home and studio.

By late March, Wright moved to the picturesque village of Fiesole in the hills on the outskirts of Florence.[73] The lively expat community of writers and artists there drew Wright to the area.[74] Villino Belvedere, the small, traditional "cream-white" stucco dwelling

6.7 Wright's drafting room in Italy, 1910. On the back wall are drawings for the Wasmuth portfolio. From left to right: plan for Mrs. (William) Martin, Oak Park, plate XIX; plan for F. W. Little, Peoria, plate XXVIII; (behind the plant) Plan for Dana house, plate XXXI(b); (above) typical low-cost suburban dwelling, plate XXIII; (below) boathouse for University of Wisconsin Boat Club, plate LV. Photographer unknown. Taylor Woolley Photograph Collection, Special Collections, J. Willard Marriott Library, University of Utah.

he rented, exhibited little applied ornamentation beyond plants and the functional elements of cornices, shutters, and railings. The indigenous structure, appearing like it had been there for centuries, clearly fit Wright's category of a flower sung into being by the roadside that he would praise in the introduction of the Wasmuth Portfolio.[75] After visiting the residence in late March 1910, Mascha von Heiroth described it as charming with its lovely little garden that featured a pool and a terrace area, protected from the summer sun by an arbor of yellow roses, that yielded impressive views of Florence.[76] The beautiful landscape might have reminded Wright of the stunning extended views from the Lloyd Jones farms in Spring Green, something that he grew to miss with the transformation of Oak Park from open prairie into residential lots.

Wright and the two young designers put in long days in the poorly lit, cold makeshift drafting room of the Italian villino preparing drawings for publication.[77] The labor significantly differed from that in the suburban studio, with little actual architectural designing carried out. Producing approximately one hundred plates for the publication involved taking a "mixed lot" of photographs, watercolors, and line drawings of projects by Wright, Mahony, Drummond, and others and turning them into "totally coordinated plates." With crow quill pen on tracing paper, they "worked at modifying, building up, corrections, simplifying, and converting all of the material" into a unified whole as Wright revisited the first major chapter of his life's oeuvres.[78] A photograph believed taken by Woolley shows drawing boards, scrolls of paper, and a number of large completed drawings pinned up along a wall. A large round vessel of leafy branches sat on the table—as in Oak Park, select bits of nature provided inspiration.[79]

With much of the preparation work for the portfolio complete, Wright sent Lloyd and Taylor Woolley off to explore Italy. Before Lloyd returned to the United States in March he joined his father in France, where they experienced the gardens of Versailles and the Tuileries and studied the design of the ornate, neoclassical Petit Palais (in which, surprisingly, his father took great interest).[80] Woolley remained in Europe until August to help complete the work on the portfolio drawings.

During his early months in Italy, Wright made several short trips to Germany to consult with people at Wasmuth and to visit Mamah.[81] In late spring he traveled to Leipzig to bring her to Fiesole.[82] The couple relaxed and took walks among the scenic hills and fields as Catherine battled the press and neighborhood gossip in Oak Park. Wright worked on the Wasmuth publications, while Mamah studied Swedish and Italian and translated Ellen Key's writings into English.[83] Wright and Cheney began to contemplate their future lives together more seriously, and over the next couple of months the couple likely traveled together. Wright claimed to have attended the *Passion Play* in Oberammergau, Germany, performed every few days throughout the late spring and summer of 1910.[84] On 20 July he visited the American consulate in Rome to apply for an emergency temporary passport. He falsely proclaimed "under oath" his intent to travel with his wife "Mamah Borthwick *Wright*" to Turkey.[85] It is doubtful, however, that they ever visited that country.[86]

During this time, Wright experienced a great emotional struggle between the guilt he felt in deserting his family and his strong desire to be with a woman who could provide greater intellectual stimulation. Both he and Cheney had found solace in the words of Ellen Key, who expressed her unconventional liberal views on love and marriage in *The Morality of a Woman*, which Cheney was translating into English. Key's work began, "Love is moral even without legal marriage, but marriage is immoral without love."[87] These words helped the couple to justify their actions.

Wright expressed his extreme frustration with societal pressures in letters to several former clients who had become close friends.[88] On Independence Day 1910, he wrote to his mother that he was "troubled and perplexed." He informed her that he had thought at one time he and Mamah were above social

6.8 Frank Lloyd Wright, duplicate passport application, issued 20 July 1910, American consulate, Rome. "United States, Passport Applications, 1795–1925," National Archives and Records Administration, Washington, DC.

norms and that he could "keep what was good in the life that was and go forward to a new life" but found instead that he lived in a world still arranged on a moral code "inadequate for certain Souls as the old science is inadequate for new achievements."[89] The two lovers began to realize they could not continue to hide from their previous lives and would eventually have to face returning to the United States and the social restraints that dictated their earlier lives. Wright, however, started formulating a public front that suggested he and Mamah planned to return to their respective families in Oak Park and he also to his Chicago Avenue studio. Wright wrote Charles Ashbee, "The fight has been fought—I am going back to Oak Park to pick up the thread of my work and in some degree of my life where I snapped it. I am going to work among the ruins—not as any woman's husband but as the father of the children—to do what I can for them."[90]

In fact Wright and Cheney had devised a plan to live together without spectacle. The architect revealed the germ of his idea to live away from the prying Chicago press and among the security of kin in Spring Green, Wisconsin, in the letter to his mother. He wanted to farm a tract of land next to that of his brother-in-law Andrew Porter, but his own situation was "too discouraging to contemplate any such luxury."[91] Not one to pass up the luxuries of life, however, within a year a busy construction site appeared on the land Wright mentioned, as he created a new residence for himself and Cheney christened Taliesin.

Wright's Return to Oak Park

In September 1910, after consulting with his contacts at Ernst Wasmuth, Wright visited Ashbee in London. Then, after a year in self-exile, he returned to the United States, arriving in Chicago by train on 8 October 1910.[92] Mamah remained in Europe protected by the Atlantic Ocean from the growing media circus in Chicago.[93] The architect returned with a new persona. William Martin, who had helped Wright bring his belongings from the train station, described Wright's appearance as akin to the man on the Quaker Oats package, "except his coat—was like an outing coat. Knee

trousers, long stockings, broad brimmed brown hat, cane and his lordly strut."[94]

Wright briefly moved back home but never formally reopened his adjoining studio. Primarily concerned with resolving financial issues and ensuring the distribution of the Wasmuth publications, Wright also had to bring his relationship with Catherine to some resolution. For a second time he asked her for a divorce, and once again she refused. By January Wright had left again for Europe, sailing in style on the RMS *Lusitania*, to take care of issues with the production of the Wasmuth publications and to reconnect with Cheney.[95]

Viewing himself as a prodigal son, Wright informed his mother that if he returned to his past life, it would be seen as a "triumph" for institutions outraged by his actions. He shared with her (in third person) his intimate feeling of being a weak son "infatuated sexually, but had his passion drained and therewith his courage."[96] While Wright felt gut-wrenching guilt for what he had done, it was a self-centered tirade with no recognition of the emotional anguish his actions had caused his children or his wife, just complaints about the financial cost of providing for their needs.[97] He wrote:

Lloyd has had two trips to the continent, I have just sent Catherine money to bring her to Ashbee's for a couple of months visit in their home, (which will be more to her than a college education I am sure) expecting to bring her home this fall, the children have their pony still—and what they can have lacked in money or luxuries is beyond the reach of my imagination. . . . David wrote that he could not take lessons in the flute I sent him for "they had no money.["] Catherine that her lessons must stop for "they had no money." Her mother that the girl must be dismissed for they had no money—that creditors were pressing for the bills unpaid etc etc. There would never be an end to it. It is a constantly increasing load—which as a matter of course for the priviledge [sic] of being a father I owe to the children—they owe me nothing. They have been so taught in fact they feel that but for their father's extravagances they would all have had much more.[98]

6.9 Frank Lloyd Wright dressed like the Quaker Oats man. DeLonge Studios. Frank Lloyd Wright and Family Photographs, IM2373, Wisconsin Historical Society.

If Wright had not been traveling first class while on his trips to Europe, staying at the Plaza in New York City and the Hotel Adlon in Berlin, and taking luxury liners, he undoubtedly would have been in a better financial situation to take care of the needs of his children and revive his architectural practice. Wright later admitted to his misplaced priorities, viewing buildings as his primal legacy in a way most parents view their flesh and blood children. While his time in Europe gave Wright the opportunity to reflect on his Oak Park–era work, he found the trip detrimental not only to his finances and family life but also to his immediate architectural career. While he continued to believe in the concept of a home studio, the specific conditions of his early suburban experiment proved, he realized, not to be the most suitable version for him.

7

WRIGHT'S FURTHER DEVELOPMENTS OF THE HOME STUDIO CONCEPT

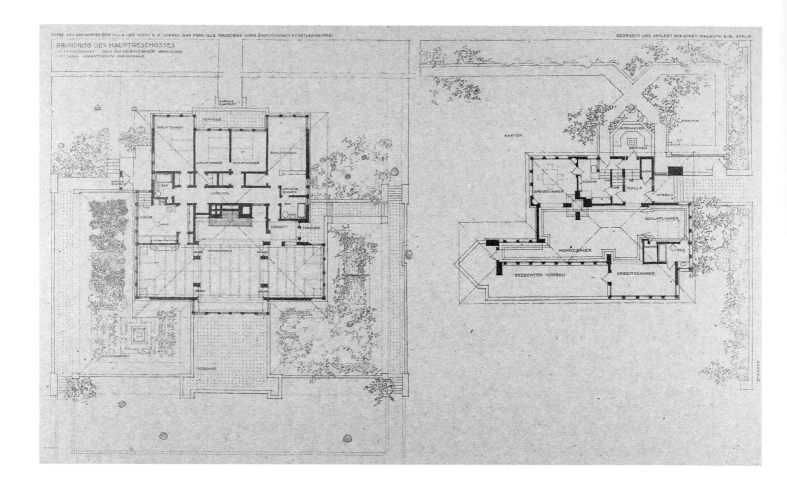

7.1 Plan of the Cheney residence (left), with Wright's "One-Story House for an Artist," next door to the right. Plate XXX(b), *Ausge-führte Bauten und Entwürfe von Frank Lloyd Wright*, 1910. Special Collections, J. Willard Marriott Library, University of Utah.

At last, my work was alongside my home where it has been ever since.

FRANK LLOYD WRIGHT (1943)

In several letters to Darwin Martin in November 1910, Wright alluded to the fact that he had left Cheney and was dutifully returning to his wife, acting as "honestly toward all as a man in my impossible situation can act."[1] In reality, however, Wright had no intention of reconciling with Catherine, or even separating from Mamah, and was busy with plans to build his new residence and workplace in Wisconsin. In the time he had been with Cheney, Wright had, in fact, explored the concept of an architect's home studio beyond the bounds of his actual residence and office in Oak Park several times. Three unrealized projects, created for different locations and conditions, as well as his soon-to-be-built home in Spring Green incorporated a studio space where he could intertwine his personal and professional lives. However, it was a life with Mamah, not Catherine, that he envisioned. Attempting to realize this desire, in 1911 he transformed his former studio into a new home for the family he was leaving behind, signaling to them, as well as to the community, the permanence of his departure.

Wright published the first of his unrealized home and studio projects in *Ausgeführte Bauten und Entwürfe von Frank Lloyd Wright*. Curiously, the plan of the small complex labeled "One-Story House for an Artist," appears on the same page as the plan for the residential design Wright created for Mamah and her husband in 1903. It was as if his new bachelor home studio was to be built right next door to his mistress's domicile.[2] The architect later added "Artist's Cottage/1906" to a drawing of a different version of the design.[3] Both schemes show a large living room with a bedroom on one end that could be closed off by folding doors. A small office opens off the living room to the front of the house, and a dining room projects from the opposite side of the room toward the rear. As with the Cheney house, a large protective hipped roof covers the residence. The roof of a long porch, running in front of the living room, ends in a pointed "prow" similar to Wright's Robie house design.

A second project with drawings dated February and March 1910 was for a small-walled villa in Italy, undoubtedly to serve as a romantic hideaway for the illicit couple.[4] Wright likely produced the design when contemplating his move to Fiesole.[5] He rendered at least two versions of this project, which feature different rooflines.[6] The more developed flat-roof scheme presents a cozy home studio protected from the street by a tall wall. While a bay projecting from the house incorporated the wall into its front facade, most of the residence was set back, forming an L-shaped plan and allowing space for a private walled garden. Wright located the living quarters in the rear of the residence and an office in the projecting front wing on the ground level. A row of bedrooms lined a hallway on the floor above. Large frieze panels on the exterior feature bas-relief figures. In at least one of the drawings the sculpture appears vaguely reminiscent of the row of figures on the Augustan *Ara Pacis* in Rome, or possibly those on one of the Cantoria panels created in the 1430s by Luca della Robbia in Florence. The presence of a reproduction of one of the panels in his Oak Park

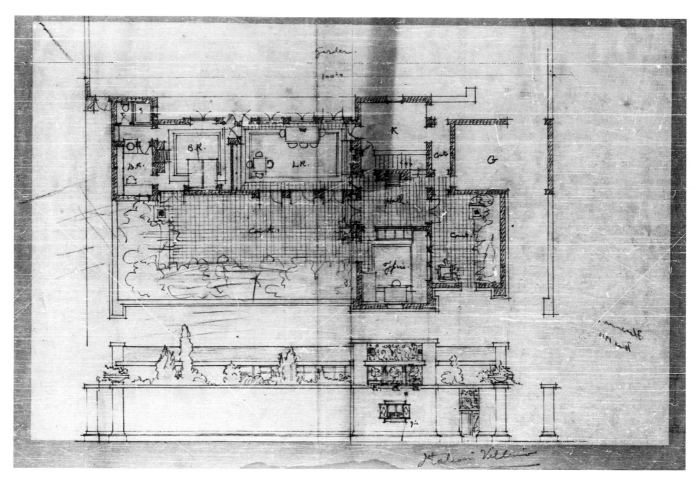

7.2 Wright's home and studio design for Fiesole, Italy. Taylor Woolley Collection, Special Collections, J. Willard Marriott Library, University of Utah.

office reflects Wright's admiration of this Renaissance-era work prior to experiencing the original in person.

A third home and studio project, for a site on Goethe Street in Chicago, most likely produced after Wright returned to the United States, illustrates the impact of his time in Italy.[7] The design may have been for a winter residence that Mamah hinted at in a letter to Ellen Key, in which she referred to Taliesin as their "summer house."[8] For a deep, narrow urban site, Wright designed a multilevel townhouse that, with its central light court and roof garden, was reminiscent of the inward-focusing Florentine palazzos and reflective of his increased desire for privacy.[9] In fact, the exterior of the building presented a vertical adaption of his flat-roofed Fiesole design: the large bas-relief panels of figures placed between the windows on the second and third floors as well as the cornice and capped end piers all appear borrowed from his earlier design. An enclosed forecourt leads to a large drafting room at the front

of the building behind large windows, while a "musician's balcony" overlooks a two-story living room in the center of the house, recalling both the Dana house and the balcony in the playroom of his own home.

Although Wright never built any of these projects, he continued his design exploration of personal residence and workplaces for different site conditions in the realized home studio design for Spring Green. Having recognized while in Italy that returning to Oak Park and suburban life with Catherine was an untenable option, the architect began planning his relocation to south central Wisconsin. Just as he had escaped the congestion of Chicago for the open spaces of Oak Park in 1889, Wright now sought to flee the claustrophobic social environment of the suburb in search of solace in his rural childhood community, completing the circle that began almost a quarter century earlier and symbolically providing closure on the Oak Park era of his career.

Taliesin

So, when family-life in Oak Park in that spring of 1909, conspired against the freedom to which I had come to feel every soul entitled and I had no choice would I keep my self-respect, but go out, a voluntary exile, into the uncharted and unknown deprived of legal protection to get my back against the wall and live, if I could, an unconventional life—then I turned to the hill in the Valley as my Grandfather before me had turned to America—as a hope and haven.

FRANK LLOYD WRIGHT (1943)

Upon returning to the Midwest from his second trip to Europe in March or possibly the very beginning of April 1911, Wright arranged to have his mother purchase land for him in the beautiful Helena Valley, his boyhood haunt just outside of Spring Green.[10] He probably chose to acquire the land through his mother to hide the fact that he was building a new residence for himself and Mamah from his creditors, especially Darwin Martin, and to keep it out of Catherine's reach in a divorce settlement.[11] Wright imagined this home and studio as a refuge where he and Cheney could escape the turmoil resulting from their societal misdeeds that would likely have continued to hound them if they had lived together in the Chicago area.[12] Perhaps he desired to create a place that would replicate the respite he had found with Mamah in Fiesole. While Wright had previously explored on paper designs for a personal residence and workspace within diverse landscapes that differed greatly from suburban Oak Park, the pastoral hills and valley in Wisconsin offered yet another setting in which he carried out the exercise, this time realizing a significantly more sophisticated resolution.

Wright claimed that as a boy he had learned every line and feature of the landscape around Spring Green, including the topography of its undulating, unglaciated hills.[13] It had been the setting of many of his most

7.4 View of the Wisconsin River near Spring Green, Wisconsin. Photographer unknown. Taylor Woolley Collection (WHI-29051), Wisconsin Historical Society.

fundamental life lessons and where he felt closest to his god and his most important teacher, "Nature, with a capital N."[14] Now, at a time when he was again searching for answers, both on how to live his life and how to advance his architectural development and career, he found comfort in the familiarity of the stunning rural landscape.

The site Wright chose for Taliesin was a hill located to the north of the Hillside Home School and Tan-y-deri. While his prairie house designs reflected the flatness of Illinois, in Wisconsin the architect wanted the building to "belong to that hill, as the trees and the ledges of rock did, as Grandfather and Mother had belonged to it in their sense of it all."[15] The hill had been one of Wright's favorite places growing up.[16] It was here he studied the formal and structural characteristics of plants and searched for prairie crocuses in the early spring.[17] As with his temporary haven in Italy, the hill offered commanding views—not of a magnificent Renaissance city but of the rolling landscape that

his uncles farmed, marked by several of his own earlier designs. In place of the Arno, just to the north of the property ran the gently flowing waters of the Wisconsin River.

Wright developed the design of Taliesin in the spring of 1911. By May construction was already under way. Unlike Wright's suburban Oak Park home or his compact designs for Fiesole or Goethe Street in Chicago, the basic layout of his Wisconsin home studio, with its extended hipped-roofed wings wrapping around a higher central courtyard, reflected the broad, open expanses of its rural location. Following the natural contours of the landscape, the plan stepped diagonally across the site, breaking from the axial rigidity that limited his earlier Oak Park residential designs created for lots defined by the Jeffersonian grid.[18] As in the large projects the architect had produced for clients like the Coonleys and the McCormicks, the wings and courts of the complex formed separate zones demarcating different functions. At Taliesin, the wings

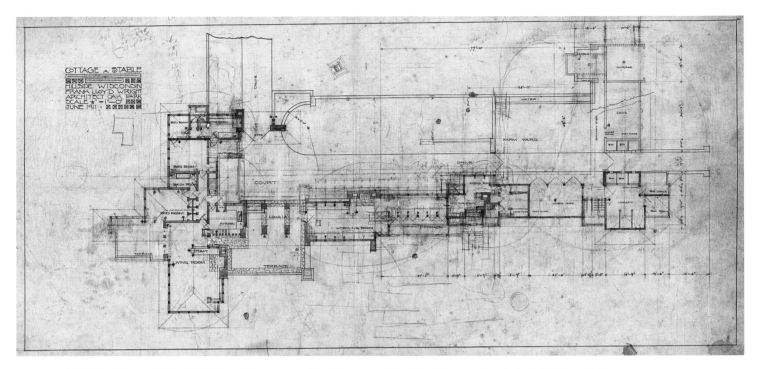

7.5 Taliesin I, plan. TAL 1104.003, Avery Architectural & Fine Arts Library, Columbia University, New York. © 2020 Frank Lloyd Wright Foundation, Scottsdale, AZ. All rights reserved.

housed private living spaces, a large workroom, and assorted animal pens and garages.[19]

The presence of stables and the garages reflected the expanded role of Wright's domicile. He wrote that Taliesin should be "a complete living-unit" that included a garden and a farm, in addition to "a real workshop and a good house."[20] He rejected his previous suburban conditions and looked to his agrarian roots for inspiration. Like Thomas Jefferson at Monticello, he began envisioning himself as an elite gentleman farmer heading a self-sustaining country estate. In doing so, he followed a tradition that extends back even earlier than Pliny the Younger, the aristocratic Roman who wrote fondly of several such residences in the first century. This tradition continued in the Renaissance rural villas and garden estates Wright observed in Italy.[21] He must have envisioned practicality in such a property. If he experienced a lean stretch architecturally, he could turn to agriculture for sustenance and income.

Wright's time in Europe reinforced his fundamental belief that buildings should directly respond to the conditions of their locale. His choice of materials for Taliesin reflected a profound knowledge of the region. The building was constructed by as many as three dozen laborers who hauled native yellow limestone from a quarry only a mile away.[22] They carefully stacked the stone like sculptors creating stratified walls that echoed the natural formations of the material. While the stone tied the building to its site, the use of plaster and wood gave it a stylistic affinity to the architect's earlier residential designs.

The residence embraced the hillside near, but not on, the top of the crest. Wright had developed the preference for situating a building on the "brow" of a hill when living in Fiesole. He wrote to Charles Ashbee in July 1910, "I have been very busy here in this little eyrie [nest] on the *brow* of the mountain above Fiesole––overlooking the pink and white, Florence spreading in the valley of the Arno below."[23] Nearby, Michelozzo's large country villa in Fiesole, commissioned by Cosimo de' Medici in the 1450s with terraced pleasure gardens that stepped down the hill, offered a grander example of a building ideally situated at brow level.

7.6 Courtyard of Taliesin I with *Flower in the Crannied Wall* sculpture. Photographer unknown. PH 6414 (3), Taylor Woolley Collection, Wisconsin Historical Society.

Unlike his small, suburban Oak Park lot, here he had access to acres of land in which to shape the environment surrounding his architecture. His landscape design at Taliesin presented a hierarchy of different types of gardens and water features that more closely mimicked what could be found in the gardens of an Italian villa than in the less structured arrangement of plants on his Oak Park property. It presented what scholar Neil Levine called "the impression of a gradual transition from the rational order of built form to the free and natural beauty of the surrounding landscape."[24]

In December 1911, Wright moved with Cheney into Taliesin, where he began to pick up the pieces of his tattered life. It was not an easy task, as there were children, former clients, and others who continually reminded Wright of the life he left behind. His daughter Frances, for example, made a desperate plea for her father to return to Oak Park for Christmas with the family.[25] Not swayed, the self-centered Wright spent the day with Mamah in Wisconsin. A journalist for the *Chicago Tribune* reported his heartless decision in a syndicated article, picked up by papers ranging from the *Des Moines News* to the *Fairbanks Citizen* in Alaska, writing, "Apparently, Mr. Wright did not feel any regret he was not present in the Oak Park house where his lawful wife and their six children were spending Christmas." The piece went on to express Wright's views on marriage, his mistress, his children, his clients, and how he had chosen to live his life. The architect arrogantly informed the journalist, "Laws and rules were made for the average. The ordinary man cannot live without rules to guide his conduct." Wright, however, viewed himself above the average, ordinary man, having "displayed the ability to see and feel the higher and better things of life."[26] Stories of his personal life eventually moved off of page 1, and in Spring Green Wright found breathing space that allowed him to continue to reflect and build upon lessons learned in his Oak Park studio.

7.7 Sketch showing the Oak Park studio remodeling, ca. 1911. Reid Addis.

The Transformation of the Oak Park Studio into a Home

Although Wright was in the process of permanently leaving Oak Park, he retained an interest in the studio building and began considering remodeling it into a residence for his family around the same time he was planning his new home in Wisconsin. Wright was at least contemplating alterations to the studio by October 1910, when Darwin Martin wrote, "Your ambition to build improvements on your premise is ill-timed … You want to show Oak Park that Wright isn't all in. You want to put one over on them. In short, brutally short, your vanity is working. Do not despise the community. Be humble. If you cannot be ordinary be as ordinary as you can."[27] Two days later, Wright arrogantly responded, "I do not care two pins … what Oak Park thinks of my state,—whether I am up or down.

In fact, they will be asked for exactly nothing—they never were much of an asset, spiritually or otherwise, and that little is written off as a total loss at the start." Of his home and studio, he said: "I want money to cut my living expenses in two and turn a place that is going to ruin fast and is nothing now but a source of expense into a business proposition for the family, making it income paying property."[28] Despite lamenting his lack of funds, Wright transformed the original house into rental property to provide a source of income for Catherine and their four youngest children still in her care and the former studio into a new residence for them. To support the remodeling, as well as the construction of Taliesin and various travels, he sold Japanese prints, as well as used them, along with the Oak Park property, as collateral for loans from Martin, Francis Little, and others.[29]

The remodeling was in part an attempt by Wright

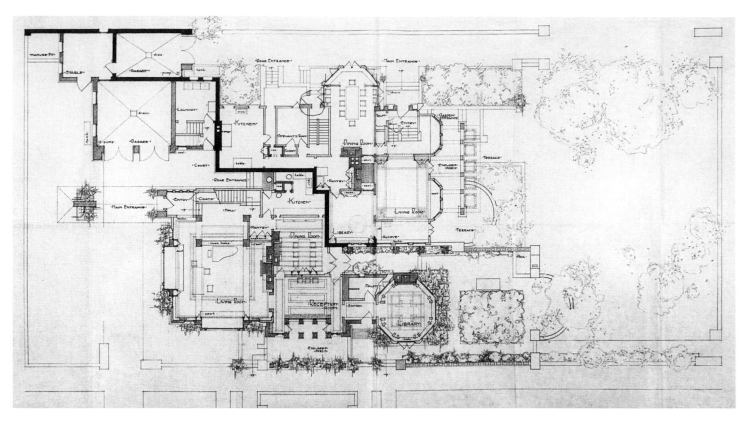

7.8 Oak Park property, first floor plan with the firewall and the conversion of the studio into a residence, as well as the garage addition to the southeast (upper left) and the walled garden to the west of the studio, ca. 1911. TAL 1125.006, Avery Architectural & Fine Arts Library, Columbia University, New York. © 2020 Frank Lloyd Wright Foundation, Scottsdale, AZ. All rights reserved.

to turn the public spotlight off his personal life and back onto his professional work. This did not quite go as planned, as in early September 1911, a headline on page one of the *Chicago Examiner* proclaimed, "Wright Divides Home to Protect His Soul." The article revisited some of the details of his "platonic" trip to Europe with "Mrs. Martha Borthwick Cheney." In addition to announcing Cheney's divorce, the piece described how the architect was "slashing apart the shell of his home just as two years ago the heart of it was separated." It reported that Mrs. Wright and the children were to occupy the larger half of the house, with Mr. Wright using the other half as his domain when not in Hillside (Spring Green), "where the most exquisite architectural concoction that has ever sprung from Mr. Wright's fancy is taking shape as his new studio home."[30]

Work on the Oak Park building appears to have been well under way, if not completed, by mid-November 1911 when Darwin Martin sent Catherine $2,000 to help cover expenses for iceboxes, electricians, and painters. This was likely part of a $4,000 loan to the Wrights secured by a deed of trust on the property. At the time, Catherine reported that they owed one carpenter four weeks' back pay.[31] There had been no funds in the couple's bank account despite Martin having loaned Wright $16,000 for the remodeling less than five months earlier.[32] Wright, meanwhile, ignored both the bills that were being sent to his Wisconsin address and messages from his wife, who was being besieged by contractors "hourly by the 'phone and door-bell."[33]

As with many other details about the studio, there is conflicting evidence about when the remodeling took place. It was also in November 1911 when William Purcell brought Hendrik Berlage by the studio while the Dutch architect was in town on a lecture tour.[34] As Wright was away, Purcell recalled that it was probably Isabel Roberts who showed them the studio but that he had been there "so many times under so many different circumstances" that he did not recall the details vividly.[35] In any case, it is surprising that he did not remember either major construction underway or a completed remodeling on his visit.[36]

Responding to an additional request for funds in January 1912, Martin told Wright that he had already loaned him more than he thought the architect could afford to borrow but then admitted that he was "weak enough" and offered to provide an additional loan if Wright could find a "good endorser."[37] Probably unable to locate one, Wright declined. The following April Martin repeated his concerns about the amount he had loaned Wright and the great possibility that he would not be paid back.[38] Wright took great offense but then offered to send Martin $8,000 worth of Japanese prints for an additional $4,000 loan. Martin agreed. However, when he received the box of prints, he exclaimed, "It's such a little box!" Still, he immediately sent out a $1,000 check "with which to facilitate the completion of the Oak Park work."[39] Maybe influenced by Martin's words, the next week Wright reported that he had paid $650 to the plumber, $391.80 to the plasterers, and paid off several other smaller bills to have mechanics' liens removed from the Oak Park property. He then asked Martin to send him $2,500 more, "as it all can be used to good advantage right away."[40]

Even though Wright no longer had his architectural office in the former studio, the physical structure continued to serve as an as an exploratory workshop and an advertisement for his practice. During this time, Wright made major aesthetic as well as functional modifications to the building. The limited records of the alterations do not reveal if he employed any of the former studio designers to help carry out the work. Changes he made to the original home were relatively minor and revolved around the entry and the living room. He created a carriage entrance on the south side, altered the staircase, and removed the original front door. He also squared off the octagonal bay on the northwest corner of the living room and placed a new door in the center of the west facade. It opened up onto the front porch, now covered by a roof supported by four brick and wood piers.

More dramatic alterations took place in the former studio, in part due to its change in function. Wright

installed a floor over the drafting room balcony opening to increase the usable square footage on the upper level. At the same time, he squared off the octagonal form of the second floor to gain the space needed to create four bedrooms. To her father's horror and without his consent, daughter Catherine, who disliked the natural woodwork, covered hers with white enamel paint and installed flounced curtains of organdy or cretonne in the windows, similar to what her friend Mad had across the street.[41] On the main floor, Wright transformed the drafting room into a living room, giving his abandoned family a place to gather. He replaced the original arched fireplace facade of Chicago common brick with a rectangular one of Roman brick recalling those he had produced for the Robies and several other clients in the later years of the studio.[42] He also projected the first-floor windows outward to provide additional illumination, since closing off the balcony had eliminated light from the clerestory windows above. The Fresnel globes of the hanging fixtures

7.9 Llewellyn in front of the Oak Park home surrounded by construction materials during the 1911 remodeling. Photographer unknown. H82, Gift of Llewellyn Wright, Frank Lloyd Wright Trust.

7.10 Oak Park home living room prior to restoration, showing the inglenook and 1911 carriage entrance, 1975. Photographer unknown. Frank Lloyd Wright Trust.

7.11 Bedroom on the second floor of the former Oak Park studio drafting room, with a Japanese print desk and chairs of Wright's design, ca. 1911. Photographer unknown. H16, Frank Lloyd Wright Trust.

7.12 The Wright family living room in the former Oak Park studio drafting room, ca. 1911. Photographer: Henry Fuermann and Sons.

he replaced with a simple exposed bulb design. No longer used to protect architectural drawings or Japanese prints, the fireproof vault on the southern wall was removed. Two piers, added to the southern half of the room to support the additional weight of the second floor, helped to visually break up the square space.[43] Furnishings and decorative objects, including a pastel by Charles Corwin, moved from the original living room helped to visually transform the drafting room into the heart of the new residence.

Wright made major changes to his studio office as he converted it into the family's dining room. The addition of a bedroom for Catherine directly above rendered the skylight useless, so he removed it. He also eliminated the staircase leading down along the west wall to the toilet room in the basement of the original home.[44] Other changes included converting the long desk that had dominated the office into a dining table, even though it offered no legroom at the projecting end.[45] He also installed plane wall sconces, possibly samples or overruns of those specified for secondary spaces of the Robie house. Another major alteration to the new dining room consisted of adding openings in the south wall to provide additional light into the original corridor between the home and studio, which became the family's kitchen. The passageway, which had never been heated or considered a functional room prior to this time, proved to be extremely problematic. Daughter Catherine remembered it as "a nice wet kitchen." The old willow tree that grew within the

7.13 The Wright family dining room in the former Oak Park studio office with new windows and French doors leading to the walled "Italian" garden, ca. 1911. Photographer: Henry Fuermann and Sons. H46, TAL 8901.0028, Avery Architectural & Fine Arts Library, Columbia University, New York.

7.14 French doors in the former Oak Park studio office that led to the walled "Italian" garden, ca. 1978. Note that the large clerestory windows have been replaced by clear glass. Photographer unknown. BL133-1, Frank Lloyd Wright Trust.

space creaked and swayed, not allowing for a water-tight roof. The icebox "placed lovingly in the arms of the tree" also leaked, leading to a great deal of mopping of the magnesite floor.[46]

Less is known about the specific alterations Wright made to the reception hall and library. The fireplace on the south wall of the library appeared around this time, if not earlier. Cabinets lining the hallway to the library were removed. A bathroom south of the hall and an exterior door on the north, installed at some point between 1909 and 1925, probably appeared in 1911 when Wright removed the stair to the basement. The studio's

reception area appears to have remained unaltered except possibly for the removal of the large plan desk.[47]

Some changes, such as the new Roman brick fireplace, illustrate that Wright went far beyond making modifications just to meet the building's changing functions. On the west wall of the new dining room, the architect removed windows and added French doors with an abstract composition of geometric forms suggesting influences not only of Froebel but also Japan and possibly the work of the Secessionists in Europe. The doors opened to an exterior walkway between the octagonal library and the original home.

The passage led to a new enclosed walled "Italian" garden just west of the library recalling the private garden in Wright's Fiesole home studio scheme.[48] The art glass design of the doors extended across mullions into a sidelight and clerestory windows, creating a unified whole, with the sidelight panel recalling a geometrically abstract vine.[49] This practice of producing a comprehensive glass design that extends over a series of windows was soon more fully realized in the clerestories and triptych of his Coonley Playhouse design (see figure C.3).[50]

The exterior of the studio was significantly altered beyond squaring the upper level of the drafting room. Wright completely closed off the original studio entrance on Chicago Avenue and added a cantilevered canopy that extended to the sidewalk. This provided a sense of enclosure similar to the porch underneath the cantilevered second floor at the nearby Laura Gale house, designed by Wright just prior to his departure for Europe. The porch provided a protected place where Catherine and the children sat on many hot evenings and eavesdropped on passersby.[51] As in the design for his unrealized Fiesole residence, Wright added a tall wall along the street between the former studio entrance and Forest Avenue to enclose the garden. The wall helped provide privacy from curious neighbors and the investigative press. He also added a porte cochere at the southeast corner of the former drafting room, leading to a large new garage and stable addition east of the house built in part on a forty-foot strip of land he received from his mother in May 1911.[52] New exterior decorative features included raised brick planters on both the north and east sides of the drafting room. To fill the existing niches on the second floor of the building, Wright once again turned to artist Richard Bock.

Interestingly, the sculptures Bock produced recall works he had previously created for the Larkin building years earlier. Like those, each of the identical works featured two prepubescent boys with flowing hair referred to as "Hermes" in a heraldic composition. While the figures in Buffalo kneeled below large globes, holding banners as they faced outward with the neutral gaze of an ancient Greek kouros statue, in Oak Park slightly older boys flanked trees as they blankly looked down upon the viewer. The composition itself was reminiscent of the first project Bock carried out for the building––the stork panels at the studio entrance. Whereas the open book is missing, the tree (of knowledge) and scroll are both present. In the new composition, the boys take the place of the birds.[53]

While works Wright completed within a few years of his return from Europe, such as Midway Gardens and the Coonley Playhouse, incorporate design characteristics that clearly reflect his time abroad, the late 1911 remodeling of the Oak Park studio exhibited little obvious evidence of Wright's time in Europe. One exception was the new walled garden and its art glass doors and windows. There are several potential contributing factors for this lack of influence in addition to Wright respecting the existing character of the complex's design. Unlike his trip to Japan in 1905, where he was engaged in the culture and clearly looking at what Japanese art and architecture could teach him, Wright's time in Europe was largely focused on escape and retrospection. This, combined with his previous rejection of European historicism, may have led him to consciously avoid looking for influences or immediately processing what he had observed. Additionally, the conditions he returned to, in particular the chaos of his personal life, did not lend themselves to deep architectural contemplation.

It is not clear when Catherine and the children moved into the former studio, but it may not have been until the end of 1912 or even later. Letters between Wright and Darwin Martin (who had loaned the architect over $25,000 by this point) reveal significant delays in finding a tenant for the Forest Avenue home.[54] Wright was to use revenue from the rent to pay Martin back, which gave the architect less incentive to find a tenant.[55] Also unhelpful was the architect returning to Japan in January 1913 in pursuit of the commission for the Imperial Hotel. Upon his departure he informed Martin he was leaving his lawyer, Sherman M. Booth, in charge of "the sales and renting campaign."[56] After his return, Wright claimed that the house would bring in $1,800 per year, a figure well above what the market would support. Even after being offered at only seventy-five dollars a month, it sat unrented.[57] Martin asked Wright about prospects for

7.15 Photograph shows the cantilevered canopy added in the 1911 remodeling above the former Oak Park studio entrance. Photographer unknown. Historic American Buildings Survey, IL-1099, Library of Congress.

7.16 Construction of the garden wall along Chicago Avenue, ca. 1912. H261, Frank Lloyd Wright Trust.

7.17 Exterior of the former Oak Park studio drafting room with new windows and sculptures by Richard Buck, post 1911. Photographer unknown. H735, Frank Lloyd Wright Trust.

renting the house in spring 1914, mentioning that the first of May was "renting time at Oak Park," yet still it remained vacant.[58] Finally, in 1915 Alfred MacArthur, business manager of the *Oak Leaves* (and brother of playwright Charles MacArthur and future philanthropist John D. MacArthur), moved into the home.

Catherine Wright did not leave a record of what she thought about living in the converted studio other than mentioning in 1915 that, as her children were beginning to scatter, it was too expensive to keep on her limited income. She did, however, write wistfully about her former home shortly after MacArthur moved into it with his young family, telling Darwin Martin, "[T]he MacArthurs have made it most pleasant for us and have been anxious to live in the old house much as we did — enjoying the playroom and the fireplaces and the other features which meant so much to us. They are beginning a little family and it is great joy to know that it again will serve a growing group of children."[59] This was not, however, to be the case. Alfred's young wife Josephine became ill and was eventually confined to the front room that had been Wright's early office. Living space over the 1911 garage added sometime before she succumbed to her illness in 1917 provided bedrooms for their two children, a maid's room, and a bathroom. MacArthur's daughter Georgiana re-

called going through the playroom to reach the additional rooms.[60] A doorway to the left of the playroom
fireplace connected the original home to the addition.
Evidence of this "secret passage" is clearly visible in
photographs taken shortly before the restoration and
today in the slight color differentiation of the restored
brick in this area from that of the original walls elsewhere in the room.

In 1918, with only Llewellyn left at home, Catherine
and her youngest son moved out of the studio residence, living nearby on Oak Park Avenue for about
a year before moving into an apartment in Chicago.
As she transformed from a youthful teenager into a
middle-aged matron, Catherine had tried hard to be a
supportive wife. She dutifully bore Wright six children,
lovingly tending to their physical, emotional, and educational needs. Her desire to be a contributing member of the community led to her involvement in many
civic organizations, including Hull House, work she
continued after her marriage fell apart.[61] Yet Wright
found her companionship limited compared with the
stimulating, intimate interactions he experienced with
Mamah Cheney. By turning his back on the confining
conditions he perceived in both his relationship with
Catherine and his suburban studio, Wright opened the
door for a new chapter in his life personally and pro-
fessionally.

CONCLUSION: LEGACY OF THE OAK PARK STUDIO
Dissemination and Manipulation

I am better qualified by my experience in every way to do stronger work than before. What I have seen and felt in the old world … has mellowed many harsh crudities and rubbed off many corners. I think I am a stronger man and a better architect. But that remains to be proven.

FRANK LLOYD WRIGHT (1910)

With his return to the United States in 1911, Wright sought closure for what would become the first "golden age" of a long, prolific career. His time in Oak Park comprised an extremely productive phase of his professional life made possible by his home-work situation. When he departed for Europe in 1909, he had already designed well over 250 buildings.[1] Publication of the work led to considerable recognition in the United States and in architectural communities further afield. With the dissemination of the Wasmuth publications, the work created in the suburban studio was about to reach an even broader audience.

Though Wright himself went on to achieve even greater acclaim, it took years to recover the momentum of the early years of his Oak Park practice. While the home studio had once afforded him a sense of fertile unity between his personal and professional lives, that unification had evaporated. In an attempt to gain it back, he redefined the equation of his life by replacing several key factors, most notably his intimate partner and his physical setting.

When he finally dissolved his architectural office, he did not gently close the door; rather, he slammed it shut, separating himself from his design community and attempting to derail the professional trajectories of those who had worked for him. Wright viewed his

architectural explorations and processes as solely his own property. He quickly and viciously circulated the opinion that his former employees, as well as other young architects creating prairie-style designs, were "disciples, neophytes, and quacks," unethically producing cheap, "half-baked, imitative" versions of his own, unique organic architecture, but without its spirit or soul.[2] He accused them of stealing his personal architectural forms without understanding the underlying principles, which, he claimed, he alone had developed.[3] In April 1911, Wright wrote Taylor Woolley, "I am working day and night myself—I will not try any of the old guard again I think. A McArthur wanted to come in but I hesitate to begin the old game again in the old way. . . . [A]ll the architects about here are inimical––nothing to expect of them or of those whom I once regarded as my own architectural family––but that is natural and not a total loss."[4] Wright, however, did go on to rehire Harry Robinson that October, demanding of him his "whole time and absolute loyalty" as "the man who isn't loyal is a liability always—not an asset, no matter what he produces—and I have liabilities enough."[5] Robinson went on to manage Wright's small downtown Chicago office in the Orchestra Hall building until 1916.

While the architect's resentment toward former

employees may have begun shortly after Walter Burley Griffin's departure in early 1906, which was, at least from Wright's perspective, initially amicable, his animosity significantly grew after 1909. Having imagined himself as his employees' *Lieber Meister,* he felt betrayed and grew extremely jealous as he witnessed former "pupils" experiencing success as his own career largely stalled. Wright became especially bitter when he envisioned his former colleagues and employees attracting recognition and commissions he believed were meant for him.[6] For example, in November 1911, while he was sequestered in Wisconsin attempting to avoid the media, the *New York Herald* described William Purcell as recognizable "throughout the United States as the leader of the architectural movement against the adherents of the old school of art."[7]

During Wright's time in Europe, several former employees, including Griffin, Mahony, Robinson, McArthur, and Drummond, along with some of his early downtown colleagues, had reconnected in the offices of Steinway Hall and were assisting each other on projects as needed.[8] In some cases the commissions they worked on likely would have fallen to Wright had he been available. Being absent from the scene also limited the amount of attention given to his work and kept him from participating in events such as the Chicago Architectural Club exhibitions. In contrast, a number of his past associates received ample critical acclaim for their entries, contributing to increasingly prominent reputations.[9]

Griffin's mounting success in these years was particularly infuriating to Wright, as he continued to perceive the talented, mild-mannered architect as his subordinate. After leaving the Oak Park studio, Griffin developed a busy independent practice that included commissions ranging from residential projects to campus and town plans.[10] His growing reputation as an educator as well as an architect and landscape designer was reflected in his being offered the chair of the department of architecture at the University of Illinois in 1913. Half a world away, busy completing the largest commission of any Prairie School architect to date—the design of a new capital city for Australia—he declined the offer.[11] The acclaim for Griffin and Mahony's first-place finish in the competition to design Canberra in May 1912 was specifically difficult for Wright's

ego to endure. After their success was acknowledged in the *New York Times*, Wright began to more openly lash out at them.[12] For example, in 1916 when the Australian architectural periodical *Building* asked for confirmation that he and Griffin had been partners, Wright caustically wrote back, "Griffin as a novice in common with a few other young men was for a short time put on a profit-sharing basis by me in my work as an experiment. The experiment continued for about a year and a half. Griffin proved unsatisfactory. I was trying to develop him as an outside man. It was not his forte."[13] The negative emotions cut both ways. Mahony remained resentful toward Wright throughout the remainder of her life for the way he treated Griffin, even refusing to refer to Wright by name in her autobiography.

Education and the Wasmuth Portfolio

When finally published, *Ausgeführte Bauten und Entwürfe von Frank Lloyd Wright* constituted "the finest publication of any Architect's work in any country," Wright boasted.[14] Housed in a pair of large folios, it consists of one hundred loose 16-by-25.5-inch lithographs of delicate linear renderings luxuriously illustrating his Oak Park studio projects in color inks on gray and white paper, some with tissue overlays.[15] Wright added brief descriptions of each design and an introductory essay.[16] The smaller, less expensive *Sonderheft* depicted a slightly different group of Oak Park projects, primarily through photographs by Chicago photographer Henry Fuermann.[17] Multipage spreads of Wright's two major nonresidential works of the period, Unity Temple and the Larkin building, bookended smaller, mostly residential commissions.

Despite focusing the Wasmuth publications on designs produced in the Oak Park studio, Wright wrote not of the prairie and the characteristics that defined the prairie house as he had in his 1908 essay but only of a few of the houses' key design characteristics. Also absent from the essay was specific mention of the other studio architects and artists who contributed to the designs and project renderings; not even his son Lloyd or Taylor Woolley, who spent long hours preparing drawings for publication, were acknowledged. Instead, Wright contrasted the different forms of architecture he had witnessed in Europe with his own principles of

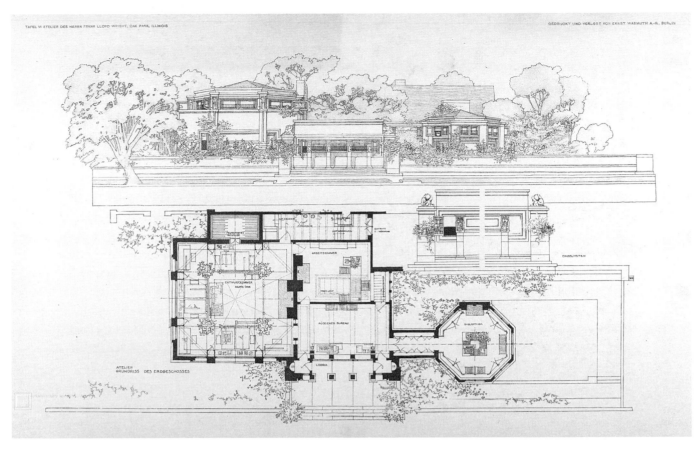

C.1 Oak Park studio from the large two-volume Wasmuth portfolio. Plate VI, *Ausgeführte Bauten und Entwürfe von Frank Lloyd Wright*, 1910. Special Collections, J. Willard Marriott Library, University of Utah.

C.2 Unity Temple with visible concrete pour marks on the facades. From the smaller *Sonderheft* publication, ca. 1911. Photographer unknown. Frank Lloyd Wright, *Ausgeführte Bauten* (Berlin: Ernst Wasmuth A.-G., 1911), 11.

organic architecture design for America. His time in Italy helped him to define more clearly the differences between training that built upon a classical past and what he viewed to be a true education bound in nature. Not surprisingly, Wright was extremely critical of the historically derived architecture that had developed out of the Renaissance. Echoing Froebel, he wrote that these soulless buildings "did not grow from within" and had "little or nothing organic in their nature."[18]

Wright placed European architecture into two broad, diametrically opposed classifications: the "highly self-conscious academic architecture" he rejected, and the more humble, primitive, indigenous architecture he favored. He imagined that the latter had developed organically out of nature and reflected the attributes of its locale in the same manner as did folklore and folksongs. He equated vernacular buildings like the ones he lived in in Italy to his own Oak Park architecture, writing that the traits of these structures are "national, of the soil . . . their functions are truthfully conceived, and rendered directly with natural feeling. . . . [T]hey are always instructive and always beautiful."[19] Education, if done correctly, the architect wrote, could provide the ability to distinguish properly between "historical imitation" and truthful "indigenous expression."[20] Instead of returning to the classicism of ancient times, modern designers should look to the machine and new technology for inspiration, as these separated the current industrial age from the past.

Wright went on to observe that, unburdened by tradition, "America, more than any other nation, presents a new architectural proposition. Her ideal is democracy, and in democratic spirit her institutions are professedly conceived. This means that she places a premium upon individuality."[21] In April 1911 he informed Woolley, who at the time was assisting in the distribution of the Wasmuth publications, that the books should be used as primers for the study of modern building design. He did not envision European colleagues or the East Coast elite as his audience but rather the unsophisticated "young man in architecture" (adapting the phrase from Louis Sullivan), such as those he had hired in the later years of his Oak Park studio, and for those in the small towns of the American heartland.[22] Wright believed that his ideas would sell themselves to these audiences. He wanted to place copies of the publications in rural public libraries and schools and in the hands of individuals ranging from building contractors and lesser architects to young mothers interested in home planning. To reach this audience, he limited illustrations primarily to plans and exterior perspectives, drawings easier to understand by laymen. He informed Woolley that the portfolio "would have more cultural effect on these people than almost anything else that could be put on their shelves."[23] For Wright, education was the route to appropriate societal change in a democracy. By exposing everyday people to the architecture and design ideology developed in the Oak Park studio, he believed he could help the United States reject parasitic transplanted follies, such as the grand neoclassical edifices of McKim, Mead and White, and adopt a new system of design training that would lead to "forms best suited to her [America's] opportunities, her aims and her life."[24]

Wright clearly understood that his recent European experiences had supplied him with a broader context from which to reflect upon the corpus of his Oak Park designs. Although his spiritual hegira had ended and he had closed his suburban studio, the personal educational vision and aims that helped to characterize his first independent office persisted. In May 1914, when the second of his "In the Cause" articles appeared, Wright was still struggling with the major upheaval resulting from his rupture from Oak Park. He had furthered his architectural explorations while carrying out the design of his new home studio in Wisconsin, the remodeling of his Oak Park property, and the few projects that entered the office from supportive clients. These included a series of designs for his lawyer Sherman Booth to be built in the north Chicago suburb of Glencoe; a large residence for Francis Little in Minnesota; a playhouse for Avery Coonley on his property in Riverside; and Midway Gardens, an entertainment complex not far from the Robie house on the South Side of Chicago for the son of longtime client Edward Waller. Wright also attempted to reestablish his architectural studio, this time from the hills of Spring Green.[25]

C.3 Coonley Playhouse, Riverside, Illinois. Gilman Lane Collection, Oak Park Public Library Special Collections.

"In the Cause of Architecture," 1914

Despite greatly benefitting from the generosity of others, whether family members or architectural colleagues or supportive clients, Wright apparently believed that one of the best ways to advance was to denigrate those around him. His 1914 "In the Cause of Architecture" article did just that. In the scathing nine-page diatribe, Wright denounced the work of his former employees and other "Prairie School" architects and the popularization of a design movement that he himself helped to define and label as the "New School of the Middle West."[26] He wrote, "There are enough types and forms in my work to characterize the work of an architect, but certainly not enough to characterize an architecture."[27]

In contrast to Wright's previous writings, he sharply balked at the use of his architectural ideas by others beyond his control. He feared his concept of organic architecture was being distilled by other designers into just another style. "*Style*," he wrote, "is a byproduct of the process and comes of the man or the mind in the process. The style of the thing, therefore, will be the man—it is his. *Let his forms alone.* To adopt a 'style' as a motive is to put the cart before the horse and get nowhere beyond the 'Styles'—never to reach *Style*."[28]

Wright alleged that architects borrowing the formal vocabulary developed in the Oak Park studio without understanding the underlying principles that defined it resulted in imitation and caricature instead of character. He described their works as "fictitious semblances—pretentiously put forward in the name of a movement or a cause" and slanderously predicted that the work carried out by these "architectural babes and sucklings" would lower "the standard of artistic integrity permanently; and demoralize all values artistically; until utter prostitution results."[29] "This is not a 'new school,' nor the way to develop one," he exclaimed. "[T]his is piracy, lunacy, plunder, imitation, adulation, or what you will; it is not a developing architecture."[30]

To prevent the average man from becoming swindled by a parasitic, "language speaking" amateur, Wright waxed righteously, someone needed to speak out. "An enlightened public opinion," he explained, "would take care of this," but because the world was not yet living in an advanced stage of culture that would not call for such plagiarism he was forced to speak up, stating, "Since disciples, neophytes and brokers will not, critics do not, and the public cannot—I will."[31] This acrimonious attitude differed greatly from his reaction when Charles White left the studio in 1905 to open his own office. White reported that Wright "talked very encouragingly to me" and "said that my employment under him gave me the right to use anything I had obtained from him."[32]

Wright's 1914 words reflected his growing disillusionment with his larger professional situation. He wrote of ethics and truth in the article, maintaining that only "artist integrity" could make "any forward movement of this nature in architecture a lasting value."[33] His behavior and writings around the end of his Oak Park era, however, exhibited little of those traits. Throughout the essay Wright presents slanderous half-truths and blatant lies.[34] Portraying himself as a lone prodigy, he selectively forgot the lively dialogues and sharing of ideas between colleagues in Steinway Hall and the ideological debates among workers in the early days of the Oak Park studio when writing, "[T]wenty-one years ago, I took my stand, alone in my field."[35]

Wright expressed sole credit for organic architecture, yet he also addressed its universal nature: "The principles . . . underlying the fundamental ideal of an organic architecture . . . are common to all work that ever rang true in the architecture of the world."[36] And

yet he exclaimed that if his work has a distinguishing trait it was individuality and that this individuality was "as irrevocably mine as the work of any painter, sculptor or poet who ever lived was irrevocably his."[37] Wright, in this instance, seems to have ignored the fact that, while an artist may create an individual form of art, his or her work more often than not is tied to a school or movement comprising multiple artists whose output exhibits some shared characteristics due to cross-fertilization and the fact that works typically reflect the place and time of their creation.

The Studio Architects

While Wright searched for new horizons, his former employees found their own challenges as they attempted to build upon the lessons they learned in Wright's employment. Barry Byrne later recalled, "When I consider the artistic integrity of the designs to which we sought to relate our developments, I can only regard the training this gave me as basic to whatever I have since been able to do in design as a practicing architect."[38] The designers who worked in the studio fit into three general categories. The first included those who remained, in Wright's words, "only long enough to acquire a smattering of form, then departing to sell a superficial proficiency elsewhere," such as McArthur and Hardin. The second category was composed of those who went on to have their own successful careers marked by original forms of what might be defined as organic architecture, like Griffin and Byrne. Most of the remainder were architects who became adept at designing prairie-style houses and later historical revival designs, including Drummond, White, and Van Bergen.[39] Reflecting on a lack of ability to produce his own architecture upon leaving the Oak Park studio in 1905, White wrote:

I told him [Wright] frankly that my present work would undoubtedly show a strong influence of his, but that he must be patient and give me time in which to work away from it. . . . I cannot hope to invent a new system of architecture at the start, and am not ashamed to have my work reflect the influence of the master, but rather,

I shall be proud to have it, providing it shows some individual qualities that would lead one to think it might some day evolve [into] something better and stronger. My ambition then, is to start with Wright's principles so far as I am familiar with them, combine with them the principles and ideals of the other strong men of the world, and try and infuse into this porridge as much of the individual spirit of Charles E. White Junior, as is possible.[40]

It was the work of the last group that gave rise to some of Wright's most spiteful comments in his 1914 essay. While the lack of personal creativity in some of those in this group may, in part, be due to limited ability, it also suggests a flaw in Wright's educational system, which, especially in later years, did not provide young designers the freedom to contemplate developing and experimenting with their own architectural ideas and forms, as academic students have some opportunity to do.

Wright admitted that he was not a teacher but rather a worker.[41] He nevertheless had provided a nurturing setting where inexperienced draftsmen could receive one-on-one guidance, if not from him then from some of the more advanced studio architects, like Griffin and Drummond. In 1908 Wright wrote,

The same formula was impressed upon all: not to imagine they were coming to school. They were coming in to make themselves as useful to me as they could.... Their living was assured [in the] meantime but they would get much or little else from the experience, as they were able. It was all up to them. The discussions in the studio—pro and con—schemes and sketches for buildings in general and more often in detail were made by myself in the midst of the studio-group, each man or boy taking over finally, as he could, whatever I assigned to him to do.[42]

Measured by personal initiative, the young designers received a sense of freedom with which they could succeed or fail, as they observed, explored, and drew.

Charles White wrote that a young architect could be given a chance in Wright's office if he was "willing to hang on by the teeth and receive his money from time to time, when W. happens to think of it." Yet White came away feeling that he owed Wright "more than money can pay" for his architectural education.[43]

White's love-hate relationship with Wright was echoed, in various proportions, by many studio employees. Designers left due to the lack of steady pay, typically finding work that was more stable but less inspiring in nature. Some, like Andrew Willatzen and William Drummond, returned, drawn back by the enticing architecture and Wright's charisma. The tide of employees, however, mostly flowed away from the studio. Growing frustration with Wright in later years became another reason for designers, including Griffin and Drummond (for the final time), to leave. Still others felt that they had learned all that they could from Wright.

Wright's departure in 1909 left a major void in the leadership of the Prairie School. None of his former employees had the architect's gift for promotion. Several former studio designers, including Drummond and Van Bergen, opened their own architectural firms. However, they were small, one- or two-man operations and not directly modeled on Wright's office. These architects initially produced prairie house designs for the Chicago area to meet a growing market due to the greater acceptance of the residential style by midwestern homeowners in the years immediately after the closing of the Oak Park studio.

This rise in interest largely resulted from increased publicity and the fact that residents in suburban communities like Oak Park and Riverside were becoming more accustomed to the simple horizontal domestic forms. Articles featuring prairie houses continued to appear in architectural publications, as well as in home magazines like *Ladies' Home Journal* and *House Beautiful*.[44] Books, such as Wright's Wasmuth publications and Charles E. White's *Successful Homes and How to Build Them* (1912) and Hermann von Holst's *Modern American Homes* (1912), which prominently featured the work of Wright, Griffin, White, and others, also helped to promote prairie style designs nationwide.[45] Soon architects not directly tied to either Wright's office or Steinway Hall, like Percy Dwight Bentley in

C.4 William Drummond's own house, River Forest, 1909. Photographer: Lisa D. Schrenk.

La Crosse, Wisconsin; Bray and Nystrom in Duluth, Minnesota; Claude and Starck in Madison, Wisconsin; Trost and Trost in El Paso, Texas; Antonin Nechodoma in Puerto Rico; and even Robert van 't Hoff and Willem Marinus Dudok in the Netherlands, began producing prairiesque designs in the Midwest and beyond.

Wright aimed his tirade in *Architectural Record* at these designers, in addition to his former employees, exclaiming, "Selling even good versions of an original at second hand is in the circumstances not good enough. It is cheap and bad—demoralizing in every sense."[46] The architect's rant reflects the disconnect between his desire to influence young designers and small-town home builders and not really wanting other architects to emulate his work.

Many of the less adventurous studio architects produced well-designed prairie-style buildings that incorporated innovative features. For example, the ba-

sic architectural vocabulary of Drummond's smaller prairie houses (including his own home in River Forest) echoed projects created in the studio. Like Wright's Laura Gale house, Drummond's early residences typically contained side entrances, a central chimney, and front porches only accessible from inside the dwelling. They also often featured hipped roofs and exterior walls of horizontal board and batten siding topped by stucco on the upper floors and wood banding on the interior walls and ceilings. But hidden storage spaces and other imaginative features, including multiple clothes chutes and porch windows that slid into wall recesses, also characterized his work.[47] Some of Van Bergen's early independent projects that resemble Wright's design for the "Fireproof House for $5000" contain his own carefully planned practical details, such as through-the-wall window-box waterers, dressers that opened into bedrooms as well as adjacent bathrooms, and innovative window hardware.[48]

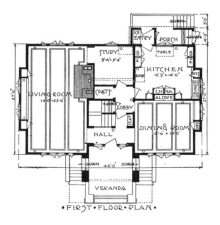

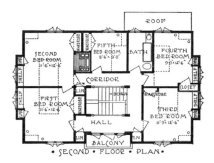

A Frame and Stucco Country House

Charles E. White, Jr., Architect, Chicago, Illinois

THIS simple yet artistic dwelling has a frame exterior with stucco on wood lath and a shingle roof. The interior design is along the same simple lines as shown in the exterior view, the woodwork being of southern pine. The house faces south. It is the home of Mr. Walter Gerts, River Forest, Illinois, and was built in 1905 at a cost of $5,500.

PLATE 26

C.5 Walter Gerts house, River Forest, Charles White, 1905. Plate 26, Hermann Valentin von Holst, *Modern American Homes* (Chicago: American Technical Society, 1912.)

C.6 Villa Henny, Huis ter Heide, Netherlands, Robert van 't Hoff, 1915. Photographer unknown. HOFF Archive, 8, Netherlands Architecture Institute.

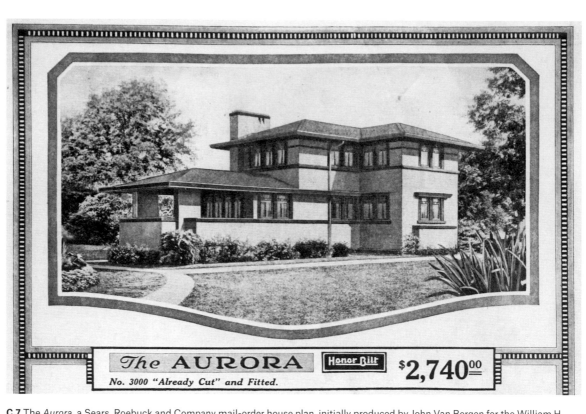

C.7 The *Aurora*, a Sears, Roebuck and Company mail-order house plan, initially produced by John Van Bergen for the William H. Griffith house, 1913. *Honor Bilt Modern Homes* (Chicago: Sears Roebuck, 1918).

By the 1920s many of these architects had given up on prairie house designs or saw them as just one stylistic solution among many. Drummond designed several picturesque English cottage and Tudor style homes in River Forest, complete with clinker bricks, steeply pitched slate roofs, and chimney pots, while Charles White, who produced a series of prairie houses in Oak Park, felt that many styles were appropriate for residential and commercial projects. In 1933 he designed the Art Deco Oak Park Post Office, constructed directly across the street from Wright's Unity Temple. Van Bergen also explored other architectural forms, including several designs for residences in the international style. He continued to create prairie houses, however, until well into the 1920s, including two designs made available through Sears and Roebuck's mail-order house service.

Several studio designers developed original architectural vocabularies as they, like Wright, incorporated new ideas and experiences in their search for an architecture that both met a commission's functional requirements and appropriately reflected its time and place. The most successful of the studio designers was Walter Burley Griffin. After Wright departed for Europe, Griffin exhibited his talents as a landscape planner in his design for the Rock Crest–Rock Glen neighborhood in Mason City, Iowa, and in his plan for the capital city Canberra. In Australia he continued an exploration of concrete begun in Wright's studio. This resulted in his patented Knitlock Blocks in 1917, a concrete block-unit design system that consisted of flat, interlocking concrete tiles in six-inch modules incorporated into a system of panels and piers.[49] Griffin had a prolific career in Australia and then in India. Before his death in 1937, he had received around forty commissions for buildings in India and, like Wright during his later career, altered his aesthetic vocabulary to reflect changes in place and local culture.

Another architect who came into his own after departing Wright's studio was Barry Byrne. Like other former studio architects, Byrne produced residential work that was eclectic, first favoring prairie style

C.8 Narain [Narayan] Singh residence, Vārānasi, India, Walter Burley Griffin, 1936. "The Magic in America," ca. 1937–49. Digital file 1_14_54a, Ryerson and Burnham Archives, AIC.

C.9 Barry Byrne with model of his design for the Church of Christ the King in Cork, Ireland, 1929.

designs, then picturesque historic forms, and finally variations of functional modernism. However, he built upon his early experiences to develop unique designs for academic and ecclesiastic commissions that addressed the needs of his own faith. Influenced by the open cubic design of Wright's Unity Temple, for which he had overseen the production of working drawings, Byrne sought to more closely integrate Catholic clergy and parishioners through innovative auditorium design. For the exteriors of his buildings, he increasingly favored expressionistic forms constructed in brick, stone, or concrete that included broad, unadorned expanses of wall accentuated with concentrated areas of ornament, resulting in an inventive architecture formally distinct from Wright's.[50] In 1929 he received international attention with the construction of his successful low-cost, concrete design Church of Christ the King in Cork, Ireland.[51] Byrne was able to use what he had learned during his formative years in the Oak Park studio as building blocks to develop creative organic design solutions that were innovative yet appropriately modern.[52]

The spiteful bitterness that Wright held for many of his former employees was a significant factor in the decline of the Prairie School in the years leading up to World War I, but it was not the only one. The development of the prairie house had slowed dramatically from its rapid formal and ideological inception by Wright and others at the turn of the century; the architect's restlessness was in part a reflection of his growing awareness of this. A reduction in the exposure of the residential form in popular publications after 1915 was another reason. After an initial rash of publicity in magazines and books, several major architectural publications, including the *Craftsman* and *House Beautiful*, that had favored the style either ceased to exist or moved from Chicago to the East Coast, where the work of less progressive, often Beaux Arts–trained architects predominated.[53]

Other reasons include the downturn of housing starts due to World War I and then the growing interest in historic building forms after the war by those who had served overseas or had viewed images of quaint European towns in newsreels and newspaper accounts of the war. Byrne identified another potential reason for the decline as the growing liberation of women and their greater preference for revival-style designs, which tended to allow for more delicate, "feminine" furnishings than did the more masculine spaces of prairie houses.[54] Byrne claimed that husbands would tend to accept his designs as logical, while their wives often rejected them as being out of fashion.[55]

Wright's Later Architectural Development

In 1914 Wright declared, "Were no more to come of my work than is evident at present, the architecture of the country would have received an impetus that will finally resolve itself into good."[56] But Wright's architectural career continued for a half a century after his departure from Oak Park. During those years he built upon the educational experiences that informed the designs born in his suburban studio, especially those lessons that grew out of close examinations of nature. For example, the underlying structural concept for many of his projects for tall buildings, including his unbuilt mile-high skyscraper and his realized Price Tower, directly borrowed from the taproot system of plants. Throughout his career, Wright continued to emphasize the concept of organic integration and celebrated the materiality and other characteristics of local landscapes as he had in Oak Park, often significantly altering his architectural vocabulary to respond to different conditions. Hence the spatial designs, choice of materials, and ornamental forms for buildings he created for sites in Japan, California, Arizona, and elsewhere differed dramatically from those he produced for suburban Chicago. In every case, however, geometrical explorations, in addition to nature, strongly informed the designs.

Wright's early interest in the use and manipulation of shapes, as revealed in the unit system of design he used to produce his prairie houses and other buildings in Oak Park, formed just the first step in a lifelong exploration of the design potential of geometric elements. After he closed the Oak Park studio, this exploration deepened to incorporate a more sophisticated examination of the symbolic meaning of forms. By 1912 Wright had reflected on symbolism and the "human ideas, moods, and sentiments" that forms represented: the circle, infinity; the triangle, structural integrity; the spire, aspiration; the spiral, organic progress; and the square, integrity. He wrote of "a certain psychic quality which we may call the spell-power of the form, and with which the artist freely plays, as much at home with it as the musician at his keyboard with his notes."[57] As in a musical composition, Wright wanted to capitalize on the transformational processes of forms as taught in Froebel exercises, with one shape evolving into another. After he left Oak Park Wright began to incorporate more elaborate decorative compositions of shapes into his architectural ornament, as revealed not only in the primary-colored circles and squares of the *Kindersymphony* windows he produced for the Coonley Playhouse but also in his designs for murals, furnishings, and tableware for Midway Gardens in Chicago and the Imperial Hotel in Japan.

Wright furthered his explorations of squares and cubes in his California concrete block houses in the early 1920s and then went on to focus on rectangles,

C.10 David Wright house, Phoenix, Arizona, Frank Lloyd Wright, 1952. Photographer: Lisa D. Schrenk.

triangles, and hexagons in his Usonian residential designs. In later years he moved on to circles, hemicycles, and spirals, producing spectacular projects that embedded a sense of movement and ever-changing visual experiences. While the Guggenheim Museum in New York City may be the most prominent example of a spiral in his architecture, he included them in other projects such as the house for his son David in Phoenix. Wright's interest in the transformative qualities of forms also led him to investigate how the rotational patterns generated in Froebel's Form of Beauty exercises could be expressed in architecture, which he explored in the designs of plans ranging from residences to skyscrapers. Near the end of his life, the architect affirmed that the memory of "the smooth cardboard

triangles and the maple-wood blocks" of the Froebel system still remained in his fingers.[58]

The Oak Park studio was a crucial venue in Wright's architectural career and a major stop on the journey he made from rural Wisconsin to urban Chicago and later back to the environment that so strongly informed his development as a youth. The suburban office also served as an important site in his evolution from a member of a community of equals at Steinway Hall to the master of his domain at Taliesin. In the process, the home studio allowed him to work within the setting for which he was primarily designing while offering an environment akin to an Old World craft workshop in an era of architectural professionalization. The studio conditions helped make possible the development of Wright's spectacular prairie houses and master works like the Larkin building and Unity Temple that offered Americans architectural solutions for the modern industrial age that clearly reflected the character of the midwestern landscape.

Wright sought to save the United States and eventually the world from what he viewed as the meaningless designs of the Beaux Arts system and later international modernism. But he also wanted to be in full control of the organic architecture realized in its place. By the later years of the Oak Park studio, Wright became conflicted between his desire to educate his workers and his competitive urges. He wanted loyal workers but scorned both "copyists" and independent designers who might achieve their own critical success in the field.

Wright's relationships with his parents and other family members played a major role in how he treated those who worked for him. After growing up encircled by adoring women, he yearned for similar attention the rest of his life. First with his studio employees and later with his Taliesin apprentices, he attempted to surround himself with admiring workers eager to contribute to his architectural explorations. However, he placed greater priority on maintaining his reputation as a leader than on directly guiding younger architects. Wright's often acrimonious reactions to departing studio employees and later apprentices likely grew out of the feeling of abandonment he experienced as an adolescent when his father deserted the family. Wright grew to view a departure as an act of betrayal. He often ostracized apprentices dismissed from Taliesin for breaking fellowship rules, as well as those who departed for other reasons. Family members who had been "under" him in his domestic life were not immune to this treatment. His older two sons, who went on to become architects in their own right, in particular, had numerous fallouts with their father as adults.

Frank Lloyd Wright evolved from a young idyllic designer into a mature architect while operating in and experimenting with his Oak Park studio, developing an original form of architecture appropriate to the modern era that built upon his experiential education experiences. The suburban workplace served as his first independent home studio, where he carried out explorations into design ideas, materials, and forms, a practice he continued throughout his life. In the process Wright honed his design ideology, his views on the proper direction of his profession, and his marketing skills and public image—all elements that had an impact on the field as other architects attempted to emulate his persona as well as his ideas. These aspects also shaped his own later career as he found great benefit in the home studio's basic structure. Those he employed in Oak Park typically went on to work in small firms or open their own offices, but none came close to replicating Wright's suburban studio, which was, like the architect himself, unique in the development of American architecture.

EPILOGUE: EVOLUTION OF THE HOME AND STUDIO POST 1911

Division and Renewal

> The building in 1974 was like a barnacled old oyster, the clarity of the shell submerged in the years of accretions—"organic" in the sense of growth over.

ANN ABERNATHY (1985)

Frank Lloyd Wright's relationship with his Oak Park home and studio did not end with his 1911 remodeling. He designed changes to the complex even after selling the property in the 1920s, suggesting the building's continual personal significance to him. That later property owners commissioned him to make alterations reflects the fact that even decades later they viewed it as an important work of architecture in spite of its much-altered state. Today the relevance of Wright's early home studio in the development of American architecture is most clearly reflected in the meticulous restoration of the building and its current use as a historic house museum.

Even though Wright gave Alfred MacArthur a contract to purchase the Forest Avenue side of the property in 1915 for $15,000, the architect did not have a clear title to his former residence.[1] Legally it was tied up in earlier loan arrangements with creditors, such as Darwin Martin, who provided substantial funds for the 1911 remodeling. Martin was willing to let Wright sell the property to MacArthur, but only if the architect signed off on a long list of stipulations, including the condition that if Wright defaulted for thirty days on either an interest or principal payment, he agreed to convey the title of the property to Martin to ob-

viate foreclosure proceedings.[2] While Wright signed the agreement, MacArthur never took ownership of the property.

Still not receiving payments on any of his loans and believing Wright was about to leave on an extended trip to Japan to carry out the Imperial Hotel commission, in February 1916 Martin politely asked of the architect's attorney, Sherman Booth, "Will not Mr. Wright before he goes, in all fairness, execute a Warranty Deed to me of the Chicago Avenue, Forest Avenue Property, and have Mrs. Wright join therein? . . . [T]here seems nothing left but either his voluntary conveyance of the property or foreclosure. Which must it be?"[3] Wright chose neither, informing Martin that he would not be leaving for at least a year and then for only a few months at a time.[4] Despite numerous mechanics' liens and deeds of trust, he maintained possession of the property for another ten years with his wife Catherine (she did not grant him a divorce until November 1922).

Catherine and various children and employees continued to inhabit the converted studio until 1920.[5] In addition to the youngest Wright offspring, this included son John in 1913, while he was overseeing his father's Chicago office and the construction of Midway

E.1 David Wright in front of the Oak Park studio garage, ca. 1915. Photographer unknown. H86a, Gift of Llewellyn Wright, Frank Lloyd Wright Trust.

Gardens. The following year, artist Alfonso Iannelli called the place home while working on decorative elements for the new entertainment venue. The artist later wrote, "[S]taying at Mr. Wright's home in Oak Park, experiencing the way I felt in his house, seeing his buildings on a winter night—snow-covered, the romance of this new simple statement of housing—there was something magical about it."[6]

At the beginning of 1919, after Catherine and Llewellyn had moved out, Viennese architect R.M. Schindler occupied the studio unit rent free while his employer was in Tokyo.[7] During his stay, the young designer helped on several of Wright's stateside projects, including the Aline Barnsdall Hollyhock House in Los Angeles. Wright encouraged him to borrow "rugs, bedding, or furniture from Taliesin" and make any "reasonable investment" to make the place comfortable.[8] Schindler discovered that the building leaked like a "sieve" and even after being armed with "oakum, putty, etc." found it comfortable only in mild weather.[9] Expected to make needed repairs to the building, he struggled through several rounds of work on the heating system, with minimal success. He also received quotes for plumbing

E.2 View of the former studio drafting room and garage addition from the east driveway, ca. 1919. Rudolph Schindler Collection, University of California, Santa Barbara.

improvements and fixing wood railings and the concrete balustrades in the front yard, although it is not clear if he had any of this work carried out.

One of Schindler's other charges from Wright was to find renters for both sides of the property. MacArthur, who continued to live in the house after his wife died, "balked" at Wright's demand for $170 in monthly rent (significantly more than appropriate in the west suburban market) and gave notice that he would vacate the unit in May 1920.[10] Schindler struggled to find tenants willing to pay the inflated rents. After creating a spreadsheet labeled "Statement Concerning Rentals of Oak Park Houses" and sending it to Wright, he finally convinced the architect the rates needed to be lower.[11] After much effort, in mid-March he rented the Forest Avenue house for $125 a month to a factory manager for the Benjamin Electric Manufacturing Company.[12] Two weeks later he rented the studio unit for the same

monthly rent to Mr. E.T. Wright (no relation), the Chicago district adjuster for the US Shipping Board.[13] To raise a bit of extra revenue, Schindler divided off the "servants' quarters" above the garage that had been part of the MacArthur unit, believing it could generate an additional $40 a month. With new occupants moving in, Schindler vacated the property on April 19 after sending Wright a telegram two days earlier with the message, "Everything Rented Going West May."[14]

Two years earlier, Wright's sister Jane and her husband Andrew Porter had purchased the Eastlake-style house next door to the studio from Anna Wright, who continued to reside there.[15] The arrangement lasted until late 1920.[16] Earlier that year Jane asked her brother to prepare a design to enlarge the residence. Drawings show the addition of a wing connecting the house to the garage of the former home and studio next door.[17] Wright attempted to unify the two stylistically different

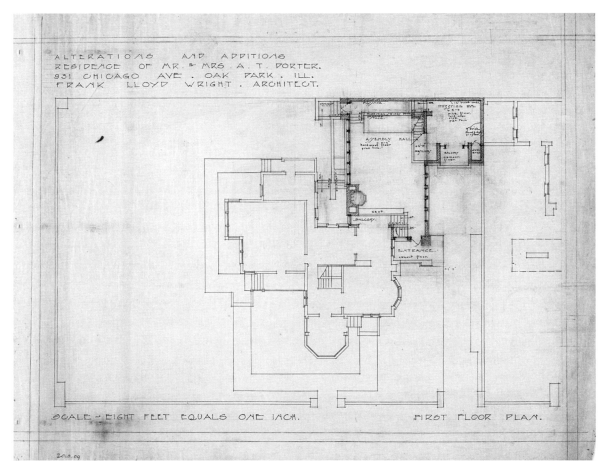

E.3 Unrealized Andrew and Jane Porter addition connecting Anna Wright's former Eastlake-style house to the garage of her son's Oak Park property, plan. TAL 2010.004, Avery Architectural & Fine Arts Library, Columbia University, New York. © 2020 Frank Lloyd Wright Foundation, Scottsdale, AZ. All rights reserved.

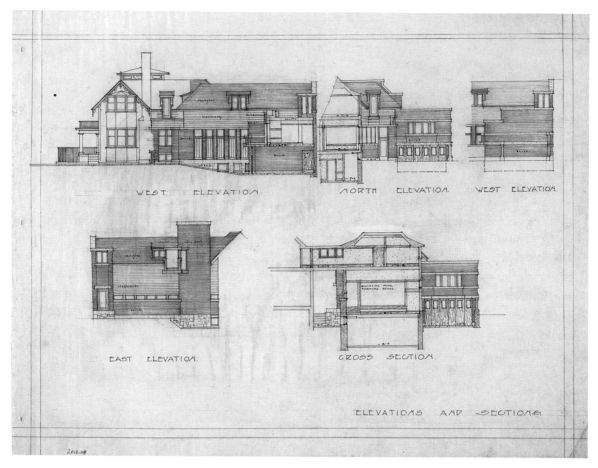

E.4 Unrealized Andrew and Jane Porter addition connecting Anna Wright's former Eastlake-style house to the garage of her son's Oak Park property, elevations and sections. TAL 2010.008, Avery Architectural & Fine Arts Library, Columbia University, New York. © 2020 Frank Lloyd Wright Foundation, Scottsdale, AZ. All rights reserved.

buildings through his choice of materials: brick on the lower levels and clapboard above, with a shingled roof. Spaces inside included a new bedroom and bathroom for Anna, along with a guest bedroom and sleeping porches on the second level. A large hardwood-floored "assembly hall" with a stage at one end and a fireplace toward the other filled most of the lower level. The main floor also included a dressing room with a darkroom to one side, above a partially sunken garage. It is not clear how the more public spaces, which recalled Wright's design for the Coonley Playhouse of 1912, were intended to be used.[18] Unfortunately, just as the Porters were contemplating construction, new neighbors to the south moved "the old Fish house" right up against the fence of the Porter property. Jane informed her brother, "[I]t seems useless to think of putting up a building there as we could have no windows that

wouldn't be against a barn or a house!!"[19] Instead of constructing the addition, in October 1920 the Porters bought the residence around the corner on Forest Avenue that Wright had designed for Arthur Heurtley eighteen years earlier.[20]

In the mid-1920s, Wright once again placed the Oak Park property on the market even though he still did not have clear title to it.[21] A sales brochure advertised, "Two unique and beautiful modern homes," to be sold separately or together, "each complete in itself and independent of the other, separated by solid brick firewall to secure absolute privacy. Both are provided with Yaryan heat, best of plumbing, drained to deep Chicago Avenue sewer and are thoroughly well built throughout."[22] To prepare the property for sale, Wright had several alterations made to the building, including connecting the small apartment above the

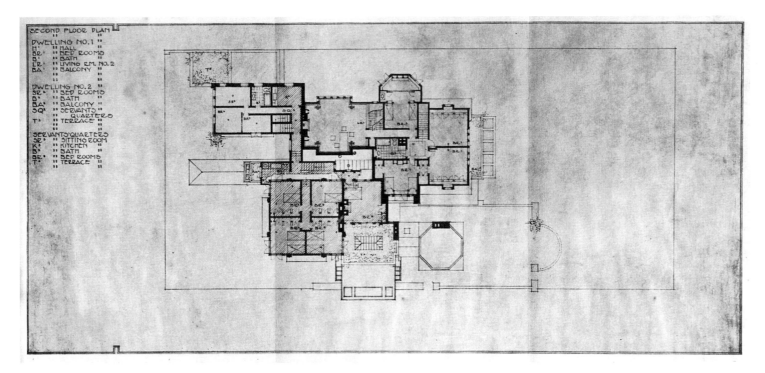

E.5 Second-floor plan of the Oak Park studio post 1911, from sales brochure "A Forest Avenue Property & A Chicago Avenue Property." Text of the brochure appears in appendix E. Oak Park Public Library Special Collections.

garage addition to the second floor of the former drafting room by a small bridge so that the space could be rented either as a separate unit or as space for servants or extra bedrooms.

This time the home and studio sold, but only with the help of Darwin Martin, who still possessed trust deeds on the property and who may have realized that the sale was the only chance he might have of recovering some of the thousands of dollars he had loaned Wright over the years. Local brokers John O. Bastear and Alva Thomas, who were already residing in the building and had begun negotiations the previous year, bought the property in 1925, purchasing it with a $28,250 loan from Martin.[23]

The building once again formed a center of artistic activity. By 1924 the former studio had become the first permanent home of the recently established Austin, Oak Park and River Forest Art League, of which Thomas was a member.[24] The league, which planned to pattern itself after the New York Art Center, applied to the Village of Oak Park to use the studio for art exhibitions, declaring: "The ART CENTER TEMPLE is to occupy the famous home of the distinguished

architect, Frank Lloyd Wright. This structure, unique in the Wright architectural style, is known far as 'the house with the trees growing through its center.' It will henceforth serve the community as a temple to art, admirably adapted for the purpose in design and location at the corner of Chicago and Forest Avenues."[25] While the application also mentions an intent to make part of the building a tea room, such use would not be allowed. On 15 October 1924 the Village of Oak Park Board of Trustees, however, did grant permission for the Art League to use the former studio as an art exhibition building.[26] The league resided at the site until around 1928.[27]

Artists had resided and worked next door in the original home even prior to the league moving in. An article in the *Oak Leaves* identified five people as inhabiting the home in 1923. Russian sculptor Samuel "Sammy" Klasstorner and painter Theodore Glass were on the first floor. Upstairs, the paper reported, painter Gladys Vinson Mitchell's studio was "arranged in convenient and artistic conjunctions with her home," while sculptor Anna Tilden's studio was "most secluded." Nell Sansom, who sang and taught

E.6 Oak Park home, ca. 1925. Photographer unknown. Gilman Lane Collection, Oak Park Public Library Special Collections.

music to children, practiced to "such success that the others declare they cannot work so well when her instrument is silent."[28] Artists continued to live in the studio until at least 1937.[29]

In 1930 a bankrupt Darwin Martin initiated a lawsuit in an attempt to try to recover money from Wright, who, he claimed, owed him $32,868.48.[30] The loan Martin made to the new owners turned out not to be any better of an investment than those to his architect. His agreement with Bastear and Thomas stipulated that they were to collect rent from the tenants and then make monthly payments of $250 on the loan with the balance due in 1930. Like Wright, Bastear and Thomas became delinquent. In the lawsuit, Martin noted "the premises have been permitted to deteriorate and fall in a bad state of repair," citing complaints about lack of heat, leaking pipes, broken sidewalks, and tenants not paying rent for months at a time.[31]

Martin threw his net wide and included a list of twenty defendants, including Bastear and Thomas and an assortment of other minor players who also might have had earlier claims against or interest in the property. Martin's underlying goal was to receive recognition as the "paramount and superior" complainant in the case, positioning him first in line to receive payment.[32] He won the case, which led to the property going into forfeiture. On 28 July 1933 the Cook County Chancery Court clerk placed the property up for auction to settle Martin's claim. The sole bid of $33,000 came from Martin's wife, Isabelle.[33] She received the certificate of sale and then turned around and sold, assigned, and transferred all rights to the property onto Martin's Buffalo Phoenix Company on 2 November 1934.[34]

The building continued to serve as rental property. In December 1938 an ad in *Oak Leaves* listed "Oak

E.7 Apartment in former balcony of the studio drafting room, ca. mid-1970s. Photographer unknown. Frank Lloyd Wright Trust.

Park's most beautiful five-room studio apartment with heated garage" at the reduced rate of $85 a month.[35] Just as it had been twenty-five years earlier, the property was still difficult to rent. Martin's son, the president of the company, like previous owners became delinquent in paying taxes on the property, and it went into foreclosure in 1943. Norman and Elizabeth Beggs then bought the former home and studio at auction for $18,000.[36]

Three years later Clyde and Charlotte Nooker purchased the property, initially living in part of the former studio and renting out the rest of the complex.[37] There were eventually six rental units in the building: the first incorporated the original living room, the home library, and pantry (used as a kitchen); the second, the home's dining room (used as a living room) and service wing; the third, the home's second floor with the playroom as a living room and the north bedroom as a kitchen; the fourth, the first floor of the former studio; the fifth, the second floor rooms of the studio that were added in 1911, with three of what had been the Wright children's bedrooms remodeled into a living room and kitchen; and the sixth, the spaces over the garage.[38]

In 1956 the Nookers hired Wright to produce designs for a new bathroom, a dressing area of Philippine mahogany, and an updated kitchen to replace the problematic one in the passageway added in the 1911 remodeling.[39] Other changes to the original studio office and library spaces, including additional built-in furniture, were probably made at this time as well (see figure P.3). The Nookers told Wright that they thought the house should be preserved. The architect retorted, "In Europe, it would be." He encouraged the couple to restore the building, telling them that he hoped they would "keep the old place from falling apart."[40] The Nookers soon began fixing art glass windows and refinishing woodwork.

Around 1966 the couple made some of the complex available to the public. They had initially lived in the former drafting room, library, and passageway areas. When they opened the building for tours, they moved to the back first floor unit that comprised the 1895 kitchen and maid's room.[41] A steady stream of people toured the building. The visit included parts of the home and the first floor of the drafting room.[42] The building, however, had to be toured in two parts, as the 1911 firewall still divided the property.[43] Due to

E.8 Former studio library before restoration with 1950s Wright-designed vanity, window in former west display case, and shag carpeting, used during Nooker era as a dressing room, 1975. Photographer unknown. BL133-2, Frank Lloyd Wright Trust.

the numerous post-1909 alterations and the fact that most of the original furniture and much of the decoration had been removed or altered, visitors found it extremely difficult to comprehend what the spaces were like when Wright lived there.[44]

In 1972, shortly after her husband died, Charlotte Nooker put the building on the market. Around this time, several women were living on the second floor in two units. They used the front room and Catherine's dayroom as bedrooms. The units shared the second-floor bathroom, while the Wrights' master bedroom served as a communal kitchen and the playroom as a living and dining area.[45] In 1974, after the Oak Park Development Corporation purchased the building and opened it to the public, the Frank Lloyd Wright Home and Studio Foundation offered its first public tour on July 17 of that year.[46]

Emergency repair work to remedy major structural issues began right away. Wright had built the studio quickly, without a proper foundation, constructing the exterior brick on the lower part of the walls as a veneer only one wythe thick. Years of neglect led to significant deterioration. The library, for example, which initially rested upon eight eighteen-inch-square brick piers spanned by concrete beams, listed four inches.[47] Early

emergency repairs included replacing the existing home roof with "one of red cedar shingles, sheet metal roofing, gutters and downspouts of lead-coated copper, rebuilding of the perimeter brick walls and chimneys, repairs to a number of art glass windows, and the addition of handrails to the interior stairways."[48]

Research on the building's complicated history also began in 1974. Students from the architectural program at the University of Illinois, Chicago, carried out a measured-drawing survey documenting the existing state of the building and produced a series of renderings used in the formation of the restoration plan.[49] In addition to the creation of as-built drawings, the Home and Studio Foundation began collecting historical photographs, furnishings, and other relevant objects, as well as memories from the Wright children and others.[50] They interviewed Lloyd, Catherine, and David Wright beginning in the mid-1970s.[51] Written documents, including descriptions by those who worked in the studio and Wright himself, as well as published sources on the architect's early career, offered many clues. The foundation incorporated the new knowledge into the training of volunteer tour guides.[52]

On Halloween 1977, the organization held a symposium of Wright family members and scholars tasked with reviewing a draft of the master plan for the building's restoration produced by architects on the Home and Studio Foundation's restoration committee and providing guidance on the future direction of the house museum.[53] A major outcome of the meeting was the decision to restore the property to its condition during 1909, the last year Wright lived and worked at the site. The foundation allowed a few practical exceptions, such as retaining the 1911 garage for a gift shop, repurposing the rental unit above as a caretaker's apartment, and turning the former maid's quarters into a catering kitchen. Three other restoration options were considered. One option included leaving the building in the state that the foundation received it, thereby maintaining the later Wright alterations to the property and then using "photographs and other simulations" to interpret the history of the building. A second option was to, in Lloyd Wright's words, "capture the spirit" and pick and choose dates for the restoration of individual rooms that could help tell the evolving history of the building and feature the choicest elements of the home and studio. A third choice was to hold rigorously to the condition of the structure in 1909, which would have meant the removal of changes that could be beneficial for the operations of a house museum, such as the garage addition.[54]

Along with "accretions" made by others, the Home and Studio Foundation removed a number of significant Wright-designed elements during the restoration, including later art glass windows and the walled garden. It then installed replicas of what was believed to have existed in 1909.[55] An example of this was the foundation's removal of Bock's original sculptures from the upper level of the exterior of the drafting room and installing replicas re-created from photographs of the artist's boulder figures to each side of the studio's entrance.[56] The decision to return the building to a specific date led to discord at times during the restoration process. For example, Lloyd Wright, who served as an architectural consultant on the project

E.9 Scholars conference in drafting room, 31 October 1977. From left to right: Bruce Goff, an unidentified National Trust for Historic Preservation observer, Theodore Sande, H. Allen Brooks, Lloyd Wright, and Eric Lloyd Wright. Photographer unknown. BL44, Frank Lloyd Wright Trust.

E.10 Entrance hall stair as originally restored to 1889 condition, ca. 1980s. Photographer: Jon Miller. BL54, Frank Lloyd Wright Trust.

until his death in 1978, fervently opposed the removal of the 1911 cantilevered canopy over the former studio entrance because of its significance in his father's design development (see figure 7.15).[57] Yet the restoration committee saw it as a major distraction from the 1909 exterior conditions and as a source of confusion for visitors attempting to make sense of the already complex building. They dismantled the cantilever.[58]

David Wright also weighed in on details of the restoration. In 1991 he insisted that a different stair configuration existed in the entry of the home at the time of his father's departure than the overscaled design of 1889. The Home and Studio Foundation initially recreated the original stair as it appeared in construction drawings and a historic photograph. David recalled a smaller stair, which provided less of a tripping hazard when moving from the entrance hall to the living room and offered more space for Wright's growing brood to remove their boots and other outerwear during the winter months. After considerable debate and a gift of financial support from David and his wife Gladys to help defray costs in January 1991, the stair was remodeled in accordance with his memories.[59]

The initial restoration of the building took thirteen years and cost more than $3 million.[60] One of the first exploits of the restoration crew involved creating a hole in the 1911 firewall to reunite the studio with the home.[61] Fortunately, Wright typically did not remove material from the building unnecessarily during his numerous remodelings, so the structure itself revealed much about the building's history.[62] Making exploratory openings often led to major discoveries, as when restoration architect John Thorpe, then living in the second-floor studio apartment, probed the attic floor above the ceiling of the southwest bedroom on the former drafting room balcony and discovered the octagon tension ring of chains Wright had designed to hold the drafting room together. It was still intact.[63]

In 1977 the Home and Studio Foundation started the major building restoration with work on the 1895 dining room.[64] After conducting extensive research on the room, the foundation reproduced the ceiling grille, added new artist canvas to the walls, and replaced missing floor tiles.[65] The return of the dining table, which Wright had given to artist Alfonso Iannelli in 1914 as partial payment for work done on Midway Gardens, and six of the eight original chairs from Taliesin helped to complete the room.[66]

Researchers often found it difficult to verify the precise condition of specific aspects of the building

E.11 "Hole in the Wall Gang," including restoration architect John Thorpe (holding a can) posing by the hole in the firewall, 1974. Photographer unknown. BL13-1, Frank Lloyd Wright Trust.

at the time Wright left Oak Park. Paint expert Robert A. Furhoff completed five separate analyses in an attempt to determine which layers of the up to twenty-five coats of paint corresponded to 1909.[67] When conflicting or insufficient information appeared about the presence of an element or specifics of its design, such as with the fireplace in the studio library, the restoration committee documented existing conditions and preserved materials where possible.[68] In addition to attempting to bring the building back to its 1909 appearance, the restoration architects and committee members also oversaw updates to help ensure the building's future survival. This included either upgrading or introducing structural, electrical, plumbing, security, heating, cooling, ventilating, and humidification systems.[69]

While the basic room arrangement of the house largely survived, the same could not be said for the studio, which underwent major restoration work between 1982 and 1987. After the stabilization of the structure, which included the excavation of a full basement under the drafting room in 1983, the restoration committee oversaw the repair of exterior surfaces and alterations to undo the 1911 changes. This included removing Catherine's bedroom over the original office

E.12 Opening in the ceiling of the second floor of the former Oak Park studio drafting room showing part of the chain tension ring still in situ, ca. 1978. Photographer unknown. BL123-1, Frank Lloyd Wright Trust.

E.13 Excavating under the studio drafting room during the restoration, 1983. Photographer unknown. BL101-2, Frank Lloyd Wright Trust.

and returning the upper part of the former drafting room's second floor to its previous octagonal form. The Home and Studio Foundation reconstructed the drafting room balcony and the arched Chicago common-brick fireplace front. Workers also replaced and repaired windows as necessary and laid a new magnesite floor throughout the studio. The organization developed a furniture plan and replicated pieces, such as the four freestanding pier cabinets and the tables and stools in the drafting room. In the library the work crew restored the fireplace, including replacing the brick front that at some point had been disassembled and its location plastered over. They also removed a layer of yellow paint from the sandblasted glass panes of the room's laylight. First-floor casement windows installed after 1909 were taken out, and the display cases fronted by panes of art glass were restored or re-created.[70] Restoration workers rebuilt the storage areas with their cork display panels and replaced light fixtures, triangular shelving, and the decorative corner piers.

On the exterior of the studio building, workers restored or replaced perimeter walls and decorative elements, including many of the the stork panels, the limestone urns, and Wright's signature plaque at the entrance, in addition to recreating the boulder sculptures in concrete.[71] While the Home and Studio Foundation's restoration committee oversaw the reconstruction process, trade specialists carried out most of the more advanced work.[72] Architects employed by the foundation and members of the restoration committee produced drawings and carefully recorded the meticulous re-creation with hundreds of documents produced and photographs taken before, during, and after each stage of the process, including recording and storing many of the building parts that were removed.

Volunteers carefully boxed and stored elements from the 1911 and later remodelings, including the art glass windows from the entrance to the walled garden. The documentation and other materials that relate to the building, as well as the careers of Wright and the other architects who worked in the studio, the lives of Wright family members, and the community, were gathered, cataloged, and placed in the foundation's Research Center, in the new basement of the drafting room. The staff architects also documented

E.14 Former studio drafting room showing the chain tension ring and restoration of the balcony opening, ca. 1985. Photographer unknown. Frank Lloyd Wright Trust.

anything of interest discovered in the restoration, with measured drawings and photographs. By 1986 the Research Center housed over twelve thousand color slides documenting the building and its restoration.[73]

With major restoration work completed, a new era of activities began in the late 1980s that focused on the development of educational programs and interpretation of the building. As part of this initiative, I was hired by the Home and Studio Foundation as education director in 1988 to develop and oversee pro-

grams and produce educational materials. As part of an NEH grant to document the building's restoration, I helped organize a second conference of prominent Wright scholars in November 1990 to receive input on the next phase of the museum's development.[74]

Over the next four years I oversaw the development of a rich assortment of educational programs, primarily carried out by dedicated volunteers, that reached hundreds of people each year.[75] One of the most successful programs for well over two decades

E.15 Studio library during the restoration showing the remains of the fireplace, ca. 1985. Photographer unknown. Frank Lloyd Wright Trust.

was a summer architectural design workshop for junior high students.[76] Within the walls of the drafting room hundreds of future architects explored the basics of building design and the architecture of Frank Lloyd Wright. Over the course of three mornings, attendees completed Froebel block exercises and designed and produced a model of a house following Wright's Usonian principles.[77] Students intently worked at drafting tables in the same space where Wright and his employees, including Marion Mahony, William Drummond, Walter Burley Griffin, Barry Byrne, Charles White, and John Van Bergen, had produced designs for such spectacular buildings as the residences for Susan Lawrence Dana, Darwin and Isabelle Martin, and Avery and Queene Coonley and larger commissions, such as the Larkin building and Unity Temple. As the students discussed their innovative design ideas, one could imagine the voices of the architects who worked in the space a century earlier echoing in the room as the studio once again served as a lively space of architectural exploration.

However, the echoes reveal a major disconnect between the Oak Park studio as restored, largely frozen in time, and its rich past. Today there is little evidence of the evolving conditions of the building and the active life that took place within to help the more than ninety thousand annual visitors comprehend its role in the architect's professional development.[78] While the Oak Park studio's complex history is extremely difficult if not impossible to present in a standard forty-five-minute tour, there are other ways that this important story can be presented. One avenue is this book. Other potential ways include the use of innovative technologies. Virtual reality, for example, can help people visualize more fully the individual spaces at different stages of the building's life. The result is a richer understanding of the multilayer historic conditions of this prominent site and the activities that took place within that contributed so significantly to the formation of Wright's ideas on building design and more broadly to the development of modern architecture in the United States.

E.16 Students producing models of their Usonian houses in the studio drafting room during a summer architectural design workshop, 2013. Photographer: Lisa D. Schrenk.

Acknowledgments

I began researching the Oak Park studio many years ago while education director for the Frank Lloyd Wright Home and Studio Foundation (when I was fortunate to have my office located on the balcony of the drafting room), building upon the previous work of many other scholars. Grant Manson's pioneering publication *Frank Lloyd Wright to 1910: The First Golden Age*, H. Allen Brooks's explorations into the Prairie School, and Leonard Eaton's scholarship on Wright's clients provided major starting points, as did early research on the Oak Park studio by volunteers of the foundation, most prominently the work of Ann Abernathy, Bill Dring, Don Kalec, the late John Thorpe, and other members of the organization's restoration committee. While employed at the foundation, I had the opportunity to engage in discussions with many academics specializing in Wright's architecture who either served on the scholars' board for the organization or came to Oak Park to complete research or present lectures on aspects relating to the architect's life and work. These included Peter Goss, Donald Hoffman, Dana Hutt, Neil Levine, Jack Quinan, Paul Sprague, David Van Zanten, and the late Leonard Eaton and Grant Manson. Anthony Alofsin strongly encouraged me to continue my work on the studio after leaving the Chicago area for the warmer environment of Texas to pursue my doctorate. More recent works on the Oak Park studio by Van Zanten and Paul Kruty greatly contributed to my understanding of the role education played in Wright's early office. Christopher Vernon generously shared insights and information on Griffin's role in the studio. Patti Cordell, Donald Morgan, Jan Korell, and Jeremy Daniels, meanwhile, furnished information relating to the Sutton house, and Sunny Hall met with me and described her experience living with several other women in an apartment on the second floor of Wright's Forest Avenue home in the late 1960s. Doug Carr, James Caulfield, Mary Jane Hamilton, Richard Heurtley, Rick McNees, and James Robinson all generously contributed photographs. Nancy Later, George Roupe, and Paul Turner provided help in shaping this work, while Kevin Harrington imparted invaluable encouragement and guidance over many years. Susannah Marie Engstrom, Caterina MacLean, and Tim Mennel at the University of Chicago Press were invaluable in the realization of this publication.

Many other colleagues and volunteers at the Frank Lloyd Wright Home and Studio provided support in the realization of this work, including Susan Allen, Cheryl Bachand, David Bagnall, Melanie Birk, Patrick Cannon, Donna Christy, Roger Christy, Lisa Dodge, Linda Gamble, Elaine Harrington, Meg Klinkow, Bill Kundert, Jack Lesniak, Ann Mahron, Judy Mason, Bill McDonald, Mary McLeod, Jerry McManus, Lisa Stern, Karen Sweeney, Janet Van Delft, Jennifer Wheeler, the late Jeanette Fields and Richard Twiss, and many more. Former Frank Lloyd Wright Home and Studio interns helped in digging for the truth, in particular Sonal Dave, Julie Jessen, and Maggie Kelly; student research assistants Bianca Bryant, Dionna Hatch, Melissa Jensen, Erica LeClaire, Andre Rioux, Katie Roch, and Juliana Seymour also greatly contributed to various aspects of the work. Keiran Murphy, Margo Stipe, and the late Bruce Brooks Pfeiffer at Taliesin were incredibly helpful, as were Pamala Casey, Mathieu Pomerleau, Janet Parks, Katherine Prater, Nicole Richard, and Christine Sala at the Avery Architectural and Fine Arts Library; Cheryll Fong and Alan Lathrop at the Northwest Architectural Archives; Dorothy Shields at the University of Michigan; Serena Washington, Kevin Whiteneir, and Mary Woolever at the Ryerson and Burnham Libraries; Bill Jerousek, Emily Reiher, Alexandra Skinner, and Leigh A. Tarullo at the Oak Park Public Library; Miriam Cady at the Henry Ford Museum; William Offhaus and Grace Trimper at the State University of New York, Buffalo; Deb Alhers, Wendy Cox, Daniel Doz, and Art Schaller at Norwich University; Cheryl Cuillier and Mary Feeney at the University of Arizona Library; Sharon Grimes at the Richard W. Bock Sculpture Museum, Greenville College; Tim Ladwig at the Milwaukee Art Museum; and Jan Cervelli, Laura Hollengreen, Robert Miller, Nancy Pollock-Ellwand, and Clare Robinson, in the College of Architecture, Landscape Architecture and Planning at the University of Arizona. Cheryl Bryan, John Dalles, and James Robinson, meanwhile, provided additional information on studio employees. Financial support for this publication included a "We the People" Summer Stipend from the National Endowment of the Humanities, a sabbatical from Norwich University, and funding from the Provost's Office; the College of Architecture, Landscape Architecture and Planning; and the School of Architecture at the University of Arizona. Additional friends and family provided various forms of assistance, including Cheryl Browne, Tom Browne, Karen Hyde, Jan Roberg, Catherine Roy, Rob Roy, and Mark Witzling. My greatest supporters have been family members, including parents, Ann and Lorenz Schrenk; siblings, Janet and Stephen; and partner, Steven Weis—yes it still does take a rocket scientist.

I am especially appreciative for the time that Wright family members shared with me. I spent an enjoyable afternoon listening to Wright's son David, at the age of ninety-nine, recall stories growing up in Oak Park when I visited him and his wife Gladys in his Phoenix home. Wright's nephew and namesake, Franklin Porter, met with me several times and generously entrusted to my care a family scrapbook that belonged to his grandmother Anna Wright, which I hand-delivered to Taliesin West for him. It now resides in the Avery Library at Columbia University, far from its proper home in Oak Park. Within its pages are family mementos, including the heartfelt letter Wright wrote to his mother while in Italy in 1910 (see appendix D) and an uncropped version of a photograph of Catherine's dayroom in the Oak Park home, which helped to initiate the reconstruction of the restored built-in wardrobes located on each side of the room so that they project slightly forward. Without the help of all of these people the creation of this long overdue book would not have been possible.

Abbreviations

AIC: Ryerson and Burnham Libraries, Art Institute of Chicago

BBC-CHM: Barry Byrne Collection, Chicago History Museum

CAP-KCC: Charles Robert Ashbee Papers, King's College, Cambridge

DMP-UB: Darwin Martin and Martin Family Papers, State University of New York, Buffalo

LEC-UMI: Leonard Eaton Collection, Bentley Library, University of Michigan

FLW-AAL: Frank Lloyd Wright Papers (Archives), Avery Architectural and Fine Arts Library, Columbia University

FLWHSF: Frank Lloyd Wright Home and Studio Foundation / Frank Lloyd Wright Trust

FLWHSRC: Frank Lloyd Wright Home and Studio Foundation Research Center

GMC-OPPL: Grant Carpenter Manson Collection, Oak Park Public Library

JLW-AAL: John Lloyd Wright Papers, Avery Architectural and Fine Arts Library, Columbia University

JLW-OPPL: John Lloyd Wright Collection, Oak Park Public Library

JSAH: *Journal of the Society of Architectural Historians*

MIT: Massachusetts Institute of Technology

MPP-AAL: Mark L. Peisch Papers, Avery Architectural and Fine Arts Library, Columbia University

RSC-GRL: Rudolf Schindler Collection, Getty Research Library

TWC-UU: Taylor Woolley Collection, University of Utah

WGPP-NWAA: William Gray Purcell Papers, Northwest Architectural Archives

WWP-UO: Walter R. B. Willcox Papers, University of Oregon

Appendix A: Architectural Designs Carried Out in the Oak Park Studio

This is not intended to be a definitive inventory but is included to present a basic picture of the work carried out in Wright's Oak Park studio. Unfortunately, only minimal office records survive and attaching specific years to projects is especially difficult, as the studio staff typically did not date drawings. Wright, however, added dates to some, often years later. Many of these additions have proven to be inaccurate. Hence, dates given here, which derive from a variety of sources, including records in the Frank Lloyd Wright Archives at the Avery Library and at the Frank Lloyd Wright Home and Studio, as well as publications by William Storrer and others, should not be considered indisputable. For more details on individual drawings, see *Frank Lloyd Wright Complete Works*, vol. 1, *1885–1916*, ed. Bruch Brooks Pfeiffer (Cologne: Taschen, 2011). An asterisk at the end of an entry indicates that the project likely remained unrealized.

Pre-1900

Frank Lloyd Wright studio	Oak Park, IL	1897–98[1]
Sue and George W. Furbeck house	Oak Park, IL	1897–98[2]
George Smith house	Oak Park, IL	1898[3]
River Forest Golf Club	River Forest, IL	1898
Mary and Edward C. Waller house remodeling	River Forest, IL	1899[4]
Abraham Lincoln Center (with Dwight Perkins)	Chicago, IL	1898–1903[5]
Joseph and Helen Husser house	Chicago, IL	1899
Aline and David Devin house	Highland Park, IL area	1898 or 1899*[6]
Mary and Edward C. Waller house remodeling	River Forest, IL	1898*
Mozart Garden restaurant remodeling	Chicago, IL	1898*
Robert Eckhart house	River Forest, IL	1899*
Cheltenham Beach Resort	Chicago, IL	1899*

1900

Jessie M. and William Adams house	Chicago, IL	1900–1901
Anna and B. Harley Bradley house ["Glenlloyd"]	Kankakee, IL	1900
Stephen A. Foster house and stable	Chicago, IL	1900
Georgiana and Warren Hickox house	Kankakee, IL	1900
Mary and Edward R. Hills house remodeling	Oak Park, IL	1900–1901
Fred B. Jones house ["Penwern"]	Delavan, WI	1900–2

Fred B. Jones barn	Delavan, WI	1900-1901
Fred B. Jones boathouse	Delavan, WI	1900
Minnie and Warren McArthur remodeling and garage	Chicago, IL	1900
Minnie and Henry Wallis cottage	Delavan, WI	1900
Dwelling	Oakland, CA	1900*

1901

Susan and E[dward] Arthur Davenport house	River Forest, IL	1901
Delia and William G. Fricke house	Oak Park, IL	1901
Nellie and Frank B. Henderson house	Elmhurst, IL	1901
Fred B. Jones gate lodge	Delavan, WI	1901
Susan and Frank W. Thomas [James C. Rogers] house	Oak Park, IL	1901[7]
Mary and Edward C. Waller gates	River Forest, IL	1901
Mary and Edward C. Waller poultry house and stables	River Forest, IL	1901
Anna and Thomas Edward Wilder Stable building	Elmhurst, IL	1901[8]
Milton H. Lowell house	Matteawan, NY	1901*
Minnie and Henry Wallis house	Riverside, IL	1901*
Minnie and Henry Wallis gatehouse	Delavan, WI	1901*
Lexington Terrace apartments	Chicago, IL	1901*[9]
"A Home in a Prairie Town"	(Ladies' Home Journal)	1901*
"A Small House with 'Lots of Room in It'"	(Ladies' Home Journal)	1901*
Quadruple block plan	(Ladies' Home Journal)	1901*
Monolithic concrete bank		1901*[10]

1902

Susan Lawrence Dana house	Springfield, IL	1902–4
Grace and Arthur B. Heurtley house	Oak Park, IL	1902
Grace and Arthur B. Heurtley cottage remodeling	Marquette Island, MI	1902
Dr. Alfred W. Hebert house remodeling	Evanston, IL	1902
Mary and George Gerts cottage	Whitehall, MI	1902
Walter Gerts cottage	Whitehall, MI	1902
Mary and Francis W. Little house I	Peoria, IL	1902–3
Winifred and William E. Martin house	Oak Park, IL	1902–3
E. H. Pitkin Summer Lodge (cottage)[11]	Sapper Island, Ontario	1902
Charles S. Ross house	Delavan, WI	1902
George W. Spencer cottage	Delavan, WI	1902
Cecelia and Ward W. Willits house	Highland Park, IL	1902–3
Hillside Home School II	Spring Green, WI	1902
Lake Delavan Yacht Club	Delavan, WI	1902
Board and Batten house	Oak Park, IL	1902*
Mary and Francis W. Little summer house	Lake Minnetonka, MN	1902*[12]
Mary and Victor E. Metzger house	Sault Ste. Marie, MI	1902*
John A. Mosher house		1902*[13]
Edward C. Waller summer house	Charlevoix, MI	1902–3*
Dial Offices remodeling	Chicago, IL	1902*
Lake Delavan Clubhouse	Delavan, WI	1902*

1903

Delta and George F. Barton house	Buffalo, NY	1903–4
Mamah and Edwin H. Cheney house	Oak Park, IL	1903
Mary and William R. Heath house	Buffalo, NY	1903–5
Robert M. Lamp house	Madison, WI	1903
Mary and Francis W. Little stable	Peoria, IL	1903
Isabelle and Darwin D. Martin carriage house	Buffalo, NY	1903–5
Isabelle and Darwin D. Martin conservatory	Buffalo, NY	1903–5
Isabelle and Darwin D. Martin pergola	Buffalo, NY	1903–5
Isabelle and Darwin D. Martin house	Buffalo, NY	1903–5
Sadie [Sarah] and Joseph J. Walser Jr. house	Chicago, IL	1903
Scoville Park Horse Show fountain (with Richard Bock)	Oak Park, IL	1903
Larkin Administration Company building	Buffalo, NY	1903–6
Artist's house		1903 (1906?)*[14]
Flora and Warren H. Freeman house	Hinsdale, IL	1903*
Charles E. Roberts block plan	Oak Park, IL	1903*

1904

Frank L. Smith [First National] bank	Dwight, IL	1904–5
Charles and Rose Barnes house	McCook, NE	1904*
Cora and Robert D. Clarke house	Peoria, IL	1904*
Robert Lamp "Dwelling for Investment"	Madison, WI	1904*
Mary and Francis W. Little house	Peoria, IL	1904*[15]
J. A. Scudder Summer Lodge (cottage) Island Encampment	d'Ours, ON	1904*
Soden house	Unknown	~1904*[16]
Clara and Herbert J. Ullman house	Oak Park, IL	1904–5*
Wood and Plaster house	Highland Park, IL	1904*
Larkin Company workmen's row housing	Buffalo, NY	1904*
Study for Brick and Concrete Building	Glencoe, IL	1904*

1905

Mary W. Adams house	Highland Park, IL	1905
Agnes and Hiram Baldwin house	Kenilworth, IL	1905
Charles A. Brown house	Evanston, IL	1905
Cora and William A. Glasner house	Glencoe, IL	1905
Thomas P. Hardy house	Racine, WI	1905
Arthur P. Johnson house	Delavan, WI	1905
Isabelle and Darwin D. Martin Gardener cottage	Buffalo, NY	1905–8
Eliza and Harvey P. Sutton house	McCook, NE	1905
Emily and Ferdinand [Fred] Tomek house	Riverside, IL	1905–6[17]
Edmund A. Cummings real estate office	River Forest, IL	1905
E-Z Polish Factory building	Chicago, IL	1905
Lawrence Memorial Library room remodeling	Springfield, IL	1905[18]
Rookery building lobby and atrium remodeling	Chicago, IL	1905
Unity Temple	Oak Park, IL	1905–9
Board and batten double house	Oak Park, IL	1905*
[Ruby and Clarence?] Darrow house	Chicago Area?	1905*[19]

T. E. Gilpin house	Oak Park, IL	1905*
Frank Martin house	Buffalo, NY	1905*
Warren McArthur apartments	Chicago, IL	1905*
Anna and Nathan G. Moore pergola and pavilion	Oak Park, IL	1905*
Clarence Buckingham office alterations	Chicago, IL	1905*
Single-story varnish factory		1905*[20]
Yahara River boathouse	Madison, WI	1905*

1906

Emma and Peter A. Beachy house	Oak Park, IL	1906
Kersey C. DeRhodes house	South Bend, IL	1906
A. W. Gridley house ["Ravine house"]	Batavia, IL	1906
Edward R. Hills house remodeling	Oak Park, IL	1906
P. D. Hoyt house	Geneva, IL	1906
Alice and George M. Millard house	Highland Park, IL	1906
Frederick D. Nichols house	Flossmoor, IL	1906
Orpha and Burton J. Westcott house	Springfield, OH	1906–8
[William H.] Pettit Mortuary Chapel	Belvidere, IL	1906–7[21]
River Forest Tennis Club rebuilding	River Forest, IL	1906
Carrie and George W. Blossom barn	Hyde Park, IL	1906*
Richard Bock residence and studio	Maywood Village, IL	1906*
Harry E. Brown residence	Geneseo, IL	1906*
Aline and David Devin summer cottage	Eliot, ME	1906*
Frazer house	Oak Park, IL	1906*
Grace Fuller house	Glencoe, IL	1906*[22]
Walter Gerts house	Glencoe, IL	1906*
Roland S. Ludington house	Dwight, IL	1906*
Joseph Seidenbecher cottage	Chicago, IL	1906*
C. Thaxter Shaw house	Montreal, QC	1906*
C. Thaxter Shaw house remodeling	Montreal, QC	1906*
Elizabeth Stone house	Lake Forest, IL	1906*

1907

Carrie and George W. Blossom garage	Hyde Park, IL	1907
Queene and Avery Coonley house	Riverside, IL	1907
Queene and Avery Coonley gardener's cottage	Riverside, IL	1907
Queene and Avery Coonley stable	Riverside, IL	1907 (rebuilt 1911)
Grace and Stephen M. B. Hunt house	La Grange, IL	1907
Nelle and Col. George Fabyan remodeling	Geneva, IL	1907
Emma Martin garage	Oak Park, IL	1907[23]
Jane and Andrew T. Porter house ["Tanyderi"]	Spring Green, WI	1907[24]
Fox River Country Club addition	Geneva, IL	1907
Larkin Company pavilion, Jamestown Tercentenary Exhibition	Norfolk, VA	1907
Pebbles & Balch store remodeling	Oak Park, IL	1907
Lake Delavan cottage	Lake Delavan, WI	1907*
Edith and Harold McCormick house	Lake Forest, IL	1907*
"Fireproof House for $5000"	(*Ladies' Home Journal*)	1907*

1908

Edward E. Boynton house	Rochester, NY	1908[25]
Edith and Edmund D. Brigham house and stable/garage	Glencoe, IL	1908–9[26]
Frances and William H. Copeland garage	Oak Park, IL	1908
Christiana and Walter V. Davidson house	Buffalo, NY	1908
Raymond W. Evans house	Chicago, IL	1908
Blanche and Eugene A. Gilmore house ["Airplane house"]	Madison, WI	1908
Lena Kent and Samuel Horner house	Chicago, IL	1908
Sophie and Meyer S. May house	Grand Rapids, MI	1908–9
Isabel and Mary Roberts house	River Forest, IL	1908
Lora and Frederick C. Robie house	Chicago, IL	1908–10
Dr. George and Eleanor Stockman house	Mason City, IA	1908
[Maurice] Browne bookstore	Chicago, IL	1908[27]
William Norman Guthrie house	Sewanee, TN	1908*
Mary and Francis Little summer house	Minnetonka, MN	1908*[28]
Mary and Francis Little boathouse, stables, gardener's cottage	Minnetonka, MN	1908*
Horseshoe Inn	Estes Park, CO	1908*[29]

1909[30]

Frank J. Baker house	Wilmette, IL	1909
Hiram Baldwin house	Kenilworth, IL	1909
Cora and Robert D. Clarke stable remodeling	Peoria, IL	1909[31]
Frances and William H. Copeland remodeling	Oak Park, IL	1909
Laura Robeson Gale house	Oak Park, IL	1909[32]
Laura Robeson Gale rental cottages I–III	Whitehall, MI	1909–10
Florence and J[ames] Kibben Ingalls house	River Forest, IL	1909
Florence and Edward P. Irving house	Decatur, IL	1909
Winifred and William E. Martin pergola	Oak Park, IL	1909
Louisa and Ingwald [Ingvald] Moe house	Gary, IN	1909–10
Oscar M. Steffens house	Chicago, IL	1909
Emily and George C. Stewart house	Montecito, CA	1909
Bitter Root Inn	Near Stevensville, MT	1909
City National Bank building and hotel	Mason City, IA	1909–10
Como Orchard Summer Colony cottages	University Heights, Darby, MT	1909
Como Orchard Summer Colony land office	University Heights, Darby, MT	1909
Como Orchards Club house	University Heights, Darby, MT	1909
W. Scott Thurber Art Gallery	Chicago, IL	1909[33]
Peter C. Stohr Arcade building	Chicago, IL	1909
Mary and Edward C. Waller bathing pavilion	Charlevoix, MI	1909
Mary Ellen Larwill house	Muskegon, MI	1909*
Isabelle and Darwin D. Martin summer cottage	Lake Erie, NY	1909*
Minnie and Joshua G. Melson house	Mason City, IA	1909*
Mary Roberts house	River Forest, IL	1909*[34]
Mary and Edward C. Waller houses	River Forest, IL	1909*
Village of Bitter Root	Bitter Root, MT	1909*
Lawton Parker studio remodeling	New York, NY	1909*
Lexington Terrace apartments	Chicago, IL	1909*[35]

1. The Oak Park studio was in operation by February 1898.
2. The George Furbeck commission was in Wright's office at the time the studio opened. His brother Rollin had already moved into the house Wright designed for him in Oak Park by October 1897.
3. The Smith house was built in 1898, although the design may date from a couple years earlier.
4. Wright produced two remodeling designs for a timber and shingle residence in River Forest owned by the Wallers that was designed by Burnham and Root in 1883, an unrealized scheme in 1898 and a realized one the following year.
5. Wright's earliest known connection to this project is a letter to his uncle Jenkin Lloyd Jones dated 15 May 1894.
6. While 1896 is often given as a date for the Devin house, it does not fit with the story of Aline Devin and young Catherine Wright (see chapter 3) or Wright's architectural development.
7. Rogers commissioned the house for his daughter Susan and her husband Frank Thomas.
8. Scholars, including Christopher Vernon, have suggested that the Wilder stables building was most likely designed by Walter Burley Griffin while in Wright's office.
9. Commissioned by Edward C. Waller.
10. Published as a brick building in *Brickbuilder* in August 1901.
11. While this commission has been labeled in different ways, including as a residence and a lodge, the terms "cottage" and "summer home" best describe the design.
12. This was a small cruciform design similar to the Charles Ross house.
13. Location unknown. Wright may have designed a house for John Mosher built in Wellington, Ohio.
14. Wright labeled the plan of this design "Artist's Cottage/1906," which he then revised and included on the same plate as the Cheney house plan in the Wasmuth portfolio.
15. Designed for a lot in Peoria on the same street as the 1903 Little house.
16. Drawing in the Frank Lloyd Wright Papers at the Avery Library dates the house "about 1904."
17. First contact between the Tomeks and the Oak Park studio may have been in 1904.
18. Commissioned by Susan Lawrence Dana in honor of her father Rheuna Lawrence within a preexisting primary school.
19. Drawings are labeled "Mrs. Darrow, North Shore." Some scholars believe that the drawings were for Ruby, the wife of Chicago lawyer Clarence Darrow, an acquaintance of Wright's. It has also been suggested that the drawings show an early scheme for the Joseph Seidenbecher house.
20. Intended location unknown.
21. Commissioned by Emma Glasner Pettit in honor of her deceased husband.
22. It is not clear if the Fuller house was actually built or remained a project.
23. Emma Martin was the second owner of the Fricke house (1901).
24. An early scheme for the Porters recalls house designs by Walter Burley Griffin around this time. Jane Porter later identified the studio architect involved in the realized design as Barry Byrne.
25. Boynton's adult daughter Beulah served as client with her father on the design.
26. The Brigham house was built of reinforced concrete. Plans and a photograph of the completed house were published in the Universal Portland Cement Company's monthly bulletin number 74 in July 1910.
27. Built in the Fine Arts Building, Chicago.
28. Wright went on to create a residential design that the Littles built on Lake Minnetonka in Deephaven, Minnesota, in 1912. Known as Northome, this house is often referred to as the Little II residence.
29. Note on one of the four drawings of this project added years later states "Willard Ashton Ranch Type Bldg. 1908."
30. Many of the 1909 studio designs were completed by others, including Marion Mahony under Hermann von Holst.
31. This was a remodeling of the stable at the Little house in Peoria that the Clarkes had bought from the Littles.
32. Laura Gale was the widow of realtor Thomas Gale.
33. Built in the Fine Arts Building, Chicago.
34. Mary Roberts is most likely the mother of Isabel Roberts.
35. Revision of the 1901 Lexington Terrace apartment project for Edward C. Waller.

Appendix B: Time Line of Architects in the Studio

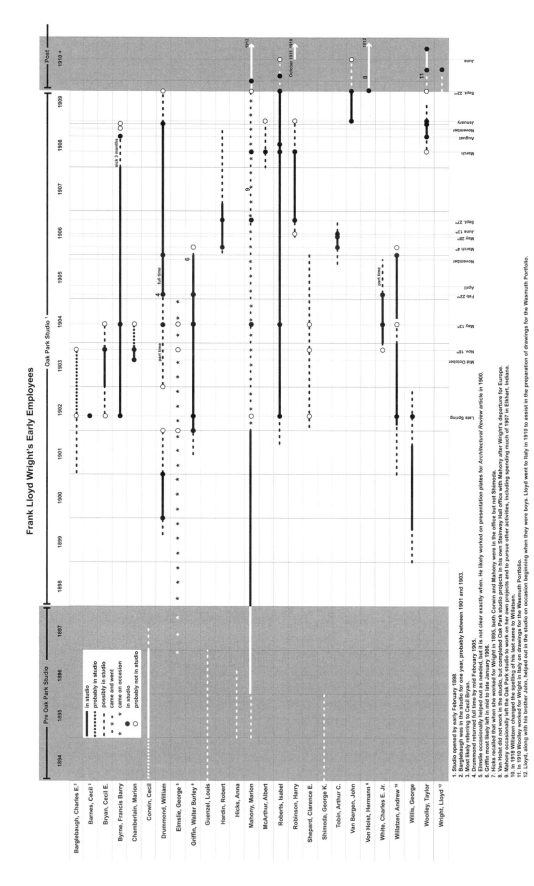

Frank Lloyd Wright's Early Employees

1. Studio opened by early February 1898.
2. Barglebaugh was in the studio for one year, probably between 1901 and 1903.
3. Most likely referring to Cecil Bryan.
4. Drummond returned full time by mid February 1905.
5. Elmslie occasionally helped out as needed. He likely worked on presentation plates for *Architectural Review* article in 1900.
6. Griffin most likely left in mid to late January 1906.
7. Hicks recalled that when she worked for Wright in 1895, both Corwin and Mahony were in the office but not Shimoda.
8. Van Holst did not work in the studio, but completed Oak Park studio projects in his own Steinway Hall office with Mahony after Wright's departure for Europe.
9. Mahony occasionally left the Oak Park studio to work on her own projects and to pursue other activities, including spending much of 1907 in Elkhart, Indiana.
10. In 1918 Willatzen changed the spelling of his last name to Willatsen.
11. In 1910 Woolley worked for Wright in Italy on drawings for the Wasmuth Portfolio.
12. Lloyd, along with his brother John, helped out in the studio on occasion beginning when they were boys. Lloyd went to Italy in 1910 to assist in the preparation of drawings for the Wasmuth Portfolio.

This time line traces the presence of the different architects who worked in Frank Lloyd Wright's Oak Park studio. In almost all cases the exact date of when they entered and departed is unknown, although there are a few dates for which a list does survive naming the office staff. In a couple cases, architects have been identified as having worked in the studio, but there is no supporting evidence to confirm their presence.

Appendix C: Biographies of Those Involved in the Oak Park Studio

In 1914, Frank Lloyd Wright wrote that "fifteen good, bad, and indifferent" architects passed through his Oak Park studio.[1] He later recalled "thirty or more" people participated in the production of his building designs there.[2] A partial list of studio draftsmen the architect published in 1908 includes Marion Mahony, William Drummond, Francis [Barry] Byrne, Isabel Roberts, George Willis, Walter [Burley] Griffin, Andrew Willatzen, Harry Robinson, Charles E. White, Jr., [Charles] Erwin Barglebaugh, Robert Hardin, and Albert McArthur. It does not, however, include people who were in the studio for a brief period, helped out only on occasion, or entered the office after 1908.[3] Over twenty-five architects and artists have been identified as working in the studio at some point between 1898 and 1909, each making his or her own contributions and experiencing their own unique relationships with their employer. Women account for at least five of Wright's early employees, a most unusual fact, as at the time few architects were willing to hire female designers. Records indicate, however, that in the final years of the studio all new hires were male, although Roberts and Mahony (intermittently) continued to work for Wright.

Many of the studio workers immigrated to the United States or were first-generation Americans with fathers in a building trade. Most had completed some formal architectural training. After departing from Wright's office, they typically continued to design prairie-style houses, often following the general trend toward a greater reliance upon historic vocabularies in the 1920s and incorporating more modern forms in subsequent years. Only a few, like Byrne and Griffin, went on to developed their own distinct architectural identity. When commissions dried up in the 1930s, first due to the depressed economy and then to World War II, several of the designers ended their careers in positions with the Works Progress Administration, the Chicago Housing Authority, or another government agency.

Oak Park Studio Architects

CHARLES ERWIN BARGLEBAUGH (1881–1927)

Charles Barglebaugh completed some formal design training in 1901 while enrolled in a preparatory program in architecture and architectural engineering at the University of Illinois Academy.[4] Although little is known about his contribution to the studio, Wright included Barglebaugh's name in his 1908 list of former employees, stating he had been in the office for one year, probably between 1901 and 1903.[5] Barglebaugh may have briefly worked for Walter Burley Griffin before heading to Houston around 1905 to work for Glenn Allen.[6] Between 1907 and 1917 he worked for the Dallas firm of Lang and Witchell designing courthouses and likely a series of prairie-styled houses, including the Higginbotham house (Dallas, ca. 1913). Its design strongly recalled Wright's William Heath house, a project on the boards around the time of Barglebaugh's employment in Oak Park.[7] During World War I, he oversaw the design of concrete ships.[8] After the war Barglebaugh formed a partnership with Lloyd R. Whitson in El Paso, with branch offices in Dallas and Houston. The firm designed several prominent reinforced concrete buildings, including the Hogg Building in Houston (1920).

CECIL ELDRIDGE BRYAN (1878–1951)

Cecil Bryan received training from his father, a builder whose work included many large homes in Russellville, Arkansas, and stations for the Continental Railroad, before moving to Chicago to attend engineering classes at the Lewis Institute.[9] Given the moniker "the Southerner" by Charles White, Bryan entered the Oak Park studio in 1902.[10] He did not stay long and had departed by May 1904, accepting a more lucrative position working as a building superintendent for Ralph Modjeski, a prominent Polish-American civil engineer and pioneer in the use of reinforced concrete and in bridge design.[11] Bryan went on to open a successful engineering office, working on designs for bank buildings, hotels, bridges, churches, waterworks, and railroad structures.[12] Believing it was "better to honor the dead above ground than in the earth," he began designing concrete mausoleums in 1912 and went on to complete approximately eighty commissions for cemeteries throughout the United States.[13] After his death in 1951 his remains were interred in his spectacular Mountain View Mausoleum in Altadena, California.

(FRANCIS) BARRY BYRNE (1883–1967)

As a young boy growing up in Chicago, Francis Xavier Ignatius Loyola Walter Barry Byrne became fascinated by the large commercial buildings he saw going up in the city and after attending the 1893 World's Columbian Exposition realized that he would be "desperately, desperately unhappy" if he could not be an architect.[14] He sought employment in the Oak Park studio after viewing Wright's designs on display in the spring 1902 Chicago Architectural Club exhibition.[15]

Although he had no prior training, Byrne learned quickly, eventually becoming responsible for producing working drawings and supervising construction. Peritonitis kept him away from the studio for three months in 1908, but he returned briefly before quitting permanently in August of that year to work for Walter Burley Griffin.[16] By November he had departed Chicago for Seattle, forming a partnership with former studio colleague Andrew Willatzen that lasted until early 1913. Byrne then moved to San Diego, living with Wright's eldest sons, Lloyd and John, but returned to Chicago in 1914 to take over Griffin's office.[17]

After serving in World War I, he opened his own architectural practice and construction company, designing buildings for Catholic institutions, including the all-girls Immaculata High School and St. Thomas the Apostle Church, both in Chicago. Learning from his work on Unity Temple,

Byrne sought to integrate Catholic clergy and parishioners in one unifying space by projecting the altar forward into the auditorium—anticipating reforms adopted at the Second Vatican Council by forty years. He increasingly favored expressionistic forms and broad and unadorned expanses of wall accentuated by areas of sculpture. With fewer commissions in the 1930s Byrne began working as a building inspector and supervisor for a government agency. He also began writing articles that appeared in both religious and design publications, including a regular column on the arts in the Catholic *America* magazine and pieces for *Liturgical Arts* and *Commonweal*.[18]

MARION LINCOLN LEWIS CHAMBERLAIN LEE (1874–1947)

Born Marion Lincoln Lewis in South Natick, Massachusetts, Chamberlain entered MIT at the age of seventeen with sophomore standing, graduating with a degree in architecture in 1896, two years after Marion Mahony, who described her friend as "a most beautiful girl of the Burne-Jones type," and in the same class as Hermann von Holst.[19] Her thesis project, "A Women's Club House," presented a grand Beaux Arts exterior topped by a mansard roof.[20] During her final year in school, she worked as a draftsman for local architect T. M. Clark.[21] Like many women studying architecture at the end of the nineteenth century, Chamberlain had a difficult time entering the field, instead finding employment as a librarian in McKim, Mead and White's recently completed Boston Public Library. She resigned in September 1898 to marry architect Herbert W. Chamberlain. The couple traveled to Europe to study architecture in Italy, where the following May Herbert contracted peritonitis and died.[22] Chamberlain returned to the United States and her librarian position. A second trip to Europe in 1903 reignited her interest in architecture, and by mid-October she had joined Mahony in Wright's studio.[23] Chamberlain's tenure in the office was brief. By the following May she was back in the East. She again worked as a librarian, including at the Avery Architectural Library at Columbia University and as dean of a college dorm, until marrying noted Boston librarian, photographer, and social reform advocate Francis Watts Lee in July 1911.[24] They had two children. Likely frustrated with the limitation of domestic life, she experienced growing anxiety, and her behavior at times became erratic. In 1928 she traveled to the Panama Canal on her own. She died nineteen years later. Her remains were interred at Mount Auburn Cemetery near Boston.[25]

WILLIAM EUGENE DRUMMOND (1876–1948)

Born in Newark, New Jersey, Drummond arrived in the Austin neighborhood of Chicago just east of Oak Park at the age of ten. After only two years of high school, he dropped out and began working with his father, a carpenter and cabinet-maker.[26] He attended preparatory classes at the University of Illinois Academy for a year prior to enrolling in the university's engineering program for the 1897–98 school year.[27] Lacking funds to continue, he spent several months working in the office of Adler and Sullivan before entering the Oak Park studio in late 1899.[28]

Drummond learned quickly, and architects highly valued his skills. In addition to Wright, he worked for Richard Schmidt in 1901 and 1902 and later part time for D.H. Burnham.[29] He continued, however, to help out in the Oak Park studio when needed, returning full time by 1905. Despite being viewed as difficult, Drummond became chief draftsman and project manager for many of Wright's commissions, including the Cheney and Robie residences, as well as the Larkin building.[30] He also worked with Barry Byrne on Wright's 1905 remodeling of the Rookery. Details of Drummond's final departure from the Oak Park studio around early 1909 involved harsh words prompted by a lack of back pay.[31]

Drummond's initial independent commission, the First Congregational Church of Austin in 1907–8, shares corner stair piers and similar decorative elements with Unity Temple, on which he was serving as job superintendent at the time. He established his own firm in fall 1909, picking up many clients, such as Avery and Queenie Coonley, who otherwise would have likely turned to Wright if available. Around 1912 he entered into a three-year partnership with architect Louis Guenzel, who had previously worked for Adler and Sullivan and may have briefly worked for Wright in the mid-1890s.[32] Drummond served as the primary designer in the firm, which produced many buildings for River Forest.[33]

In the 1910s, Drummond entered a number of design competitions, including one for the German Embassy in Washington, DC, and two sponsored by the City Club of Chicago. In 1922 he submitted an odd-looking entry to the prominent Chicago Tribune Building competition that architectural scholar Carl Condit exclaimed "defies the descriptive powers of the historian" as its "panoply of columns, garlands, and statues" culminated in an "orgiastic tower."[34] Around this time, Drummond began relying more on historical forms, as reflected in his Elizabethan-style public library (1928) and the large, picturesque Vilas (1926) and Scott (1928) houses in River Forest.

Drummond had significantly fewer commissions in the 1930s and '40s and struggled to maintain his practice. He became a specification specialist and a member of the River Forest planning commission. He remodeled the lobby and interior office spaces of the Rookery Building in 1931, completing the work with the help of Barry Byrne and Byrne's wife, Annette. Drummond's last major project consisted of a series of unrealized plans for the US Capitol building, published in a twenty-two-page pamphlet in 1946.[35]

GEORGE GRANT ELMSLIE (1869–1952)

Born in Aberdeenshire, Scotland, George Grant Elmslie immigrated to Chicago as a boy. He began his architectural training as an apprentice under William LeBaron Jenney before joining Wright in the office of Joseph Lyman Silsbee in 1887. He followed his officemate to Adler and Sullivan, working under Louis Sullivan for more than twenty years, completing much of the design and ornament for works such as the National Farmers' Bank (1907–8) in Owatonna, Minnesota. Although not a regular Oak Park studio employee, in the early years, Elmslie would help out when an extra hand was needed, such as on drawings for the 1900 *Architectural Review* article on Wright.[36]

After leaving Sullivan in 1909, Elmslie formed a partnership headquartered in Minneapolis with William Purcell, whom he had met while both were working for Sullivan, and Purcell's college friend George Feick Jr.[37] That fall they declined an offer to take over the Oak Park studio. Feick left the firm in 1912, while the other two partners continued to practice together until 1921. They designed a series of prairie-style residences, banks, and churches, primarily for small towns in the Midwest, as well as the spectacular Woodbury County Courthouse in Sioux City, Iowa (1915–17) with William L. Steele. Elmslie's independent work in the late 1920s and 1930s included a number of educational projects, highlighted by a series of campus buildings for Yankton College in South Dakota. The American Institute of Architects elected Elmslie a fellow in 1947.

WALTER BURLEY GRIFFIN (1876–1937)

Walter Burley Griffin was born in Maywood, Illinois, and attended Oak Park High School.[38] During a visit to the 1893 World's Columbian Exposition while still a teenager, Griffin became fascinated by the fair pavilions and their picturesque setting.[39] Advised by the landscape gardener O.C. Simonds to pursue a degree in architecture, as no formal program in landscape architecture yet existed, Griffin attended the University of Illinois, earning top grades in his classes, which included horticulture and forestry in addition to building design. He served as president of the school's Architect's Club and was inducted into the engineering honor society, Tau Beta Pi, before receiving a BS in architecture in 1899.[40] A few months later he found work in Steinway Hall as a part-time draftsman for Dwight Perkins. He also worked for Robert C. Spencer Jr., Adamo Boari, and Webster Tomlinson. Around the time he passed the Illinois architects' licensing examination in July 1901, Griffin accepted his first major commission, a campus plan for Eastern Illinois State Normal School in Charleston, Illinois.

Sometime in 1901, most likely in late summer, Griffin joined the Oak Park studio, possibly with some form of partnership arrangement with its owner.[41] Wright initially found a kindred spirit in the mild-mannered architect, as both men strove for a close relationship between building and nature in their work. Griffin served as office manager, supervising local construction work and producing landscape plans for several prominent projects.[42] He also completed several independent residential commissions, including the W. H. Emery house in Elmhurst, Illinois (1903). Griffin left the studio in early 1906 and opened his own office in Steinway Hall, primarily designing single-family residences for the Chicago area.[43] There he eventually reunited with Oak Park studio colleague Marion Mahony, and the two married in 1911.

Griffin's interest in town planning and landscape architecture is illustrated in his sensitive layout for Rock Crest / Rock Glen in Mason City, Iowa (1912), and in his winning entry for the design of the Australian capitol of Canberra (1912). He departed for Australia in 1913 to oversee the realization of the design. Turning down an offer to head the architectural program at the University of Illinois, he chose instead to open an office in Australia, where he worked for the next twenty-one years.[44] Projects included a series of incinerators; the community center at Newman College, Melbourne (1915–17); and the town plan for Castlecrag, a suburb of Sydney (1921–35). After receiving the commission to design a library for the University of Lucknow, he moved to India in 1935 and established a busy practice designing residential, academic, commercial, and civic buildings, including a memorial to King George V. In February 1937 Griffin underwent gall bladder surgery. Stricken with peritonitis, he died five days later.[45]

ROBERT AUGUSTUS HARDIN (1884–1977)

Born in Barren, Kentucky, Robert Hardin is one of the lesser-known members of the Oak Park studio. As a child, his family moved west, settling in Fort Worth, Texas. In 1905 Hardin registered as a special student in art and design at the University of Illinois and attended classes for less than a year.[46] Described as the "new man" in the office in March 1906, He helped to fill the void left by Griffin's departure.[47] Hardin himself left after having worked in the studio for only a year, possibly because of Wright's marital infidelities.[48] The Texan headed to California, attracted by the "simplicity and practicality of the California bungalow and bungalow courts."[49] After marrying Texan Rose Theresa Christian in 1913, he moved to the Houston area, where he worked at his older brother's lumber company. Not much is known about his later architectural career, beyond that he designed a bungalow court in 1921 on land that belonged to his wife's family.[50]

MARION LUCY MAHONY (GRIFFIN) (1871–1961)

Marion Mahony was raised in a progressive home in Winnetka, Illinois. Her father, an educator and journalist, died in 1882. Her mother, a social and educational reformer, became a prominent elementary school principal in the Chicago school system in the years following his death. Mahony's cousin, architect Dwight Perkins, likely influenced her career choice, and in 1894 she earned her degree in architecture from MIT, becoming only the second woman to do so.[51]

Unlike many of her female peers, unsuccessful in their attempts to enter the strongly male-dominated profession, Mahony easily obtained a position as draftsman just a week after graduating, as Perkins hired her to help with the working drawings for Steinway Hall. She penned enthusiastically to former classmates, "Chicago men welcome women into the profession with open arms," adding that her employer's estimate of the value of her services far exceeded her own. She confessed to earning "the lordly sum of six dollars a week."[52]

After briefly working for "two classmates who had left Tech before graduating," Mahony entered Wright's office "through Mrs. Davis [a mutual friend] at the time the Francis Apartments was on the boards."[53] Mahony went on to contribute renderings and design art glass and other decorative elements for many of Wright's Oak Park–era projects. During this time, she regularly assisted other architects and accepted her own commissions.[54] Her first major independent project was All Souls Unitarian Church in Evanston, Illinois, of 1902. Needing a break from the studio, around 1907 she spent time in Elkhart, Indiana, engaging in amateur dramatic pursuits and working with her cousin Lucy Perkins illustrating children's primers by Maud Summer.[55] In 1909 Wright asked Mahony to take over his studio. She declined but agreed to work on the projects under Hermann von Holst.

While carrying out this work in Steinway Hall, Mahony reconnected with former Oak Park officemate Walter Burley Griffin, and the two married in 1911. Although she claimed no credit for designs produced by her husband, Mahony illustrated his projects with remarkable skill, as evidenced by her stunning perspective drawings for his winning entry for the Australian capitol of Canberra of 1912.

The couple moved to India in 1936. Following Griffin's death a year later she returned to Chicago, where she focused on landscape planning and wrote her rambling autobiography, "The Magic of America." During the last years of her life she struggled financially and suffered from dementia. Mahony died in 1961 at the age of ninety.

ALBERT CHASE MCARTHUR (1881–1951)

The eldest son of Warren McArthur, client for one of Wright's "bootleg" houses, Albert attended the Armour Institute of Technology and Harvard University, studying languages, metaphysics, color theory, and mathematics.[56] He may have briefly taught math at a private school in Arizona before returning to the Chicago area and entering Wright's studio.[57] McArthur's tenure was brief. Labeled as "new" on Wright's March 1908 list of studio members, he had departed by January 1909.[58] However, he went on to work as a draftsman on some of the last Oak Park studio projects under Marion Mahony in Hermann von Holst's office.[59]

In 1912 McArthur founded a practice in the Chicago area with Arthur S. Coffin.[60] In the early 1920s he moved to Arizona to design his most prominent commission, the Arizona Biltmore resort built by his brothers, Charles and Warren McArthur Jr.[61] Albert sought Wright's assistance on the concrete block design. While in Arizona, McArthur also designed a number of houses in the Country Club neighborhood of Phoenix. In 1932, he followed his brothers to California, relocating his practice to Hollywood, where he worked until his retirement in 1940.[62]

ISABEL ROBERTS (1871[63]–1955)

Born in Mexico, Missouri, Isabel Roberts grew up in South Bend, Indiana, where her father served as deputy inspector for the city until his death in 1907.[64] From 1899 to 1901 Isabel received architectural training in New York at the prominent Beaux Arts–modeled atelier of French architect Emmanuel Louis Masqueray and his American partner Walter B. Chambers. She became one of the first pupils in the partners' new atelier specifically designed for women, which focused on interior decoration.[65] It is not clear how or exactly when Roberts entered Wright's studio, but they may have first met through family connections.[66] Barry Byrne noted her presence in the office in June 1902.[67]

Along with serving as secretary and bookkeeper, Roberts helped Griffin manage the studio and assisted with architectural drawings and produced art glass designs.[68] Her unsuccessful membership application to the American Institute of Architects in 1921 records her role as a "draughtsman with Frank Lloyd Wright of Chicago."[69] Wright corroborated this statement in a letter of support, verifying that Roberts served as his assistant in the practice of architecture for several years and that he could recommend her without reservation to anyone requiring an architect.[70] In her own correspondence with the AIA, Roberts alluded to completing design work on her own house in River Forest and the DeRhodes house in South Bend, a commission that came into Wright's office as a result of her friendship with Laura Caskey Bowsher DeRhodes.[71]

Roberts became a good friend of Wright's wife Catherine and tended the Wright children on occasions when their parents were away.[72] She remained on the payroll at the time of Wright's 1909 departure for Europe, continuing to work at the Oak Park property with John Van Bergen on projects close to completion, including the nearby Laura Gale house and the Stohr Arcade in Chicago.[73] She then worked for William Drummond for several years.[74]

Roberts later moved to Orlando, Florida, and in 1920 began a partnership with Idah A. Ryan, the first woman to graduate with an advanced degree in architecture from MIT.[75] They designed a bandshell for Orlando's Lake Eola (1924, since demolished), as well as a hotel, a library, a funerary chapel, a Unitarian church, and a series of houses and apartment buildings in a variety of styles in central Florida.[76] Roberts died of coronary heart disease in 1955. Her death certificate lists her occupation as "architect."[77]

HARRY FRANKLIN ROBINSON (1883[78]–1959)

Born in Alliance, Ohio, Harry Robinson went to high school in the rural community of Mattoon, Illinois.[79] He received a scholarship to the University of Illinois in 1901 but initially turned down the award and instead accepted a job in an architectural office in St. Paul. He entered the University of Illinois the following year, graduating in 1906 with a degree in architectural engineering. During his senior year, Robinson served as president of the Architectural Club and invited Wright to speak to the group. After the lecture the architect asked Robinson to consider working for him.[80] The young designer accepted the offer and entered the Oak Park studio by September 1906.[81]

Much of Robinson's contribution involved developing working drawings from rough preliminary sketches. A gifted artist, he produced renderings that built upon the office style developed by Birch Burdette Long and Marion Mahony before him. Concerned about deteriorating office conditions as Wright's personal life began to undermine his professional career, Robinson left the studio by January 1909 and went to work for Griffin.[82] There, he supervised draftsmen and produced working drawings and details. Robinson also assisted Griffin with several landscape plans. During these years, he submitted at least eight sets of competition drawings to building journals, including the *Brickbuilder* and *Concrete*.[83]

In October 1911, Robinson rejoined Wright, managing his Chicago Orchestra Hall office and overseeing the realization of local projects for a salary of thirty dollars per week. When rehired, his employer informed Robinson that he expected his "whole time and absolute loyalty." To Wright, embroiled in scandal and believing that other former studio associates had unjustly turned on him, this meant "to stand up for your employer and your employer's opinions before the world."[84] Robinson likely did much of the design work for the Ravine Bluff development in Glencoe, Illinois, and on the Green House in Aurora, Illinois (1911).[85]

Like a number of Wright's previous employees, Robinson left the office for good on a bitter note in late 1916, resulting from his employer not paying him his earned wages.[86] Hired by Steinway Hall architects George and Arthur Dean as chief draftsman, he supervised other employees and oversaw the development of two planned communities near Duluth: Morgan Park for the US Steel Corporation and Gary, (Minnesota), for the US Housing Corporation.[87]

Robinson officially opened his own firm in 1923 but had been working on his own projects as early as 1908 when he designed an unrealized house for his fraternity, Phi Gamma Delta, at the University of Illinois. His body of work includes St. Mary's Church in Riverside and many residences, including the James Heald house (1913) in River Forest and the Griffinesque "Elmholm" residence in Naperville, Illinois. Robinson also likely contributed to, if not outright designed, twenty-four prairie houses located on the 700 block of Williams Street just south of Chicago Avenue in River Forest (1915–16).[88]

By early 1932, Robinson closed his office due to a lack of work. After failing to find other employment, he went back to school and received a master of arts degree in social science from the University of Chicago in 1934. Robinson then took employment with the Public Housing Commission, working as a land appraiser and a liaison between the public and the Public Works Administration district man-

ager. He became a project manager for several housing projects in Chicago, including the Trumbull Park complex. After holding a series of positions in Ohio and Nebraska with the US Housing Authority between 1938 and 1942, Robinson returned to Chicago and became a senior project planner for the federal Public Housing Administration.[89] Because of mandatory employment rules, Robinson retired in 1955 at the age of 72.[90]

CLARENCE ERASMUS SHEPARD (1869–1949)

The son of a painter and a decorator, Clarence Shepard was born in Cortland, New York. He moved with his family to Kansas in 1880 and then to Chicago by the early 1890s.[91] Shepard may have begun his architectural education in Illinois before taking courses in building design at the University of California, Berkeley, in the mid-1890s.[92] While on the West Coast he studied landscape painting under James Martin Griffin. During his time in the West, he collected woven baskets by native artists that he sold to the Field Museum and the Smithsonian Institution.[93]

Back in the Midwest by 1900, Shepard worked for the Chicago Portrait Company and Moffett Studios and married Kansas City native Nella Steese Kendall the following year.[94] Shepard may have entered Wright's office in 1902, possibly working for the architect until 1905. While neither Wright nor Charles White mentioned his presence in the Oak Park studio, the 1955 *National Cyclopedia of American Biography* states that he was there, and no known records indicate that he was working elsewhere in those years.[95]

Shepard moved to Kansas City in 1905 and began working for his father-in-law at the Kendall Realty Company.[96] Two years later he passed the Kansas architectural licensing exam and opened his own firm.[97] He went on to join the faculty of the Fine Arts Institute of Kansas City between 1913 and 1917 and formed a partnership with Hardborne D. Belcher producing residential designs for the J. C. Nichols Company's Country Club and Mission Hills communities.[98] By the time he retired in 1940, Shepard had designed more than six hundred residences in a variety of idioms, including the Louis R. Gates house (1923), which shows a strong affinity to Wright's "Fireproof House for $5000" design but with Griffinesque corner piers. While Shepard embraced the prairie style for his first home in Kansas City (1928), after marrying his second wife, Arabell White Hemingway, he built a new family residence with Tudor characteristics.[99] Following his retirement from architecture, Shepard painted and served as a trustee of the Kansas City Art Institute, including as its president between 1939 and 1941.[100]

ARTHUR COLLSON TOBIN (1879–1940)

The younger brother of Catherine Tobin Wright, Arthur Tobin received his education at Armour Institute of Technology, graduating in 1896.[101] The following year he entered employment with the Armour and Company meatpackers in Chicago, beginning as an office boy for Phillip D. Armour and continuing in the sales department.[102] He left Armour to begin a brief tenure in Wright's studio in 1905.[103] According to Charles White, Tobin was "a good business man (with no experience in architecture) and a fine fellow."[104] He served primarily as the office manager, but little is known about his specific contributions beyond his involvement with Wright's Sutton house and the First National Bank of Dwight, Illinois.[105]

Tobin left the studio sometime during the second half of 1906 for a position at the General Fireproofing Company of Youngstown, Ohio.[106] Tobin's keen business skills allowed him to move quickly up the managerial ranks, heading the Chicago sales office in 1907 and soon the whole furniture sales division from Youngstown. Selected as the company's outstanding man in the office in 1912, he accompanied company president William H. Foster to Europe to develop international markets for the business.[107] In 1913, Tobin returned to Illinois to serve as chief officer for the company's successful Chicago location until his death in 1940.[108]

(HENRY) WEBSTER TOMLINSON (1870–1942)

Born in Chicago, Webster Tomlinson received a degree in architecture from Cornell and then returned to the Midwest to work for W. W. Boyington. The young architect opened an office in Steinway Hall and became a member of the Chicago Architectural Club, as well as the group Wright labeled as "the eighteen." Although there is no evidence that Tomlinson actually worked in the Oak Park studio, he had formed a partnership with Wright by early 1901 that lasted until sometime between March and July 1902. His role primarily involved taking care of business dealings and supervising construction.[109]

After leaving Wright, Tomlinson went on to design the Tudor-revival Village Hall (1905) and several houses in Lake Bluff, Illinois.[110] In 1918 he moved to Joliet and produced plans for a Presbyterian church as well as local commercial buildings and residences. He became a specialist in prison design and served as superintendent of construction for Stateville Penitentiary, overseeing construction of its panoptic design by state architect William Carbys Zimmerman.[111] Tomlinson received several design patents, including one for a wall anchoring system and another for a slide rule. He retired in 1940.

JOHN SHELLETTE VAN BERGEN (1885–1969)

Born in Oak Park, at the age of eight John Van Bergen moved with his family into a new house in Fair Oaks, a recently plotted subdivision of the growing suburb.[112] He remembered being a child "very interested in making things … homes in trees, houses underground, houses in the old barn, & houses above ground."[113] He watched the new residences going up around his own home with great fascination, including two that stood out from the rest, Wright's Rollin Furbeck house constructed down the street when he was twelve and the William Fricke house on a neighboring corner lot four years later.[114]

After graduating from Oak Park High School, Van Bergen briefly worked for a small electrical contractor in Hollywood, California. Returning home in spring 1906, he found employment with a speculative house builder.[115] Although Van Bergen had no formal architectural training and later described himself as "a very poor draftsman," Griffin hired him as an assistant in January 1907 for six dollars a week.[116] He left Griffin's office in October 1908, spending the next three months attending architectural classes at the Chicago Technical College while also working in the office of Oak Park architect E. E. Roberts.[117] When the opportunity arose to work for Wright in January 1909, Van Bergen left school and became the last known hire in the Oak Park studio.[118] After Wright's departure for Europe that fall, he supervised studio projects already under construction with Isabel Roberts.[119]

With the work for Wright complete, Van Bergen entered William Drummond's office and began attending classes again at the Chicago Technical College in preparation for taking the Illinois licensing exam.[120] He received his license in March 1911 and opened his own practice under the sloping roof of his childhood home, moving by early 1913 to a small office in downtown Oak Park.[121]

Van Bergen completed thirty-six projects between 1911 and 1917; many recall Wright's "Fireproof House for $5000" scheme.[122] The designs contained carefully worked-out details designed to make daily life easier and more comfortable. His close friendship with landscape architect Jens Jensen and his time with Griffin helped shape Van Bergen's interested in the relationship of architecture to site conditions.[123]

After serving in the army during World War I, Van Bergen reopened his practice in the northern Chicago suburb of Highland Park. He continued to promote the prairie style, producing residential plans for the surrounding communities, and designing Braeside School, the first of a series of educational buildings. In 1918 Sears and Roebuck's mail-order house service made available two of his prairie house designs for purchase: the C. Percy Skillin house as the "Carlton" and the William H. Griffith house as the "Aurora."[124] During these years Van Bergen became involved in the Architects' Small House Service Bureau, a national organization of architects that promoted quality small home design. He likely authored two prairie house designs available from the organization in 1925.[125] That same year he produced drawings for an unrealized campsite and rustic service station building as part of the "Ideal Section," a 1.3-mile-long stretch of concrete highway, marketed as being the most advanced road in the world, built by the Lincoln Highway Association near Dyer, Indiana.[126]

The Great Depression made commissions difficult to come by. In the late 1930s, Van Bergen designed and remodeled several buildings at Carleton College in Northfield, Minnesota, as partial payment for his daughter's tuition.[127] During World War II, he designed workers' dormitories for a munitions complex in Sidney, Nebraska.[128] After the war, he moved to Northfield and carried out additional work for Carleton before moving his practice back to the Chicago area in 1945. Van Bergen's later designs increasingly illustrate an influence of modern technology and design, and included concrete slab floors with radiant heat, concrete block walls, and flat roofs.[129] In 1955, he built a retirement home in Santa Barbara, California, but continued to design until experiencing a stroke in 1968.[130] Unfortunately, a fire in 1964 destroyed Van Bergen's family home and most of the drawings and records of his career.

CHARLES ELMER WHITE JR. (1876–1936)

While many sources, including his obituary in the *Oak Leaves*, state that Charles E. White Jr. received his architectural training at MIT, the university has no record of his presence there.[131] In 1894, at the age of eighteen, he began working in the office of Samuel J. Brown, a residential architect in Boston.[132] Two years later White had advanced to chief draftsman. Meatpacker Swift and Company employed him in its Boston branch in 1897 and 1898 to design and supervise the installation of refrigerators on vessels.[133] There are conflicting accounts of other positions White held before arriving in Chicago in 1902, but evidence suggests that he spent time in both Rockford, Illinois, and Steubenville, Ohio.[134] White married Alice Roberts, the daughter of Oak Park resident and early Wright client and friend Charles E. Roberts, in 1901. After the wedding, they briefly lived in Steubenville,

where White carried out work for the local gas company.[135] The couple then moved to Burlington, Vermont, where they became close friends with architect Walter Willcox.[136]

White entered Wright's employment shortly after November 1903, focusing much of his time on the Buffalo commissions. Eager to strike out on his own, by 1905 he dropped to half time in the studio, leaving the position completely to start his own firm the following year. White built a "charming little architectural office immediately west of Oak Park Avenue behind the [old] Post Office facing Lake Street" that reminded the architect himself of Noah's Ark, with "a Pilot house at both ends."[137] In 1905 White collaborated with Wright and local architect Vernon S. Watson on the River Forest Tennis Club.[138] While some of his initial houses, such as the Walter Gerts and Charles Austin residences, relied fully on a prairie-style vocabulary, soon he was blending prairie forms with more traditional elements, such as half timbering and dormers, believing that a variety of design styles were appropriate for the home.

White exhibited his independent work in the 1908 and 1909 Chicago Architectural Club exhibits, listing fifteen different commissions in the 1909 catalog.[139] In 1912, he formed a partnership with Charles Christie and began to write articles for *House Beautiful* and *Country Life in America*.[140] White was a staff member of the *Ladies' Home Journal* for ten years and authored two books: *Successful Homes and How to Build Them* (1912) and *The Bungalow Book* (1923). He joined Bertram Weber to form the partnership of White and Weber in 1923, continuing to design in a variety of styles, including the Art Deco Oak Park Post Office (1933). In his later years, when commissions were less plentiful, White became involved in several slum clearance projects on Chicago's North Side.[141] He died of heart failure in 1936, a week before the dedication of his post office building.

ANDREW CHRISTIAN PETER WILLATZEN/ WILLATSEN[142] (1876–1974)

Born in North Schleswig, at the time part of Denmark, Andrew Willatzen received training from his father, a cabinetmaker, and attended a trade school as a youth.[143] In 1901 he immigrated to the United States, settling in Illinois. He briefly worked as a carpenter in Moline and then as a mechanic in Rock Island before entering Wright's employment sometime before spring 1902.[144] While at the studio, Willatzen, on Wright's encouragement, attended evening classes in architectural engineering at the Armour Institute.[145] On 13 May 1904, Charles White wrote, "Willatzen, the Deutscher, has 'learned' the old business and gone back to Rock Island to work for his old friend. He worked a year or more here for eight dollars per, so I suppose felt he would like to handle a little more money."[146] Willatzen returned soon after but left Wright's office permanently sometime prior to March 1906 to take a position with Robert C. Spencer Jr. and then Chicago architects Pond and Pond.[147]

Willatzen moved to Spokane in 1907. After a brief stint with Harlan Thomas, he entered the firm of Cutter and Malmgren, relocating to Seattle to oversee construction of their design for the Seattle Golf and Country Club.[148] Willatzen formed a partnership with Oak Park studio colleague Barry Byrne in November 1908. Their work primarily consisted of residential designs in the city's Highlands neighborhood.[149] The firm disbanded in 1913 when Byrne headed to California.[150]

Willatzen maintained an active practice in Seattle. His design for the Sanitary Public Market Building in 1910 led him to oversee a series of alterations for Seattle's famous Pike Place Market. Like many former Oak Park studio employees, Willatzen eventually moved away from the prairie style, although he considered his last prairie house, the Martin house (1928), his best work.[151] His later designs, such as the Richard Desimone house (1959), more closely relate to the forested environment of the Pacific Northwest. A 1963 *Progressive Architecture* article addressed his sensitive use of wood.[152] Willatzen produced fewer designs in the mid-twentieth century, keeping busy managing an apartment building and studying theosophy, possibly an influence of the Griffins. He died in Seattle at the age of ninety-seven.[153]

GEORGE RODNEY WILLIS (1879–1960)

Born and raised in Chicago, George Willis was a quiet, eternally optimistic man known for taking long walks.[154] He began formal classes in architecture at the Armour Institute of Technology in 1899, around the time he entered the Oak Park studio.[155] Wright later recalled that Willis was in his employment for approximately four years, at least part of that time as head draftsman.[156] He departed in 1902 for Los Angeles to work for former Chicago architect Myron Hunt.[157] Four years later, he moved to Dallas, entering into short-lived partnerships, first with Stewart Moore and then in 1907 with J. Edward Overbeck. In search of more promising employment, Willis moved to San Antonio in 1911, securing a position with Atlee B. Ayres.[158] He likely contributed to the design of a series of Texas courthouses, including ones for Brownsville, Alice, Kingsville, and Refugio Counties. In 1917 he began practicing independently, sharing an office and occasionally working with Emmitt T. Jackson. Several

residences Willis designed around this time, including the Lemma Young (1915) and Lawrence Wright (1917) houses in San Antonio, incorporate Prairie School features. His commercial designs include the twenty-one-story Milam Building, the first fully air-conditioned office complex and the tallest brick and reinforced concrete structure in the country at the time.[159] When building commissions became scarce in the 1930s, Willis participated in several WPA projects. His later work consisted mostly of minor commercial buildings, including a series of meatpacking plants.[160]

TAYLOR AHLSTROM WOOLLEY (1884–1965)

A Mormon and native of Salt Lake City, Taylor A. Woolley began his architectural training in the local office of Ware and Treganza before heading to Chicago to take classes at the Art Institute.[161] He joined the Oak Park staff sometime between March and August 1908.[162] Toward the end of the following year he traveled to Europe to work with Wright on drawings for the *Ausgeführte Bauten und Entwürfe von Frank Lloyd Wright*. After returning to the United States, Woolley received a license to practice architecture in Utah. During the next six years, he worked in both Utah and the Midwest, including supervising the start of construction on the Henry Ford residence in Michigan for von Holst and Fyfe and, between 1915 and 1916, assisting Byrne in Griffin's Chicago office.[163]

Woolley returned to Salt Lake City, where he entered a partnership with Miles Miller and Clifford Evans in 1917 that lasted until 1922.[164] Influenced by his time with Griffin, they incorporated landscape and site designs into the scope of their services. Woolley's work in Utah, largely confined to Salt Lake City, included numerous residences, such as prairie houses for Samuel Jackson (1911–12) and William Wallace Ray (1915) based on Wright's "Fireproof House for $5000." His layout of the Gilmer Park neighborhood recalls Frederick Law Olmsted's curving streets of Riverside, Illinois. Woolley also designed a series of Church of Jesus Christ of Latter-Day Saints ward chapels and Technical High School in Salt Lake City (1911), which recalls the Larkin Company Administration Building. These projects reflect Woolley's part in the production of Wright's Wasmuth Portfolio and, after its completion, his role in its distribution in the American West.

By the 1920s Woolley's work became more eclectic, including the Elizabethan meetinghouse for the Garden Park Ward in Salt Lake City. He served as president of the Utah Chapter of the AIA in 1926 and as the state architect of Utah between 1933 and 1941. He also became the supervising architect for the This Is the Place Heritage Park, which marks the location where Brigham Young's party first entered the Salt Lake Valley. Woolley retired from architecture in 1950.

Other Architects Linked to the Oak Park Studio

CECIL BARNES (?–?)

Identified as a Texan in Byrne's list of who was in the studio in 1902, Cecil Barnes likely refers to architect Cecil Bryan.[165]

EARL CARL GROETZINGER (1885–1936)

Born to a father who owned a monument business in Chilton, Wisconsin, Earl Groetzinger exhibited artistic abilities early on, leading him to study sculpture as a student at the Art Institute of Chicago for three years beginning in 1909 under Lorado Taft and Charles Mulligan and then in New York with Gutzon Borglum.[166] Groetzinger spent most of his adult life working as a sculptor in Chilton and was particularly known for his portrait busts. In addition to his artistic pursuits, he designed residences and landscaping plans for himself and his father and contributed to the design of houses for several friends.[167] The only evidence that Groetzinger may have worked in the Oak Park studio is a document at the Frank Lloyd Wright Home and Studio about a prairie-styled house designed around 1911 for Clinton, Iowa, stating its architect, Groetzinger, was a friend of Wright's who had worked with him in Oak Park.[168] If the artist did work for Wright, it may have been in a temporary position during the last days of the studio.

ANTONIN NECHODOMA (1877–1928)

Born in Prague, the Czech immigrant Antonin Nechodoma moved to the United States in 1887.[169] He worked as a contractor in Chicago and later told potential clients that he had worked for Wright, although there is no substantive evidence supporting that he was ever in the Oak Park studio. Nechodoma lived briefly in Florida before moving to Puerto Rico in 1905 and becoming one of the most prominent early twentieth-century architects in the Caribbean. He designed in a variety of styles, including producing prairie-style buildings for Puerto Rico and the Dominican Republic that show direct influence of Wright's Wasmuth Portfolio. These include his Korber house (1919) in Miramar, which recalls the Dana house, and Casa Roig (1919) in Humacao, closely based on plates of Wright's Westcott house in Springfield, Ohio. Nechodoma died in a car crash in 1928.

FRANCIS CONROY SULLIVAN (1882–1929)

Several publications on the Oak Park studio have erroneously stated that the Canadian architect Francis Sullivan worked in Wright's office in 1907.[170] Like Barry Byrne, Sullivan had no formal architectural education. He taught himself how to draw and in 1904 he became a draftsman for a civil engineer in Ottawa. Two years later he took a position as an architect in the firm of E. L. Horwood. Sullivan departed in 1907, announcing that he was heading to Wright's studio.[171] This statement and a copy of a 1917 letter from Wright to Sullivan incorrectly dated by some past researchers to 1911 that suggests a familiarity between the two men supported the belief that Sullivan had worked for Wright in Oak Park.[172] Instead, Sullivan ended up in Oakland, California, for several months collaborating on "plans for the San Francisco pest house," for the isolation of people afflicted with communicable diseases.[173] By the start of 1908 he had returned to Ottawa.[174]

Sullivan eventually did meet Wright and worked with the architect on several Canadian projects in the 1910s, including the Banff National Park Pavilion. Sullivan shared a number of traits with Wright. His wardrobe was "loud, but immaculate" and he "bore himself with confident sureness. . . . He was dubiously blessed with a glib, lacerating tongue which he found difficult to control."[175] Byrne called him "mercurial."[176] Unfortunately, he was missing Wright's great charm and ability to capitalize on new ideas. As a result, Sullivan managed to alienate himself from others and often faced disappointment in his career.

HERMANN VALENTIN VON HOLST (1874–1955)

Born in Freiburg, Germany, Hermann von Holst arrived in Chicago in 1891 when his father, a noted political scientist, became head of the history department at the University of Chicago. The younger von Holst graduated from that institution in 1893 and then received a degree in architecture from MIT in 1896. He returned to Chicago to work in the local office of Shepley, Rutan and Coolidge, becoming head draftsman by 1900.[177] Von Holst opened his own firm in the Rookery Building in 1905. He produced work that ranged from local electric company substations to buildings for summer estates in the mountains of New Hampshire.[178] He taught architecture at the Armour Institute of Technology and at the Art Institute of Chicago during 1905–6 and contributed to four books on "Beaux Arts character" for the American School of Correspondence headquartered at the Armour Institute.[179]

In 1909 von Holst moved his offices to Steinway Hall and oversaw the completion of Oak Park studio projects, including the Irving, Amberg, and Robert Mueller houses. He also produced residential designs for C. H. Wills and Henry Ford. In 1910 he formed a partnership with MIT classmate and Oak Park native James Fyfe that lasted until 1918. During this time, von Holst published the book *Modern American Homes* (1912), which featured designs by former members of Wright's studio, including White and Griffin.[180] In the 1920s, von Holst moved to Florida, opening a practice in Boca Raton. In the late 1920s he became involved in the development of Floresta, a subdivision in Boca Raton of Spanish Revival homes, including Lavender House, his own residence of 1928. After von Holst retired from architecture in 1932, he served on the Boca Raton Council for many years and chaired the Boca Raton Town Planning Board in 1940.[181]

WILLIAM ABIJAH WELLS (1878–1938)

William Wells attended classes at the University of Kansas for one year before entering the joint program in architecture at the Art Institute of Chicago and the Armour Institute of Technology. His address on a 1901–2 school registration card was listed as "c/o Frank Lloyd Wrights [*sic*], Oak Park."[182] Wells's exact relationship to the studio is not known. By 1904, he had joined an older brother in Oklahoma City and designed the Oklahoma County Courthouse in partnership with George Berlinghof.[183] Wells went on to form a partnership with Arthur J. Williams, producing several buildings with Sullivanesque details for Oklahoma City, including the Pioneer Telephone Building (1907–8) and the Colcord Building (1909–10). He moved to Hollywood, California, in 1914, but resettled two years later in Spokane, Washington. There he worked with H. G. Ellis and John K. Dow and designed a number of school buildings, including Waitsburg High School (1927) with Henry Bertelson. Possibly building upon Griffin and Wright's interest in textile blocks, in 1924 Wells took out a patent in Australia for blocks made out of a "concrete material in rectangular, oblong form or shape design."[184] He died in 1938.[185]

Artists and Contractor

RICHARD BOCK (1865–1949)

Born in Schloppe, Germany, Richard Bock moved to Chicago as a child. Trained in cabinetmaking by his father, in the 1880s he worked as a woodcarver while taking life drawing and modeling classes.[186] He returned to Europe in 1888 to study with Fritz Schaper at the Prussian Academy of Arts in Berlin and then under Alexandre Falguière at the École des Beaux Arts in Paris.[187] Back in the Chicago area in late summer 1891, Bock began executing sculptures for the exteriors of the mining and electricity exposition halls at the 1893 World's Columbian Exposition. Five years later he received a similar commission from Dwight Perkins to produce sculpture for the Machinery and Electricity Building at the Trans-Mississippi Exposition in Omaha. Bock also created interior sculpture for Adler and Sullivan's Schiller Building. It was while carrying out this commission he met Wright.[188]

Bock's first project for the architect was a frieze for the Heller house in 1896. This led to a long series of commissions from Wright, including sculpture for the architect's own house, the Dana residence, and the Larkin building. They also codesigned the Horse Show Fountain for Oak Park. After Wright's departure to Europe, Bock worked for several other Chicago architects, including White, Drummond, Spencer, and Purcell.[189] His projects ranged from funerary monuments for Graceland Cemetery to window displays for Marshall Field and Company's State Street store. He also painted portraits, including of Illinois governor Len Small and of members of Northwestern University's dental school.[190] In 1929, he was appointed head of the Sculpture Department at the University of Oregon. Forced to retire three years later due to age, he returned to River Forest and produced one of his last major works, an unrealized design for Chicago's 1933 Century of Progress International Exposition.[191]

"DUBUOIS"

In a May 1904 letter, Charles White mentioned that a sculptor named "DuBuois" had left the studio "to do some work at St. Louis," likely for the Louisiana Purchase Exposition.[192] The full identity of this artist has not been uncovered.

ORLANDO GIANNINI (1860–1928)

Born in Cincinnati, Orlando Giannini received his initial artistic training from his father, a sculptor and co-owner of a terra cotta works. He later attended classes at the Cincinnati School of Design and worked as a stonecutter between 1876 and 1880.[193] After making a brief trip to the East Coast in 1880, he returned to Ohio and found employment with a number of different pottery and tile manufacturing companies, including Rookwood Pottery and the American Encaustic Tile Works. Around 1885 Giannini secured a position as a foreman and designer for Adams and Westlake, a brass and bronze foundry that primarily manufactured railroad supplies and hardware. The company's vice president was Wright's future client Ward Willits.

Giannini may have produced murals for Wright in the 1890s, including two in the master bedroom of the architect's own home and one for the Chauncey Williams house in River Forest.[194] By 1897 Giannini had established an art glass firm with Fritz Hilgart. The company carried out glass designs for at least five of Wright's projects, including the Thomas, Willits, McArthur, and Cheney houses.[195] He also produced three glass panel mosaics designed by artist Blanche Ostertag for the Husser house in 1903. The firm additionally created art glass for other Prairie School architects, including Robert C. Spencer Jr. and the partnership of Purcell and Elmslie.

Around 1904, Giannini developed a relationship with the William Day Gates's American Terra Cotta Company and carried out several of the establishment's designs for the St. Louis exposition, including art glass shades for Teco lamps. Giannini may have also designed the company's art glass display pavilion exhibited at the fair in the Palace of Varied Industries. By 1907 he had left the firm and moved to La Jolla, California, where he continued his work as an artist until his death in 1928.

BURCH BURDETTE LONG (1878–1927)

Born in Columbia City, Indiana, Burch Burdette Long moved to Chicago as a teenager and began an apprenticeship in architecture. His first independent project was a small pavilion for Mariano Park in Chicago, a commission he won through a design competition in 1895.[196] Long worked for architect Richard Schmidt from 1898 to 1900.[197] Colleagues quickly recognized his exceptional drawing ability, and Long soon became a specialist in architectural renderings. He had a studio in Steinway Hall, and it was most likely there that he produced a number of exterior perspectives for Wright around 1901 and 1902. Long's eye-catching pen-and-ink renderings, which clearly reflect his interest in Japanese art, heavily influenced the later rendering style of the Oak Park studio.

After winning the Chicago Architectural Club's Travelling Scholarship in 1913, Long headed to Europe. Upon his return, he settled in New York City and produced architectural renderings for major building projects, including Henry Bacon's Lincoln Memorial in Washington, DC, and Bertram Goodhue's Cathedral of the Incarnation in Baltimore. In 1906 he illustrated a series of designs by Stanford White after the prominent architect's untimely death.

In addition to producing renderings, Long designed and painted murals for the New York pavilion at the 1915 Panama-Pacific Exposition in San Francisco and for the William Penn Hotel in Pittsburgh. The artist's immense talent led the Architectural League of New York to establish a major architectural drawing competition in his name after he unexpectedly died from pneumonia in 1927. The Birch Burdette Long Memorial Prize was awarded annually until 1972.[198]

GEORGE MANN NIEDECKEN (1878–1945)

A third-generation German American, George Niedecken trained as a teenager with Richard Lorenz at the Wisconsin Art Institute in Milwaukee before becoming a student in the decorative arts program under Louis Millet at the Art Institute of Chicago in 1897–98.[199] He then traveled to Europe, where he witnessed the work of the Secessionists. In late 1899 he began studying under Alphonse Mucha in Paris but briefly returned to Wisconsin after his father died in May 1900. During a second trip to Europe in 1901–2 he visited Italy, likely attending the Prima Esposizione Internazionale d'Arte Decorativa Moderna in Turin, which prominently featured art nouveau designs.[200] Niedecken returned to Milwaukee in 1902 to teach decorative arts at the Wisconsin School of Arts, The following year he taught classes in decorative designs at the Milwaukee Art Student's League.

By the spring of 1904, Niedecken had returned to Chicago to produce work for Wright. During this time he created the frieze for the Dana house dining room. He also produced a number of interior presentation renderings, including of the Dana house. In 1907, Niedecken left the studio, later informing one of his apprentices that he departed because "the work was too much like mission work; he needed to make money."[201] Niedecken then joined his brother-in-law, John Walbridge, to form the Niedecken Walbridge Company. The Milwaukee firm completed work for several of Wright's late Oak Park–era interiors, including for the Tomek, Coonley, Robie, and May houses. After Wright's departure for Europe, Niedecken created furnishings and other interior decorative elements for the Amberg and Irving houses. In the mid-1910s he also completed work on the interiors of Wright's Fredrick Bogk residence in Milwaukee and the Henry Allen house in Wichita, Kansas.

Niedecken produced decorative designs for other prairie-style buildings, including Drummond's Brookfield kindergarten; Robert Spencer's Denkmann-Hauberg house in Rock Island, Illinois; and William Purcell's own house in Minneapolis. He also carried out work designed by George

Elmslie for Louis Sullivan's Henry Babson house in Riverside, Illinois, including a grandfather clock.[202] He went on to serve as a trustee for the Milwaukee Art Institute, and in 1932 Niedecken was elected president of the Wisconsin Chapter of the American Institute of Interior Decorators.

BLANCHE ADELE OSTERTAG (1872–1915)

Born in St. Louis, Missouri, Blanche Ostertag briefly took classes at the St. Louis Art Museum before sailing to Europe in 1894.[203] She studied painting in Paris at the prominent Julian and Delacluse academies and in the private studio of Louis-Joseph-Raphaël Collin. Her work was exhibited at both the Salon de Champ-de-Mars and the official Salon de Champs-Élysées.[204] Ostertag returned to the United States shortly before November 1896, settling in Chicago, where she opened a studio across the street from Steinway Hall in the Athenaeum Building.[205] Dwight Perkins described Ostertag as "a whirlwind, a steam engine, a wild Indian, and a coquette all combined."[206] She quickly broke away from her formal academic training and began experimenting with various media, including etchings and pastels. She developed a reputation for her commercial monotypes and produced illustrations for books, magazine covers, calendars, and posters, including images for Carson Pirie Scott and Company advertisements.[207] She also painted the *Old Indian Fort*, a mural in the Chicago and North Western Railway Passenger Depot (1899) in Green Bay, Wisconsin.

Ostertag created decorative works for Wright's Husser house, including the spectacular gold and glass mosaic fireplace mantel featuring wisteria realized by Orlando Giannini. Before its installation in the residence, it appeared at the 1900 Chicago Architectural Club exhibition to great acclaim.[208] The artist designed other decorative elements for Wright commissions. At the club's 1903 show she exhibited decorative panels from the Husser house dining room and in 1908 entered a figure of Michael from a group titled "The Everlasting Covenant," listed as having been created for the "Hall of J. J. Husser."[209]

Ostertag's reputation as an artist quickly spread beyond Chicago. She went on to paint several prominent murals, including *Sailing the Claremont* for the art nouveau interior of the New Amsterdam Theatre (1902–3) in New York City, and served on the jury that selected exhibits for the Fine Arts Department at the 1904 Louisiana Purchase Exposition in St. Louis.[210] The 1910 US Federal Census recorded Ostertag as residing with her mother and sister in Manhattan, listing her occupation as "oil-painting artist" and her sister Rosa as

"architect."[211] Ostertag died in New York City on 13 November 1915 after battling uterine cancer.[212]

ALBERT LOUIS VAN DEN BERGHEN (1850–1921)

Born in Vilvorde, Belgium, Albert Van den Berghen studied at the School of Fine Arts in Brussels. He immigrated to the United States in 1876 and worked with the sculptor Augustus Saint Gaudens in New York before moving to Washington, DC, sometime before 1880. While residing in the capital, he produced decorative sculpture for the Congressional and War and Navy Libraries building, including corner figures representing Science, Peace and War, Commerce, and Industry for the latter library.[213] Van den Berghen briefly lived in Philadelphia before heading to Chicago to work on several projects for the 1893 World's Columbian Exposition. He taught at the School of the Art Institute for four years. An associate member of the Chicago Architectural Club, Van den Berghen exhibited three models in the club's 1896 annual show. He produced plasterwork for Marshall Field and Company and in 1899 a model of Chicago's Fort Dearborn for the Chicago Historical Society.[214] In 1902 Van den Berghen created the bronze relief *Spirit of the Waves* for the hall fireplace mantel of Hugh Garden's Madlener house in the Gold Coast neighborhood of Chicago.[215]

Van den Berghen moved to River Forest sometime prior to 1899.[216] Charles White noted the presence of the "talented and eccentric artist" in the studio the following year.[217] Van den Berghen had a kind, quiet disposition and a free spirit that gained him the title of "hermit sculptor of River Forest."[218] Richard Bock recalled him wearing his hair long, with "a full beard, trimmed very much in the image of Christ."[219] The artist's only known work for Wright was his unsuccessful sculpture representing the poem "Flower in the Crannied Wall" for the Dana house.

Van den Berghen continued to produce sculptures throughout his life. One of his last works, a full-size model for a statue of Abraham Lincoln, was cast in bronze multiple times by the American Art Bronze Foundry, including for monuments in Racine, Wisconsin, and Clinton, Illinois.[220]

MARGARET ELLEN "MAGINEL" WRIGHT (ENRIGHT BARNEY) (1881–1966)

Beginning in 1897 Wright's younger sister Maginel took classes at the Art Institute of Chicago and became a book illustrator, initially with the Barnes-Crosby Company of Chicago. She went on to illustrate over sixty children's books, beginning with *The Twinkle Tales* in 1906 and later such classics as *Hans Brinker or the Silver Skates* and *Heidi*. She also provided illustrations for magazines, creating cover art for *McClure's* and *Ladies' Home Journal*. In addition to producing her own work on the drafting room balcony of the studio, Maginel also helped out on art glass designs. Her more personal works include a pastel believed to show Catherine Wright with a brood of Wright children and their friends and the draft of an invitation to a studio event.[221]

In 1911 Maginel moved to New York with her first husband, illustrator and cartoonist Walter J. "Pat" Enright. The following year she became a member of the Society of Illustrators. After Maginel divorced Enright, she married Hiram Barney, who died in 1925. When work became less plentiful in the 1930s, she began creating women's clothes and accessories, including felt slippers and shoes. Maginel continued to produce art throughout her long life and in 1962, at the age of eighty-five, had a solo show in New York City. Three years later, she published *The Valley of the God-Almighty Joneses*, a memoir about her maternal relatives.

PAUL F. P. MUELLER/MÜLLER (1864–1934)

Born to a baker, Mueller was baptized in the Evangelic church in Wiebelskirchen, Germany, as Paul Friedrich Philipp Müller.[222] As a young teenager he studied at the school of mining and engineering in the coal mining region of the Saar Basin near the French border. He passed the polytechnic entrance exam but left school in 1878 and worked in the machine department of the local Heinitz coal mine for two years.[223] Mueller planned to enter a government school of mining to train to become a mining officer, but his father, hoping for a more promising future, decided to relocated the family to the United States. They settled in Chicago in 1881.

After arriving in the Midwest, Mueller spent six weeks working as a machinist before meeting August Fiedler, a local architect who, after witnessing his "facilities in drawing" employed the young immigrant.[224] The bright young man, later remembered as a walking encyclopedia, went on to work for various architects and draftsman and reported being "engaged by the Aetna Iron Company; Clark, Raffner & Company, and S.S. Wetner, engineers; also superintended the erection of steel structures."[225] He worked for Joseph Lyman Silsbee, probably as a draftsman, and briefly worked for Adler and Sullivan in 1883. He returned in 1886 to help with the steel construction for the Auditorium Building. Mueller later reported that after being at the firm for only six weeks, Dankmar Adler promoted him to office foreman, a position he held for the next seven years.[226] Wright probably first met Mueller while working in Silsbee's office, and it may have been the young German engineer who suggested to Wright that he seek employment with Adler and Sullivan.[227]

Between 1891 and 1896 Mueller worked for the Probst Construction Company as a "secretary and consulting engineer."[228] His responsibilities likely included supervising the construction of pavilions for the 1893 World's Columbian Exposition. In 1897 Mueller became an independent contractor, primarily working on large, nonresidential buildings.

With firsthand knowledge of Mueller's ability to successfully realize complex building designs, Wright relied upon the contractor to oversee the construction of his larger projects, including the E-Z Polish Factory, the Larkin Company building, and Unity Temple. Like Griffin, Mueller often served as a facilitator between the temperamental architect and his clients.

Even though Mueller's involvement in the realization of Unity Temple resulted in his bankruptcy, he continued to work for Wright, including on Midway Gardens and the Imperial Hotel. Toward the end of his life, Mueller spent time at Wright's Arizona camp Ocatillo in the capacity of contractor manager for the architect's unrealized resort San Marcos in the Desert. Mueller's last project with Wright, Westhope, a house in Tulsa, Oklahoma, designed in 1930, also resulted in major financial difficulties for the contractor.[229] After completing work on the house, Mueller returned to Illinois. With little available work due to the depressed economy, he became a building inspector for the city of Chicago. Mueller had a heart attack while at a job site and died in 1934.[230]

Appendix D: Letter from Frank Lloyd Wright to Anna Lloyd Wright, 4 July 1910

[This letter, found in a scrapbook assembled by Anna Lloyd Wright beginning in 1909 that once resided in the family collection of Frank Lloyd Wright's nephew Franklin Porter, is now part of the Frank Lloyd Wright Archive at the Avery Library. A red square and "Frank Lloyd Wright" appear at the top of first page. The handwritten text is in green ink.][1]

Dear Mother,

I have not replied to letters from Jennie and Maginel and am aware that I have written you no word for four months. I have had all your letters—I think—two from Maginel and three from Jennie. My neglect of them does not mean that I am insensible of what they contained or that it did not touch me and help me. I have been so troubled and perplexed that I have not known what to write? It might be one thing one day another thing the next. Meanwhile however the work of the publication has prospered. It's going to be all I expected and more. There will be twenty five plates entirely from my own hand work done here beside all the re-drawing, retouching, arranging and rearranging, the editing etc. I can not leave until September, early in September, probably as the proofs are daily coming back to me for correction and I find much to do on them. There is the article still to finish, and six more plates. There will be one-hundred in all. I am depending upon this to give my feet a more secure footing when I come back. I do not like to return without it. The financial return from it should be considerable. I received the card with the note of the birth of Jennie's second son and the name. Jennie certainly nails her colors to the mast and had courage to name the child after a brother in disgrace. It was like her though and through this perhaps we see Jennie as she really is. I am sorry Andrews [sic] affairs are in such a tangle—but I think eventually he will get what is due in salary at least; and perhaps the farm may be a good thing after all. I would like to farm it beside him—with that tract of Reiders and Uncle Thomas' farm joined together. But my situation is too discouraging to contemplate any such luxury. I have learned, at least this year that I must earn at least $5,000.00 every year to keep two boys in college and pay household expenses at the rate they have gone in my absence. This with no account of my own needs. Catherine has this year—without counting clothes, rent, interest, taxes or anything, paid out $275.00 per month for household expenses merely—Lloyd has had two trips to the continent, I have just sent Catherine money to bring her to Ashbee's for a couple of months visit in their home, (which will be more to her than a college education I am sure) expecting to bring her home this fall, the children have their pony still—and what they can have lacked in money or luxuries is beyond the reach of my imagination. I had left certain bills to be paid out of the funds, that the work would bring due when completed. But apparently this work has gone to pot in my absence as out of the six thousand dollars it should have brought, it has cost $1400 to complete it, and what with one thing and another, about 600.00 dollars is all I get. The clients all beat their accounts with excuses where they can find a hair to hang to—so I have there [sic] bills still in my hands—You should hear no talk about the family lacking money however—they have paid some of these bills, but since last September 23rd 1909 to June 21st 1910 they have had in cash from me $4500.00. The sum I gave you above as the true household account is taken from Catherine's accounts. This without the money given to the children direct—I mention this so that you may have no worry over reports of no money, family unprovided for, etc etc, which of course reach you. David wrote that he could not take lessons in the flute I sent him for "they had no money.["] Catherine that her lessons must stop for "they had no money." Her mother that the girl must be dismissed for they had no money—that creditors were pressing for the bills unpaid etc etc. There would never be an end to it. It is a constantly increasing load—which as a matter of course for the priviledge [*sic*] of being a father I <u>owe</u> to the children—they owe me nothing. They have been so taught in fact they feel that but for their father's extravagances they would all have had <u>much more</u>. This doesn't look much like a farm for me. The personalities of the children are dear to me—just the same, and I must make the struggle—I can see in no way how I can do otherwise than let this load drop and die to them one and all if I were to find <u>the happiness</u> in the life I planned and hoped to lead anew <u>that alone would justify it</u> for myself and others. ~~For this I have written~~ I had one time thought that in time I might keep what was good in the life that was and go forward to a new life—The world is not yet arranged on that basis I find—<u>but</u> Someday it will be—the present moral code is as inadequate for certain Souls as the old science is inadequate for new achievements. Life is not a thing to be lumped and legislated for in the lump—when we progress beyond the mob stage—Eternal verities are not alone those within the group of present majorities—some lie beyond—let us hope . . I have written only to Ashbee and Guthrie and Little—since I came away. Ashbee wrote me inviting urgently and so repeatedly that I wrote to tell him all. He wrote a fine friend's letter to me in reply. Guthrie wrote me a long appeal to listen to the voice of reason—the expedient—he seems to care something for me as does Ashbee. I dread the aspect my return must wear. I am the prodigal—whose return is a triumph for <u>the institutions</u> I have outraged. A weak son who infatuated sexually, but had his passion drained and therewith his courage, and so abandoning the source of his infatuation to whatever fate may hold for her—probably a hard lonely struggle in the face of a world that writes her [down?] as an outcast to be shunned,—or a craven return to another man, his prostitute for a roof and a bed and a chance to lose her life in her children, that something—some shred of self-respect may clothe her nakedness—While I return to my dear wife and children, who all along "knew I would" and welcomed by my friends with open rejoicing and secret contempt.

Why must this be so? It is the character given it by my own people; those who should know me best, and therefore it is <u>authentic</u>. Why could it not have worn the semblance of its truer aspect that scorn might not be added to the natural effects of ideals, lost life sacrificed and hopes dead? Anyone, who lets, by his acts the outer world touch in any way upon his affections must submit to having them vulgarized, brutalized and spit upon by the mob—but when ones [*sic*] own people give him over—ticketed and labeled libertine and weakening in a frantic and unseemly to [*sic*] effort to save him what can be said. Love is blind, but when love lies parallel to self-interest—of what is it incapable?

This burns out of my heart something that grew there once and still grows there but to wither and burn at the thought—always.

The truth might have been easily death to the idea that I had <u>eloped</u> with the wife of my friend or that she had "taken me from my family." She had left her home forever three months before she went away with me as her husband knew. You knew and Catherine knew that ~~if~~ I was going to take her anyway with me as soon as I could, as I had declared openly to you both and to her husband a year before I did take her. There was no deception that makes the "runaway match["] of the yellow journal any where. She went with me knowing what you knew and Catherine knows that I would in any case have separated from Catherine—though I might have continued under the same roof with her for the sake of the children—but even that I had told you I was determined not to do—She told her husband one year before she went away with me that she would go with me married or not whenever I could take her. Marriage was never a condition with her any more that it was with me—except that in order to work, I felt this most take place when it might if it might. It seemed at one time (owing [?] to requests of her husband solely) as though this were to be made a condition—and I so misunderstood it my self [*sic*] for a time but this was never her stipulation nor did she ever hide behind it—I may be the infatuated weakling, she may be the child-woman inviting harm to herself and others—but nonetheless the basis of this whole struggle was a desire for a fuller measure of life and truth at any cost—and as such an act wholly sincere—and respectable—within—whatever aspect it may have worn without. This by my return I discredit because I seemingly endorse the character made for it publicly by those, ~~to~~ whom by my returning to them I seem to endorse—This bitter draught seems to me—almost—more than I can bear—The last weight of a degradation otherwise not hopeless. I turn from it in disgust, and hard as it was to throw down what I had worked hard for twenty years to build up it is doubly hard to go to work again among the ruins—poorer in heart, in mind, in pocket—robbed even of the sustaining sense of the truth when dealing such a foul blow to the women who trusted her all to me in the struggle as I do when I endorse the character ~~my~~ made publicly for her by those for whom I leave her. ~~For.~~ I enclose the letter written a week or more—ago to Catherine telling her the basis upon which I wish to come to my work and the children—I think it is well you should know it. My absence has given me a perspective at least of the things the children have not had from me—nor from their mother. You know well enough what they are—I need not to repeat them—It may be too late to do anything worthwhile now—but I am a house divided against itself by circumstances I can not control—I can face them and down them or go down with them trying to get whole again within—but again is not the word. I have always as you know lived a divided life, but always with a hope—undefined—but a hope. Now it will be without the hope and so, perhaps more useful to others. Those who have "the claim." Give my love to all—Aunt Nell's word on Christmas received in Paris made me her "favorite young nephew"—once more. I would like to see you and she and Aunt Jennie take a cottage for three months here in this garden spot of earth. I would know how to tell you, how you could get most out of it—Love to Jennie and hers, Maginel and hers—I suppose I may look forward to seeing you all again before long—As always, Frank.

July 4, 1910
Villino Belvedere
Fiesole
Italy

Appendix E: Text of Sales Brochure for Home and Studio Property

FOR SALE AT OAK PARK A FOREST AVENUE PROPERTY & A CHICAGO AVENUE PROPERTY
Semi-detached dwellings For sale separately or together, partly furnished.

Two unique and beautiful modern homes, each complete in itself and independent of the other, separated by solid brick firewall to secure absolute privacy. Both are provided with Yaryan heat, best of plumbing, drained to deep Chicago Avenue sewer and are thoroughly well built throughout.

The Forest Avenue house was formerly the home of an Architect and is carefully and artistically designed and provided with furniture designed for the house. The interior is finished in quarter sawed oak—floors and trim, and painted sand finished walls throughout. There is a marble floor in the bath room, tile floor in the dining room, and in all of the rooms much delicately executed detail, rarely found in any American building.

The whole has a distinction of style and quality throughout not common to American homes and will not go out of fashion—a home which possesses the sort of character that grows more valuable with age. The arrangement is thoroughly convenient and modern in every respect.

The second story contains a large family living and music room, wainscoted with brick and oak, covered by a panel vaulted ceiling—perforated by fretted skylight—a mural decoration in the tympanum to the East. There is a recess for [a] grand piano, a large fire place, and the room has balconies, bookcases, a sunny bay to the south, cross ventilation and appropriately designed light fixtures. The whole made as beautiful as possible for the sake of its cultural effect upon the children. The north and south bed rooms are not less notable.

The dining room and main floor living room with its library alcoves are also carefully and richly worked out in a simple and distinguished style. The windows are all casements, fitted with quietly designed pattern glass. A covered porch is screened within the surrounding terraces overlooking small gardens and the lawn. There is a garden entrance at the front and a general carriage entrance and toilet at the side of the living room on the ground level.

It was originally in advance of the times in point of style and was built at a cost of about $18,000.00, without architect's fees, when building was much less than its present cost and was remodelled [sic] and repaired last year at a cost of fifty seven hundred dollars more. The property has a frontage of 88 3-10 feet on Forest Avenue, Oak Park's finest residence street. The lot is entirely surrounded by low masonry walls surmounted by low wooden screens. A cement drive from Forest Avenue leads to a brick garage—fitted with Bowser tank and pump, drain and special catch basin. Terraces and small gardens are used in the setting of the home and the whole harmoniously related to the Chicago Avenue house, which adjoins on the north.

The Chicago Avenue dwelling, formerly erected at a cost of nine thousand dollars to serve as the studio of the architect, was entirely rebuilt last year and extensive additions made at a further cost of fifteen thousand four hundred dollars, also without architect's fees. The lot has a frontage of 140 feet on Chicago Avenue. A fireproof garage and laundry entirely brick, wainscoted in white enameled brick, with servant's quarters or small flat above, and also a small stable to the rear were added.

The foundations throughout are solid concrete, the courts paved with cement. The structure of the dwelling is about half brick and half frame aside from the solid brick party line fire wall. The whole is covered by four-ply gravel roofs, and copper flashings. The interior trim is of soft wood, stained brown, with furniture and fittings designed to match. The walls are sand finished plaster, painted four coats. The floors are of permanent material, monolithic-magnesite, and polished with wax. The plumbing, lighting fixtures and drainage are of the latest approved type, connected to deep Chicago Avenue sewer. The proximity of the car line to the north and of the house to the south has been so considered in laying out the interior that the occupants are defended from the one and unconscious of the other. The masonry walled courts between the buildings are treated as enclosed gardens—the one opening from the dining room being fitted as are many Florentine gardens. It is enclosed on two sides by high walls, surmounted by balustrades, furnished with stone vessels for shrubs, a small pool and fountain set at the end of the garden.

The octagonal library and the hall are both top lighted as well as side lighted. Sun enters freely into every room in the house, five of the rooms have south light and all are cross ventilated.

The octagonal library is arranged with a direct and separate entrance and connected as it is with the hall, and adjoining toilet room, would well serve as a professional man's office in connection with the residence. The kitchen is top lighted and ventilated and is reached by rear court from the garage.

The servant's sleeping rooms are designed apart from the family rooms and may be reached from the kitchen by the main stairway or by an outside door from the court.

This arrangement was made to enable a serving man and wife to occupy these rooms while doing the work of the house or to provide additional bed rooms in case of need. The stable occupies the far corner of the lot and will accommodate a saddle horse and pony. The garage has room for two cars. The carriage entrance is at the ground level, entered from the cement drive which passes through the garden and is convenient in every way. A screened-in-porch joins the hall on the north and is designed to secure privacy from the street. The whole property is surrounded by low masonry walls and upper screens of wood. Cement window gardens, trellises, and terraced gardens are a feature of the exterior and no expense has been spared to create within the walls a worthy artistic atmosphere, dignified and rare, comparable with the best of the old world homes and with all, an absolutely modern, convenient, practicable dwelling place.

The exterior is a dignified and interesting expression of the interior and related harmoniously to the Forest Avenue property to the south.

In both homes there is to be found something money is seldom able to buy in America—a genuinely artistic environment, intelligently wrought out, in course of time, with painstaking care, and that will be more distinguished for genuine beauty and even more desirable fifty years from to-day than it is today. Both properties are for sale at a sacrifice. They will not be thrown away but will be sold at a price substantially less than their actual cost. The figures of cost given here will be vouched for. Both properties will be open for inspection by appointment only on Wednesday and Saturday of each week by arrangement with Frank H. Lune, E. H. Taintor or S. E. Kent of Oak Park or arrangements for inspection may be made by calling Harrison 457.

The property is situated at the corner of Chicago Avenue and Forest Avenue, Oak Park, Illinois.

Appendix F: Title Record of Oak Park Home and Studio Property

Kettlestrings Addition to Harlem, Block 2, Lot 20, Oak Park, Illinois.

Source: Cook County, Illinois, Recorder of Deeds

KETTLESTRINGS ADD to HARLEM a SUB NORTHERN
PART NW¼ SEC. 7-39-13.

BLOCK 2 — LOT

Missing text from bottom of the page:

79 11521526 Mun C Cir Ct Buffalo Phoenix Corp 11-2-36 12-11-34 W 205 ft

80 Anna Wright E 125 ft

Notes

Prologue

1. For more on the feminine, nurturing environment of the studio, see David Van Zanten, "Frank Lloyd Wright's Kindergarten: Professional Practice and Sexual Roles," in *Architecture: A Place for Women*, ed. Ellen Perry Berkeley (Washington, DC: Smithsonian Institution Press, 1989), 55–61, and reprinted in *Not at Home: The Suppression of Domesticity in Modern Art and Architecture*, ed. Christopher Reed (London: Thames and Hudson, 1996), 92–97.

2. In January 1887 it was reported in the Chicago periodical *Building Budget* that the "old-fashion system of apprenticeship was at an end; that it was opposed to the genius of our institutions ... and not generally sustained by the laws of the different States; and that a return to it was not really practicable." *Building Budget* 3 (January 1887): 1–2.

3. The property title during the years Wright owned the home and studio was almost always tied up in deeds of trust and lawsuits. See appendix F.

4. Ann Abernathy, "Outline: Restoration Alternatives, Goals, Procedures," August 1985, 1, FLWHSRC.

5. Ann Mahron, past president of the organization, in Wes Venteicher, "Frank Lloyd Wright Home and Studio Celebrating 40 Years of Tours," *Oak Leaves*, 15 July 2014. Alvin Nagelberg, "Frank Lloyd Wright's Former Home at 951 Chicago Av. in Oak Park Up for Sale," *Chicago Tribune*, 5 October 1972.

6. A copy of the photograph is in the collection of the FLWHSRC.

7. Eric Lloyd Wright, foreword to Zarine Weil, ed. *Building a Legacy: The Restoration of Frank Lloyd Wright's Oak Park Home and Studio* (San Francisco: Pomegranate, 2001), vi.

8. The owner's son also threatened to sell some of the art glass. Don Kalec to author, 30 August 2016.

9. The dismantling took place in 1972.

10. The property was purchased for $168,000 from Clyde and Charlotte Nooker, who had acquired it in 1946. Weil, *Building a Legacy*, 17.

11. The foundation was renamed the Frank Lloyd Wright Trust in December 2013.

12. "Trust Acquires Wright Home," *Preservation News* 15 (October 1975): 1; Bob Trezevant, "Laying the Foundation for Historic Preservation: A Timeline, 1946–Present," *Wednesday Journal*, 25 November 2014, available at http://www.oakpark.com/News/Articles/11-25-2014/Laying-the-foundation-for-historic-preservation/; Nagelberg, "Former Home." The organization purchased back the building in May 2012. On the restoration, see Frank Lloyd Wright Home and Studio Foundation, *The Plan for Restoration and Adaptive Use of the Frank Lloyd Wright Home and Studio* (Chicago: University of Chicago Press, 1978), hereafter *Plan for Restoration*, and Weil, *Building a Legacy*.

13. US Department of the Interior, National Park Service, Interagency Resources Division, "Guidelines for Evaluating and Documenting Traditional Cultural Properties," *National Register Bulletin* 38 (1985): 11–12.

Introduction

1. Neighborhood children, including John Lloyd Wright, pried apart the spindles to free the balls to serve as hockey pucks. Baxter and L. Wright, interview by Don Kalec, FLWHSRC. John Lloyd Wright to Dad [Frank Lloyd Wright], 12 March 1945, JLW-AAL. Historic Photographs show the fence missing balls. H135 and H96A, FLWHSRC. A rendering of the studio in *House Beautiful* in 1899 shows a solid wall, although Wright did not replace the fence until late in the life of the studio.

2. As described in Chicago Architectural Club, *The Chicago Architectural Annual Published by the Chicago Architectural Club: A Selection of Works Exhibited at the Art Institute in March of the Year One Thousand Nine Hundred and Two* (Chicago: Chicago Architectural Club, 1902).

3. Wright never offered a precise definition for "monogoria" but used it several times in his autobiography to describe the meaningless "monotonous iterations" of the suburban Queen Anne house. Frank Lloyd Wright, *An Autobiography*, 2nd ed. (New York: Duell, Sloan and Pearce, 1943), 80.

4. Frank Lloyd Wright, *Ausgeführte Bauten und Entwürfe von Frank Lloyd Wright*, (Berlin: Verlegt bei Ernst Wasmuth A. G., 1910; repr., New York: Rizzoli, 1986), 15. On how the Midwest has been perceived over time, see: William Barillas, *The Midwestern Pastoral: Place and Landscape in Literature of the American Heartland* (Athens: Ohio University Press, 2006).

5. For more on the history of the term, see Christopher Vernon, "Introduction to the Reprint Edition," in Wilhelm Miller, *The Prairie Spirit in Landscape Gardening* (1915), ed. Robin Karson (Amherst: University of Massachusetts Press/ Library of American Landscape History, 2002), ix–xxx, and Brooks, *The Prairie School: Frank Lloyd Wright and His Midwest Contemporaries* (Toronto: University of Toronto Press, 1972), 10–13.

6. Christopher Vernon to author, 7 September 1994.

7. In 1908 Wright published a list of propositions that define his prairie houses. Frank Lloyd Wright, "In the Cause of Architecture," *Architectural Record* 23 (June 1908), 156–57. Reprinted in *In the Cause of Architecture*, ed. Frederick Gutheim (New York: Architectural Record Books, 1975), 54–55.

8. Charles White to Walter Willcox, 16 November [1903], 6, WWP-UO. Several of the White letters, with some translation errors, appear in Nancy K. Morris Smith, ed., "Letters, 1903–1906, by Charles E. White, Jr. from the Studio of Frank Lloyd Wright," *Journal of Architectural Education* 25 (Fall 1971): 104–12.

9. Charles White to Walter Willcox, 15 May 1904, 13–14, WWP-UO.

10. Robert C. Spencer Jr., "The Work of Frank Lloyd Wright," *Architectural Review* (Boston) 7 (June 1900): plate 38.

11. For a discussion of previous scholarship on the studio, see introduction to the bibliography.

12. William Purcell to H. [L.] Morgan Yost, 22 March 1947. WGPP-NWAA.

13. Barry Byrne, "On Frank Lloyd Wright and His Atelier," *AIA Journal* 39 (June 1963): 111.

14. David Gebhard and Harriette Von Breton, *Lloyd Wright Architect: Twentieth Century Architecture in an Organic Exhibition* (Santa Barbara, CA: Standard Printing of Santa Barbara, 1971), 15.

15. David Wright, "Musing Memories," 30 July 1991, FL-WHSRC.

16. Hugh Downs and the National Broadcasting Company, *Broadcast Wisdom: A Conversation with Frank Lloyd Wright*, interview, 17 May 1953.

17. Catherine W. Baxter to Grant Manson, 6 November 1966, 2, GMC-OPPL; Catherine Wright Baxter to Grant Manson, 13 May 1959, 2, GMC-OPPL.

18. Barry Byrne to Mark Peisch, 13 May 1957, BBC-CHM.

19. Barry Byrne, *America* 69 (19 June 1943): 305.

20. George Elmslie to Talbot Hamlin, 25 June 1941, 3, WGPP-NWAA; G. G. Elmslie to Frank Lloyd Wright, 12 June 1936, in *JSAH* 20:3 (October 1961): 141–42.

21. When Manson exclaimed, "Mr. Wright, you can't do that!" the architect responded "Well, why not? Who else? It's my design!" Grant Carpenter Manson, "The Wonderful World of Taliesin: My Twenty Years on Its Fringes," *Wisconsin Magazine of History* 73 (August 1989): 35. For more on Wright and his relationship to drawings, see: Bruce Brooks Pfeiffer, "Tre disegni inediti di Frank Lloyd Wright," *Domus* 713 (1990): 72–75.

Chapter 1

1. Robert McCarter, *Frank Lloyd Wright* (London: Phaidon, 1997), 11.

2. Wright, *Autobiography*, 2nd ed., 13.

3. Ibid., 422–23.

4. Ibid., 9.

5. Wright later stated that the only authors on architecture he respected in his youth were Ruskin and Eugène Emmanuel Viollet-le-Duc. William Wesley Peters to Donald Hoffmann, 11 April 1967, cited in Donald Hoffmann, "Frank Lloyd Wright and Viollet-le-Duc," *JSAH* 28:3 (October 1969): 173.

6. Wright, *Autobiography*, 2nd ed., 15.

7. Frank Lloyd Wright, "Architecture and Music," *Saturday Review of Literature* 40 (28 September 1957): 72.

8. Wright, *Autobiography*, 2nd ed., 167.

9. Ibid., 26.

10. It is highly likely, however, that the family was already aware of this progressive educational method, as Froebel's student Margarethe Schurz had founded the first kindergarten in the United States twenty years earlier in Watertown, Wisconsin, only ninety miles from Spring Green and a mere nine miles from Ixonia, where the Lloyd-Jones family first settled in the state. Maginel Wright Barney, *The Valley of the God-Almighty Joneses* (Spring Green, WI: Unity Chapel Publications, 1986), 36.

The great regard for progressive educational practices like Froebel's in Wright's mother's family revealed itself later in his aunts' Hillside Home School, a progressive boarding school with a curriculum largely based on hands-on activities and explorations in nature. Several of Wright's children attended the school, and he designed buildings for it in 1887 and 1901–2. Mary Ellen Chase, *A Goodly Fellowship* (New York: Macmillan, 1939), 100–102, 116.

11. Wright, *Autobiography*, 2nd ed., 13–14. For more on the Froebel exhibit at the 1876 exposition, see Nina C. Vandewalker, "Excerpt from the Kindergarten in American Education," (New York, 1908) in *Nine Commentaries of Frank Lloyd Wright*, ed. Edgar Kaufmann Jr. (Cambridge, MA: MIT Press for the Architectural History Foundation, 1989), 10.

12. Friedrich Froebel, *Froebel's Chief Writings on Education Rendered into English*, trans. Samuel Sigmund Fechheimer Fletcher and James Welton (London: Edward Arnold, 1912), 50.

13. Norman Brosterman, *Inventing Kindergarten* (New York: Harry N. Abrams, 1997), 12.

14. The series of gifts progressed from solids to points: (1) six yarn balls in the colors of a rainbow; (2) a sphere, a cube, and a cylinder, all of wood with loops so that they can be hung from a wooden frame; (3) through (6) wooden blocks in cubes and rectangular and triangular shapes; (7) geometric cardboard pieces reminiscent of tangrams; (8) sticks in different lengths; and (9) peas or small wooden balls.

15. Frank Lloyd Wright, *A Testament* (New York: Bramhall House, 1957), 20.

16. Lloyd recalled playing with Froebel blocks and colored paper on the grids, as well as undertaking activities involving patterns of "circles, squares and triangles painted in red, yellow and blue" on the playroom floor (Some of the markings, including a large circle, are just barely visible in figure 1.3). See *Oak Park Reporter*, 8 January 1892, 4, and Catherine Wright [Baxter], interview, 1 November 1975, FL-WHSRC. Kate's family commissioned two summer houses from Wright in 1902.

17. Shortly after he completed the playroom addition, Wright hung a series of balloon-like glass globes from the ceiling above the balcony. These appear in several photographs of the room taken around 1895–96 (see figure 3.13). "Successful Houses III," *House Beautiful* (15 February 1897):

64–69 plus plates; Alfred H. Granger, "An Architect's Studio," *House Beautiful* 7 (December 1899): 36–45.

18. Thomas C. Hines Jr., "Frank Lloyd Wright—the Madison Years: Record versus Recollection," *Wisconsin Magazine of History* 50 (Winter 1967), 115.

19. Frank Lloyd Wright, *An Autobiography*, 1st ed. (London: Longmans, Green 1932), reprinted in *Frank Lloyd Wright Collected Writings*, ed. Bruce Brooks Pfeiffer (New York: Rizzoli, 1992), 2:150.

20. Ibid.

21. Grant Manson noted that Wright had "picked up some inkling of the fascination of Japanese art" from Silsbee, "whose suburban house in Edgewater was filled with the sort of Orientalia that 'advanced' people" were beginning to collect in the 1880s. Grant Carpenter Manson, *Frank Lloyd Wright to 1910: The First Golden Age* (New York: Van Nostrand Reinhold, 1958), 35. See also Kevin Nute, *Frank Lloyd Wright and Japan: The Role of Traditional Japanese Art and Architecture in the Work of Frank Lloyd Wright* (New York: Van Nostrand Reinhold, 1993).

22. He shared the work space with George Elmslie, who had followed him from Silsbee's office. Brendan Gill, *Many Masks: A Life of Frank Lloyd Wright* (New York: G. P. Putnam's Sons, 1987), 83–84.

23. Louis H. Sullivan, "What Is the Just Subordination, in Architecture Design, of Details to Mass?" lecture presented 2 April 1887, in Sullivan, *Kindergarten Chats and Other Writings* (New York: Dover Publications, 1968), 183.

24. Wright, *Autobiography*, 2nd ed., 103.

25. Louis H. Sullivan, "The Young Man in Architecture," *Inland Architect and News Record* 35 (June 1900): 38–40, reprinted in Louis Sullivan, *Kindergarten Chats and Other Writings* (New York: Dover Publications, 1968), 214–23 and Robert Twombly, ed., *Louis Sullivan: The Public Papers* (Chicago: University of Chicago Press, 1988), 131–44.

26. Eric M. Nicholls to Mark Peisch, 5 November 1964, MPP-AAL.

27. Sullivan, *Kindergarten Chats*, 100.

28. Wright had been staying with his uncle Jenkin Lloyd Jones. The 1887 Chicago city directory lists Wright's address as 3921 Vincennes Avenue, a block from his uncle's church. Lesley Martin to author, 30 May 2017.

29. Wright, *Autobiography*, 2nd ed., 65–66.

30. Rudyard Kipling, *From Sea to Sea: Letters of Travel* (Garden City, NY: Doubleday, Page, 1913), 421. The Hooghly is a distributary of the Ganges River in an industrial area of West Bengal, India.

31. Leonard Eaton, *Two Chicago Architects and Their Clients: Frank Lloyd Wright and Howard Van Doren Shaw*

(Cambridge: MIT Press, 1969), 12. Beginning in November 1901 central Oak Park was heated by a Yaryan system, which used the hot water discharged from steam engines that generated electricity for the area. Wright's property, located at the end of the line, did not receive much heat from it during the winter, so the architect installed a supplemental coal gravity furnace. David Wright remembered tending the basement furnace with "coal being chuted into the boiler room via a ground level window in the basement." David and Gladys Wright, interview by Don Kalec, 8 October 1975, 1, FLWHSRC.

32. At the time, Kitty, as she was often called, was a "gay-spirited, sunny-haired" eighteen-year-old who came from a Unitarian family. Wright, *Autobiography*, 2nd ed., 77

33. Chapin, the first woman awarded a doctor of divinity degree in the United States, was a major early figure in the suffragette movement and served as chairman of the Woman's Congress on Religion at the 1893 World's Columbian Exposition. Jeanette Fields, "First Woman Minister Brought Wright to Village," *Wednesday Journal*, 27 May 1991.

34. Wright, *Autobiography*, 2nd ed., 79.

35. Between 1870 and 1910 Oak Park's population grew from approximately 500 to 19,500. Jean Guarino, *Oak Park: A Pictorial History* (St. Louis: G. Bradley, 1988), 11–12; Frank Lloyd Wright Home and Studio Foundation, *Frank Lloyd Wright Home and Studio Foundation Volunteer Manual*, 13th ed. (Oak Park, IL: Frank Lloyd Wright Home and Studio Foundation, 1989), sec. 5: 3.

36. For more on Wright's purchase of Blair's property, see: Christopher Vernon, "John Blair, Landscape Gardening and the Prairie School," *Wright Angles: Newsletter of the Frank Lloyd Wright Home and Studio* 29:2 (2003): 3–7.

37. Lloyd Wright to Linn Cowles, 3 February 1966, 1, FLW-AAL.

38. It was common to place houses on the north half of large lots to allow for maximum southern exposure, as was done at the Nathan Moore and Peter Beachy residences designed by Wright down the street from his property.

39. Wright signed a $5,000 contract with Louis Sullivan ($2,875 for the property and $2,125 for construction of the house) on 20 August 1889, part of a complex transaction between Sullivan, the Wrights, and the Blairs. Grant Manson recorded that on 11 September 1889 a building permit was issued to "Frank Lloyd Right [*sic*]" for a $4,000 wood dwelling on lot 20, block 2 of Kettlestring's Addition to Harlem. Robert Monk, "The Oak Park Home of Frank Lloyd Wright: The Beginning," draft 13 March 1993, FLWHSRC; Arlene Sanderson, "Anniversary Recalls Significant Dates," *Wright Angles:*

Newsletter of the Frank Lloyd Wright Home and Studio 14:4 (Fall 1988): n.p. For more on the contract, see Meg Klinkow, "Back to Those Days of Yesteryear: Purchasing the Land and Home," 7 September 1989, FLWHSRC.

40. Louis Sullivan with Frank Lloyd Wright, "Agreement," 19 August 1889, copy in the FLWHSRC.

41. If he did not own a copy himself, Wright likely had access to it in either Silsbee's or Sullivan's office. Vincent J. Scully, Jr., *The Shingle Style and The Stick Style: Architectural Theory and Design from Richardson to the Origins of Wright*, rev. ed. (New Haven, CT: Yale University Press, 1971), 159.

42. Wright may have acquired the plaster details from C. Hennecke and Company of Milwaukee, which opened a Chicago branch in 1887 not far from the architect's downtown office, or ordered them from P. P. Caproni and Brother of Boston, which issued yearly catalogs for their plaster casts between 1892 and 1915.

43. The other quote, "Good friend, around these hearthstones speak no evil word of any creature," appeared in James Lane Allen's 1895 novel *Aftermath*, in which the author described the text as running around an arch across a chimney. Wright likely added it to the fireplace front after reading Allen's work. Allen, *Aftermath* (New York: Harper and Brothers, 1895), 37.

44. John Lloyd Wright, *My Father Who Is on Earth* (New York: G. P. Putnam's Sons, 1946), 15.

45. "Office of F. L. Wright," note card, GMC-OPPL; Wright, *Autobiography*, 2nd ed., 123. The Schiller Building was located at 109 Randolph Street.

46. Wright, *Autobiography*, 2nd ed., 123–24.

47. See "Building News Synopsis," *Inland Architect & News Record*, July 1891, 73, and June 1892, 66.

48. Wright, *Autobiography*, 2nd ed., 130.

49. Both Corwin and Wright had projects listed in *Inland Architect* in 1894. "Synopsis of Building News," *Inland Architect & News Record* 3 (March 1894): 24.

50. Born in Caeslin, Germany, in 1860, Guenzel received his architectural training in Berlin. He immigrated to the United States and entered the office of Adler and Sullivan in 1892, where he met Wright. Two years later he formed a partnership with Harley Seymour Hibbard while possibly helping Wright with his new practice. In 1912 he went into partnership with Oak Park studio architect William Drummond. Wilbert R. Hasbrouck, "The Architectural Firm of Guenzel and Drummond," *Prairie School Review* 1:2 (1964): 5; Brooks, *The Prairie School*, 267.

51. Shimoda studied architecture in Japan before traveling to San Francisco in September 1888, where he may have worked as a draftsman for Daniel Burnham. Several years later he moved to Chicago to work on the Hōōden for the Columbian Exposition. After the fair closed, he designed several Japanese gardens for Chicago, including ones for Jackson and Lincoln parks, exhibiting the Lincoln Park design and a church at the 1895 Chicago Architectural Club show. Two years later Shimoda became one of the first architects licensed in Illinois but returned to Japan the following year. For more on Shimoda, see Kikutaro Shimoda, *"Ideal Architecture … Business Building … Barrack …"* (Tokyo: n.p., 1928).

52. Wright later claimed that shortly afterward the two men had words in the hall and he ended up kicking Shimoda and throwing him down a flight of stairs. Wright, *Autobiography*, 2nd ed., 124.

53. Anna Cordelia Hicks (Brackett) recalled that both Corwin and Marion Mahony were in the office when she was there. Hicks attended MIT for one year, leaving school to marry. Manson, Hicks note card, GMC-OPPL; *Bulletin of the M.I.T. Boston Register of Former Students with an Account of the Alumni Association* 50 (May 1915): 61.

54. On Mahony's upbringing, see Alice T. Friedman, "Girl Talk: Feminism and Domestic Architecture at Frank Lloyd Wright's Oak Park Studio," in *Marion Mahony Reconsidered*, ed. David Van Zanten (Chicago: University of Chicago Press, 2011), 22–49.

55. *1894 Class Book, M.I.T.,* 1898, as quoted in Susan Fondiler Berkon, "Marion Mahony Griffin," in *Women in American Architecture: A Historic and Contemporary Perspective*, ed. Susana Torre (New York: Whitney Library of Design, 1977), 75.

56. Paul Lautrup, Daniel Burnham's chief draftsman and one of the top renderers in Chicago, created a small watercolor of the Winslow house and a color exterior of the Francis Apartments that was signed by both Wright and Lautrup. Artist Ernest Albert painted a watercolor of Wright's Oak Park home, as well as five of the six entries Wright submitted to the Chicago Architectural Club exhibition at the Art Institute of Chicago in 1894. The watercolor is now in Avery Archives at Columbia University. In 1895 Wright hired Hugh Garden and Cecil Corwin's brother Charles to create a large watercolor perspective of his Cheltenham Beach project. Robert Spencer likely painted the watercolor of the McAfee house that appeared in *Architectural Review* in 1900. Paul Kruty, "Graphic Depictions: The Evolution of Marion Mahony's Architectural Renderings" in Van Zanten, *Mahony Reconsidered*, 54, 153n13.

57. Wilbert R. Hasbrouck, *The Chicago Architectural Club: Prelude to the Modern* (New York: Monacelli Press, 2005), 213.

58. Perkins, thirty, had worked for D. H. Burnham and Company, while Spencer, thirty-two, and Hunt, twenty-nine, had spent time in Boston at Shepley, Rutan, and Coolidge. Hasbrouck, *Chicago Architectural Club*, 214.

59. They included Adamo Boari, Walter Burley Griffin, Henry Holt, Francis Kirkpatrick, Roy Lippincott, Marion Mahony, George Kikutaro Shimoda, and Webster Tomlinson. The architectural renderers Birch Burdette Long and Jules Guerin were also present. Hasbrouck, *Chicago Architectural Club*, 215.

60. Wright, *Testament*, 35; Robert C. Spencer Jr. to Grant Manson, 3 March 1940, GMC-OPPL.

61. Mark L. Peisch, *The Chicago School of Architecture: Early Followers of Sullivan and Wright* (New York: Random House, 1964), 37.

62. On the Arts and Crafts connection to Wright's Oak Park studio, see Jack Quinan, "Frank Lloyd Wright in 1893: The Chicago Context," in *Frank Lloyd Wright: In the Realm of Ideas* (Carbondale: Southern Illinois University Press, 1988).

63. Growing out of the Aesthetic Movement in England, the House Beautiful concept offered an approach to design that reacted against historicism and the rise of industrialization by accentuating the innate beauty of nature and simple decorative forms to achieve a profound spiritual quality and sense of harmony in residential designs. Between 1896 and 1898, Wright and his early client William Winslow designed and hand-printed an exquisitely crafted limited edition of the essay "The House Beautiful." Written by William C. Gannett, a Unitarian clergyman and social reformer, the work described the role of aestheticism and good craftsmanship in creating an ideal home and family life. William C. Gannett, *The House Beautiful* (River Forest, IL: Auvergne, 1896-97).

64. Wright provided a partial list of the group's members: "Bob [Robert] Spencer, [James] Gamble Rogers, [Frank] Handy and [Jeremiah Kiersted] Cady, Dick [Richard] Schmidt, Hugh Garden, Dean [probably George Dean], [Dwight] Perkins, and [Howard Van Doren] Shaw." Wright, *Testament*, 34. See also Chicago Architectural Club, *The Chicago Architectural Annual* (1902).

65. Wright, "Cause," (1908), 156.

66. On the Arts and Crafts Movement in Chicago, see Richard Guy Wilson, "Chicago and the International Arts and Crafts Movements: Progressive and Conservative Tendencies," in *Chicago Architecture 1872-1922: Birth of a Metropolis*, ed. John Zukowsky (Munich: Prestel-Verlag, 1987), 208–27.

67. Chicago area artists and craftsmen had been encouraged to exhibit their work and share their ideas at the settlement house. Hasbrouck, *Chicago Architectural Club*, 222.

68. After Wright left his family, Catherine became actively involved with Hull House.

69. Chicago Arts and Crafts Society members included Wright, Marion Mahony, Dwight Perkins and his wife, illustrator Lucy Fitch Perkins, Robert C. Spencer Jr., Irving Pond and his brother Allen, and Myron Hunt. *Chicago Architectural Club, Catalogue of the Eleventh Annual Exhibition by the Chicago Architectural Club at the Art Institute of Chicago, March 23rd to April 10th 1898* (Chicago: Chicago Architectural Club, 1898), 553–56. See also Hasbrouck, *Chicago Architectural Club*, 223.

70. Artist Richard Bock recalled that the intimate audience was made up of "Miss Jane Addams, Professor Lubin [*sic*] of the University of Chicago, Hugh M. Garden, Birch Burdett [*sic*] Long, the office staff, Mrs. Wright, Mrs. Bock and Myself." Richard Bock, *Memoirs of an American Artist, Sculptor, Richard W. Bock*, ed. Dorathi Bock Pierre (Los Angeles: C.C. Publishing., 1989), 89. Wright also recalled the attendance of Professor Zueblin and Professor Triggs. Wright, *Autobiography*, 2nd ed., 132. For more on Wright's "The Art and Craft of the Machine" lecture and essay, see Joseph M. Siry, "Frank Lloyd Wright's 'The Art and Craft of the Machine': Text and Context," in *The Education of the Architect*, ed. Martha Pollak (Cambridge, MA: MIT Press, 1997), 3–36.

71. On the Chicago Architectural Club, see Hasbrouck, *Chicago Architectural Club*.

72. Wright exhibited in all but two of the Chicago Architectural Club's annual exhibitions between 1894 and 1902, then did not appear until 1907 when he had thirty-eight entries, including works from the Dana, Coonley, and Darwin Martin houses, Unity Temple, and the Larkin building.

73. *American Architect and Building News* 76 (26 April 1902): 29–30.

74. He used a photograph of the library and drawings from the 1900 *Architectural Review* article to illustrate his studio.

75. For example, Wright's early ornament for many of his buildings, such as the Heller and Husser houses, incorporated the type of leafy vegetation common to Louis Sullivan's designs.

76. Wright used Roman brick as early as 1889 for the living room fireplace of his Oak Park home. He first used bands of windows on the front of the second floor of his own home in an 1890 remodeling.

77. J. L. Wright, *My Father*, 15.

78. Analysis revealed more than ten layers of paint from 1909 or before. "Three Decades of Renovating Wright," *Wednesday Journal Special Section*, 31 March 2004; Robert A. Furhoff, "Frank Lloyd Wright Home and Studio Site Investigation," September 1985, FLWHSRC.

79. Historic Photograph H220, FLWHSRC.

80. Barney, *Valley*, 134.

81. Olgivanna Wright, *The Shining Brow: Frank Lloyd Wright* (New York: Horizon, 1960), 46.

82. Sarah Booth Conroy, "The Right Home for Wright's Son," *Washington Post*, 13 July 1974, in Patrick J. Meehan, *Frank Lloyd Wright: Remembered* (Washington, DC: Preservation, 1991), 236.

83. David Hanks, *The Decorative Designs of Frank Lloyd Wright* (New York: E. P. Dutton, 1979), 19.

84. Ann Abernathy and Don Kalec, Room Descriptions of the Frank Lloyd Wright Home and Studio, Restoration Documentation Files, FLWHSRC.

85. Catherine (Wright) Baxter and Lloyd Wright, interview by Don Kalec, June 1975, FLWHSRC.

86. J. L. Wright, *My Father*, 16.

87. Don Kalec to author, 22 August 2016. On clothing and other decorative designs by Wright, see Carma R. Gorman, "Fitting Rooms: The Dress Designs of Frank Lloyd Wright," *Winterthur Portfolio* 30:4 (Winter 1995): 259–77.

88. The fireplace received a similar treatment with a framed shelf just below the ceiling, made possible by the flue receding horizontally into the wall before heading upward to the chimney.

89. H. H. Richardson's Glessner house in Chicago has a similar multifaceted bay facing south for plants. Elaine Harrington, to author, 18 May 2016.

90. Ibid.

91. Frank Lloyd Wright, *The Japanese Print: An Interpretation* (Chicago: Ralph Fletcher Seymour, 1912), revised and enlarged ed. (New York: Horizon Press, 1967), plate 25. The print was sold after Wright's death to the UCLA Grunwald Center for the Graphic Arts, Hammer Museum.

92. The exact height of the original wall is unknown; however, it did not divide the central semicircular window. Both David and young Catherine Wright remembered the boys throwing pillows over the wall while the girls hosted slumber parties on the other side. David Wright, conversation with author; Catherine W. Baxter to Don Kalec, 25 March 1976, FLWHSRC.

93. As pointed out by David Hanks, Wright likely based the leaded pattern of the dining room windows on glass designs illustrated in plates 72 and 74 of the book H. Carot, *Kunstverglasungen*, (Berlin, 1886). Hanks, *Decorative Designs*, 53–55.

94. Windows of the original design still exist in the cabinets that surround the playroom fireplace.

95. Floral motifs in art glass designs were popular in Victorian houses and favored by several Prairie School architects, including George Maher.

Chapter 2

1. H57, FLWHSRC, also 9506.01/9307.01, FLW-AAL. William Purcell, who grew up on Forest Avenue, recorded that he had become fascinated by Wright's work when at the age of fourteen in 1894 he saw a little pen-and-ink drawing of the Oak Park studio. Yet it is unlikely Wright created that rendering before 1897. Perhaps Purcell had seen the sketch on the playroom mural drawing. William Gray Purcell, *Parabiographies, Volume for 1910*, job date 3 January 1912, H. S. Adams, Oak Park, WGPP-NWAA; Henry-Russell Hitchcock, *In the Nature of Materials, 1887–1941: The Buildings of Frank Lloyd Wright* (New York, Duell, Sloan and Pearce, 1942), plate 38.

2. Wright, *Autobiography*, 2nd ed., 138.

3. *Construction News* (Chicago), 6 (9 February 1898): 121.

4. Wright to Uncle Jenkins, 25 February 1898. FLW-AAL. Conflicting evidence points to several different dates for the studio. Early scholars such as Robert Twombly often gave 1895 as the date for the building's construction. Grant Manson noted that just prior to 1 March 1898, permit number 3461 was issued to Frank Lloyd Wright for an $1,800 frame dwelling on "W1/2 lot 2, Block 1, Kettlestrings," the second lot south of Chicago Avenue on the east side of nearby Grove Avenue. It has been suggested that this permit, which no longer exists, was for the studio. The houses on the given site do not appear to have been designed by Wright. Robert C. Twombly, *Frank Lloyd Wright: An Interpretive Biography* (New York: Harper and Row, 1973), 102. Grant C. Manson, "Cicero Building Permit Files," notes, 9 January 1939, GMC-OPPL.

5. Only a small percentage of architects who exhibited at the Chicago Architectural Club shows had their offices in the suburbs. The few other designers who opened offices in Oak Park included E. E. Roberts (1893), H. C. Fiddelke (1894), Charles White (1905), and John Van Bergen (1911).

6. Wright, *Autobiography*, 2nd ed., 138. Wright later told apprentices at Taliesin that he extended his work output by at least 33 1/3 percent by avoiding the daily trip into the city. Yukio Futagawa, ed., *Frank Lloyd Wright Monograph 1887–1901* (Tokyo: A.D.A. Edita, 1986), 1:33.

7. Announcement of the opening of the Oak Park studio, ca. 1898.

8. US Patents #27,977 to #28,015 were filed for the designs in October 1897 and issued that December.

9. While the 1898 *Lakeside Directory* lists Wright as residing in Room 1123 of the Rookery, as early as February 1898 he identifies Room 1119 as his office on his studio stationary. On 1 May 1899 he moved to room 1104 and then occupied room 435 from 25 September 1899 until 30 April 1900. The departure of the Luxfer Company from the building may have contributed to at least one of the moves. *Lakeside Annual Directory of the City of Chicago* (Chicago: Chicago Directory, 1898); Grant Manson, "The Rookery: Further Information from Mary P. Harman," GMC-OPPL; Mary P. Harman to Grant Manson, n.d. GMC-OPPL.

10. Contract between E. Arthur Davenport and Webster Tomlinson on behalf of Frank Lloyd Wright and Webster Tomlinson for a house on Ashland Avenue in River Forest, Illinois, FLWHSRC; *Lakeside Annual Directory of the City of Chicago* (Chicago: Chicago Directory, 1901).

11. Barry Byrne recalled that Wright had no Chicago office between 1902 and 1908, and between 1902 and 1907 Wright does not appear in the Chicago business directories. Barry Byrne, undated notes, possibly to H. Allen Brooks, Barry Byrne folder, FLWHSRC.

12. Grant Manson, "Offices of F. L. Wright, Steinway Hall, Chicago," note card, GMC-OPPL.

13. Announcement of the opening of the Oak Park studio, ca. 1898.

14. In 1915, a writer noted extreme difficulties in securing "satisfactory office space in down-town Chicago where any expression of individuality is possible." "The Work of Guenzel and Drummond," *Western Architect* 21 (February 1915): 15.

15. Kevin Harrington suggested the idea that Wright sought to avoid having his time dominated by managerial activities.

16. David Van Zanten writes about the nurturing environment of the studio in "Frank Lloyd Wright's Kindergarten."

17. Sharon Darling, *Chicago Furniture Art, Craft, & Industry, 1833–1983* (W. W. Norton, 1984), 225–26.

18. "The Kalo Foundation of Park Ridge," available at http://iannellistudios.org/kalo_history.html.

19. In 1887, an editorial in *American Architect and Building News* observed, "[T]he late Mr. [Henry Hobson] Richardson was the only American architect in extensive practice . . . who carried on business in his own home." Quoted in James O'Gorman, "Henry Hobson Richardson and Frank Lloyd Wright," *Art Quarterly* 32 (July/August 1969), 311.

20. Richardson likely first became familiar with the idea of a home architectural office during his brief tenure studying at the École des Beaux-Arts in Paris beginning in 1860, as the École educational system included ateliers, where established masters guided students in their design education, at times within the educators' own homes. That Wright used Richardson's studio as a source was first suggested by James O'Gorman in "Richardson and Wright."

21. James O'Gorman, *Three American Architects: Richardson, Sullivan, and Wright, 1865–1915* (Chicago: University of Chicago Press, 1991), 6. Richardson's studio also appeared in the 17 December 1884 issue of *American Architect and Building News*.

22. Sullivan's copy was auctioned off along with some of his other possessions on 29 November 1909. O'Gorman, "Richardson and Wright," 313n26.

23. Wright, *Autobiography*, 1st ed., 172, 300.

24. Richardson's signature appears on a check to Dwight Perkins dated a week before the Boston architect's death in 1886, suggesting that he may have worked in Richardson's office while at MIT. Hasbrouck, *Chicago Architectural Club*, 117n29. Additional information about the Brookline office could have reached Wright through MIT graduates Myron Hunt and Robert C. Spencer Jr. Although Richardson had died by the time they finished their formal studies, the two men both went on to work for the renowned architect's successor firm, Shepley, Rutan and Coolidge, in its Chicago branch office. Hasbrouck, *Chicago Architectural Club*, 156, 214.

25. This led architect P.B. Wight to describe the studio at the time of Richardson's death in 1887 as having an exterior that resembled a barracks or a hospital. He thought the interiors, however, to be "most interesting." P.B. Wight, "H.H. Richardson," obituary, *Inland Architect and Building News Record* 7 (May 1886): 59.

26. Edward Hale, "H.H. Richardson and His Work," *New England Magazine* 11 (December 1894): 513–14 as referenced in Mary Alice Molloy, "Richardson's Web: A Client's Assessment of the Architect's Home and Studio," *JSAH* 54:1 (March 1995): 14, 22n46.

27. In the mid-1880s, Richardson, realizing the great danger from fire to his immense collection of books, photographs, and art, installed the large "fireproof" library. Wight, "H.H. Richardson," 59, 61.

28. Mariana Griswold Van Rensselaer, *Henry Hobson Richardson and His Work* (Boston: Houghton, Mifflin, 1888; repr., New York: Dover, 1969), 125.

29. Elaine Harrington, "At Home in the Studio: H.H. Richardson and F.L. Wright," abstract draft, August 1991, copy in author's collection. Luca della Robbia created *Cantoria* (choir balcony) between 1431 and 1438 for Santa Maria

del Fiore, the cathedral in Florence. Richardson's library also included an image of the *Winged Victory of Samothrace*. Plaster copies of the Hellenistic sculpture appear in photographs of Wright's drafting room and playroom and of a number of his other early residential projects.

30. O'Gorman, "Richardson and Wright," 311.

31. Van Rensselaer, *Henry Hobson Richardson and His Work*, 123.

32. Ibid., 126.

33. Mahony's decision to design a dwelling instead of a large civic building stemmed from her interest in residential architecture. She later wrote, "When in my last year at Tech I was called upon to do a thesis drawing I rebelled and told the head of the Architecture Department I couldn't do that sort of thing, that perhaps I wasn't an architect. He said well wasn't there something I would be interested to do. And I said well domestic work was the only thing that appealed to me, and he said well do the home of an architect but doll it up a bit. So I did. My theme was an *architects* [sic] *dwelling* with a connecting motif to his studio office." Marion Mahony Griffin, "original typescript notes for '*The Magic of America*,' c. 1945," as published in James Weirick, "Marion Mahony at M.I.T.," *Transition* 25 (Winter 1988), 50–51. A definitive edition of Mahony's "The Magic of America" was never commercially published. Draft versions exist at the Ryerson and Burnham Libraries of the Art Institute of Chicago and the New-York Historical Society. A collated edition of the texts is available online at http://www.artic.edu/magicofamerica/moa.html. The drawings of Mahony's thesis project are at the MIT Museum.

34. Marion Mahony, "The House and Studio of a Painter" (bachelor's thesis, MIT, 1894), 3–8. On Wright's debt to this project, see Weirick, "Marion Mahony at M.I.T.," 48–54.

35. Granger, "An Architect's Studio," 36–45. Wright treated the photographs of his studio as artistic undertakings. Much like a Froebel block exercise, he assembled furniture and decorative elements in a carefully constructed aesthetic composition void of people, so how the studio spaces looked on a typical day is undocumented. Only one known historic photograph of the office includes a person (artist Albert Van den Bergen; see figure 3.11). For more on Wright's photography, see Jack Quinan, "Frank Lloyd Wright, Photography and Architecture," *Frank Lloyd Wright Quarterly* 2:1 (Winter 1991): 4–7, and Jack Quinan, "Wright the Photographer," in Melanie Birk, ed., *Frank Lloyd Wright's Fifty Views of Japan: The 1905 Photo Album* (Rohnert Park, CA: Pomegranate Artbooks, 1996), 73–88.

36. Historic photographs H171 and H87, FLWHSRC.

37. Wright carved a version of this early logo on the water table of the Winslow house likely several years before he built the studio. Today a reproduction plaque exists on his Oak Park office, as the architect took the original with him to Spring Green and placed it at an entrance to the property.

38. Mahony claimed authorship of the idea and drawing for the stork capitals, although notations on the drawing suggests Wright's hand. Marion Mahony Griffin to William Purcell, n.d., WGPP-NWAA; Kalec to author, 22 August 2016.

39. Wright labels the storks as "wise birds" on the design drawing for the panels (see figure 2.7).

40. Both Jonathan Lipman and Robert McCarter suggested Wright based the plan on a part of the Baths of Caracalla in Rome, but the plan exhibits only vague similarities, and it is doubtful Wright would have imitated a classical building for such a personal work.

41. See photograph 9506.019, FLW-AAL.

42. Spencer, "Work of Frank Lloyd Wright," 65.

43. After Bock produced the stork capitals for the studio's entrance loggia Wright came up with the idea to create the crouching figures. John Lloyd Wright later described the Boulder figures as "man struggling to pull his beard from the earth." John Lloyd Wright Collection Inventory, JLW-AAL. The artist found a model named Clap able to hold the necessary "difficult and neck breaking" position, and Bock began creating the works in an "all-glass room" on the top floor of the Rookery Building. To prevent Wright from trying to alter the figure, Bock locked the architect out of the studio. Edward Waller soon found out about the "naked man" in the building and gave the artist a "terse order to get out, bag and baggage." Bock, *Memoirs of an American Artist,* 67–68.

David Wright and his siblings referred to the figures as "The Thinkers" after Auguste Rodin's figure and said that his father also thought of them that way. D. Wright, conversation with author. Bock had seen the Rodin sculpture in 1891 while studying in France. Bock, *Memoirs of an American Artist,* 25.

44. While the suggested permit for the studio notes an $1,800 frame dwelling, a later sales brochure states that the studio was originally constructed for $9,000 (see appendix E). Wright, however, likely inflated the price to increase the perceived worth of the property. "For Sale at Oak Park: A Forest Avenue Property & A Chicago Avenue Property: Semi-Detached Dwelling for Sale Separately or Together, Partly Finished," sales brochure, 4, JLW-AAL and JLW-OPPL.

45. Don Kalec, "The Frank Lloyd Wright Studio," lecture, The Frank Lloyd Wright Home and Studio Foundation Volunteer Training Course, 10 February 1990.

46. Granger, "An Architect's Studio," 39.

47. Ibid., 40–41.

48. Spencer, "Work of Frank Lloyd Wright," plate 38. In 1902 the Chicago Architectural Club catalog described the walls as "of the simplest materials, soft woods and rough plaster. Stained in deep tones, polychromatic in arrangement." Chicago Architectural Club, *The Chicago Architectural Annual* (1902). After workers stripped numerous coats of paint from the studio woodwork during the restoration, the need for its heavy staining became apparent, as Wright had used four different colors of basswood (red, yellow, brown, and white) in the addition. Abernathy, "Outline," 12; Karen Sweeney to author, 19 July 1993.

49. Restoration workers placed large steel beams into the floor of the balcony in reaction to the disastrous collapse of the atrium balconies at the Hyatt Regency Kansas City in July 1981.

50. Kalec to author, 30 August 2016.

51. Granger, "An Architect's Studio," 40. Granger's color descriptions match data from paint analyses carried out during restoration by Robert Furhoff.

52. The floor appears smooth in a photograph taken soon after construction. The 1900 *Architectural Review* article describes it as brown linoleum. Historic photograph H10, FLWHSRC; Spencer, "Work of Frank Lloyd Wright," plate 38.

53. Wright, *Autobiography,* 1st ed., 278.

54. A state-of-the-art climate control system was installed at the property around 1990, ending the use of the windows for ventilation.

55. Prismatic glass globe fixtures were relatively new. The architect's understanding of their benefits undoubtedly stemmed from his work for the Luxfer Prism Company.

56. While the vault included a steel door, its walls consisted of brick and the floor and ceiling of concrete. Kalec to author, 22 August 2016.

57. Spencer, "Work of Frank Lloyd Wright," 69.

58. Like those in his home, Wright likely acquired the casts from either C. Hennecke and Company or P. P. Caproni and Brother.

59. The quote appears in photos taken throughout the life of the space as a drafting room. Wright may have hung quotes on the other three faces of the balcony, but if he did no evidence of them survives. Kalec to author, 22 August 2016.

60. The pattern of the fabric, "Campion," was one of three William Morris designs used in Richardson's library. Elaine Harrington to author, 19 July 1993.

61. Restoration architects believe Wright designed the hinged panels so the narrow top piece could fold down onto the lower panel and then both could open up together to provide fuller access to drawings stored inside. The architect used similar cabinets and hardware at Taliesin but later switched to storing his drawings in flat files. Ann Abernathy and Don Kalec, room descriptions, in Restoration Documentation Files, FLWHSRC; Kalec to author, 29 August 2016.

62. Granger, "An Architect's Studio," 41–43.

63. Lloyd Wright claimed the room never functioned as a neighborhood library. *Plan for Restoration,* 30.

64. It is not clear when Wright installed the skylight. A cloth shade that may be covering a skylight in the photograph of the office in Granger's article suggests its early presence. Granger, "An Architect's Studio," 43.

65. Austrian sculptor Franz Klein produced the mask in 1812.

66. Brooks, *The Prairie School,* 79.

67. Wright had a well-deserved reputation for not paying his employees on time.

68. Griffin, Mahony, and Drummond executed personal commissions in an "open and above-board matter [*sic*]" while part of the studio staff. Barry Byrne to Mark Pesch [Peisch], draft, ca. 1958, 4, BBC-CHM; David T. Van Zanten, "The Early Work of Marion Mahony Griffin," *Prairie School Review* 3:2 (1966): 6.

69. Charles E. White Jr. to Walter Willcox, Thursday night, [20 May 1904], 4, WWP-UO; Laytha Sue Haggard Kothmann, "George Willis, Prairie School Architect in Texas" (master's thesis, University of Texas at Austin, 1988), 7.

70. Frank Lloyd Wright to Lewis Mumford, 7 April 1931, FLW-AAL. Years later Elmslie reminded Wright of his contribution, writing, "I was loyal to you too. You have forgotten how often I went to Oak Park to do a bit of drawing for you." G.G. Elmslie to Frank Lloyd Wright, 12 June 1936, published in *JSAH* 20:3 (October 1961): 141–42.

71. Leisa Jayne, "George Willis: A Brief Account of His Life and Works," 7 December 1981, unpublished report in the George Willis reference file at the Alexander Architectural Archives, University of Texas at Austin.

72. White to Willcox, 15 May 1904, 6. Niedecken visited the studio primarily in conjunction with his work on murals for the Dana and Coonley residences. Byrne to Peisch, 13 May 1957.

73. Giannini created the murals in the north bedroom of Wright's home and carried out art glass designs for many of Wright's prairie houses, while Ostertag produced a glass fireplace mural for the Husser house around 1899.

74. White to Willcox, 15 May 1904, 5.

75. Barney, *Valley,* 134.

76. E. Harrington to author, 19 July 1993.

77. D. Wright to Kalec, 9 February 1978, FLWHSRC; Baxter and L. Wright, interview by Kalec.

78. John remembered the makeshift darkroom up on the balcony, while David recollected it being in the vault. John Lloyd Wright, memo, December 1968, JLW-AAL; D. Wright to Don Kalec, 9 February 1978.

79. According to Barry Byrne, around this time Wright also engaged in some form of partnership agreement with Walter Burley Griffin. Byrne to [Peisch], ca.1958, 3.

80. For more on the Abraham Lincoln Center, see Joseph Siry, "The Abraham Lincoln Center in Chicago," *JSAH* 50:3 (September 1991): 235–65.

81. A lighthearted account of their partnership appears in "Mosaics," *Inland Architect and News Record* 37 (March 1901): 16.

82. Both Wright and Tomlinson listed their offices as "Oak Park and 17 Van Buren Street, Chicago." "Selected Miscellany: In General," *Brickbuilder* 10 (January 1901): 20; *Construction News* (Chicago) 12 (23 February 1901): 121.

83. *Construction News* (Chicago) 12 (23 February 1901): 121. A drawing of the house dated January 1901 acknowledges Tomlinson as collaborator. Grant Manson, "Davenport House," note card, GMC-OPPL.

84. The Davenport house was mentioned on page 121 of the 23 February 1901 issue of *Construction News,* the Henderson house on page 781 in the 16 November 1901 issue, and the Fricke house on page 89 of the 8 February 1902 issue. The Fricke drawings in the Frank Lloyd Wright Archives are signed "Frank Lloyd Wright and Webster Tomlinson, Architects." The Bradley and Hickox houses were also published under the two architects' names. The regular reporting of Wright's work in *Construction News* ended at the same time the partnership with Tomlinson dissolved, suggesting that Tomlinson was responsible for sending information to the publication. Manson, "Webster Tomlinson," note card, GMC-OPPL; Grant Manson, "Fricke House," note card, GMC-OPPL.

85. Webster Tomlinson to Grant Manson, 10 January 1940, GMC-OPPL.

86. Webster Tomlinson to Grant Manson, 19 January 1940 and 14 February 1940, GMC-OPPL.

Chapter 3

1. Other architects producing prairie-style designs in the western suburbs of Chicago between 1900 and 1917 include Lawrence Buck, George Elmslie, William Purcell, E.E. Roberts, Robert C. Spencer Jr., Thomas Tallmadge, and Vernon Watson, as well as former studio architects Barry Byrne, William Drummond, Walter Burley Griffin, Harry Robinson, John Van Bergen, and Charles E. White Jr.

2. Spencer, "Work of Frank Lloyd Wright," 61–62.

3. Wright removed some of the banding in later remodeling. The changes in banding are visible in photos taken of the drafting room published in 1899 and 1900 (see figures I.5, 2.9, and 4.6).

4. Wright claimed that Daniel Burnham offered to finance his architectural studies at the École des Beaux-Arts and Rome, but he declined. Wright, *Autobiography*, 2nd ed., 126.

5. Paul Kruty, "Walter Burley Griffin and the University of Illinois," *Reflections: The Journal of the School of Architecture* 9 (Spring 1993): 33.

6. Suzanne Ganschinietz, "William Drummond: I. Talent and Sensitivity," *Prairie School Review* 6:1 (1969): 6. In 1899 Chicago annexed Austin into the city.

7. Brooks, *The Prairie School*, 80; Ganschinietz, "William Drummond," 7. Drummond later claimed responsibility for both the Hickox and Bradley houses. His limited formal architectural training, however, makes this assertion doubtful. Dr. Alan M. Drummond, "William E. Drummond Works with Frank Lloyd Wright: 1899–1910," typescript, 17 March 1968, as recorded in Ganschinietz, "William Drummond," 7. Other early studio projects Drummond reported having worked on include the Husser, Waller, and Dana houses, the River Forest Golf Club, and the Wolf Lake Amusement Park. Barry Byrne to [H.] Allen Brooks, 2 April 1962, BBC-CHM.

8. Wilbert R. Hasbrouck, "The Architectural Firm of Guenzel and Drummond," *Prairie School Review* 1:2 (1964): 7.

9. Byrne to [Peisch], ca. 1958, 1; Barry Byrne to Mark Peisch, 3 May 1951. BBC-CHM. Wright may have hired Griffin earlier that year but probably not before Drummond's initial departure. The 1916–17 volume of *Who's Who in America* lists Griffin as a junior partner with Wright between 1901 and 1905, and Griffin himself reported in 1918 that he had worked with Wright between 1901 and 1905. *Who's Who in America*, 9 (Chicago: A.N. Marquis, ca. 1917), 1003–4; Franklin W. Scott, ed., *The Semi-Centennial Alumni Record of the University of Illinois* (Chicago: R.R. Donnelly and Sons, 1918), 120.

10. For more on Griffin's education, see Kruty, "Walter Burley Griffin and the University," 32. On Griffin's early career, see Paul Kruty, "Chicago 1900: The Griffins Come of Age," in *Beyond Architecture: Marion Mahony and Walter Burley Griffin: America, Australia, India*, ed. Anne Watson (Sydney: Powerhouse, 1998), 10–25.

11. Wright acknowledged in 1916 that there had been an experimental profit-sharing arrangement with Griffin for about a year and a half but it did not work out. "Canberra Royal Commission," *Building* (A), 19 (October 1916): 50, as quoted in Donald Leslie Johnson, *The Architecture of Walter Burley Griffin* (Melbourne: Macmillan, 1977), 22.

12. Byrne to [Peisch], ca. 1958; H. Allen Brooks, ed., *Prairie School Architecture: Studies from "The Western Architect"* (Toronto: University of Toronto Press, 1975), xiv.

13. For example, Wright's lack of interest in the particulars led Ward Willits to look to Griffin for answers about issues such as plumbing lines and electrical wires. Gill, *Many Masks*, 186–87. Wright's sister Maginel remembered Grace Heurtley turning to Griffin when she was getting nowhere with Wright. Maginel Wright Barney, interview by Mark L. Peisch, 17 February 1958, as quoted in Alasdair McGregor, *Grand Obsessions: The Life and Work of Walter Burley Griffin and Marion Mahony Griffin* (London: E-Penguin, 2014), 95–96. Griffin also interceded numerous times during disagreements between Wright and Darwin Martin.

14. Wright designed two houses built by the Littles that are referred to today as the Little I and Little II houses. Griffin's signature along with the title of "landscape architect" appears on several of the Darwin Marin house planting plans, and Christopher Vernon has identified the architect's handwriting on two landscape plans of the Willits grounds. In January 1914, Griffin wrote to Wilhelm Miller that he was responsible for the landscape design for the William Martin house, and Martin's daughter Lois Martin Mann remembered seeing Griffin "around the house and gardens supervising and consulting with her father on different occasions." Christopher Vernon, "'Expressing Natural Conditions with Maximum Possibility': The American Landscape Art (1901–c.1912) of Walter Burley Griffin," *Journal of Garden History* 15:no. 1 (1995): 45n65–67. For more on Griffin's impact on landscape designs in the studio, see Charles E. Aguar and Berdeana Aguar, *Wrightscapes: Frank Lloyd Wright's Landscape Designs* (New York: McGraw-Hill, 2002), 46–138.

15. The plan for Eastern Illinois State Normal School dates to 1901, but Griffin may have begun working on it earlier. Christopher Vernon to author, 21 July 2015 and 14 May 2018.

16. Brooks, *The Prairie School*, 82.

17. Isabel Roberts, Application for Membership, AIA Archives; Joy Wallace Dickinson, "Roberts Brought Wright Style to Region's Landmark Buildings," *Orlando Sentinel*, 11 September 2011.

18. Byrne to [Peisch], ca. 1958, 1; White to Willcox, 15 May 1904, 5.

19. Brooks, *The Prairie School*, 82.

20. Mahony listed her occupation in the *Lakeside Annual Directory of the City of Chicago* in 1902 and 1903 as a teacher, as noted in Van Zanten, "Early Work of Marion Mahony Griffin," 6.

21. "Wood in Architecture," *Progressive Architecture* 44 (June 1963): 112.

22. Charles Williams, interview by Norman Johnston and Hermann Pundt, Conversation #1, 7 August 1974, 7, Architecture and Urban Planning Library, University of Washington Libraries. Williams was a former employee of Willatzen.

23. "Wood in Architecture," 112; Brooks, *The Prairie School*, 82.

24. Wright wrote that he employed Barglebaugh for approximately one year between 1901 and 1903. Wright, "Cause" (1908), 164. The only known record to mention Shepard working for Wright is "Shepard, Clarence Erasmus," in *National Cyclopedia of American Biography* (New York: James T. White and Co., 1955; repr. Ann Arbor, MI: University Microfilms, 1967), 40:348–49.

25. Sally Kitt (Anderson) Chappell and Ann Van Zanten, *Barry Byrne, John Lloyd Wright: Architecture and Design* (Chicago: Chicago Historical Society, 1982), 10.

26. Byrne, *America* 69, 305.

27. Wright, *Autobiography*, 1st ed., 278.

28. Barry Byrne to Mark Peisch, 21 April 1955, BBC-CHM; Byrne to [Peisch], ca.1958, 3; Brooks, *The Prairie School*, 82.

29. Brooks, *The Prairie School*, 82; Byrne to [Peisch], ca. 1958.

30. White to Willcox, 16 November [1903], 7, WWP-UO.

31. Barry Byrne, "The Chicago Movement," paper delivered before the Illinois Society of Architects, 28 November 1939, typed manuscript in the Ricker Architectural Library, University of Illinois, 4.

32. Byrne, "The Chicago Movement," 4; Barry Byrne, undated notes, possibly to H. Allen Brooks, Barry Byrne folder, FLWHSRC.

33. Barry Byrne, "The Drawings of Frank Lloyd Wright," review, *JSAH*, 22 (May 1963), 108–9; Byrne to [Peisch], ca. 1958, 3.

34. Byrne to [Peisch], ca. 1958, 3.

35. Ibid., 1.

36. Barry Byrne remembered both Griffin and Wright enjoyed sparring. Richard Bock noted that he and Wright also relished debating with each other. Byrne to [Peisch], ca. 1958; Bock, *Memoirs of an American Artist*, 82.

37. Wright's debating style undoubtedly also grew out of feelings of self-importance, built up by his doting mother and other female family members and reinforced by early employers and colleagues impressed with his talents and taken in by his charm.

38. Illinois was the first state to adopt a licensing law for architects. Having been "grandfathered in," Wright did not have to take the exam. See Paul Kruty, "'A New Look at the Beginnings of the Illinois Architects' Licensing Law," *Illinois Historical Journal* 90 (Autumn 1997): 154–72.

39. Brooks, *The Prairie School*, 80.

40. Mahony's feelings of great bitterness toward Wright later in her life likely influenced her statement. Marion Mahony Griffin, "The Magic of America," 4:42.

41. Purcell, *Parabiographies*, 3 January 1912.

42. As quoted in Van Zanten, "Early Work of Marion Mahony Griffin," 10.

43. Mahony's note is in the Eric Nicholls Collection, National Library of Australia, MS 9957, file 17, box 3. David Van Zanten informed me of its existence. A second sketch illustrating a comparison between Griffin's layout and Wright's in the Grant Manson Collection at the Oak Park Public Library includes six lots. The diagrams representing Griffin's idea show houses at the edge of the properties, while Wright's houses are in the middle of the individual lots with what appears to be an alley dividing the block in half. These diagrams may be in Manson's hand. GMC-OPPL.

44. On Wright's quadruple-block layouts, see Neil Levine, *The Urbanism of Frank Lloyd Wright* (Princeton, NJ: Princeton University Press, 1916), 3–115.

45. A number of scholars have noted the significant change in the role of landscape in Wright's designs around the time of Griffin's arrival. See Aguar and Aguar, *Wrightscapes*, 55–59.

46. Purcell, *Parabiographies*, 3 January 1912.

47. Mahony Griffin, "Magic," 4:21. Mahony likely provided Purcell with much of his information on the situation, as he was away attending Cornell University at the time of the Thomas commission. This house is also known as the James C. Rogers residence, after the client who commissioned the home for his daughter Susan and her husband Frank Thomas; see F. W. Fitzpatrick, "Chicago," *Inland Architect and News Record* 45 (June 1905): 47.

48. Mahony Griffin, "Magic," 420.

49. Purcell, *Parabiographies*, 3 January 1912.

50. Mahony later recalled, "[A]lthough the design was charming it was not the right answer, this was not the proper plan for the location, words which meant nothing to the designer who was only an architect, to whom town planning was a closed book." Mahony Griffin, "Magic," 4:20.

51. Purcell, *Parabiographies*, 3 January 1912.

52. Wright later observed that "a little height on the prairie was enough to look like much more," and that "every detail as to height becomes intensely significant." Frank Lloyd Wright, *The Natural House* (New York: Horizon, 1954), 15.

53. Mahony Griffin, "Magic," 4:20.

54. Ibid., 3:180.

55. Christopher Vernon identified Griffin as the author of the rendering. Today drawing PIC/9929/1516 LOC Album 1092/12 is part of the Eric Milton Nicholls Collection at the National Library of Australia, available at https://trove.nla.gov.au/version/42217069.

56. Griffin also likely played a significant role in Wright's Henderson house, another Elmhurst commission. These houses were not far from the site of the residence he soon designed for William Emery and Emery's future wife, Thomas Wilder's daughter Marjorie. Christopher Vernon to author, 28 July 2015. The Wilder drawings appear in Futagawa, *Frank Lloyd Wright Monograph*, 1:220–21.

57. Byrne to Peisch, 3 May 1951. It was not until May 1904 that the concept of using a unit system to design a building is articulated in the context of Wright's work. White to Willcox, 15 May 1904, 9.

58. Mahony Griffin, "Magic," 3:318.

59. Spencer, "Work of Frank Lloyd Wright," 67.

60. White to Willcox, 15 May 1904, 10.

61. McGregor, *Grand Obsessions,* 120.

62. Bock, *Memoirs of an American Artist,* 81. For more on Van den Bergen, see Mary Jane Hamilton, "Albert Van den Berghen: An Elusive Figure in American Sculptural History," *Wright Angles: Newsletter of the Frank Lloyd Wright Home and Studio* 33 (May–July 2007): 3–7.

63. Van den Berghen initially received the commission because Bock had been too busy. Ibid.

64. The McHughs lived across Forest Avenue. Baxter and L. Wright, interview by David Kalec; D. Wright, "Musing Memories."

65. J. L. Wright, *My Father,* 27–28.

66. Jackson lived in the rear of a Chicago pickle factory, where he made his furniture from orange crates, originating, according to John, the "Unit System of Furniture." J. L. Wright, *My Father,* 32; David Wright to Don Kalec, 12 February 1976.

67. J. L. Wright, *My Father,* 32.

68. Bruno Möhring stopped by in 1904 while he was overseeing the German presentation at the St. Louis exposition, and Kuno Francke visited most likely in February 1908. Wright, *Autobiography,* 2nd ed., 161–62; White to Willcox, 15 May 1904, 6; L. Wright to Cowles, 3 February 1966, 2.

69. White to Willcox, 15 May 1904, 7.

70. J. L. Wright, *My Father,* 32.

71. L. Wright to Cowles, 3 February 1966, 2.

72. Wright, *Autobiography,* 2nd ed., 138.

73. Wright's employees, who ate meals in the studio, did enter the residence on occasion, such as after 1904 to play the Cecilian player piano. David and Gladys Wright, interview by Don Kalec 8 October 1975, 2; Baxter and L. Wright, interview by Kalec; John S. Van Bergen, interview by Grant Manson, 19 February 1940, GMC-OPPL.

74. The youngest, Robert Llewellyn, did not arrive until 1903.

75. David Wright, conversation with author; Catherine (Wright) Baxter to Don Kalec, n.d., FLWHSRC.

76. Wright, *Autobiography,* 2nd ed., 116.

77. Byrne, *America,* 305.

78. J. L. Wright, *My Father,* 27.

79. Barry Byrne, "Search for Delight," in *Division Street: America,* ed. Studs Terkel (New York: Pantheon Books, 1967), 260.

80. Wright, *Autobiography,* 2nd ed., 117. The date of 1896 is typically given for the Devin residence design, but if that was the case the studio would not yet have been constructed and Catherine would have been only two or three years old. A slightly later date for the design makes more sense both in terms of the story and in how the Devin design fits into Wright's architectural development.

81. Barney, *Valley,* 134–35.

82. Wright, *Autobiography,* 2nd ed., 117.

83. J. L. Wright, *My Father,* 43; Baxter and L. Wright, interview by Kalec.

84. Bock, *Memoirs of an American Artist,* 90.

85. Baxter and L. Wright, interview by Kalec; "A Lovely Wedding," *Oak Park Reporter,* 28 June 1900, 4.

86. Wright's uncle, Reverend Jenkin Lloyd Jones, officiated. "A Lovely Wedding"; "June Weddings," *Oak Park Vindicator,* 29 June 1900, 1.

87. Baxter and L. Wright, interview by Kalec.

88. Maginel recalled that her brother "spent days arranging the furniture and decorating the room with autumn leaves and flowers." Barney, *Valley,* 140.

89. Lloyd Wright in Meehan, *Frank Lloyd Wright,* 228–29.

90. Wright, *Autobiography,* 2nd ed., 138.

91. Marion Mahony Griffin to William Purcell, 7 August 194[7]?, WGPP-NWAA; Wright, *Testament,* 36.

92. David and Gladys Wright, interview by Kalec, 8 October 1975.

93. H. Allen Brooks, "Frank Lloyd Wright and the Wasmuth Drawings," *Art Bulletin* 48 (June 1966): 194.

94. Byrne, *America,* 305.

95. The sculpture is shown already rotated in a December 1899 photograph (see figure I.1). Granger, "An Architect's Studio," 41; historic photograph H37, FLWHSRC.

96. The drawing Wright produced of the studio for *Architectural Review* illustrates the two boulder figures as mirror images. Spencer, "Work of Frank Lloyd Wright," 65.

97. The original studio urns framed the entrance to the home after 1905. Historic photograph H113, FLWHSRC.

98. For a diagram of this pathway, see Grant Hildebrand, *The Wright Space: Pattern and Meaning in Frank Lloyd Wright's Houses* (Seattle: University of Washington Press, 1991), 37.

99. Wright, "Cause" (1908), 158. For a detailed study on Wright's clients, see Eaton, *Two Chicago Architects and Their Clients*.

100. Eaton, *Two Chicago Architects and Their Clients*, 32–39.

101. Ibid., 89.

102. Martin served as president of the Oak Park Kindergarten Association in 1908, while Queene established the Avery Coonley School in 1906, for which Wright designed a building several years later.

103. The Heurtleys lived on Forest Avenue until Arthur's retirement in 1920, when Wright's sister Jane and her husband Andrew Porter purchased the property.

104. Arthur lived in River Forest until 1894, when he and his wife moved to Oak Park. Jack Lesniak, "Arthur B. Heurtley," unpublished training manual for the 2002 Wright Plus house walk, 2.

105. Eaton, *Two Chicago Architects and Their Clients*, 96–98.

106. "Leader in Matters Musical," *Oak Leaves*, 31 March 1906, 28, as quoted in Lesniak, "Arthur B. Heurtley," 2.

107. Manson, *Frank Lloyd Wright to 1910*, 68; D[arwin] D. M[artin] to Mr. Larkin, 20 March 1903, DMP-UB; "Wright Returns to Oak Park Wife," *Chicago Tribune*, 9 October 1910, 1.

108. Manson, *Frank Lloyd Wright to 1910*, 68.

109. D.D.M. [Martin] to Larkin, 20 March 1903.

110. Arthur Heurtley to Richard Heurtley, 13 October 1902, as quoted in Lesniak, "Arthur B. Heurtley," 5.

111. "Wright Returns to Oak Park Wife," 1.

112. Wright often blamed contractors and changes in clients' desires for cost overruns, even though the rise in building expenses typically had more to do with his practice of talking clients into more expensive designs and furnishings than initially agreed upon.

113. Manson, *Frank Lloyd Wright to 1910*, 79.

114. White to Willcox, 15 May 1904, 11–12.

115. Wright, *Autobiography*, 2nd ed., 70–71; White to Willcox, 15 May 1904, 11–12.

116. Wright, "Cause" (1908), 161.

117. Frank Lloyd Wright, "In the Cause of Architecture, I: The Logic of the Plan," *Architectural Record* 63 (January 1928): 49.

118. White to Willcox, 15 May 1904, 10.

119. The earliest evidence of Wright using a grid is a drawing for an unrealized 1896 development plan for a site seven blocks to the east of his home (TAL 9705.006). Laid out like graph paper, the grid, however, does not appear to have played a major role in his design process.

120. White to Willcox, 15 May 1904, 10.

121. Wright, "Cause" (1908), 160.

122. Barry Byrne to H. Allen Brooks, 20 July 1962, BBC-CHM.

123. Five main categories of drawings produced in Wright's office include conceptual sketches, preliminary studies, presentation drawings, developmental drawings, and working drawings. Pfeiffer, "Tre disegni."

124. The drawing (TAL 0208.04), labeled with the number three in the upper righthand corner, is in the Frank Lloyd Wright Archives and appears in Futagawa, *Frank Lloyd Wright Monograph*, 1:195.

125. Ibid., 129.

126. Byrne, "On Frank Lloyd Wright," 110. Wright had renderings of his built works produced from photographs as early as 1894 when Ernest Albert created his watercolor of the architect's home based on a photograph (plate 11 in Hitchcock, *In the Nature of Materials*). Wright used this practice in the production of a number of the plates for the Wasmuth Portfolio.

127. Louis Rasmussen produced a rendering of the Abraham Lincoln Center. For more on presentation renderings in the Oak Park studio, see Brooks, "Wasmuth Drawings," 193–202, and Kruty, "Graphic Depictions," 50–93.

128. Architect William Purcell remembered Elmslie working on many of Wright's presentation drawings prior to 1900, claiming that the touch of his pen can easily be identified in Spencer's June 1900 *Architectural Review* article. William Purcell, "Notes on Frank Lloyd Wright Home and Studio," WGPP-NWAA. In reference to the article, Elmslie himself noted on a handwritten copy of a letter Purcell wrote to Wright's son Lloyd, "I did some drawings and all of the printing as I remember on that issue for F.L.W." Purcell to Lloyd Wright with added notation by George Grant Elmslie, 2 April 1939, WGPP-NWAA.

129. Brooks, "Wasmuth Drawings," 193. Paul Kruty suggests that other architects, including Robert C. Spencer Jr., Birch Burdette Long, Marion Mahony, Hugh Garden, or Charles Corwin, may have contributed to the plates. Kruty, "Graphic Depictions," 57.

130. The Frank Lloyd Wright Trust owns several of Wright's early sketches. Others appear in Gannett, *The House Beautiful*. Brooks noted that the evergreens in the Husser drawing in particular show similarities with ones that appear in a drawing signed by Wright dated 1887. Brooks, "Wasmuth Drawings," 201. Kruty suggests that Spencer or Mahony, both of whom received training in Beaux Arts techniques at MIT, introduced the *analytique* style of presentation to Wright. Kruty, "Graphic Depictions," 54, 57.

131. However, details from the studio and Winslow plates reappear in the 1902 Chicago Architectural Club catalog, and other studio architects, including Mahony and Robinson, produced *analytique* drawings after departing the studio.

132. Wright, *Autobiography*, 2nd ed., 131. Near the end of his life Wright referred to Long rather disparagingly as "clever boy renderer." Wright, *Testament*, 34.

133. Futagawa, *Frank Lloyd Wright Monograph*, 1:162. Two non-Wright works authored by Long during this period, a cover illustration for the 1901 Chicago Architectural Club catalog and an entry in a competition for an American Embassy published in the catalog the following year, include similar uses of color washes over line drawings.

134. Brooks, "Wasmuth Drawings," 194, 202.

135. TAL 0209.002, published in *Frank Lloyd Wright Complete Works*, vol. 1, *1885–1916*, ed. Bruce Brooks Pfeiffer (Cologne: Taschen, 2011), 156–57. Another drawing of the Metzger house has the text "good by Boari" below the house, a reference to Adamo Boari, the Italian architect who spent several years working in Steinway Hall. Published in Futagawa, *Frank Lloyd Wright Monograph*, 1:214–15.

136. "Monographs on Architectural Renderers: X. The Work of Birch Burdette Long," *Brickbuilder* 23 (November 1914): 274.

137. Frank Lloyd Wright to C.R. Ashbee, 3 January 1902, CRA/1/11, CAP-KCC.

138. Wright, *Ausgeführte Bauten*, 18.

139. With the death of her father in 1901, the widowed Susan Lawrence Dana inherited a substantial fortune. Local architect Samuel J. Haines supervised construction of the house. Aguar and Aguar, *Wrightscapes*, 9.

140. Donald Hoffmann, *Frank Lloyd Wright's Dana House* (Mineola, NY: Dover Publications, 1996), 17.

141. The Dana gallery was labeled the "Studio" in the working drawings. Early accounts of social events hosted by Dana also referred to the gallery as a studio, and many years later Wright labeled a photograph of the room using the same term. Hoffmann, *Frank Lloyd Wright's Dana House*, 94n6.

142. The plaster frieze's green color gives it the appearance of weathered copper.

143. The poem had great meaning for Wright due to its suggestion that one may come to know God through carefully examining and developing an understanding of nature. He included the poem in *The House Beautiful* (1896–98) and later prominently displayed a copy of Bock's sculpture at Taliesin.

144. Charles E. White Jr. to Walter Willcox, 19 May [1904], 4, WWP-UO.

145. The bas-relief presents stratified layers of abstract clouds horizontally dividing a circle of figures of various ages surrounding a vessel from which water pours.

146. White to Willcox, 19 May [1904], 5.

147. Cheryl Robertson, *Frank Lloyd Wright and George Niedecken: Prairie School Collaborators* (Milwaukee: Milwaukee Art Museum, 1999), 11; Cheryl Robertson, "Mural Painting and the New Art," *Tiller* 1 (March–April 1983): 49.

148. White to Willcox, [20 May 1904], 1.

149. Niedecken signed the mural. Hanks, *Decorative Designs*, 215. Other murals Niedecken created for Wright's clients include the birch trees and fern mural in the Coonley house, the hollyhock mural in the Meyer May house, the pine tree mural in the David Amberg residence, and the sumac and prairie flower mural for the Edward Irving house. Robertson, *Wright and Niedecken*, 59n11.

Chapter 4

1. White to Willcox, 15 May 1904, 8.

2. White to Willcox, 16 November [1903], 1, WWP-UO.

3. Clarence Shepard may have also been in the studio during the early part of this era. Barry Byrne mentions a "Barnes" helping out on drawings for the Larkin building, but he was probably referring to Cecil E. Byran. Byrne to [Peisch], ca. 1958, 3.

4. White to Willcox, [20 May 1904], 4.

5. Mahony Griffin, "Magic," 4:156.

6. Sally Beddow to author, 16 May 1990; Patricia J. Fanning, *Artful Lives: The Francis Watts Lee Family and Their Times* (Amherst: University of Massachusetts Press, 2016), 135.

7. "Herbert W. Chamberlain, Obituary," in *Technology Review*, vol. 1 (Cambridge, MA: Association of Alumni and Alumnae of MIT, 1899), 389.

8. Other Chicago-area contacts include Hermann von Holst and his partner, James Fyfe (a native of Oak Park), both members of Chamberlain's architecture class at MIT. Berkon, "Marion Mahony Griffin," 75. The two Marions corresponded regularly for decades as part of a round-robin letter group that consisted of eight women from MIT. Mahony Griffin, "Magic," 2:202.

9. Fanning, *Artful Lives*, 194n22.

10. White to Willcox, 15 May 1904, 4.

11. While it has been suggested that that White attended MIT the University has no record of his enrollment. "Charles Elmer White, Jr.," in *The Book of Chicagoans: A Biographical Dictionary of Leading Men and Women of the City of Chicago* (Chicago: A.N. Marquis, 1911), 716.

12. Alice R. White to Will[iam] Purcell, Sunday, n.d. WGPP-NWAA.

13. Purcell to Yost, 22 March 1947.

14. Purcell, *Parabiographies*, 3 January 1912; William Purcell to Leonard Eaton, 15 March 1956, LEC-UMI and WGPP-NWAA. While Wright's unfavorable reputation in the community for not paying his debts to local merchants likely began earlier, it appears that his wandering eye did not cause a neighborhood scandal until around the time of his trip to Japan.

15. Byrne to [Peisch], ca. 1958, 3–4. Later Willatzen claimed responsibility for the interior of the Darwin Martin house. Alan Grainger, "Mr. Andrew Willatsen," Student Papers on the Architecture of Puget Sound: 1959–1970s, Architecture and Urban Planning Library, University of Washington Libraries, 1972, available at http://cdm16786 .contentdm.oclc.org/cdm/ref/collection/archps/id/2744. Willatzen stated that he based his Rookery designs on plates published in Gray's *Handbook of Ornament*, likely referring to Franz Sales Meyer, *A Handbook of Ornament* (1888), which he recalled as being one of Wright's standard reference works. Several of the plates include designs similar to the metal work and marble of the Rookery's atrium staircase. Grainger, "Mr. Andrew Willatsen," 2.

16. Byrne to [Peisch], ca. 1958, 3; White to Willcox, 15 May 1904, 8.

17. Artists present during this period include Albert Van den Berghen, Richard Bock, Wright's sister Maginel, and "DuBuois." White to Willcox, 15 May 1904, 3.

18. Bryan went to work for the civil engineer Ralph Modjeski, while Willatzen briefly moved to Rock Island.

19. White to Willcox, 13 February [1905], 4, WWP-UO.

20. W. Martin to D. Martin, [20 May 1904], DMP-UB.

21. White informed Willcox that the space had been torn up for so long that he had not had the opportunity to take any photographs but would do so when they were settled back in the studio. The following week, he told Willcox that he had taken photographs of Niedecken and Mahony and would send them later. Unfortunately, no such photographs have been uncovered. White to Willcox, 15 May 1904, 14; Charles White to Walter Willcox, [21 May 1904], 1, WWP-UO.

22. Jack Quinan, *Frank Lloyd Wright's Larkin Building: Myth and Fact* (Cambridge, MA: MIT Press for the Architectural History Foundation, 1989), 56, 142.

23. Frank Lloyd Wright to Ludington, ca. 1905-06, FL-WHSRC. Note indicates original in the Burnham Library, AIC.

24. A historic drawing of the plan desk shows designs for female figures on the sides of the desk holding scrolls. These figures apparently were never executed. Historic drawing H72, FLWHSRC.

25. The laylights still exist in situ.

26. A photograph of the room published in *House Beautiful* suggests that the office may have had a skylight as early as 1899.

27. *Oak Leaves,* 16 July 1904, 8.

28. The Fresnel glass in the globes directs light through an array of tiny prisms, much like the glass blocks that Wright had previously designed for Luxfer.

29. Drawing H84. JLW-AAL.

30. The shelving, approximately six inches thick and two feet wide, forms a "#."

31. Evidence uncovered during the restoration, including plastered walls, wood trim, hooks, and a toilet base, identify the location of a toilet room and a possibly a place to hang coats or laundry in the basement of the home. A staircase from the passageway between the home and studio to the basement, labeled *toiletten* in the plan of the studio published in *Ausgeführte Bauten* in 1910, suggests the original way down to the toilet room. Wright likely added the staircase from the reception hall to make the toilet more directly accessible to visiting clients; however, it does not appear in any studio drawing or photograph until the Wasmuth Portfolio, where it is labeled *z. schrankzimmer* (to closet or cloakroom). Restoration workers discovered the framing of the passageway stair. Unfortunately, evidence of its exact configuration was destroyed when the foundation remodeled the space. Kalec to author, 22 August 2016; Karen Sweeney to author, 10 October 2016. Also see Abernathy and Kalec, room descriptions.

32. Byrne, "On Frank Lloyd Wright," 110. Lloyd Wright confirmed the lack of direct teaching by his father in the Oak Park studio, recalling many years later that the architects "learned from actual work on the project with him [Wright], as a pencil in his hand.... He had no intention of formally educating them in any cultural development except as they found it out in the process with which he was involved and in which he involved them." Lloyd Wright, radio broadcast, Bruce Radde's Radio Program, KPFA-FM (Berkeley, CA), in Meehan, *Frank Lloyd Wright,* 223.

33. Byrne to Peisch, 21 April 1955.

34. Byrne, "On Frank Lloyd Wright," 109.

35. Martin Hackl, *The Work of John S. Van Bergen, Architect.* 3rd ed. (Oak Park, IL: Martin Hackl, 2001), 7.

36. Byrne to Peisch, 3 May 1951. Byrne recalled: "The situation in the studio, as it affected those of us who came there to work and to learn by working, was a uniform one, and I can truthfully state that my status and my apparent worth (qualified as that was by the fact that on entering I possessed only the rudiments of drafting ability) soon put me on the level of those who had come from the Armour Tech and University of Illinois Schools of Architecture." Byrne, "On Frank Lloyd Wright," 109.

37. John Ruskin, *Seven Lamps of Architecture* (Sunnyside, Orpington, Kent: G. Allen, 1889), chapter 3, sect. 24, page 101.

38. Scholars believe that at least nine of the round urns, executed by James A. Miller and Brother, were produced in two variations. "Design and Decoration: An Important and Rare Urn by Frank Lloyd Wright," available at http://www.wright20.com/auctions/2015/11/design-masterworks/20.

39. John Lloyd Wright to Grant Manson, 14 April 1959, 1, GMC-OPPL.

40. White to Willcox, 16 November [1903], 3.

41. White to Willcox, 15 May 1904, 2.

42. Wright, *Autobiography*, 2nd ed., 116.

43. Wright, "Cause" (1908), 162.

44. McCarter, *Frank Lloyd Wright*, 215.

45. The original hook was discovered in situ during the restoration.

46. Wright designed the door so that when raised it would block the route up to the balcony, preventing falls through the opening. Sweeney to author, 10 October 2016.

47. Peisch, *Chicago School*, 42–43.

48. The name "Cecilian" referred to a line of high-quality pianos and player pianos built and sold by the Farrand Piano Company of Detroit, Michigan.

49. White to Willcox, [21 May 1904], 1–2. WWP-UO.

50. Catherine Dorothy Wright Baxter, radio broadcast, "Frank Lloyd Wright: The Shining Brow," Bruce Radde's Radio Program, KPFA-FM (Berkeley, CA), in Meehan, *Frank Lloyd Wright*, 234. Wright's son John remembered that his father would pump Beethoven by the roll until the player finally collapsed. J. L. Wright, *My Father*, 28.

51. Barney, *Valley*, 133.

52. David Gebhard, *Purcell & Elmslie: Prairie Progressive Architects* (Salt Lake City: Gibbs Smith, 2006), 12.

53. White to Willcox, [23 May 1904], 1. WWP-UO.

54. A photograph of the sculptural group appears in Bock's autobiography. Bock, *Memoirs of an American Artist*, 80.

55. White to Willcox, [23 May 1904]; Bock, *Memoirs of an American Artist*, 79–80.

56. E. Harrington to author, 19 July 1993.

57. Frank Lloyd Wright to Mr. Martin, 6 October 1904, reprinted in Bruce Brooks Pfeiffer, ed., *Letters to Clients:*

Frank Lloyd Wright (Fresno, CA: Press at California State University, 1986), 13–14. Brooks, *The Prairie School*, 91.

58. Barry Byrne to Mark Peisch, 8 June 1955, BBC-CHM.

59. Anthony Alofsin, *Frank Lloyd Wright, Art Collector: Secessionist Prints from the Turn of the Century* (Austin: University of Texas Press, 2012), 8.

60. *History of the Louisiana Purchase Exposition* (St. Louis: Universal Exposition Publishing Company, 1905), 237; *The Greatest of the Expositions Completely Illustrated: Official Views of the Louisiana Purchase Exposition* (NP: np, ca. 1904), 92.

61. *The Greatest of the Expositions*, 92; *History of the Louisiana Purchase Exposition*, 238.

62. Wright was particularly intrigued with the designs of Joseph Maria Olbrich, whose work he later sought out in Europe.

63. William Purcell, "Dr. H. P. Berlage," to Leonard K. Eaton, 1 March 1956, 2–3, LEC-UMI.

64. Displays in the pavilion included Japanese furniture; cut velvet wall hangings; paintings on silk and paper; and plans, sections, and elevations of contemporary Japanese architecture. Anthony Michael Alofsin, "Frank Lloyd Wright: The Lessons of Europe, 1910–1922" (Ph.D. diss., Columbia University, 1987), 13; *The Greatest of the Expositions*, 35, 37.

65. For more on Japanese exhibits at the exposition, see Imperial Japanese Commission to the Louisiana Purchase Exposition, *The Exhibition of the Empire of Japan: Official Catalogue* (St. Louis.: International Exposition, 1904).

66. [Darwin Martin] to Wright, 30 December 1905, DMP-UB.

67. David Wright to Goshorn, 12 November 1975, FL-WHSRC.

68. Wright, *Autobiography*, 2nd ed., 194.

69. Darwin Martin to Wright, [mid-December 1904], DMP-UB. There are several other letters written by Walter Burley Griffin on 15 December 1904 in the Martin papers that mention Wright's illness.

70. White to Willcox, 13 February [1905], 6.

71. Ibid., 5.

72. Llewellyn did not recognize his mother when his parents returned three months later. Elizabeth [Kelher] Wright to Meryle Secrest, published in Meryle Secrest, *Frank Lloyd Wright: A Biography* (New York: Alfred A. Knopf, 1992), 187.

73. White to Willcox, 13 February [1905], 4.

74. Birk gives February 14 as the departure date, although a couple of weeks before Wright had informed client Frank Smith that he would be departing on February 15. Birk, *Frank Lloyd Wright's Fifty Views of Japan*, 19; Frank Lloyd Wright to Frank Smith, 25 January 1905. The First National Bank of Dwight Collection, AIC. The *Oak Leaves* announced their departure, while the *Reporter Argus*, another local paper, recorded their return three months later on Sunday, May 14. "Mr. and Mrs. Frank Lloyd Wright Left Last Week … ," *Oak Leaves*, 25 February 1905, 22; "About the Village," *Reporter Argus*, 20 May 1905, 4. For a detailed itinerary, photographs, and other information about his 1905 trip to Japan, see Birk, *Frank Lloyd Wright's Fifty Views of Japan.*

75. Manson, *Frank Lloyd Wright to 1910*, 35.

76. Near the end of his life Wright maintained that he did not see the Hōōden, stating that he "despised the fair, went there but one afternoon, came away angry and bewildered." Introduction to "Influence or Resemblance" (1953), *Frank Lloyd Wright Collected Writings*, 5:70.

77. Many of the objects in the pavilion were sold rather than shipped back to Japan. The plate appears in photographs of the library as early as the December 1899 issue of *House Beautiful.* It was given to the Frank Lloyd Wright Trust by David Wright around 1990. (See figure 2.12. The plate also appears in figure 5.13.)

78. Marion Mahony Griffin, interview by Grant Manson, January 1940, GMC-OPPL.

79. An *onigawara* is an ornamental tile located at the end of a roof ridge. The Power Company cottage also strongly echoed a design that came out of the Oak Park studio for a realized remodeling of a cottage for Arthur Heurtley dated 1902 but without the ridge ornament.

80. Arthur Wesley Dow, *Composition: A Series of Exercises in Art Structure for the Use of Students and Teachers*, 9th ed. (1899; repr., Garden City, NY: Doubleday, Page, 1920), 3–5.

81. Ibid.

82. "Work of Frank Lloyd Wright—Its Influence," *Architectural Record* 18 (July 1905): 65.

83. Photographs that Wright took on his 1905 trip to Japan are now in the collection of the Frank Lloyd Wright Preservation Trust and published in Birk, *Frank Lloyd Wright's Fifty Views of Japan.*

84. The Willitses' son shared this information with Meg Klinkow, as noted in Quinan, "Wright the Photographer," 78, 122n12; Edgar Tafel, ed., *About Wright* (New York: Wiley, 1993), 85.

85. Manson, *Frank Lloyd Wright to 1910*, 39.

86. Frank Lloyd Wright, transcript of Sunday morning print party talk, 21 March 1954, 8–9, Frank Lloyd Wright Archives, as quoted in Julia Meech, *Frank Lloyd Wright and the Art of Japan: The Architect's Other Passion* (New York: Harry N. Abrams, 2001), 39.

87. Frank Lloyd Wright, "The Japanese Print Party," tape transcript, Taliesin, 20 September 1950, as quoted in Nute, *Frank Lloyd Wright and Japan*, 108.

88. Wright, *Autobiography*, 2nd ed., 194. Tatami mats are woven reed mats, approximately one by two meters that became the basic unit of traditional Japanese architecture beginning in the eighteenth century.

89. David Wright donated to the home and studio collection, in addition to the scrapbook of photographs Wright took in Japan, a lacquer *jubako* (a tray box) with Wright's red square logo outlined in gold, books on Japanese prints, blue and white ceramics, *chyogami* (wood block prints) of flower and plant patterns, a red *furoshiki* (a scarf in which to carry things), and examples of origami folded into *noshi* (a gift decoration). Elaine Harrington, "Frank Lloyd Wright and the Art of Japan," *Frank Lloyd Wright Home and Studio Foundation Volunteer Newsletter,* March 1992, 9. For more on the Wrights' collection of Japonism, see Margaret Klinkow, "Wright the Collector," in Birk, *Frank Lloyd Wright's Fifty Views of Japan*, 103–20.

90. Jack Quinan, *Frank Lloyd Wright's Martin House: Architecture as Portraiture* (New York: Princeton Architectural Press, 2004), 25.

91. Byrne, "Drawings of Frank Lloyd Wright," 108.

92. Byrne to Purcell, 5 March 1956, WGPP-NWAA.

93. Barry Byrne to H. Allen Brooks, 24 April 1962, BBC-CHM.

94. Mahony Griffin to Purcell, n.d.

95. Bock, *Memoirs of an American Artist*, 83–84.

96. Byrne to [Peisch], ca. 1958, 3; Brooks, *The Prairie School*, 80.

97. "Frank Lloyd Wright" to dear Mr. Martin, 18 January 1904, DMP-UB.

98. Walter Burley Griffin to D. D. Martin, 30 March 1905; Walter Burley Griffin to D. D. Martin, 11 April 1905, DMP-UB.

99. Wright informed Martin, "The general scheme has been determined.… All that remains to be done for that particular portion of the work is for Mr. Griffin to complete the diagram in detail.… You will probably receive it from him in a day or so." Wright to Martin, 6 October 1904, 13–14. Several of the drawings for the Martin house landscape in the Frank Lloyd Wright archive include Griffin's signature with the title "landscape architect."

100. Frank Lloyd Wright to D.D.M. [Martin], 2 November 1905, DMP-UB; *Darwin D. Martin House Cultural Landscape Report* (Honeoye Falls, NY: Bayer Landscape Architects, ca. 2015), 59–60; Vernon, "'Expressing Natural Conditions," 27.

101. These included an elaborated sculptural program for the Larkin building featuring bas-relief panels, capitals, and globes fronted by young lads supporting banners that said "Larkin" on top of the exterior piers, and two sculptures, *Spring* and *Winter*, for the Darwin Martin house.

102. Byrne to [Peisch], ca. 1958, 3. The window design for the pergola at the Darwin Martin house and the living and dining room ceiling fixtures of the Barton house are stylistically reminiscent of Mahony's work.

103. White to Willcox, 15 May 1904, 3.

104. Byrne, "Drawings of Frank Lloyd Wright," 109; Byrne to Peisch, 3 May 1951.

105. White to Willcox, 4 March [1906], 4, WWP-UO.

106. Byrne, "Drawings of Frank Lloyd Wright," 109.

107. Claude Bragdon, "Harvey Ellis: A Portrait Sketch," *Architectural Review* (Boston) 15 (December 1908): 177.

108. Robinson owned a copy of the *Architectural Review* issue.

109. More than four hundred drawings for Wright's Buffalo commissions survive in the Frank Lloyd Wright Archives.

110. For detailed accounts of Wright's Buffalo projects, see various publications by Jack Quinan and Patrick J. Mahoney.

111. For more on Darwin Martin and his relationship with Wright, see Quinan, *Martin House.*

112. Wright later designed a building for the E-Z Polish Factory down the street from the company's original 1891 site.

113. Hubbard worked at the Larkin Company until 1893, when he left to establish the Roycroft. Patrick J. Mahoney, *Frank Lloyd Wright's Scholarly Clients: William and Mary Heath* (Buffalo: Buffalo State College, E. H. Butler Library, 2015), 13.

114. Wright designed the Heath house, completed in May 1904, three months before the Bartons moved into their new home.

115. Andrews, who had grown up near the Heath family in Illinois, was related to William Heath through marriage to Heath's sister Ina.

116. Darwin D. Martin to Elbert Hubbard, 19 September 1902, as published in Quinan, *Larkin Building*, 4. Elbert wrote back that he was "glad to say that I know of Brother Wright of Oak Park. He is certainly a genius in his line, and no man admires him more than I." Elbert G. Hubbard to Darwin Martin, 20 September 1902, DMP-UB.

117. William E. Martin to Darwin D. Martin, 22 October 1902, DMP-UB.

118. Ibid.

119. D.D.M. [Martin] to Larkin, 20 March 1903. Wright likely knew that John Larkin had an interest in hiring Adler and Sullivan. For more on Wright's pursuit of the Larkin commission see, Quinan, *Larkin Building*, 7.

120. Darwin Martin, memorandum, DMP-UB; Quinan, *Martin House*, 25, 30.

121. [Darwin Martin] to W. E. Martin, 26 January 1903, DMP-UB.

122. Ibid.

123. Everett K. Martin, Darwin's nephew, told this to Jack Quinan. Jack Quinan, *Frank Lloyd Wright's Buffalo Venture* (Petaluma, CA: Pomegranate Communications, 2012), 42. The fact that Wright significantly altered the presentation of the William Martin house design in the Wasmuth Portfolio seems to support this statement.

124. D.D.M. [Martin] to Larkin, 20 March 1903.

125. Ibid.

126. [Martin] to Wright, 26 March 1903, DMP-UB.

127. D.D.M. [Martin] to Larkin, 20 March 1903.

128. Ibid.

129. Ibid.

130. Walter B. Griffin to D. D. Martin, 30 July 1903, DMP-UB.

131. Mahony also stated that the Barton house was the first complete design she produced in the Oak Park office. The design, with its tripartite public rooms, was revised again a couple years later for the DeRhodes house. Mahony Griffin, "Magic," 4:75b, 361.

132. Mahony later claimed that the design of the Larkin building belonged to Griffin. Marion M. Griffin to William [Purcell], ca. 1951, WGPP-NWAA.

133. Quinan, *Buffalo Venture*, 54.

134. Darwin [Martin] to [William Martin], 14 August 1903, DMP-UB.

135. Frank Lloyd Wright to D.D. Martin, 14 January 1904, DMP-UB.

136. Darwin [Martin] to [William Martin], 14 August 1903; Quinan, *Buffalo Venture*, 54. Similarly, William Heath requested a house costing $10,000. Wright submitted a design that he finally admitted might cost $15,000 to build. A bid from a local contractor came in at $28,000. In July 1903 Wright sent a letter "in ill-taste" demanding Heath pay for services involved in producing the impractical design. [Darwin Martin] to W.E. Martin, 21 July 1905, 3, DMP-UB.

137. Frank Lloyd Wright to Darwin Martin, 24 August 1904, as quoted in Quinan, *Buffalo Venture*, 22.

138. White to Willcox, 15 May 1904, 12–13.

139. The eight-feet figure for the basement height included the six-inch thickness of the first floor. William Martin to D.D. Martin, 19 September 1905.

140. Ibid.

141. D.D.M. [Darwin Martin] to W.E. Martin and Frank Lloyd Wright, 21 September 1905, DMP-UB.

142. William Martin to D.D. Martin, 19 September 1905; W. Martin to D. Martin, 12 September 1905, DMP-UB.

143. W. Martin to D. Martin, 12 September 1905.

144. There were over three hundred letters between Darwin Martin and Wright during the design and construction of the Barton and Martin houses, most from Martin. Quinan, *Martin House*, 25.

145. W. E. Martin to Darwin D. Martin, 20 May 1904, DMP-UB.

146. [Darwin Martin] to W. E. Martin, 1 July 1904, DMP-UB.

147. W. E. Martin to Darwin D. Martin, 4 August 1904, DMP-UB.

148. The Blue Sky Mausoleum, "The Story Behind Blue Sky Mausoleum: Two Exceptional Men and an Extraordinary Friendship," http://www.blueskymausoleum.com/the-story/.

Chapter 5

1. Wright to Darwin Martin, 18 May 1905, DMP-UB.

2. White to Willcox, 4 March [1906], 4.

3. Wright to Darwin Martin, 28 December 1905, DMP-UB. Wright often portrayed himself as being at a loss for cash. On 16 May 1906, he wrote to Martin that he was "awfully in the whole [sic]" and needed "money awfully." Nine days later he wrote a one-line note: "You are incorrigible, but I love you just the same. Send the money." Both as quoted in Pfeiffer, *Letters to Clients*, 15.

4. David remembered his father laying the prints out on tables on the balcony when Frederick W. Gooken [Gookin] and other Japanese print experts visited. D. Wright to Kalec, 9 February 1978.

5. The screen appears in drawing TAL 0601.001, published in *Frank Lloyd Wright. Complete Works*, ed. Bruce Brooks Pfeiffer (Cologne: Taschen, 2011), 1:253.

6. For more on the exhibit, see Frank Lloyd Wright, *Hiroshige. An Exhibition of Colour Prints from the Collection of Frank Lloyd Wright* (Chicago: Art Institute of Chicago, 1906). Wright also contributed to a second, larger exhibition of Japanese prints at the Art Institute in 1908.

7. "River Forest Women's Club," *Oak Leaves*, 10 February 1906; "Unity Club of Unity Church," *Oak Leaves*, 24 March 1906, 12.

8. For more on Mahony's renderings, see Kruty, "Graphic Depictions," 51–93.

9. White writes, "Marion Mahoney [sic] has been doing great work, (the Unity Perspectives are hers)." White to Willcox, 4 March [1906], 4. For more on the composition of these renderings and their relationship to Japanese prints, see "The Woodblock Print and the Geometric Abstraction of Natural, Man-Made, and Social Forms," in Nute, *Frank Lloyd Wright and Japan*, 100–119.

10. Twenty-eight of the works Wright exhibited in the 1906 Art Institute exhibition were of Hiroshige's birds and flowers prints. Wright, "Hiroshige," n.p.

11. Brooks, "Wasmuth Drawings," 194.

12. An unsigned watercolor rendering of the house by Louis Rasmussen is almost identical in composition. For more on this drawing, see Kruty, "Graphic Depictions," 69–75. An almost identical version of this drawing appears as plate 43 of the Wasmuth Portfolio, one of five original drawings from the publication found in Robinson's own portfolio. The other four drawings were of the Stewart and Adams houses, the George E. Millard house, the Isabel Roberts and the E. C. Waller Summer houses, and the Richard W. Bock studio. Robinson also had in his portfolio the original copy of the rendering of the Bock studio that appeared in Wright's 1908 "In the Cause of Architecture" article on which the Wasmuth version was based. James Alexander Robinson, *The Life and Work of Harry Franklin Robinson, 1883—1959* (Hong Kong: Hilross Development, 1989), 42–48. Charles and Berdeana Aguar address the presence of the Zen concept of "hide-and-reveal" in Wright's work in *Wrightscapes*, 100.

13. Brooks, "Wasmuth Drawings," 193–94.

14. Robinson, *The Life and Work of Harry Franklin Robinson*, 20.

15. Wright also gave prints to Drummond and Willatzen in lieu of pay. Alan Grainger, "Mr. Andrew Willatsen," 4.

16. H. Allen Brooks, interview, in *Walter Burley Griffin: In His Own Right*, PBS, http://www.pbs.org/wbgriffin/brooks2.html. Paul Kruty suggested that the issue resulted from "bad blood" between Griffin's parents and the Ullmans. Kruty, "Walter Burley Griffin: An Architect of America's Middle West," in *Walter Burley Griffin in America* (Urbana: University of Illinois Press, 2001), 20.

17. Brooks, *The Prairie School*, 81.

18. Brendan Gill mentions a $5,000 loan, but scholars have questioned its existence, suggesting that Wright's debt to Griffin was the result of a short-lived profit-sharing agreement between them. Gill, *Many Masks*, 185; Christopher Vernon to author, 14 September 1994. Griffin received at least some of his final payment in monetary funds. At the end of March 1906, Wright wrote to Griffin that the check he had given him recently "would be better held until the Monday or Tuesday following" and that he hoped Griffin would not find this "inconvenient." Frank Lloyd Wright to Walter Burley Griffin, 29 March 1906, as quoted by Christopher Vernon to author, 14 February 2016.

In 1910, while in Italy working on drawings for the Wasmuth Portfolio, Wright wrote to Griffin stating that he had heard an "unpleasant rumor" that Griffin was dissatisfied "with the nature of the 'deal'" of being paid in prints. He claimed that he had been totally unaware of Griffin's feelings and that he always felt that he had treated him "not only fairly, but well," viewing his "time, travel, and flair" that went into acquiring the prints as a gift to Griffin. Wright then offered to buy back the prints, giving Griffin his money owed plus 6 percent interest and 20 percent profit. The letter, which may never have been sent, was found in Taylor Woolley's papers. Frank Lloyd Wright to Walter [Burley Griffin], 10 June 1910, TWC-UU.

19. Surviving correspondence between members of the Oak Park studio and those involved in the bank project for Dwight, Illinois, suggests that Griffin departed sometime between January 5, when he sent a note about hardware to the client, and the end of that month, when Arthur Tobin began writing to clients in Griffin's place. The First National Bank of Dwight Collection, Ryerson and Burnham Archives, AIC. Between these dates either Isabel Roberts or Wright signed correspondence headed to Dwight. A letter between Wright and Darwin Martin dated March 1 alludes to Griffin possibly still providing his expertise for Martin's landscape plans, but Griffin had definitely resigned from the studio by March 4. Frank Lloyd Wright to Darwin Martin, 1 March 1906, DMP-UB; White to Willcox, 4 March [1906], 4.

20. Aguar and Aguar, *Wrightscapes,* 104.

21. Christopher Vernon to author, 3 November 2015. The author expresses her deep gratitude to Christopher Vernon for sharing this material.

22. Wright to Griffin, 29 March 1906.

23. Wright had encouraged White to establish his practice either in the Loop or in a northern Chicago suburb, most likely to avoid local competition from him. He called White a fool to anchor himself to Oak Park. White to Willcox, 4 March [1906], 3. That Wright continued to be supportive of White after he left the studio was due in part to White's father-in-law, Charles E. Roberts, being an important client and friend of Wright's.

24. Byrne to Peisch, 3 May 1951; Byrne to [Peisch], ca. 1958, 3.

25. White to Willcox, 4 March [1906], 5.

26. Ibid. Byrne recalled that Drummond left around the time that he himself departed in August 1908, yet Van Bergen recalled Drummond still being in the office in 1909. Drummond also contributed to the completion of studio work after Wright left for Europe. Brooks, *The Prairie School,* 86; Byrne to Peisch, 21 April 1955.

27. Wright, "Cause" (1908), 164.

28. Charles Leroux, "Like Father, like Son, Lloyd Comes Home Making the Wright Impression," *Chicago Tribune,* 18 October 1976.

29. Gebhard, *Purcell & Elmslie,* 14.

30. According to Darwin Martin, "Mrs. Martin learned this from Mrs. Wright." D.D.M. [Martin] to Larkin, 20 March 1903.

31. White noted, "Griffin has resigned and will practice in Chicago. His place is taken by Wright's brother in law…. Willatzen resigned to go work for Robert Spencer for Thirty dollars." White to Willcox, 4 March [1906], 4.

32. Ibid.

33. "Arthur C. Tobin," obituary, *Chicago Tribune,* 19 February 1940, 16.

34. His initial wage was $780 per year. Robinson, *The Life and Work of Harry Franklin Robinson,* 18–19.

35. Hardin was enrolled in the Art and Design Program during the summer of 1905 and designated as a special student during the regular school term. He did not finish the school year, as he was working in the Oak Park studio by March 1906. *Annual Register July, 1905-July, 1906, with Announcements for 1906–1907* (Urbana: University of Illinois, 1906), 420, 432.

36. Mahony Griffin, "Magic," 4:261, 264.

37. One was Maud Summers, *First Reader* (New York: Frank D. Beattys, 1908).

38. Wright had designed one of his "bootleg" houses for Albert's father Warren McArthur in the South Kenwood neighborhood of Chicago in 1892.

39. Van Bergen, interview by Manson, 19 February 1940.

40. L. Wright to Cowles, 3 February 1966, 2–3.

41. John Van Bergen to H. Allen Brooks, August 1966, as quoted in Hackl, *The Work of John S. Van Bergen,* 6–7; Robinson, *The Life and Work of Harry Franklin Robinson,* 20. Wright must not have been too upset about Robinson's departure, as he rehired the young architect in October 1911 to manage his Chicago Orchestra Hall office and in 1912 wrote him in a holiday card, "To a faithful architectural son; Harry—May he live long and prosper." Robinson, *The Life and Work of Harry Franklin Robinson,* 42.

42. Van Bergen, interview by Manson, 19 February 1940.

43. Darwin [Martin] to Wright, 30 December 1905, DMP-UB. It is not clear to which property Martin was referring. Wright acquire a forty-foot strip of land from his mother east of his property on which to build a garage, but not until 23 May 1911. The other borders of his lot were fixed.

44. Bock incorporated the horizontal leaded glass panes into his home studio "high like clerestory windows with wide sills under them," on which he placed "small sculptures and blooming plants." He incorporated one of the smaller vertical windows in a door. Bock, *Memoirs of an American Artist,* 92–93.

45. A photograph of the studio exterior (Avery FLW 4775.027; see figure 3.16) from around 1906 that includes the brick entrance wall and the original wood fence to each side shows two levels of diamond-paned clerestories on the drafting room but just one level of windows on the library. Meanwhile, a similar photograph published in the March 1908 "In the Cause" article reveals two levels of diamond-pane clerestories in both areas. Leaves on the trees in the photo suggest a date before November 1907.

46. It is not clear if Wright added the grilles when he installed the second row of windows or shortly afterward.

47. Drawing H63/TAL 9506.002.

48. Drawing H63/TAL 9506.002 also showed possible ideas for altering the studio entrance.

49. Frank Lloyd Wright, *Two Lectures on Architecture* (Chicago: Art Institute of Chicago, 1931), 62.

50. Kalec to author, 30 August 2016.

51. Wright probably installed the laylight when he covered over the upper row of clerestories. Kalec to author, 22 August 2016.

52. TAL 9506.007. "For Sale at Oak Park."

53. Abernathy and Kalec, room descriptions; Jack Lesniak to author, 5 February 2016.

54. Kalec to author, 30 August 2016. Lloyd claimed that the fireplace was not there until after the conversion of the studio into an apartment. David had no recollection of a fireplace in the library while growing up, even after the family moved into the studio in 1911. David Wright to Don Kalec, 19 April 1977, FLWHSRC; Lloyd Wright to Don Kalec, 20 May 1977, FLWHSRC.

55. Wright, "Cause" (1908), 158.

56. Ibid., 164–65.

57. Byrne to Purcell, 5 March 1956.

58. Byrne, "On Frank Lloyd Wright," 110.

59. Byrne, "Drawings of Frank Lloyd Wright," 109.

60. W. Martin to D. Martin, 4 August 1904.

61. Barry Byrne to H. Allen Brooks, 10 October 1962, as quoted in Brooks, *The Prairie School*, 82; Byrne to [Peisch], ca. 1958, 2–3.

62. Joe Robinson, interview by Carol Kelm, 21 February 1989, FLWHSRC.

63. Anne Sloan, "Homing in on the Heights: Residents and Developers Vie for the Heart of a Historic Houston Neighborhood," *American Bungalow* 68 (November 2010–February 2011): 72.

64. Wright, "Cause" (1908), 164.

65. Ibid.

66. Byrne completed at least some of the working drawings for the Hunt house.

67. Jane Porter to Barry Byrne, 30 March [1953?], BBC-CHM. According to Byrne scholar Vincent Michael, the year was most likely 1953. Other possibilities are 1936 and 1942. Vincent Michael to author, 2 July 2015.

68. The McCormick residence would have been Wright's largest residential commission to date.

69. Wright, "Cause" (1908), McGraw-Hill reprint, 117.

70. Byrne, "Drawings of Frank Lloyd Wright," 109.

71. Wright predated the design to 1906 on a 1929 rendering, but Robie did not acquire the site until 8 April 1908. He signed off on the working drawings the following March. Donald Hoffmann, *Frank Lloyd Wright's Robie House: The Illustrated Story of an Architectural Masterpiece* (New York: Dover, 1984), 21.

72. For more on the Robie House entrance procession, see Aguar and Aguar, *Wrightscapes*, 127–28.

73. Wright, *Autobiography*, 2nd ed., 252.

74. Wright, "Cause" (1908), 157. Wright expressed this idea repeatedly. E.g., Frank Lloyd Wright to Mr. Martin, 27 March 1903, reprinted in Pfeiffer, *Letters to Clients*, 8.

75. Wright acknowledged the legacy of the Guthrie design in both the Roberts and Baker residences in the Wasmuth Portfolio under the plate note for the Isabel Roberts house. Wright, *Ausgeführte Bauten*, 19. For more on these houses, see Patrick J. Mahoney, *Frank Lloyd Wright's Walter V. Davidson House: An Examination of a Buffalo Home and Its Cousins from Coast to Coast* (Buffalo: Buffalo State College, E. H. Butler Library, 1911).

76. Patrick Cannon, *The Complete Buildings of Frank Lloyd Wright in Oak Park and River Forest, Illinois* (San Francisco: Pomegranate, 2006), 107. Drummond, for example, claimed a major role in the design of the Isabel Roberts house, as did Roberts herself. Mahoney, *Davidson House*, 60.

77. The copies of the letters from the Suttons to Wright that exist today are pencil drafts in Eliza's hand and not the actual letters. Since the responses from Wright's office are directed to "Sir," Harvey may have actually signed the sent copies. Unfortunately, there are no dates on the drafts. A similar cache of letters in the Ryerson and Burnham Libraries at the Art Institute of Chicago documents the design and construction of the Frank L. Smith Bank building in Dwight, Illinois. For more on the Sutton house, see Donald Morgan and John Altberg, *The Sutton House, McCook, Nebraska* (Hastings, NE: Cornhusker, 2008).

78. Studio members involved in these correspondences include Wright, Griffin, Drummond, Tobin, Byrne, and Roberts. "A Wright House on the Prairie," *Prairie School Review* 2:3 (1965): 5–19.

79. The couple first contacted Wright by writing to the magazine's editor in mid-1902. While a bill for the design was paid on 11 January 1904, the house was never built. Morgan and Altberg, *The Sutton House*, 9.

80. Since the response to the letter was dated 8 February 1905, the Suttons most likely wrote their original request in late January. "A Wright House on the Prairie," 6–7.

81. Griffin then laid out charges for sketches (2.5 percent of total cost) and for a complete set of plans and specifications. Ibid., 7.

82. Griffin to the Suttons, 24 March 1905, reprinted in Morgan and Altberg, *The Sutton House*, 15.

83. The scheme strongly recalled Griffin's cottage design for the Elmhurst Electric and Power Company.

84. Drummond to the Suttons, 18 April 1905, reprinted in Morgan and Altberg, *The Sutton House*, 18–19.

85. "A Wright House on the Prairie," 10–11.

86. The delay was caused by the death of her son. Mrs. Harvey (Eliza) Sutton to "Burnham Lib. of Arch.," 26 December 1939, AIC.

87. "A Wright House on the Prairie," 11; Sutton to Burnham Lib., 26 December 1939.

88. "A Wright House on the Prairie," 16. Donald Morgan identified that the "$300.00" was handwritten over "$260.00," suggesting that Wright raised the amount from what had been originally typed, probably by Isabel Roberts or one of the other studio employees. Donald Morgan to author, 24 January 2020.

89. Morgan and Altberg, *The Sutton House*, 3–4.

90. These include the balcony of the Laura Gale house in Oak Park, the roof overhang from the 1911 remodeling of the Oak Park studio, and, most notably, the dramatic terraces of Fallingwater.

91. "A Wright House on the Prairie," 6, 15, 18. Cost-cutting changes included using wood shingles in place of tiles on the roof and stucco instead of brick on the exterior walls. Morgan and Altberg, *The Sutton House*, 44.

92. Sutton to Burnham Lib., 26 December 1939. According to the Sutton family, Wright visited the house after it was built and was extremely displeased with changes made by the clients that departed from the design. Patty Cordell to author, 16 November 2019.

93. The other Wright-designed buildings named to the list are the Robie house, Taliesin, the Aline Barnsdall Hollyhock house, Fallingwater, the Herbert and Katherine Jacobs house, Taliesin West, and the Solomon R. Guggenheim Museum.

94. The only major architectural article on Unity Temple at the time consists of descriptive text from a church brochure reprinted in *Inland Architect and News Record* in December 1908. A photograph of the sanctuary also appears in the issue. "Our Illustrations," *Inland Architect and News Record* 52 (December 1908): 77.

95. Frank Lloyd Wright, *An American Architecture*, ed. Edgar Kaufmann (New York: Horizon, 1955), 75. On the design and construction of Unity Temple, see Joseph Siry, *Unity Temple: Frank Lloyd Wright and Architecture for a Liberal Religion* (New York: Cambridge University Press, 1996), and David M. Sokol, *The Noble Room: The Inspired Conception and Tumultuous Creation of Frank Lloyd Wright's Unity Temple* (Oak Park, IL: Top Five Books, 2008). Robert McCarter's published discussions of Unity Temple, such as "Frank Lloyd Wright and the Nature of Concrete," *Ptah* 1 (2001): 3–19, are also valuable in understanding the significance of the church in Wright's architectural development.

96. Siry, *Unity Temple*, 59.

97. Ibid., 70.

98. "Frank Lloyd Wright Chosen," *Oak Leaves*, 16 September 1905, 13.

99. Siry, *Unity Temple*, 80; *The New Edifice of Unity Church, Oak Park, Illinois, Frank Lloyd Wright, Architect*, illustrated pamphlet (Oak Park, IL: Unitarian Universalist Church, 1906).

100. Wright, *Autobiography*, 1st ed., 212.

101. Ibid., 215.

102. Wright, *Autobiography*, 2nd ed., 157.

103. Wright reported that the early preliminary studies were lost, so there is limited visual documentation of his initial designs; see Wright, *Autobiography*, 2nd ed., 158. In 1962 Barry Byrne wrote that the plan of Unity Temple remained relatively unchanged, but Wright's first scheme for the building included a saucer-shaped dome. Byrne to Brooks, 20 July 1962.

104. The 23 September 1905 issue of *Construction News* reported that Wright had prepared plans for a new building in Oak Park for Unity Church that "will be one-story and basement of brick and stone" (235).

105. Wright, *Autobiography*, 1st ed., 215–16.

106. White alluded to this debt when he wrote to Willcox about Unity Temple: "The motif, as you will note, is an evolution of Wright's Studio. An entrance in a link connecting a dominant, and subordinate mass." White to Willcox, 4 March [1906], 4.

107. Wright, *Autobiography*, 2nd ed., 155.

108. The path of approach was mirrored on the east side of the building.

109. One could also reach the stairs from the side street just before the large urn.

110. During their 1905 trip to Japan, the Wrights and Willitses visited Tokyo and Nagoya, both with early seventeenth-century castles. Masami Tanigawa, "The Wright's 1905 Itinerary," in Birk, *Frank Lloyd Wright's Fifty Views of Japan*, 19.

111. Wright's use of this pattern of compression then release and the manipulation of other elements in the playroom, such as the low window seats, proportioned for children, make the room appear significantly larger in photographs and in people's memories. John Lloyd Wright recalled that, as a child, his "first impression upon coming into the playroom from the narrow, long, low-arched, dimly lighted passageway that led to it was its great height and brilliant light. The ceiling twenty feet high formed a perfect arch springing from the heads of groups of windows which were recessed in the Roman brick walls." J. L. Wright, *My Father*, 16. David Wright, meanwhile, recalled children's parties in the playroom around a twenty-foot Christmas tree during the holidays. D. Wright to Kalec, 17 August 1984. In reality the floor-to-ceiling height at the top of the barrel vault is only fourteen feet, seven inches. Karen Sweeney to author, 22 February 2016.

112. Wright, "Cause" (1908), 212.

113. Parishioners with fussy infants could sit in one of these lower "cloisters" and make a quick departure if needed.

114. While the play of half levels was more in keeping with the character of Griffin's architecture than Wright's, it is not clear what, if anything, he contributed to this design before his departure from the studio.

115. The idea to locate the pulpit in this way may have originated from Reverend Johonnot. Siry, *Unity Temple*, 99.

116. Wright described the path of discovery sequence at Unity Temple in *Autobiography*, 2nd ed., 155.

117. For more on this play of two- and three-dimensional forms, see Sidney K. Robinson, "Architectural Evolution of Unity Temple," foreword to *The Noble Room: The Inspired Conception and Tumultuous Creation of Frank Lloyd Wright's Unity Temple*, by David M. Sokol (Oak Park, IL: Top Five Books, 2008), xi–xlii.

118. Wright, *Autobiography*, 2nd ed., 206.

119. Manson, *Frank Lloyd Wright to 1910*, 7–9.

120. Although he published the bank in the *Brickbuilder* in 1901 as being "constructed entirely of brick" the rendering shows monolithic, not brick, walls. Frank Lloyd Wright, "The 'Village Bank' Series. V," *Brickbuilder* 10 (August 1901): 19. "Other concrete projects Wright developed around this time included an apartment building for Warren McArthur on the South Side of Chicago and a large estate for Harold McCormick.

121. Wright hid the concrete frame of the E-Z Polish Factory behind a façade of buff-colored brick.

122. Frank Lloyd Wright to Ludington.

123. McCarter, "Frank Lloyd Wright and the Nature of Concrete," 10. The lines of the pours were visible on the facades until 1961, when the building was covered with Albitol, a stucco-like bonding agent. On alterations to Unity Temple, see Siry, *Unity Temple*, 247–50.

124. White to Willcox, 4 March [1906], 3.

125. Byrne to [Peisch], ca. 1958, 2; William A. Storrer, *The Frank Lloyd Wright Companion* (Chicago: University of Chicago Press, 1993), 92.

126. Byrne, "Drawings of Frank Lloyd Wright," 108–9. The drawing is #0611.004 in the Frank Lloyd Wright Archives.

127. The actual dedication service was not held until 26 September 1909, three days after Wright left Oak Park for Europe. In March 1908 Wright informed the church that Paul Mueller had put nearly $11,000 more into the construction of the building than what he was to receive. Wright to Trustees of Unity Church, 20 March 1908, Unity Temple Collection, Oak Park Public Library. Later, Wright dismissed the contractor's dire financial situation stating that Mueller "[d]oesn't lose much on it in the end. It is exciting to him to rescue ideas, to participate in creation. And together we overcame difficulty after difficulty in the field, where an architect's education is never finished." Wright, *Autobiography*, 1st ed., 217.

128. Wright, *Autobiography*, 1st ed., 217.

129. Editors of *Architectural Record*, introduction to Wright, "Cause" (1908), 4.

130. Ibid., 161–62.

131. Ibid., 4.

132. Ibid., 158–59.

133. Harriet Monroe, "In the Galleries," *Chicago Examiner*, 13 April 1907.

134. Charles E. Illsley, "The Larkin Administration Building, Buffalo," *Inland Architect and News Record* 50 (July 1907): 4.

135. Russell Sturgis, "The Larkin Building in Buffalo," *Architectural Record*, 23 (April 1908): 312, 317. Earlier, when offered "a complete number" from *Architectural Record*, Wright explored the idea of including an article authored by Sturgis. After meeting the critic, however, he felt that Sturgis did not understand the work of the Oak Park studio and wanted to find a younger man to write the piece. In the end, Wright wrote what became his 1908 "In the Cause of Architecture" essay himself. White to Willcox, 16 November [1903], 1–2; White to Willcox, 15 May 1904, 8.

136. Wright, "Cause" (1908), 163–64.

137. White to Willcox, 13 February [1905].

138. Wright, "Cause" (1908), 164.

Chapter 6

1. The Bankers' Panic of 1907 began in mid-October. Many financial institutions across the country ended up in bankruptcy.

2. Frank Lloyd Wright to Charles Robert Ashbee, CRA/1/21, 3 January 1909, FLW-AAL and CAP-KCC. (According to Neil Levine, the correct date of the letter is 3 February 1909.)

3. Most of the original investors of the project were faculty from the University of Chicago who purchased ten-acre lots on which to build summer cabins. For more on Wright's Montana projects, see, Randall LeCocq, *Frank Lloyd Wright in Montana: Darby, Stevensville, and Whitefish* (Helena, MT: Drumlummon Institute, 2013).

4. Wright, *Ausgeführte Bauten*, 19.

5. Grant Manson, "John Van Bergen," note card, GMC-OPPL.

6. LeCocq, *Frank Lloyd Wright in Montana*, 11.

7. Manson, *Frank Lloyd Wright to 1910*, 207.

8. LeCocq, *Frank Lloyd Wright in Montana*, 7–8.

9. Ibid., 17.

10. Frank Lloyd Wright to Darwin D. Martin, 2 December 1908, DMP-UB.

11. Barry Byrne to Sally Chappell, 25 October 1966, in Sally Anderson Chappell, "Barry Byrne: Architecture and Writings" (Ph.D. diss., Northwestern University, 1968), 9.

12. Van Bergen recalled that the visitor was Henry Ford, but this is extremely doubtful, as he and his wife did not start thinking seriously about building a new home until 1912. Barry Byrne, meanwhile, recalled that Wright had met Wills right before the architect departed for Europe. Miriam Cady to author, 7 December 2015; Van Zanten, "Early Work of Marion Mahony Griffin," 18.

13. Hermann von Holst to Grant Manson, 16 February 1940, GMC-OPPL.

14. Manson, *Frank Lloyd Wright to 1910*, 165, 201–2; Alofsin, "Lessons of Europe," 22.

15. Wright, *Autobiography*, 2nd ed., 110–11.

16. "Stoutly Defends Erring Husband," *Chicago Tribune*, 8 November 1909, sec. 1: 7.

17. While Purcell recalled prior to Wright's departure that there had been no cloud on the architect's fame or character beyond the confines of the neighborhood, "Wright was continuously the center of neighborhood gossip on Forest Avenue." [William Purcell], "Biographical—F. L. Wright," page B, WGPP-NWAA.

18. Wright's marital infidelities reportedly led to Robert Hardin leaving the office, most likely sometime in 1907 or 1908. Sloan, "Homing In."

19. According to Wright, Catherine told him he would have to wait a year, but when the year was over, she declined to give him the divorce. *Autobiography*, 2nd ed., 163.

20. Charles Ashbee journal, 21 December 1908, CRA/1/20, CAP-KCC.

21. Janet Ashbee journal, [December] 1908, CRA/3, CAP-KCC, as quoted in Gill, *Many Masks*, 202.

22. Charles Robert Ashbee to Frank Lloyd Wright, 25 December 1908, CRA/1/20, CAP-KCC; Alan Crawford, "Ten Letters from Frank Lloyd Wright to Charles Robert Ashbee," *Architectural History* 13 (1970): 66.

23. Wright to Ashbee, 3 January 1909.

24. Unfortunately, the exact details of Wright's initial contact with Wasmuth are unknown. Company records did not survive the Second World War. Neil Levine, *The Architecture of Frank Lloyd Wright* (Princeton, NJ: Princeton University Press, 1997), 66. For more on the various editions and number of copies of Wright's Wasmuth publications, see Anthony Alofsin, *Frank Lloyd Wright's Lost Years, 1910–1922: A Study of Influence* (Chicago: University of Chicago Press, 1993), 76–77.

25. Early in 1909, Wright wrote to Charles Ashbee of his temptation to "desert" Oak Park. Wright to Ashbee, 3 January 1909. Levine, *The Architecture of Frank Lloyd Wright*, 444n30.

26. Word likely reached Oak Park a few days later, as a note added to the letter reads "copy to W.E.M. 9/18/09. N.T.," suggesting that Martin notified his brother William of Wright's imminent desertion. Frank Lloyd Wright to Mr. Martin, 16 September 1909, DMP-UB.

27. Wright later alluded to having left Oak Park on 20 September 1909. Frank Lloyd Wright to C.R. Ashbee, 24 July 1909, CRA/1/12, CAP-KCC. Several scholars have erroneously endorsed that date. Wright was still in the Chicago area on July 22 when he signed the contract with von Holst. The September 25 issue of the *Oak Leaves* recorded July 23 as the date of his departure, noting, "Frank Lloyd Wright left Thursday for Germany to superintend publication of a book to contain his architectural work. He expects to be absent a year, and the work may take even longer." "Announcements," *Oak Leaves*, 25 September 1909, 32.

28. Edwin Cheney claimed in his testimony during his divorce proceedings that Mamah left him on 28 June 1909.

29. On the application Wright "solemnly swore" that he last left the United States on 3 October 1909. Frank Lloyd Wright, duplicate passport application, issued 20 July 1910, American Consulate, Rome, "United States, Passport Applications, 1795–1925." Images, FamilySearch, http://FamilySearch.org, National Archives and Records Administration, Washington, DC. Unfortunately, records for passengers leaving the United States for that period are not complete, and the ship he and Cheney departed on has not been identified.

30. Baxter to Manson, 6 November 1966.

31. John Lloyd Wright to Dad [Frank Lloyd Wright], 12 March 1945, JLW-AAL.

32. J. L. Wright, *My Father*, 53–54.

33. "Contract between Frank Lloyd Wright and Hermann V. von Holst," 22 September 1909, WGPP-NWAA; Isabel Roberts to William Gray Purcell, 12 October 1909, WGPP-NWAA. Von Holst sent his copy of the contract to William Purcell in 1951. Purcell kept a copy, giving the original to the Burnham Library. H. V. von Holst to William Purcell, 25 May 1951, WGPP-NWAA. A transcript of the contract appears in Alofsin, *Lost Years*, 311–12.

34. Brooks, *The Prairie School*, 86. Problems with contractors arose on projects Van Bergen worked on, largely due to his inexperience and the fact that Wright had collected final fees on projects prior to his departure. Van Bergen, interview by Manson, 19 February 1940.

35. Mahony Griffin, "Magic," 4:20; Byrne to Peisch, 21 April 1955; Brooks, "Wasmuth Drawings," 199.

36. William Purcell to John [Jager?], 25 June 1941, WGPP-NWAA. Purcell wrote that he told Wright that he would discuss the matter with his partner. When he brought up the topic, George Elmslie said at once, "Willie, don't you touch it, you'll get burnt sure." After their refusal, he reported that Wright had "never been more than barely decent" to either him or Elmslie. [William Purcell,] "Wright," draft of paper on Frank Lloyd Wright, 2, WGPP-NWAA. Wright left Adler and Sullivan in early 1893. Robert Twombly, *Louis Sullivan: His Life and Work* (Chicago: University of Chicago Press, 1986), 235, 495n8.

37. Roberts wrote, "You will be interested in knowing that Mr. H. V. Von Holst, a Chicago architect whom you may know, has taken charge of this office and we think the work will be cared for nicely during Mr. Wright's absence." She signed the note "Isabel Roberts, Sec'y." Roberts to Purcell, 12 October 1909.

38. A member of the class of 1896, Hermann von Holst had studied architecture at MIT along with Marion Chamberlain and his eventual partner James Fyfe.

39. Wright, *Autobiography*, 2nd ed., 164.

40. Van Bergen, interview by Manson, 19 February 1940.

41. The contract listed commissions under three headings: "Work Under Construction," "Probable & Prospective," and "Work in Hand." "Contract between Wright and Von Holst, AIC."

42. "Contract between Wright and Von Holst." For more

on von Holst's office and the completion of the Wright commissions, see Paul Kruty and Paul E. Sprague, *Marion Mahony and Millikin Place: Creating a Prairie School Masterpiece with the Help of Frank Lloyd Wright, Herman Von Holst, and Walter Burley Griffin* (St. Louis: Walter Burley Griffin Society of America, 2007).

43. If David was referring to the studio library and not the home study, then it is likely that Wright had already constructed the fireplace. David Wright to Papa [Frank Lloyd Wright], n.d. (David alluded to Christmas presents being sent, suggesting December 1909 or early January 1910.)

44. Manson, "Van Bergen," note card.

45. Von Holst to Manson, 16 February 1940.

46. Mahony Griffin, "Magic," 4:20.

47. Van Zanten, "Early Work of Marion Mahony Griffin," 13; Kruty and Sprague, *Marion Mahony and Millikin Place*, 18. A recent graduate of the architecture program at Cornell University, Lippincott worked briefly for the firm of Spencer and Powers in 1912 before becoming Griffin's chief draftsman. In 1914 he married Griffin's sister Genevieve and moved to Australia with Mahony and Griffin. Arselia Bessie Martin [Swisher] received degrees in architectural engineering in 1909 and architectural decoration in 1910 from the University of Illinois.

48. Mahony Griffin, "Magic," 4:20.

49. Von Holst recalled Wright giving him just a sketch of the Irving house, which Mahony identified as her work, noting that 'Wright had done nothing on it." Von Holst to Manson, 16 February 1940; Grant Manson, "E. P. Irving House," note card, GMC-OPPL.

50. Both of these projects, as well as residential buildings for C. A. Brown, Mr. Smith, Mr. Wood, Mr. Stiles, and C. S. Church appear under the heading of "Probable and Prospective" in the contract. Other projects completed for Wright include the Copeland, Robie, Zale, Ingalls, Steffens, May, Coonley, Baldwin, and Hardy houses, as well as the Stohr Arcade, the Thurber Galleries, and the City National Bank. "Contract between Wright and Von Holst"; Silber, Isaacs, Silber, and Wooley to Kerr and Kerr, 7 July 1911, WGPP-NWAA. A transcript of the letter appears in Alofsin, *Lost Years*, 316–17.

51. Von Holst to Manson, 16 February 1940.

52. Purcell, "Wright" draft, 2, WGPP-NWAA.

53. Manson, "J. S. Van Bergen."

54. Purcell, "Wright" draft, 4.

55. Manson, "J. S. Van Bergen."

56. In an attempt to extract additional funds, Wright wrote to Darwin Martin that his practice "will yield me nothing for months and months—the statement [from von Holst] sent to Heath is uncollectible except the work in his hands and if that goes through he will pay me when it is finished a year or two from now." Frank Lloyd Wright to Darwin D. Martin, 22 November 1910, FLW-AAL.

57. Silber et al. to Kerr and Kerr, 7 July 1911.

58. "Leave Families; Elope to Europe: Architect Frank Lloyd Wright and Mrs. Edwin H. Cheney of Oak Park Startle Friends," *Chicago Tribune*, 7 November 1909, 1, 4; Manson, *Frank Lloyd Wright to 1910*, 212n2. The article reported that, upon their departure, the couple indicated they planned to head to Japan, likely an attempt to throw anyone tracking them off their path. For an in-depth study on Wright's time in Europe, see Alofsin, *Lost Years*.

59. Purcell to John [Jager?], 25 June 1941.

60. John Lloyd Wright later wrote, "I remember the humiliation and lonesomeness I felt at Hillside School when I heard the whisperings and read accounts of the first scandal. It produced a curious feeling of emptiness." Llewellyn, meanwhile, attending the progressive Francis Parker School in Chicago, was largely shielded from the turmoil. J. L. Wright, *My Father*, 54; "Summary of Video Interview with Mrs. Robert Llewellyn Wright (Betty)," 29 March 1992, FLWHSRC. Per young Catherine's experience, Brooks Bruce Pfeiffer to Anthony Alofsin. Alofsin, *Lost Years*, 337n107. Still reeling from the fallout of her father's iniquitous actions, on her eighteenth birthday the following January, Catherine wrote to him in Europe that she hoped to go away to school in the fall, "either East or South," as she could "not endure another year at Oak Park High." Catherine Wright to Father [Frank Lloyd Wright], 12 January [1911].

61. Frances Barbara Wright to Papa [Frank Lloyd Wright], 19 November 1911, FLW-AAL.

62. Wright to A. Wright, 4 July 1910.

63. Catherine Wright quoted in Finis Farr, *Frank Lloyd Wright: A Biography* (New York: Scribner, 1961), 117, with no citation.

64. "Oak Park Awaits Wright," *Chicago Tribune*, 24 September 1910, 9.

65. On the day after his return, the minister of the First Presbyterian Church in Oak Park "damnably blamed" Wright from the pulpit, telling the congregation that the architect had lost "all sense of morality and religion." Ibid.

66. Wright, *Testament*, 84.

67. Alofsin, *Lost Years*, 31.

68. Taylor Woolley recalled, "Mr. W and Mrs Borthwick separated in Paris." Evidence suggests that Cheney traveled to Nancy, France, possibly on her way to Leipzig. Taylor

Woolley to Blossom Holm [Woolley's daughter], 2 July 1955, copy in possession of Peter Goss; Wright, *Autobiography*, 2nd ed., 366.

69. Woolley to Holm, 2 July 1955. Well educated, Mamah received a BA in 1892 and a master's degree in teaching in 1893 and was fluent in both French and German. She was head of the Port Huron Public Library in Michigan when Edwin B. Cheney met her. Alofsin, "Lessons of Europe," 47n108.

70. Frances Wright to Papa [Frank Lloyd Wright], Thursday, 10 [February] 1910, FLW-AAL.

71. Frank Lloyd Wright, "Studies and Executed Buildings," in Wright, *Ausgeführte Bauten*, n.p.

72. For more on Wright's time in Italy, see Ron McCrea, *Building Taliesin: Frank Lloyd Wright's Home of Love and Loss* (Madison: Wisconsin Historical Society Press, 2012).

73. Wright had moved to Fiesole by 27 March 1910, as confirmed by a letter he wrote on 31 March. Maria Sophie "Mascha" von Heiroth, diary, 1 April 1910, as published in McCrea, *Building Taliesin*, 30; Frank Lloyd Wright to Charles Ashbee, 31 March 1910, CRA/1/20, FLW-AAL and CAP-KCC.

74. Other foreigners living near Wright included the British writer Violet Paget, the married art historians Bernard Berenson and Mary Costelloe, English architectural critic Geoffrey Scott, and the British garden designer and architect Cecil Ross Pinsent. Levine, *The Architecture of Frank Lloyd Wright*, 67.

75. Wright, "Studies and Executed Buildings."

76. Maria Sophie "Mascha" von Heiroth, diary, 1 April 1910, as published in McCrea, *Building Taliesin*, 30. Wright describes the house and his time with Mamah there in Wright, *Autobiography*, 2nd ed., 164–65; See also Alofsin, *Lost Years*, 50.

77. According to Lloyd, Woolley completed half of the reworked renderings for the portfolio. Peter Goss, "Taylor Woolley and the Wasmuth Folios," recording, FLWHSF Lecture Series, Oak Park, Illinois, 24 October 1990.

78. L. Wright to Cowles, 3 February 1966, 4.

79. The photograph likely shows Wright's work room in Fiesole. Photograph, TWC-UU.

80. L. Wright to Cowles, 3 February 1966, 5.

81. Ibid., 4.

82. Woolley to Holm, 2 July 1955.

83. Alofsin, *Lost Years*, 50.

84. Frank Lloyd Wright to Darwin Martin, n.d. [1911], DMP-UB.

85. Author's emphasis. Wright, duplicate passport application.

86. They likely were heading to Austria to see the work of the Viennese Secessionists and, not wanting to be hounded by the American press, repeated the ploy they had carried out the previous November, when Wright had erroneously announced that he and Cheney were planning to head to Japan, not Europe.

87. Ellen Key, *The Morality of a Woman and Other Essays*, trans. Namah [*sic*] Bouton Bothwick (Chicago: Ralph Fletcher Seymour, 1911), 5. For more on Key's ideas and how they were viewed by Wright and Cheney, see Anthony Alofsin, "Taliesin: To Fashion Worlds in Little," in *Wright Studies*, vol. 1, *Taliesin 1911–1914*, ed. Narciso G. Menocal (Carbondale: Southern Illinois University Press, 1992), 44–65.

88. Wright wrote to his mother that besides her he had only written to Charles Ashbee, William Guthrie, and Francis Little. He additionally wrote several letters to Darwin Martin. Wright to A. Wright, 4 July 1910.

89. Wright to A. Wright, 4 July 1910.

90. Frank Lloyd Wright to Charles Robert Ashbee, 31 March 1910, FLW-AAL and CAP-KCC; Frank Lloyd Wright to Charles Robert Ashbee, 8 July 1910, CRA/1/20, CAP-KCC.

91. Wright to A. Wright, 4 July 1910.

92. Wright left from Hamburg on 25 September 1910, arriving in the United States on 6 October 1910. "Wright Returns to Oak Park Wife," 164.

93. Alofsin, *Lost Years*, 66.

94. W. E. Martin to D. D. Martin, 10 October 1910, DMP-UB.

95. Frank Lloyd Wright to Darwin D. Martin, 21 January 1910, DMP-UB; Alofsin, *Lost Years*, 308. Mamah did not return to the United States until June 1911. McCrea, *Building Taliesin*, 25.

96. Wright to A. Wright, 4 July 1910.

97. The pain was deep. Catherine disclosed to Janet Ashbee two days after Wright's return home that he had arrived with "many beautiful things. Everything but his heart. I believe I could be more brave if I felt any justice in the present arrangement.... Each morning I wake up hoping it to be the last and each night I hope may prove to be eternal.... He is happy to be with the children and oh! How happy they are to have him back." Catherine Wright to Janet Ashbee and C. R. Ashbee, 12 October 1910, as published in Gill, *Many Masks*, 213.

98. Wright to A. Wright, 4 July 1910.

Chapter 7

1. Wright to D. Martin, 22 November 1910; Frank Lloyd Wright to D. D. Martin, 29 November 1910, FLW-AAL.

2. A similarly interesting juxtaposition appears in the illustration section of Wright's 1908 "In the Cause of Architecture" essay. A rendering of a "Residence of Mr. H. [*sic*] H. Cheney" was located directly above a photograph of Wright's Oak Park studio library. Wright, "In the Cause of Architecture" (1908), reprint, 108.

3. A plan and exterior of the earlier version numbered 0311 in the Frank Lloyd Wright Archives appear in vol. 1 of *Frank Lloyd Wright. Complete Works*, 170.

4. Below a rendering of the design labeled "Studio for the Architect, Florentine Study, Florence, 1910" was faintly printed "VILLA: Florence, Italy—Via Verdi, Madame Illingsworth—1910. Feb." The Englishwoman Elisa Illingworth was the owner of the Villa Belvedere, the property Wright was renting in Fiesole. Drawing #1005.001, FLW-AAL.

5. Neil Levine has suggested a potential site for the villa was the property just west of Michelozzo's fifteenth-century Villa Medici. Levine, "Frank Lloyd Wright's Own Houses and His Changing Concept of Representation," in *The Nature of Frank Lloyd Wright*, ed. Carol R. Bolon et al. (Chicago: University of Chicago Press, 1988), 33.

6. Seven drawings exist for the two studies. On the individual drawings, see Levine, *The Architecture of Frank Lloyd Wright*, 69–70, 445n48.

7. The site was not far from the small brick Georgian coach house the architect rented at 25 East Cedar Street in 1914–15. Levine, "Wright's Own Houses," 34.

8. Mamah Borthwick Cheney to Ellen Key, undated, ca. December 1911, as quoted in McCrea, *Building Taliesin*, 32n20.

9. Up to this point, Wright's inward-looking buildings were larger, nonresidential designs, such as the Oak Park studio, the Larkin building, and Unity Temple.

10. The valley is also known as Jones Valley. Anna Lloyd Wright purchased 31.561 acres just across the Wisconsin River from Spring Green for $2,274.88 from Joseph and Justina Rieder. Joseph Rieder and Wife [Justina] to Anna Lloyd Wright, Warranty Deed, 30:590, signed 10 April 1911, recorded 22 April 1911, Register of Deeds, County Court House, Iowa County, Dodgeville, Wisconsin.

11. When Wright informed Martin about this purchase in mid-April, he deliberately misled him, writing, "I helped Mother buy a small farm up country on which she had a contract for purchase and had paid $500.00, hoping to sell her Oak Park property to redeem her contract; it expired Saturday and I went up with her to close it and see about building a small house for her." Frank Lloyd Wright to Darwin D. Martin, 23 April 1911, DMP-UB. While the initial plans identified the design as a "Cottage for Mrs. Anna Lloyd Wright," a later set dropped Anna's name from the title block.

12. The name *Taliesin*, as Wright explained, means "shining brow" in Welsh, the language of his Lloyd Jones ancestors, but also references the poetic druid-bard of Welsh legends. While in Oak Park, the Wright family owned a copy of the four-volume set of Richard Hovey's *Launcelot and Guinevere: A Poem in Dramas*, the last volume being *Taliesin: A Masque*. Each of the volumes bears the inscription "Frank Lloyd Wright, Oak Park, February 1908" along with a red square stamp. Margaret Klinkow, *The Wright Family Library* (Oak Park, IL: FLWHSRC, 1994), 7. For a bibliographic database of books that Frank Lloyd Wright owned or had access to, see Paul Turner, "Frank Lloyd Wright's Library," at https://flwlibrary.sites.stanford.edu/.

13. Wright, *Autobiography*, 2nd ed., 167. Unlike much of the Upper Midwest, southwest Wisconsin, including the area around Spring Green, was not covered by glaciers during the last ice age, leaving a landscape that is referred to as the Driftless Area or Paleozoic Plateau, noted for its lack of invasive materials typically left when glaciers recede.

14. Frank Lloyd Wright, interview by Mike Wallace, *The Mike Wallace Interview Show*, CBS, 1 September 1957.

15. Wright, *Autobiography*, 2nd ed., 168.

16. His sister Maginel recalled, "Mother knew the hill that was Frank's favorite. She bought the land from whichever of the Uncles owned it, and made a present of it to Frank. He loved the site." Barney, *Valley*, 141.

17. Wright, *Autobiography*, 2nd ed., 167.

18. For more on Wright's use of diagonals in his building layouts, see Neil Levine, "Frank Lloyd Wright's Diagonal Planning," in *In Search of Modern Architecture: A Tribute to Henry Russell Hitchcock* ed. Helen Searing (Cambridge, MA: MIT Press, 1982), 245–77.

19. Wright to Ashbee, 8 July 1910.

20. Wright talked romantically of growing orchards of apple and plum trees, berry bushes, abundant rows of asparagus and rhubarb, opulent vines of grapes, and a melon patch. He planned to also raise bees; a variety of fowls, including hens, ducks, and geese, as well as swans and exotic peacocks; gentle Holstein cows; and well-schooled horses. Wright, *Autobiography*, 2nd ed., 169–73.

21. While no known archeological evidence exists of Pliny's villas, his detailed descriptions provide great insight into the design and siting of such complexes. See Pliny the Younger, *Letters,* trans. William Melmoth, revised by F. C. T. Bosanquet (New York: P. F. Collier and Son, 1909–14), vol. 9, part 4.

22. Wright, *Autobiography*, 2nd ed., 170.

23. Author's emphasis. Wright to Ashbee, 8 July 1910.

24. Levine, *The Architecture of Frank Lloyd Wright*, 90. For more on the landscape at Taliesin, see ibid., 90–92.

25. F. B. Wright to Papa, 19 November 1911.

26. "Spend Christmas Making 'Defense' of 'Sprit Hegira,'" *Chicago Tribune* 26 December 1911, 1.

27. [Darwin Martin] to Frank Lloyd Wright, 28 October 1910, DMP-UB.

28. Frank Lloyd Wright to D. D. Martin, 30 October 1910, DMP-UB.

29. Wright had also requested a loan of $20,000 at 6 percent interest for two years from John Larkin in October 1910. He informed Larkin that he would use the funds to tide him over until he was able to sell copies of the Wasmuth publications in the United States. He reported that $5,000 would be used to convert the Oak Park property into two units, and $9,000 would pay off an earlier loan secured by some of his Japanese prints. It appears that Larkin ignored the request. Frank Lloyd Wright to John Larkin, 21 October 1910, DMP-UB. According to a later sales brochure for the Oak Park property, the cost of the 1911 remodeling was $15,400. Wright, however, was known to inflate figures. "For Sale at Oak Park," 4.

30. "Wright Divides Home to Protect His Soul," *Chicago Examiner*, 8 September 1911, 1.

31. [Darwin Martin] to Frank Lloyd Wright, 18 November 1911, DMP-UB.

32. Wright later informed Martin that all of the money went to the remodeling. Although unlikely, if true, he spent over $20,000 on the studio remodeling, four times what he told Larkin he would need for the project in October 1910. F. Wright to D. D. Martin, 3 October 1913, DMP-UB.

33. D. D. Martin to C. Wright, 18 November 1911, DMP-UB.

34. Purcell reported the visit took place in November 1910, but other records indicate that Berlage did not travel to the United States until 1911. Purcell, "Dr. H. P. Berlage," to Eaton, 1 March 1956, 7. The *New York Times* recorded a H. P. Berlage departing New York on 12 November 1911 on the *Nieuw Amsterdam*. "Passengers For Europe," *New York Times*, 12 December 1911, 11.

35. Purcell, "Dr. H. P. Berlage," to Eaton, 1 March 1956, 7.

36. That Purcell does not remember their time in the studio is a bit odd, as years later he offered a detailed account of the other places he had visited with Berlage. This included stops to see Charles White in his Lake Street, Oak Park, studio and Walter Burley Griffin in his Chicago office. Christopher Vernon, "Berlage in America: The Prairie School as 'The New American Architecture,'" in *The New Movement in the Netherlands, 1924–1936,* by Jan Molema (Rotterdam: 010 Publishers, 1996), 138–40.

37. [Darwin Martin] to Frank Lloyd Wright, 24 January 1912, DMP-UB.

38. Frank Lloyd Wright to D. D. Martin, 2 April 1912, DMP-UB.

39. [Martin] to Wright, 24 April 1912.

40. F[rank]. Wright to D. D. Martin, 30 April 1912, DMP-UB. The next day, Martin sent the Wrights a promissory note for a second $1,000 to be paid in four years. A photocopy of it is in FLWHSRC.

41. Baxter and L. Wright, interview by Kalec; J. L. Wright, *My Father,* 53.

42. While the restoration architects initially thought Wright may have carried out this change prior to 1909 due to its aesthetics, explorations during the restoration revealed that the Roman bricks were integrated into the 1911 building fabric and had not been present while the balcony was in place. As originally built, the fireplace did not draw properly and smoke entered the drafting room, so Wright added a new, more efficient firebox and damper during the 1911 remodeling. Kalec to author, 30 August 2016.

43. Abernathy and Kalec, room descriptions.

44. This was done to help separate the studio residence from the rental spaces in the original home. Additionally, a double wythe brick firewall was built to prevent flames from spreading from one residence to the other. *Plan for Restoration,* 40.

45. Historic photograph H46, FLWHSRC.

46. Baxter to Kalec, 25 March 1976.

47. Historic photograph H163, FLWHSRC.

48. *Plan for Restoration,* 40. Wright stated that the secluded outdoor space was like many Florentine gardens, "enclosed on two sides by high walls, surmounted by balustrades, furnished with stone vessels for shrubs, a small pool and fountain set at the end of the garden." "For Sale at Oak Park," 5.

49. The green glass is of a middle to light tone featuring a "cat's paw" effect. Elaine Harrington, notes to author, 18 May 2016.

50. Wright based the art glass design for the "kinder-symphony" windows at the playhouse, a small school for the Coonleys' daughter and friends, on a parade from the vantage point of a small child complete with geometric forms representing balloons, confetti, and flags.

The 1911 studio windows were removed during the building restoration. Sashes that could be were reused, although the cames were replaced, as the originals were pitted and had

deteriorated to a state that they could not be replated with a copper coating as they had originally been treated. Kalec to author, 22 August 2016.

51. Baxter and L. Wright, interview by Kalec.

52. Cook County, Illinois, Recorder of Deeds, chain of title for Lot 20 in Block 2 of Kettlestrings' Addition to Harlem, document 4785720, 23 May 1911.

53. Unfortunately, neither Wright nor Bock ever explained the meaning behind the sculptures.

54. Martin had loaned Wright $16,000 in June 1911 and another $4,000 the following November against the Oak Park property, as well as at least two other loans for $2,500, and a sight draft signed by both Frank and Catherine Wright to Martin for $1,000 dated 1 May 1912. In a 1915 letter to Catherine, Martin informed her that her husband had never paid him a dollar on the loans owed him, which at the time totaled $25,283.25 in principal plus $5,636.64 in interest. Darwin Martin to Catherine Wright, 3 December 1915, DMP-UB. The Cook County recorder of deeds shows no payments made to the 1911 loans against the property. (See appendix F.)

55. E. Sanderson to D. D. Martin, 6 March 1912, DMP-UB.

56. Frank Lloyd Wright to D. D. Martin, 10 January 1913, DMP-UB.

57. D. D. Martin to Frank Lloyd Wright, 8 October 1913, DMP-UB.

58. D. D. Martin to Frank Lloyd Wright, 24 May 1914, DMP-UB; notes, Owners and Tenants File, FLWHSRC.

59. Catherine Wright to D. D. Martin, 29 November 1915, DMP-UB. A daughter (Georgiana) was born to the MacArthurs in December 1914, followed by a son (Robert) in 1916.

60. Don Kalec, memorandum to Bill Dring, John Thorpe, and Paula Nelson, "Meeting and Interview with Georgiana Hansen (MacArthur) and Jean Bletzer (Tobin) May 24, 1977, at the Home and Studio," 1 June 1977, FLWHSRC. The passageway presented a significant breach in the firewall added in 1911. Interestingly, this opening does not appear in the second-floor plan included in the post-1911 sales brochure for the property. Kalec to Dring, Thorpe, and Nelson, 1 June 1977.

61. Catherine also volunteered for the American Red Cross during World War I and later became a case-work supervisor for Jessie Binford's Juvenile Protective Association.

Conclusion

1. From 1885 through 1909, Wright produced around 160 built designs and more than 110 unrealized ones. Well over 175 of the projects were designed at the Oak Park studio. Jack Lesniak to author, 2 August 2016.

2. Wright, "In the Cause of Architecture, Second Paper" (1914), 407.

3. Wright, "Cause" (1914), 407.

4. Frank Lloyd Wright to Taylor Woolley, 22 April [1911]. TWC-UU.

5. Wright to Robinson, 18 October 1911, reprinted in Robinson, *The Life and Work of Harry Franklin Robinson*, 35.

6. After Wright returned from Europe, he attempted to secure Darwin Martin's assistance in stealing the Childe Harold Wills commission away from von Holst. Wright to D. Martin, 25 October 1910, DMP-UB.

7. Alongside a copy of the article belonging to the architect, Purcell later scribbled: "Gosh! I occupied no such place in 1911. Did not join A.I.A. until 1913." "Architects Reply to Foreign Critic," *New York Herald*, 19 November 1911, copy in WGPP-NWAA.

8. Harry Robinson joined Griffin's office in Steinway Hall in the summer of 1908. The following fall, when von Holst began overseeing the Oak Park studio commissions, Mahony, Drummond, and McArthur were also employed in the building.

9. Hasbrouck, *Chicago Architectural Club*, 385.

10. In addition to carrying out designs for Mason City, Griffin worked on a range of projects, including houses in Chicago; a library for Anna, Illinois; the Trier Center Neighborhood of Winnetka, Illinois; the town of Idalia, Florida; and campuses for the University of New Mexico and the Wisconsin State Normal School, Milwaukee.

11. Kruty, "Walter Burley Griffin and the University," 38–39.

12. "American Designs Australian Capital. Walter B. Griffin of Chicago Wins the First Prize of $8,750 in the Competition. Complete in Every Detail City of the Radial Type Provided for—First Instance of a Great Town Being So Laid Out in Advance," *New York Times*, 24 May 1912.

13. "Canberra Royal Commission," *Building* (A) 19 (October 1916): 48, as quoted in Johnson, *Griffin*, 22.

14. Advertising prospectus for *Ausgeführte Bauten und Entwürfe von Frank Lloyd Wright*, n.p., n.d., FLW-AAL, as quoted in Alofsin, *Lost Years*, 92.

15. Wright gave one of the twenty-five limited-edition, deluxe versions printed on Japanese paper to his son John, who donated it to the Oak Park Public Library. An inscription inside reads, "To John, from father, who hopes to approve his son's studies and executed buildings some day."

16. Although dated "Florence, May, 1910" in the German edition and "Florence, Italy, June, 1910" in the English version, Wright did not complete the essay until December 1910, several months after he returned to the United States. Alofsin, *Lost Years*, 88.

17. Many of the photographs previously appeared in the March 1908 issue of *Architectural Record*.

18. Wright, "Studies and Executed Buildings."

19. Ibid. Undoubtedly, Wright wrote this with the sting of Russell Sturgis's *Architectural Record* Larkin building article still in the back of his mind.

20. Alofsin, "Taliesin: To Fashion Worlds in Little," 54.

21. Wright, "Studies and Executed Buildings."

22. Wright to Woolley, 22 April [1911].

23. Ibid.

24. Wright, "Studies and Executed Buildings."

25. He maintained a small Chicago office in the Orchestral Hall building after his return in 1911.

26. Wright, "Cause" (1908), 156.

27. Wright, "Cause" (1914), 408.

28. Ibid., 413.

29. Ibid., 407.

30. Ibid., 410.

31. Ibid., 407.

32. White to Willcox, 13 February [1905], 3.

33. Of ethics, he wrote, "[W]e hear something occasionally, but only in regards to the relation of architects to each other when a client is in question—never in relation to sources of inspiration…. Ethics that promote integrity in this respect are as yet unformed and the young man in architecture is adrift in the most vitally important of his experiences, he cannot know where he stands in the absence of any well-defined principles on the part of his confreres or his elders." Wright, "Cause" (1914), 406–7.

34. Wright's false statement that employees came to him "all entirely inexperienced and unformed" offers just one example of this. Ibid., 410.

35. He went on to explain, "I entered a field he [Louis Sullivan] had not, in any new spirit, touched—the field of domestic architecture—and began to break ground and make the forms I needed, alone, absolutely alone." Ibid., 406.

36. Ibid.

37. Ibid., 408.

38. Byrne, "On Frank Lloyd Wright," 110.

39. Wright, "Cause" (1908), 164.

40. White to Willcox, 13 February [1905], 3–4.

41. Wright, "Cause" (1914), 410.

42. Wright, *Autobiography*, 2nd ed., 237–238.

43. White to Willcox, 4 March [1906], 7.

44. *House Beautiful* published numerous articles by Prairie School architects Robert C. Spencer Jr. (between 1905 and 1909) and Charles White Jr. (between 1910 and 1914).

45. Oak Park studio architects represented in Hermann von Holst's *Modern American Homes*, for example, include White, Mahony, and Griffin, as well as Wright. Other architects whose Prairie School work was featured amid examples of colonial and bungalow designs include Lawrence Buck, Henry Holsman, George Maher, E. E. Roberts, Robert C. Spencer Jr., and Vernon Watson.

46. Wright went on to state of his own former employees, "[O]ne left off here, another added there, with varying intent—in some a vain endeavor to reindividualize the old types; in others an attempt to conceal their origin, but always—ad nauseam—the inevitable reiteration of the features that gave the original work its style and individuality…. [B]adly modified inorganic results seem to satisfy their authors' conception of originality; and banalities of form and proportion are accordingly advertised in haste as work of creative architects of a 'new school.'" Wright, "Cause" (1914), 409–10.

47. Ganschinietz, "William Drummond," 13, 16.

48. James Muggenberg, "John Van Bergen: The Wunderkind No One Noticed: Revelations of the Prairie School's Overlooked Genius," *Chicago Guide* 23 (April 1974): 132.

49. The blocks could be mass-produced in a wide range of designs and assembled in unlimited variations, resulting in a flexible low-cost construction method. Wright, who developed a concrete block system of his own in the early 1920s, likely borrowed from Griffin's innovations. James Birrell, *Walter Burley Griffin* (Brisbane: University of Queensland Press, 1964), 146. For more on Wright's "borrowing" of this concept, see Donald Leslie Johnson, *On Frank Lloyd Wright's Concrete Adobe: Irving Gill, Rudolph Schindler and the American Southwest* (Surry, England: Ashgate, 2013).

50. Alfonso Iannelli produced most of the ornament for Byrne's buildings. Chappell, "Barry Byrne," 11.

51. Recognized as the "first overtly modern church to be built in Ireland," it appeared alongside Karl Moser's modern concrete masterpiece, St. Anthony in Basel, Switzerland, in *Architectural Record*. "Portfolio of Current Architecture," *Architectural Record*, 65 (May 1929): 435–66. Paul Larmour, as quoted in Vincent L. Michael, *The Architecture of Barry Byrne: Taking the Prairie School to Europe* (Urbana: University of Illinois Press, 2013), 95.

52. For more on Barry's Byrne's career, see Michael, *Barry Byrne*.

53. *House Beautiful* moved its headquarters from Chicago to the East Coast in 1911 and the *Craftsman* ceased to exist in 1916. By 1915 *House Beautiful* had turned completely away from Prairie School designs. H. Allen Brooks, paper read at the 20th International Congress in New York, 11 September 1961, 13.

54. Byrne, "The Chicago Movement." Chicago architect Thomas Tallmadge also listed changes in family dynamics as a major reason for the decline in prairie style commissions. Brooks, paper, 11 September 1961, 12.

55. Brooks, paper, 11 September 1961, 12. For more on the demise of the Prairie School, see Brooks, *The Prairie School*, 336–48.

56. Wright, "Cause" (1914), 409.

57. Wright, *The Japanese Print*, 117–18.

58. Wright, *Testament*, 19.

Epilogue

1. Alfred MacArthur to Darwin D. Martin, 16 April 1915, DMP-UB; Martin to C. Wright, 3 December 1915.

2. Darwin D. Martin to Frank Lloyd Wright, 26 April 1915, DMP-UB. The story of Wright's Oak Park property is complex, with numerous liens, deeds of trust, and lawsuits recorded during the years he owned it and even afterward, with Darwin Martin typically in the middle due to the many loans he made to his architect (see appendix F).

3. [Darwin Martin] to Sherman M. Booth, 29 February 1916, DMP-UB.

4. Frank Lloyd Wright to Darwin D. Martin, 28 February 1916, DMP-UB.

5. It appears that both Catherine and Frank maintained ownership of the Oak Park property after their divorce, as separate entries exist for each in the Cook County record of title when the property was sold to John Bastear and Alva Thomas in 1925. Cook County, Illinois, Recorder of Deeds, chain of title for Lot 20 in Block 2 of Kettlestrings' Addition to Harlem, Document 8975059, 17 June 1911; Document 8975060, 10 February 1911.

6. Alfonso Iannelli to John Lloyd Wright, 25 April 1961, Folder XXVIII: Midway Gardens, JLW-AAL.

7. *Plan for Restoration,* 42.

8. Wright to Schindler, 28 December 1918, RSC-GRL.

9. Schindler to Wright, 10 January 1920, RSC-GRL.

10. Schindler to Wright, 21 January 1919, RSC-GRL.

11. "Statement Concerning Rentals of Oak Park Houses," RSC-GRL.

12. Schindler to Wright, 17 March 1920, RSC-GRL.

13. Schindler to Wright, 31 March 1920, RSC-GRL.

14. Schindler to Wright, 17 April 1920, RSC-GRL.

15. The transfer took place on 19 April 1918. Cook County, Illinois, Recorder of Deeds, chain of title for Lot 20 in Block 2 of Kettlestrings' Addition to Harlem, Document 6308467, 19 April 1920.

16. On 1 December 1920 they sold the property to Jay and Margaret Bliss. Cook County, Illinois, Recorder of Deeds, chain of title for Lot 20 in Block 2 of Kettlestrings' Addition to Harlem.

17. Drawings 3114.1, 3114.2, 3114.3, FLW-AAL.

18. Possibilities include the home of a local civic group or a school (Andrew Porter had served as an administrator for the Hillside Home School). For more on the Oak Park home and studio's history during the 1920s and 1930s, see Bill McDonald, "Frank Lloyd Wright Home and Studio," Wright Plus House Report, 2018, FLWHSRC.

19. Jen [Jane Wright Porter] to Frank [Lloyd Wright], 20 July 1920, FLW-AAL.

20. Rudolph Schindler had informed Wright in February 1920 that Mrs. Heurtley had requested a sketch showing how to enclose their second-floor porch, as the couple prepared to put the house on the market for $60,000 and move to California. Rudolph Schindler to Frank Lloyd Wright, 28 February 1920. RSC-GRL.

21. "For Sale at Oak Park," 1. Wright still had not paid Darwin Martin back for earlier loans.

22. Ibid. The brochure included plans for the building drawn by Wright's son John. *Plan for Restoration,* 42.

23. Records show two entries in the title chain, possibly due to the Wrights' divorce a couple years earlier. One from "Catherine L. Wright et al." to John O. Bastear in January 1925 and a second from "Frank L. Wright and wf." to Bastear on 10 February 1925. Bill McDonald to author, 16 February 2019.

24. Established in 1921, the Art League held meetings in a variety of locations before moving into the former studio. Thomas taught children's art classes for the organization. McDonald, "Wright Plus," 40.

25. Village of Oak Park, Illinois, Permit Processing Department, historical files (microfiche) for 951 Chicago Avenue, Oak Park, Illinois; McDonald, "Wright Plus," 41.

26. Village of Oak Park, historical files; McDonald, "Wright Plus," 42.

27. Today the descendent of the organization, the Oak Park Art League, resides at 720 Chicago Avenue, Oak Park.

28. Lois Wine, "Wright's Home Is Studio: Local Artists Make Over Frank Lloyd Wright Residence into Art Rendezvous," *Oak Leaves,* 6 January 1923, 48.

29. In 1937 the village informed Mr. C.D. Lunceford that he needed to remove the sign "Lunceford Studios" from the window of the former home, as the property was not zoned for business. McDonald, "Wright Plus," 42.

30. Cook County, Illinois, Municipal Circuit Court, case 205695, Darwin D. Martin v. John O. Bastear, August 27, 1930.

31. Ibid.

32. McDonald, "Wright Plus," 43–44.

33. Ibid., 45. This was likely just a transfer of title, as Darwin Martin, who had lost most of his wealth in the 1929 stock market crash, had written to Wright the previous year that he did not even have the six dollars to purchase a copy of the architect's autobiography. Darwin Martin to Wright, 24 March 1932, DMP-UB.

34. Cook County, Illinois, Masters Deed, Book 31592, 75.

35. "To Rent," classified ad, *Oak Leaves,* 22 December 1938.

36. McDonald, "Wright Plus," 46.

37. Don Kalec to author, 10 April 2016.

38. *Plan for Restoration,* 42-43.

39. Drawings of these changes may exist, as an offer was once made to sell them to the Home and Studio Foundation, but the asking price was too high. Kalec to author, 30 August 2016.

40. Frank Lloyd Wright Home & Studio (1889–1897 - S.002-004), photographs, *Wright Library,* available at http://www.steinerag.com/flw/Artifact%20Pages/PCHome&Studio.htm.

41. Kalec to author, 10 April 2016.

42. *Plan for Restoration,* 43; Nagelberg, "Former Home."

43. Even though the firewall is no longer intact, visitors still typically tour the building in two parts.

44. *Plan for Restoration,* 43.

45. Sunny Hall to author, 24 May 2016.

46. Venteicher, "Frank Lloyd Wright Home." For more on the transfer of the building's ownership. See Weil, *Building a Legacy,* 17–21.

47. Jeanette Fields, "Volunteers Renovate Wright in the Nick of Time," in "Three Decades of Renovating Wright," *Wednesday Journal Special Section,* 21 March 2004, 38. The brick foundation walls were replaced during the restoration using concrete. Abernathy, "Outline," 13.

48. These initial projects took approximately two years to complete. John Thorpe, "Wright Studies Outline: The Restoration and Adaptive Reuse of the Frank Lloyd Wright Home and Studio," (1990), 2, FLWHSRC.

49. Ibid., 2. More than 250 "as-built" drawings were reproduced by the time the restoration was fully underway. Weil, *Building a Legacy,* 43.

50. The restoration committee collected over three hundred historic photographs, drawings, and sketches. Thorpe, "Wright Studies," 2.

51. Documentation of the interviews is available in the FLWHSRC.

52. The organization refers to tour guides of the Oak Park home and studio as *interpreters,* reflecting Lloyd Wright's comment to the early trainees that they were "to *interpret* the grammar of the building." Trezevant, "Laying the Foundation."

53. Participants included H. Allen Brooks, Arthur Drexler, Richard Frank, Bruce Goff, Frederick Gutheim, Wilbert Hasbrouck, John Howe, Paul Sprague, Lloyd Wright, and

Eric Lloyd Wright. Additional written comments on the master plan came from Vincent Scully, Edgar Kaufmann Jr., Grant Manson, Elizabeth Wright Ingraham, David Wright, and employees of the National Trust for Historic Preservation, among others. Thorpe, "Wright Studies," 3.

54. *Plan for Restoration,* 60.

55. Abernathy, "Outline," 3.

56. "Insights from Preservation," Research Center Exhibit, October 1990, FLWHSRC.

57. Lloyd viewed the decision as a "criminal act," believing the overhang to be the first cantilever of his father's career, even though it postdates the cantilevers at the Sutton and Laura Gale houses. "Scholars' Conference: Summary of Adaptive Use and Restoration," 31 October 1977, FLWHSRC.

58. Eric Lloyd Wright, foreword to Weil, *Building a Legacy,* vi.

59. No known photographs of this configuration exist, and the 1911 remodeling that replaced the front door with a side "carriage" entrance eliminated physical clues to its existence. The change made functional sense, as the architect, no longer using the front room upstairs as an office, did not need to impress potential clients entering through the front door. Kalec to author, 22 August 2016.

Also, while John Lloyd Wright recalled that "'Skinny' Giannini from Italy painted American Indians in brilliant colors on the walls of Papa's bedroom," and the paintings were discovered under later layers of paint during the restoration, David was adamant that the Indian murals in his father's bedroom were not present while he was growing up. J. L. Wright, *My Father,* 34; David Wright, notes made on letter from Don Kalec to David and Gladys Wright, 16 March 1987, FLWHSRC.

60. "Three Decades of Renovating Wright," 37; Kalec to author, 22 August 2016. In 1987, the Frank Lloyd Wright Home and Studio Foundation received a National Honor Award from the American Institute of Architecture for the restoration.

61. As a result of their participation in this event, the volunteers were known by the moniker of "the Hole in the Wall Gang."

62. For example, when Wright constructed the studio, he cut down trees that were in the way but did not remove the stumps. They remained until the new studio basement was added during the restoration. When he built the 1911 firewall between the home and studio, he just bricked over the original shingled wall. During the restoration, when the firewall was disassembled in front of the home bathroom, the volunteers discovered the pre-1911 bay window bricked over on one side and plastered over on the other. While the glass in the sash was broken, a new uninstalled pane was left leaning next to it waiting for a never-realized repair. Kalec to author, 10 April 2016; Abernathy, "Outline," 3.

63. For John Thorpe's description of the chain harness discovery, see "None of Us Had Done That Before, but That Didn't Stop Us," John Thorpe interview, 7 August 1997, copy in FLWHSRC.

64. The foundation hired an outside architectural firm to produce the contract documents. Over the next year they also involved members of twelve different trades in the restoration process of the dining room at a cost of approximately $55,000. Thorpe, "Wright Studies," 2.

65. Workers revealed the dark green paint of the original kitchen when they stripped the dining room wallpaper. Kalec to author, 10 April 2016.

66. Catherine took the chairs when she moved out at the end of 1918 and eventually gave them to Llewellyn. He returned the chairs to his father in 1953. At the time of the restoration Olgivanna Wright gave six chairs to the Home and Studio Foundation. Taliesin later returned the two remaining ones to the organization as a long-term loan. Weil, *Building a Legacy,* 70; David Jameson, *Alfonso Iannelli: Modern by Design* (Oak Park, IL: Top Five Books, 2013), 294.

67. It did not help that to give his walls visual depth and a sense of life to the surfaces, Wright often used numerous overlays of paint. Furhoff, "Studio Site Investigation." In the post-1911 sales brochure for the property, he notes the walls were "sand finished plaster, painted four coats." "For Sale at Oak Park," 4.

68. Weil, *Building a Legacy,* 34.

69. Thorpe, "Wright Studies," 2.

70. Of the three original art glass–fronted bookcases in the library, one to the south had been replaced by the fireplace and the one to the west altered by the addition of a window to provide a link to the outside when the space was used by the Nookers. Kalec to author, 30 August 2016.

71. Thorpe, "Wright Studies," 4.

72. In addition to hundreds of volunteers, led by architects John Thorpe, Don Kalec, Ann Abernathy, Bill Dring, Jack Lesniak, Andrew Bober, Carl Hunter, and Karen Sweeney, a series of expert craftsmen and contractors participated in the restoration. For a list see, Weil, *Building a Legacy,* 146–48.

73. While these slides may be available for consultation, currently no catalog for them exists. Kalec to author, 22 August 2016; Restoration Documentation Meeting, notes, 21 October 1986, FLWHSRC. Much of the initial research for this book relied upon the important Research Center collection.

74. Participants included Anthony Alofsin, Dennis Doordan, Kevin Harrington, Donald Hoffmann, Don Kalec, Neil Levine, Jack Quinan, Sidney K. Robinson, David Van Zanten,

John Vinci, Richard Wesley, and Wim de Wit, with presentations made by Elaine Harrington, Don Kalec, Meg Klinkow, Lisa Schrenk, and John Thorpe.

75. During the 1990–91 fiscal year, the Home and Studio Foundation reached over four thousand people through its educational programs (not including tours, use of Research Center, or curriculum materials provided to schoolteachers). They included a speaker's bureau, a lecture series, and excursions to Wright-related sites for adults; a junior interpreter program for preteens from a neighborhood school; Froebel block workshops for all levels; and Saturday morning exploratory classes for kindergarteners through sixth graders. I also established an internship program for university students interested in pursuing careers in the fields of architectural history, historic preservation, and museum studies. Lisa D. Schrenk, "The Frank Lloyd Wright Home and Studio Foundation Educational Programs: Number of People Reached Directly by Educational Programs," ca. 1991, copy available in FLWHSRC.

76. I had significant help from Sharon Gabor, a former teacher and staff member of the Home and Studio Foundation, and Jerry McManus, an architect and longtime foundation volunteer, who led this program for many years.

77. In 1989, the first year of the revised workshop, the Museum of Science and Industry constructed a full-size model of one of Wright's Usonian Automatic houses. Since most of the local students knew something about Wright's prairie houses, having them explore his later Usonian designs both helped to expand their knowledge of the architect's work and allowed for the use of a gridded surface, which provided a needed set of guidelines to make it possible for them to design and then build a model of their house in just three mornings.

78. Illinois Office of Tourism, "Illinois Tourism Kicks Off National Travel & Tourism Week Announcing New Illinois Frank Lloyd Wright Trail," 7 May 2018, available at https://media.enjoyillinois.com/press-releases/illinois-tourism-kicks-off-national-travel-and-tourism-week-announcing-new-frank-lloyd-wright-trail-in-illinois/.

Appendix C

1. Wright, "Cause" (1914), 410.

2. Wright, *Autobiography,* 1st ed., 198.

3. Wright, "Cause" (1908), 164.

4. *The Alumni Quarterly and Fortnightly Notes of the University of Illinois* (Urbana: University of Illinois, 1918), 4:371.

5. Wright, "Cause" (1908), 164; John W. Leonard, *Who's Who in Engineering: A Biographical Dictionary of Contemporaries* (New York: John W. Leonard, 1925), 119.

6. Leonard, *Who's Who in Engineering* (1925), states that Barglebaugh worked for Griffin during 1903–4. Although Griffin was carrying out independent work at the time, he was still employed in Wright's studio.

7. *Houston Architectural Survey* (Houston: Southwest Center for Urban Research, 1980), 6:1421, 1:37; "Dallas' Swiss Avenue Historic District Opens Doors Saturday, Sunday," *Dallas Morning News*, 10 May 2013.

8. Leonard, *Who's Who in Engineering* (1925), 119.

9. The Lewis Institute, established in the mid-1890s, offered a four-year high school program of technical subjects and liberal arts and two years of college-level work in arts and engineering. It merged with the Armour Institute of Technology in 1940.

10. White to Willcox, 15 May 1904, 4. Cecil Bryan was listed in the 1903 Oak Park directory with the occupation of architect. *City Directory of Oak Park* (Oak Park, IL: Delos Hull, 1903), 33.

11. White to Willcox, 15 May 1904, 4.

12. Cheryl Bryan to author, 23 July 2016.

13. "Buildings: Prospective Work," *Engineering and Contracting* 42 (July–December, 1914): 42. For more on Bryan, see "Community Mausoleums: The Architecture of Cecil E. Bryan," Finding and Preserving Your History, http://preservingyourhistory.blogspot.com/2015/04/community-mausoleums-architecture-of.html.

14. Byrne, "Search for Delight," 259. For more on Barry Byrne, see Chappell and Van Zanten, *Barry Byrne*, and Michael, *Barry Byrne*.

15. He had also read Wright's essay "The Art and Craft of the Machine." Michael, *Barry Byrne*, 10.

16. Chappell, "Barry Byrne," 9.

17. Chappell and Van Zanten, *Barry Byrne*, 11. During the three-year partnership, the two men did not collaborate on projects. Barry Byrne to Peter Harrison, 15 July 1957, BBC-CHM; Byrne to Peisch, 3 May 1951.

18. Michael, *Barry Byrne*, 117.

19. Mahony Griffin, "Magic," 4:156. Chamberlain did not attend MIT in 1894 but returned as a senior in 1895. Beddow to author, 16 May 1990; Marion Lincoln Lewis (Chamberlain), "Application for Employment," Personnel Office, Boston Public Library. On Chamberlain, see Fanning, *Artful Lives,* 131–48.

20. Marion Lincoln Lewis (Chamberlain), "A Women's Club House," elevation, senior thesis, Department of Architecture, Non-Circulating Collection, 3, Thesis Archives and Special Collection, Institute Archives, MIT.

21. Chamberlain worked for Clark from September 1895 to July 1896. Lewis (Chamberlain), "Application."

22. "Herbert W. Chamberlain, Obituary," 389.

23. As quoted in Fanning, *Artful Lives,* 139. White to Willcox, 16 November [1903], 1.

24. Rhode Island Board of Agriculture, *Twentieth-Fifth Annual Report of the State Board of Agriculture Made to the General Assembly at Its January Session, 1910* (Providence, RI: E. L. Freeman, State Printers, 1910), 21; Fanning, *Artful Lives,* 140–41.

25. Fanning, *Artful Lives,* 144–45.

26. Hasbrouck, "Guenzel and Drummond," 5.

27. C. J. Roseberry, *University of Illinois Directory for 1929* (Urbana-Champaign: University of Illinois, 1929), 252.

28. Ganschinietz, "William Drummond," 6.

29. Brooks, *The Prairie School,* 80; Ganschinietz, "William Drummond," 7; Hasbrouck, "Guenzel and Drummond," 7.

30. Byrne to [Peisch], ca. 1958, 3.

31. Brooks, *The Prairie School,* 86.

32. Ibid., 267; Hasbrouck, "Guenzel and Drummond," 5.

33. Byrne to Peisch, 8 June 1955.

34. Carl W. Condit, *The Chicago School of Architecture: A History of Commercial and Public Building in the Chicago Area, 1875–1925* (Chicago: University of Chicago Press, 1964), 209n46.

35. William Eugene Drummond, *Our National Capitol: An Architect Proposes Minor Additions to Capitol and Extensive Changes within Its Environment Area* (Chicago: National Capitol, ca. 1946).

36. Wright, *Testament,* 36.

37. For more on Elmslie's later career, see David Gebhard, *Purcell & Elmslie.*

38. For more on Griffin, see the Walter Burley Griffin Society and the Walter Burley Griffin Society in America, as well as publications by Donald Leslie Johnson, Paul Kruty, David Van Zanten, and Christopher Vernon.

39. Walter Burley Griffin, "A Eulogy of System," *City Club Bulletin* 7:6 (17 February 1914): 66.

40. Kruty, "Walter Burley Griffin and the University of Illinois," 32.

41. Christopher Vernon to Jack Lesniak, 20 June 2016. Paul Kruty gives the date as July 1901.

42. These included the Willits house in Highland Park and Martin commissions in Oak Park and Buffalo.

43. Brooks, *The Prairie School,* 81, 117.

44. Johnson, *Griffin,* 11, 13.

45. Ibid., 13. Griffin was buried in an unmarked grave (plot II, number 163) at Nishatganj in Lucknow. A marker now identifies the site.

46. *Annual Register, July, 1905–July, 1906,* 420, 432.

47. White to Willcox, 4 March [1906], 4.

48. Wright, "Cause" (1908), 164. Charles White recorded that Hardin's college tuition had been "paid by a fellow townsman in Texas, who had thrown him over since he had become so 'degraded' as to go into Wright's," alluding to his employer's growing negative reputation. White to Willcox, 4 March [1906], 4.

49. Sloan, "Homing In," 72.

50. Ibid.

51. The first was Sophia Hayden Bennett, who graduated in 1890. For more on Mahony, see Van Zanten, *Mahony Reconsidered.*

52. As quoted in Berkon, "Marion Mahony Griffin," 75.

53. The architects were probably John J. Flanders and William Carbys Zimmerman; see Berkon, "Marion Mahony Griffin," 75. Marion Mahony Griffin, interview by Grant Manson, January 1940.

54. Byrne to Peisch, 3 May 1951.

55. Mahony Griffin, "Magic," 4:261, 264.

56. A member of Harvard's class of 1905, McArthur did not graduate from the institution, possibly leaving after only two years due to poor health. "McArthur, Albert Chase," in *National Cyclopedia of American Biography,* (New York: James T. White, 1954), 39:432.

57. Ibid.

58. Wright, "Cause" (1908), 164. McArthur was not mentioned in the list of architects in the studio when Van Bergen entered in January 1909. Brooks, *The Prairie School,* 85.

59. Van Zanten, "Early Work of Marion Mahony Griffin," 13.

60. "McArthur," 39:432.

61. Brooks, *The Prairie School,* 85.

62. "McArthur," 39:432.

63. Roberts erroneously listed her birth year as 1874 on her application for membership in the American Institute of Architecture. Isabel Roberts, Application for Membership, American Institute of Architects, 11 September 1921.

64. Orange County Department of Health, Orlando, Florida, Certificate of Death for Isabel Roberts, 1955; John A. Dalles, "The Pathbreaking Legacy of Ryan and Roberts," *Reflections from Central Florida* 7:3 (Summer 2009): 9.

65. Roberts, Application for Membership; Dickinson, "Roberts Brought Wright Style."

66. Roberts's former neighbor in Orlando, Kathryn Williams, informed the author that Roberts's family in Iowa had known Wright. Her family, however, was most likely living in Indiana, not Iowa. Kathryn N. Williams, letter to author, 25 August 1990.

67. Brooks, *The Prairie School,* 82.

68. Byrne to [Peisch], ca. 1958; Robert C. Twombly, *Frank*

Lloyd Wright: His Life and His Architecture (New York: John Wiley and Sons, 1979), 111.

69. Roberts stated on the application form that she was employed as a draftsman between 1902 and 1914. In addition to working for Wright, she wrote that she was employed as a draftsman for "1 year with Guenzel & Drummond, 1 year or more with William Drummond—Chicago." Roberts, Application for Membership.

70. "Frank Lloyd Wright to Anyone, Anywhere," 6 August 1920, AIA Archives. Both John Van Bergen and Hermann von Holst signed Roberts's AIA membership application and also wrote letters endorsing her abilities as an architect. Roberts, Application for Membership, copy in FLWHSRC.

71. Isabel Roberts to William Stanley Parker, Secretary of the American Institute of Architects, 11 September 1921, AIA Archives, Washington, DC.

72. Williams to author, 25 August 1990. Wright's daughter Catherine remembered many of the other studio workers also as family friends. Catherine B[axter] to Mr. [Don] Kalec, 5, n.d., FLWHSRC.

73. Brooks, *The Prairie School,* 85–86.

74. Roberts, Application for Membership.

75. Beddow to author, 16 May 1990.

76. "Miss Roberts, Bandshell Designer Dies," *Orlando Evening Star,* 28 December 1955, sec. 1: 1; Mr. and Mrs. Blenus Williams, interview by Mr. and Mrs. Webb Thorpe, 5 December 1977, FLWHSRC.

77. Orange County, Certificate of Death for Isabel Roberts, 1955.

78. While discrepancies regarding Robinson's year of birth exist, his son's birth certificate and other family records list it as 1883. Robinson, *The Life and Work of Harry Franklin Robinson,* 18.

79. For more on Harry Robinson, see Robinson, *The Life and Work of Harry Franklin Robinson.*

80. Ibid., 18–19.

81. Joseph R. Robinson, conversation with son of Harry Robinson by Carol Kelm, 12 February 1989. Copy of transcript in FLWHSRC.

82. Brooks, *The Prairie School,* 82.

83. Robinson, *The Life and Work of Harry Franklin Robinson,* 20–21.

84. Wright to Robinson, 18 October 1911, as quoted in Robinson, *The Life and Work of Harry Franklin Robinson,* 35.

85. Robinson was the architect for later additions. Ibid., 22.

86. Ibid., 19, 21.

87. Ibid., 24.

88. Authorship of these houses has not been confirmed. Robinson's involvement in this project is primarily based on the fact that a small rendering of a block of the houses appeared in his personnel records and that plans for many of the houses were found in his portfolio. Some scholars have argued that the houses are actually Wright designs. James Robinson to author, 14 June 2019; Blair Kamin, "The Mysterious 29 Frank Lloyd Wright Sleuths Are on the Trail of Who Designed Houses in River Forest and Other Chicago Suburbs," *Chicago Tribune,* 6 July 2008.

89. Robinson, *The Life and Work of Harry Franklin Robinson,* 26–27.

90. Because Robinson's birthdate was incorrectly recorded in his federal record as 1885, he was able to work two year beyond the mandatory retirement age of seventy. "Harry Robinson," obituary, *Chicago Tribune,* 19 August 1959; J. R. Robinson, conversation with author, 12 February 1989.

91. Wornall Homestead, "Our Homes," available at http://www.wornallhomestead.org/our-homes/.

92. Ibid., 4.

93. "Shepard," 40:348.

94. Ibid., 340:48–49.

95. Ibid., 348.

96. Ibid.

97. Ibid.

98. Mazee Bush Owens, *The Kansas City Art Institute and School of Design: A History of Community Achievement: 1885–1964,* (Kansas City: n.p., 1965), 8. Several houses Shepard designed for the Mission Hills neighborhood of Kansas City were published in architectural journals during the 1920s, including in the January 1920 issue of the *Western Architect* and the March, April, July, and October 1925 and May 1927 issues of *An American Architect.*

99. "Shepard," 40:349. The aunt of author Ernest Hemmingway, Arabell provides another link to Oak Park, as Ernest Hemingway grew up in the Chicago suburb and was a classmate of Wright's daughter Frances.

100. Owens, *Kansas City Art Institute,* 66–67.

101. "Tobin, Arthur Collson," *National Cyclopedia of American Biography* (New York: James T. White, 1947), 33:543.

102. "Tobin," 33:543; John W. Leonard, ed. "Arthur C. Tobin," *The Book of Chicagoans: A Biographical Dictionary of Leading Men and Women of the City of Chicago* (Chicago: A.N. Marquis, 1917), 678.

103. "Tobin," 33:543.

104. White to Willcox, 4 March [1906], 4.

105. Tobin's contribution to the Sutton house is documented by letters dated May and June 1906 he authored to the clients. "A Wright House on the Prairie," 5–19. He also wrote a series of letters to the clients of the Dwight, Illinois, bank project between 31 January and 26 May 1906. These letters are now located in the Ryerson and Burnham Libraries, AIC.

106. *The GF News: Fifty Years of Progress* (n.p.: General Fireproofing, 1952), 20.

107. "Tobin," 33:543.

108. Ibid.; *GF News*, 20.

109. Webster Tomlinson to Grant Manson, 10 January 1940, GMC-OPPL.

110. Manson, "Tomlinson."

111. John M. Lamb, "The Architecture of Punishment: Jeremy Bentham, Michael Foucault and the Construction of Stateville Penitentiary, Illinois," 7, typed manuscript, John M. Lamb Collection, Howard and Lois Adelmann Regional History Collection, Lewis University, available at https://www.lewisu.edu/imcanal/JohnLamb/section_40.pdf.

112. For more on Van Bergen, see Hackl, *The Work of John S. Van Bergen.*

113. Van Bergen to Charles [Chick] Masterson, (draft), 10 April 1968, as published in Hackl, *The Work of John S. Van Bergen*, 4.

114. Hackl, *The Work of John S. Van Bergen*, 4.

115. Linda Legner, "John Van Bergen: The Wunderkind No One Noticed: Revelations of the Prairie School's Overlooked Genius," *Chicago Guide* 23 (April 1974):, 127–28.

116. Van Bergen to Brooks, August 1966, 7; Brooks, *The Prairie School*, 85.

117. Muggenberg, "John Van Bergen: The Wunderkind," 127, 131.

118. Brooks, *The Prairie School*, 85.

119. Ibid., 149.

120. Ibid., 179.

121. Muggenberg, "John Van Bergen: The Wunderkind," 131–32; "Residence—$4,500," *Construction News* (Chicago) 35 (28 June 1913): 21. Van Bergen located his office in Room 1 of the Caldwell Building at 801 South Boulevard, Oak Park. "Personal," *American Contractor* 34 (22 February 1913): 87.

122. Hackl, *The Work of John S. Van Bergen*, 8.

123. Jensen and Van Bergen occasionally collaborated and worked in each other's studios. James Muggenberg, "John Van Bergen: The Prairie Spirit into the Mid-Twentieth Century," *Prairie School Review* 13:1–4 (1976): 14–15.

124. The houses were published in the catalog *Honor Bilt Modern Homes* (Chicago: Sears, Roebuck, 1918). A version of the Aurora was built at 6416 Grand Vista Avenue, Pleasant Ridge, Cincinnati, Ohio, in 1926.

125. For more on the Architects' Small House Service Bureau see Lisa D. Schrenk, introduction to *Your Future Home* (Washington, DC: American Institute of Architects Press, 1992), v–xxiv.

126. Sponsored by US Rubber Company, the *Ideal Section* was built to also showcase the best in "lighting, safety, and landscaping" and included modern sidewalks, lights, curbs, bridges, and culverts. Brian Butko, *Greetings from the Lincoln Highway: A Road Trip Celebration of America's First Coast-to-Coast Highway* (Lanham, MD: Globe Pequot, 2019), 108–9.

127. Muggenberg, "John Van Bergen: The Prairie Spirit," 15.

128. Ibid.

129. Muggenberg, "John Van Bergen: The Wunderkind," 132.

130. Marty Hackl to author, 9 February 2020; Muggenberg, "John Van Bergen: The Prairie Spirit," 16.

131. Beddow to author, 16 May 1990; Jessie Combs Scheffler, MIT Office of the Registrar, letter to author, 10 July 2015. The earliest identified reference to White attending MIT is the 1911 edition of the *Book of Chicagoans*, which asserts that he finished his education by doing special work at MIT. His 1936 obituary states that he graduated from the university, while Paul Sprague's 1986 book on the architecture of Oak Park claims that he graduated from MIT in 1895 with a BS in architecture. Henry F. Withey and Elsie R. Withey, *Biographical Dictionary of American Architects, Deceased* (Los Angeles: New Age, 1956), 650; Leonard, "Charles Elmer White, Jr.," 716; "Death of Charles E. White, Noted in Architecture," *Oak Leaves*, 20 August 1936; Paul E. Sprague, *Guide to Frank Lloyd Wright & Prairie School Architecture in Oak Park* (Chicago: Chicago Review Press, 1986), 94.

132. For information on Brown, see Beleden, Bristol, CT, National Register of Historic Places Inventory Nomination Form, 8 February 1981, Item 8, page 1.

133. Withey and Withey, *Biographical Dictionary*, 650.

134. White's obituary states that White had worked as an engineer and architect for street railway companies in Ohio and then in Illinois, while the *Book of Chicagoans* notes that he had been employed as an architect for the American Gas Company of Philadelphia in 1899 and 1900 and had an independent practice in Boston from 1900 to 1902. "Death of Charles E. White"; Leonard, "Charles Elmer White, Jr." 716.

135. Alice R. White to Will Purcell, Sunday, n.d. WGPP-NWAA. Charles Roberts was an influential member of the Unity Temple building committee.

136. It is not clear if White worked for Willcox while in Burlington or if they were just friends.

137. White to Willcox, 4 March [1906], 3; Vernon, "Berlage in America," 138–39.

138. Jeanette S. Fields, ed., *A Guidebook to the Architecture of River Forest* (River Forest, IL: River Forest Community Center, 1981), 45. White was part of the design committee for the Oak Park Country Club in 1914, along with E. E. Roberts and Norman Patton and studio colleague William Drummond.

139. White exhibited seven designs the previous year.

140. Sprague, *Guide to Frank Lloyd Wright & Prairie School Architecture*, 95.

141. Withey and Withey, *Biographical Dictionary*, 650.

142. In 1918 Willatzen changed the spelling of his last name to Willatsen due to growing anti-German sentiment during World War I. Brooks, *The Prairie School*, 82.

143. Grainger, "Mr. Andrew Willatsen," 1.

144. "Wood in Architecture," 112; Brooks, *The Prairie School*, 82.

145. Grainger, "Mr. Andrew Willatsen," 2.

146. White to Willcox, 15 May 1904, 4.

147. White to Willcox, 4 March [1906], 4.

148. Henry C. Matthews, *Kirtland Cutter: Architect in the Land of Promise* (Seattle: University of Washington Press, 1998), 193.

149. Brooks, *The Prairie School*, 82; Chappell, "Barry Byrne," 10.

150. Byrne reported that they disbanded the firm as although they were friends who had "mutual respect" for one another, they were "not suited in temperament and differed widely in our ideas and architectural objectives." Barry Byrne to Sally Chappell, 25 October 1966, as quoted in Chappell, "Barry Byrne," 10.

151. Grainger, "Mr. Andrew Willatsen," 5.

152. "Wood in Architecture," 112–13.

153. Grainger, "Mr. Andrew Willatsen," 3.

154. Kothmann, "George Willis, Prairie School Architect in Texas," 3, 7. For more on Willis, see Kothmann and Jayne, "George Willis."

155. Willis enrolled in the joint program between the Armour Institute and the Art Institute of Chicago in 1899, taking classes for three years. Kothmann, "George Willis," 1.

156. Wright, "Cause" (1908), 164; White to Willcox, [20 May 1904], 4; Brooks, *The Prairie School*, 82.

157. White to Willcox, 15 May 1904, 4; White to Willcox, [20 May 1904], 4.

158. Kothmann, "George Willis," 3.

159. Chris Carson and William B. McDonald, eds., *Guide to San Antonio Architecture* (San Antonio: San Antonio Chapter of the American Institute of Architects, 1986), 50.

160. Kothmann, "George Willis," 5.

161. Taylor Woolley was listed in "The Art Institute of Chicago Circular of Instruction of the School of Drawing, Painting, Modeling, Decorative Design, Normal Instruction, Illustration and Architecture for 1909," AIC.

162. Brooks, *The Prairie School*, 82.

163. Peter L. Goss, "The Prairie School in Utah," *Prairie School Review* 12:1 (1975): 6.

164. Clifford Evans, Woolley's brother-in-law, also worked for Wright in the mid-1910s, after the Oak Park studio closed. Ibid., 6–7.

165. Byrne to [Peisch], ca. 1958, 3.

166. "Earl Groetzinger," obituary, *Chilton Times*, 30 April 1936.

167. Ibid.

168. Ted Pierce to the Research Center, n.d., FLWHSRC.

169. For more on Nechodoma, see Thomas S. Marvel, *Antonin Nechodoma, Architect, 1877–1928: The Prairie School in the Caribbean* (Gainesville: University Press of Florida, 1984).

170. H. Allen Brooks mentioned Sullivan's possible presence in the Oak Park studio. Brooks, *The Prairie School*, 85.

171. Martin Birkhans, "Francis C. Sullivan, Architect," *Journal of the Royal Architectural Institute of Canada* 39 (March 1962): 32.

172. Closer inspection of details in the letter, such as the mention of Wright taking Miriam (Noel?) and the Porter children to the circus in Madison, indicates that the letter dates from 1917 and not 1911. Frank Lloyd Wright, copy of letter to Fras [Francis C. Sullivan], 10 September 1911 [1917?], John Lloyd Wright Collection, Avery Library, Columbia University.

173. Birkhans, "Francis C. Sullivan, Architect," 10.

174. Ibid., 32.

175. Ibid.

176. Birkhans had written to Byrne asking him if he remembered Sullivan in Wright's office. Unfortunately, while Byrne mentioned that John Lloyd Wright knew Sullivan well, he did not answer Birkhans's question. Barry Byrne to Martin Birkhans, 3 February 1964, BBC-CHM.

177. "News from the Class," *Technology Review* 2 (1900): 374.

178. Bryant Franklin Tolles Jr., *Summer Cottages in the White Mountains: The Architecture of Leisure and Recreation, 1870 to 1930* (Hanover, NH: University Press of New England, 2000), 128–29.

179. "News from the Class," *Technology Review* 7 (1905): 253; Rick Twiss, "Hermann Valentin von Holst, Architect," 9 and 16 April 1988, copy available in FLWHSRC.

180. Hermann Valentin von Holst, *Modern American Homes* (Chicago: American Technical Society, 1912).

181. Donald W. Curl, "Boca Raton's Old Floresta," *Spanish River Papers*, 5:2 (February 1988): n.p.

182. Ronald Lanier Ramsey, "William Wells: Towers in Oklahoma," *Prairie School Review* 8:4 (1971): 6.

183. Ibid.

184. Australian patent AU1924019252, 21 August 1924, description available at http://www.ipaustralia.com.au/applicant/william-abijah-wells/patents/AU1924019252/.

185. Ramsey, 13.

186. For more on Richard Bock, see Bock, *Memoirs of an American Artist*.

187. Donald Hallmark, "Richard W. Bock, Sculptor Part I: The Early Work," *Prairie School Review* 8:1 (1971): 5.

188. Ibid., 7, 9.

189. Ibid., 6.

190. "The Richard W. Bock Sculpture Collection," pamphlet, Greenville College, Greenville, Illinois, ca. 1990. Also see Bock, *Memoirs of an American Artist*, 102–3, 108.

191. "Bock Sculpture Collection."

192. White to Willcox, 15 May 1904, 5.

193. Hanks, *Decorative Designs*, 203.

194. John Lloyd Wright identified Giannini as the artist of the murals of Native Americans in the master bedroom. J. L. Wright, *My Father*, 34. Giannini most likely also painted the *Fisherman and the Genie* mural in the playroom, although Wright identified the artist as Charles Corwin, the brother of his friend architect Cecil Corwin, on the back of a photograph of the playroom. Photograph 9307.002, FLW-AAL.

195. Hanks, *Decorative Designs*, 203–5.

196. "Monographs on Architectural Renderers," 274.

197. Brooks, *The Prairie School*, 50n13.

198. Bishop, n.p.

199. Robertson, *Wright and Niedecken*, 11.

200. Ibid.; Cheryl Robertson, *The Domestic Scene (1897–1927): George M. Niedecken, Interior Architect*, 2nd ed. (Milwaukee: Milwaukee Art Museum, 2008), 26.

201. Alexander Bick to the Prairie Archives, 9 July 1981, as quoted in Robertson, *Wright and Niedecken*, 14.

202. Robertson, *Wright and Niedecken*, 61, 80.

203. For more on Ostertag, including copies and links to various articles on the artist, see "Creator: Blanche Ostertag," *Tenth Letter of the Alphabet*, 9 December 1913, available at http://alphabettenthletter.blogspot.com/2013/12/creator-blanche-ostertag.html.

204. Isabel McDougall, "Blanche Ostertag, Artist," in *The Book Buyer* (New York: Charles Scribner's Sons, 1903), 25:309–10.

205. McDougall, "Blanche Ostertag, Artist," 25:311.

206. Dwight Perkins to Lucy Perkins, 25 September 1898, as quoted in Wilbert R. Hasbrouck, "Influences on Frank Lloyd Wright: Blanche Ostertag and Marion Mahony," *Journal of Illinois History* 15 (Summer 2012): 76.

207. McDougall, "Blanche Ostertag, Artist," 25:311.

208. *Daily Inter Ocean* (Chicago), 21 March 1900. Ostertag likely worked on the renderings for the 1900 *Architectural Review* article on Wright. Hasbrouck, "Influences on Frank Lloyd Wright," 83–84. Several similar glass mosaic mantels in other Prairie School houses are not believed to be the work of Ostertag but that of George Niedecken or Orlando Giannini, including in Wright's Darwin Martin house and in George Maher's Blinn house in Pasadena. Jeannine Love, "Blanche Ostertag: Another Wright Collaborator," *Frank Lloyd Wright Newsletter* 4:2 (1981): 14–15.

209. Chicago Architectural Club, *Book of the Annual Exhibition of the Chicago Architectural Club* (Chicago: Chicago Architectural Club, 1908): n.p.

210. "Art Jury Completes Work," *St. Louis Republic*, 7 April 1904, 2.

211. *1910 U.S. Federal Census*, 6 May 1910.

212. "Blanch Ostertag," death certificate, Department of Health of the City of New York, 16 November 1915.

213. *Madlener House: Tradition and Innovation in Architecture* (Chicago: Graham Foundation, 1988), 34.

214. "Replica of the Original Fort Dearborn," *Chicago Tribune*, 5 March 1899, 1.

215. *Madlener House*, 34–35.

216. "Replica of the Original Fort Dearborn," 1.

217. White to Willcox, 15 May 1904, 5; Bock, *Memoirs of an American Artist*, 81.

218. "Replica of the Original Fort Dearborn," 1.

219. Bock, *Memoirs of an American Artist*, 81.

220. "The Racine Sesquicentennial Committee and the Lincoln Fellowship of Wisconsin," brochure, ca. 1998, available (along with a copy of Van den Berghen's death certificate) in the folder "Statues of Abraham Lincoln: Albert Van den Berghen, Racine, Wisconsin," Lincoln Financial Foundation Collection; also available at https://archive.org/stream/statuesofabrahavlinc#page/n41/mode/2up.

221. The pastel is in the collection of the Frank Lloyd Wright Trust.

222. Much of the known historical details about Mueller's early life come from his own testimony recorded in the court document US Circuit Court of Appeals for the Seventh Circuit, October Term, 1925, no. 3733, Chicago Auditorium Association v. Mark Skinner Willing and the Northern Trust Co., as Trustees, 448, as reprinted in "Testimony of Paul P. Mueller, Testified in Court," in *Nine Commentaries of Frank*

Lloyd Wright, ed. Edgar Kaufmann Jr. (Cambridge, MA: MIT Press for the Architectural History Foundation, 1989), 42–62. Also see Andrew Saint, "Frank Lloyd Wright and Paul Mueller: The Architect and His Builder of Choice," *Architectural Research Quarterly* 7:2 (June 2003): 157–67.

223. Dana Hutt, "Paul F. P. Mueller," research paper, University of Texas at Austin, 1993, 3.

224. Ibid.

225. Kaufmann, 42.

226. Ibid.

227. Hutt, "Paul F. P. Mueller," 4–5.

228. Kaufmann, 43.

229. Saint, "Frank Lloyd Wright and Paul Mueller," 166.

230. Hutt, "Paul F. P. Mueller," 21.

Appendix D

1. I am indebted to the late Franklin Porter for sharing this letter with me and entrusting it and the rest of the Anna Lloyd Wright scrapbook to my care, allowing me to document the fascinating contents of the scrapbook for myself and for the Frank Lloyd Wright Home and Studio Foundation before delivering it to the Taliesin Archives for him.

Bibliography

Previous Discussions of Wright's Oak Park Studio

The first descriptions and images of Wright's Oak Park studio appeared in print shortly after its completion in 1898 beginning in the December 1899 issue of *House Beautiful*. This was quickly followed by Robert C. Spencer Jr.'s critical essay on Wright's early work in June 1900. Wright himself described aspects of his home studio several times, including in two *Architectural Record* essays (March 1908 and May 1914) and in the various editions of his autobiography. Yet many of the early major scholarly explorations of Wright's oeuvre mention the suburban workplace only briefly or not at all.

Grant Manson's pioneering *Frank Lloyd Wright to 1910: The First Golden Age* (1958) attempted to remedy this deficiency with a thorough historical study of Wright's early career, including an appendix identifying some of his Oak Park office employees. Yet Manson's work reflects both the blessings and the limitations of researching a "living subject." Fourteen years later, H. Allen Brooks published his groundbreaking *The Prairie School: Frank Lloyd Wright and His Midwest Contemporaries* (1972), placing the Oak Park studio in the larger context of developments in progressive midwestern architecture. Like Manson, Brooks was able to engage with a number of people directly involved in the Oak Park studio. Several subsequent biographies incorporate the Oak Park studio into the larger story of Wright's life, including books by Robert Twombly, Brendan Gill, and Meryle Secrest.

During the restoration of Wright's suburban home and studio in the 1970s and 1980s a group of architects and architectural historians including Ann Abernathy, Elaine Harrington, Donald Kalec, Karen Sweeney, and John Thorpe carried out detailed research that primarily focused on the physical complex and resulted in several concise publications. Abernathy and Thorpe authored *The Oak Park Home and Studio of Frank Lloyd Wright* (1988), a thin, full-color book that includes brief descriptions and photographs of the restored building. Elaine Harrington, a former curator of the site, offers a descriptive essay in *Frank Lloyd Wright Home and Studio, Oak Park (Opus 23)* (1996), while Zarine Weil gives insight into the restoration in *Building a Legacy: The Restoration of Frank Lloyd Wright's Oak Park Home and Studio* (2001).

With the building restoration largely completed in 1988, shorter scholarly discussions on specific aspects of the Oak Park studio began appearing. These include Neil Levine's essay "Frank Lloyd Wright's Own Houses and His Changing Concept of Representation" (1988), Paul Kruty's "At Work in the Oak Park Studio" (2003), and David Van Zanten's "Frank Lloyd Wright's Kindergarten: Professional Practice and Sexual Roles" (1996), in which he explores the concept of Wright's office as an architectural kindergarten. Yet none of these works extensively explore the evolution of the building nor the activities that took place within.

Abernathy, Ann. "Outline: Restoration Alternatives, Goals, Procedures." August 1985. FLWHSRC.

Abernathy, Ann, and Don Kalec. Room Descriptions of the Frank Lloyd Wright Home and Studio. Restoration Documentation Files, FLWHSRC.

Abernathy, Ann, and John Thorpe. *Oak Park Home and Studio of Frank Lloyd Wright*. Oak Park, IL: Frank Lloyd Wright Home and Studio Foundation, 1988.

"About the Village." *Reporter Argus* (20 May 1905), 4.

Aguar, Charles E., and Berdeana Aguar. *Wrightscapes: Frank Lloyd Wright's Landscape Designs.* New York: McGraw-Hill, 2002.

Allen, James Lane. *Aftermath.* New York: Harper and Brothers, 1895.

Alofsin, Anthony Michael. "Frank Lloyd Wright: The Lessons of Europe, 1910–1922." Ph.D. diss., Columbia University, 1987.

———. *Frank Lloyd Wright, Art Collector: Secessionist Prints from the Turn of the Century.* Austin: University of Texas Press, 2012.

———. *Frank Lloyd Wright's Lost Years, 1910–1922: A Study of Influence.* Chicago: University of Chicago Press, 1993.

———. "Taliesin: To Fashion Worlds in Little." In *Wright Studies,* vol. 1, *Taliesin 1911–1914,* edited by Narciso G. Menocal. Carbondale: Southern Illinois University Press, 1992. 44–65.

The Alumni Quarterly and Fortnightly Notes of the University of Illinois. Vol. 4. Urbana: University of Illinois, 1918.

"American Designs Australian Capital. Walter B. Griffin of Chicago Wins the First Prize of $8,750 in the Competition." *New York Times,* 24 May 1912.

"Announcements." *Oak Leaves,* 25 September 1909, 32.

Annual Register July, 1905–July, 1906, with Announcements for 1906–1907. Urbana: University of Illinois, 1906.

"Architects Reply to Foreign Critic." *New York Herald,* 19 November 1911. Copy in WGPP-NWAA.

"The Art Institute of Chicago Circular of Instruction of the School of Drawing, Painting, Modeling, Decorative Design, Normal Instruction, Illustration and Architecture for 1909." AIC.

"Art Jury Completes Work." *St. Louis Republic,* 7 April 1904, 2.

"Arthur C. Tobin." Obituary. *Chicago Tribune,* 19 February 1940, 16.

Ashbee, Charles. Journal. CRA/1/20, CAP-KCC.

Australian patent AU1924019252, 21 August 1924. Description available at http://www.ipaustralia.com.au /applicant/william-abijah-wells/patents/AU1924019252/.

Barillas, William. *The Midwestern Pastoral: Place and Landscape in Literature of the American Heartland.* Athens: Ohio University Press, 2006.

Barney, Maginel Wright. *The Valley of the God-Almighty Joneses.* Spring Green, WI: Unity Chapel, 1986.

Baxter, Catherine Dorothy Wright. "Frank Lloyd Wright: The Shining Brow." Radio broadcast, Bruce Radde's Radio Program, KPFA-FM (Berkeley, CA). In *Frank Lloyd Wright: Remembered,* edited by Patrick J. Meehan. Washington, DC: Preservation, 1991. 231–34.

Beleden House, Bristol, CT. National Register of Historic Places Inventory Nomination Form, 8 February 1981, Item 8, page 1.

Berkon, Susan Fondiler. "Marion Mahony Griffin." In *Women in American Architecture: A Historic and Contemporary Perspective,* edited by Susana Torre. New York: Whitney Library of Design, 1977. 75–79.

Birk, Melanie, ed. *Frank Lloyd Wright's Fifty Views of Japan: The 1905 Photo Album.* Rohnert Park, CA: Pomegranate Artbooks, 1996.

Birkhans, Martin. "Francis C. Sullivan, Architect." *Journal of the Royal Architectural Institute of Canada* 39 (March 1962): 32.

Birrell, James. *Walter Burley Griffin.* Brisbane: University of Queensland Press, 1964.

"Blanch Ostertag." Death certificate. Department of Health of the City of New York. 16 November 1915.

Bock, Richard. *Memoirs of an American Artist, Sculptor, Richard W. Bock.* Edited by Dorathi Bock Pierre. Los Angeles: C.C. Publishing, 1989.

Bragdon, Claude. "Harvey Ellis: A Portrait Sketch." *Architectural Review* (Boston) 15 (December 1908): 173–82.

Brooks, H. Allen, ed. "Frank Lloyd Wright and the Wasmuth Drawings." *Art Bulletin* 48 (June 1966): 193–202.

———. Interview. In *Walter Burley Griffin: In His Own Right.* Corporation for Public Broadcasting, 1998. http:// www.pbs.org/wbgriffin/brooks2.html.

———. Paper read at the 20th International Congress of the History of Art, New York, 11 September 1961.

———. *Prairie School Architecture: Studies from "The Western Architect."* Toronto: University of Toronto Press, 1975.

———. *The Prairie School: Frank Lloyd Wright and His Midwest Contemporaries.* Toronto: University of Toronto Press, 1972.

Brosterman, Norman. *Inventing Kindergarten.* New York: Harry N. Abrams, 1997.

Building Budget 3 (January 1887): 1–2.

"Building News Synopsis." *Inland Architect & News Record,* July 1891, 73.

"Building News Synopsis." *Inland Architect & News Record,* June 1892, 66.

"Buildings: Prospective Work." *Engineering and Contracting* 42 (July–December 1914): 41–42.

Bulletin of the M.I.T. Boston Register of Former Students with an Account of the Alumni Association. Vol. 50, May 1915.

Butko, Brian. *Greetings from the Lincoln Highway: A Road Trip Celebration of America's First Coast-to-Coast Highway.* Lanham, MD: Globe Pequot, 2019.

Byrne, Barry. *America* 69 (19 June 1943): 305.

——. "The Chicago Movement." Paper delivered before the Illinois Society of Architects, 28 November 1939. Typed manuscript in the Ricker Architectural Library, University of Illinois.

——. "The Drawings of Frank Lloyd Wright." Review. *JSAH* 22 (May 1963), 108–9.

——. "On Frank Lloyd Wright and His Atelier." *AIA Journal* 39 (June 1963): 109–12.

——. "Search for Delight." In *Division Street: America*, edited by Studs Terkel. New York: Pantheon Books, 1967. 259–66.

Cannon, Patrick. *The Complete Buildings of Frank Lloyd Wright in Oak Park and River Forest, Illinois*. San Francisco: Pomegranate, 2006.

Carson, Chris, and William B. McDonald, eds. *Guide to San Antonio Architecture*. San Antonio: San Antonio Chapter of the American Institute of Architects, 1986.

[Chamberlain, Lee], Marion Lincoln Lewis. "Application for Employment." Personnel Office, Boston Public Library, Boston, MA.

——. "A Women's Club House." Elevation. Senior thesis, Department of Architecture. Non-Circulating Collection 3, Thesis Archives and Special Collection, Institute Archives, MIT, Cambridge, MA.

Chappell, Sally Anderson. "Barry Byrne: Architecture and Writings." Ph.D. diss. Northwestern University, 1968.

Chappell, Sally Kitt [Anderson], and Ann Van Zanten. *Barry Byrne, John Lloyd Wright: Architecture and Design*. Chicago: Chicago Historical Society, 1982.

Chase, Mary Ellen. *A Goodly Fellowship*. New York: Macmillan, 1939.

"Chicago." *American Architect and Building News* 76 (26 April 1902): 29–30.

"Chicago." *Construction News* (Chicago) 12 (16 November 1901): 780–81.

Chicago Architectural Club. Book of the Annual Exhibition of the Chicago Architectural Club. Chicago: Chicago Architectural Club, 1908.

——. *Catalogue of the Eleventh Annual Exhibition by the Chicago Architectural Club at the Art Institute of Chicago, March 23rd to April 10th 1898*. Chicago: Chicago Architectural Club, 1898.

——. *The Chicago Architectural Annual Published by the Chicago Architectural Club: A Selection of Works Exhibited at the Art Institute in March of the Year One Thousand Nine Hundred and Two*. Chicago: Chicago Architectural Club, 1902.

City Directory of Oak Park. Oak Park, IL: Delos Hull, 1903.

Condit, Carl W. *The Chicago School of Architecture: A History of Commercial and Public Building in the Chicago Area, 1875–1925*. Chicago: University of Chicago Press, 1964.

Construction News (Chicago) 6 (9 February 1898): 121.

"Contract between Frank Lloyd Wright and Hermann V. Von Holst." 22 September 1909. WGPP-NWAA.

Cook County, Illinois, Municipal Circuit Court. Case 205695, Darwin D. Martin v. John O. Bastear. 27 August 1930.

Cook County, Illinois, Recorder of Deeds. Chain of title for Lot 20 in Block 2 of Kettlestrings' Addition to Harlem. Document 4785720, 23 May 1911.

——. Chain of title for Lot 20 in Block 2 of Kettlestrings' Addition to Harlem. Document 8975059, 17 June 1911.

——. Chain of title for Lot 20 in Block 2 of Kettlestrings' Addition to Harlem. Document 8975060, 10 February 1911.

——. Chain of title for Lot 20 in Block 2 of Kettlestrings' Addition to Harlem. Document 6308467, 19 April 1920.

"Community Mausoleums: The Architecture of Cecil E. Bryan." Finding and Preserving Your History, http://preservingyourhistory.blogspot.com/2015/04 /community-mausoleums-architecture-of.html.

Conroy, Sarah Booth. "The Right Home for Wright's Son." *Washington Post*, 13 July 1974. In *Frank Lloyd Wright: Remembered*, edited by Patrick J. Meehan. Washington, DC: Preservation, 1991. 234–39.

Crawford, Alan. "Ten Letters from Frank Lloyd Wright to Charles Robert Ashbee." *Architectural History* 13 (1970): 64–76, 132.

"Creator: Blanche Ostertag." *Tenth Letter of the Alphabet*, 9 December 1913. Available at http://alphabettenthletter .blogspot.com/2013/12/creator-blanche-ostertag.html.

Curl, Donald W. "Boca Raton's Old Floresta." *Spanish River Papers* 5:2 (February 1988): n.p.

Daily Inter Ocean (Chicago), 21 March 1900.

"Dallas' Swiss Avenue Historic District Opens Doors Saturday, Sunday." *Dallas Morning News*, 10 May 2013.

Dalles, John A. "The Pathbreaking Legacy of Ryan and Roberts." *Reflections from Central Florida* 7:3 (Summer 2009): 8–9.

Darling, Sharon. *Chicago Furniture Art, Craft, & Industry, 1833–1983*. New York: W. W. Norton, 1984.

Darwin D. Martin House Cultural Landscape Report. Honeyoye Falls, NY: Bayer Landscape Architects, ca. 2015.

"Death of Charles E. White, Noted in Architecture." *Oak Leaves*, 20 August 1936.

"Design and Decoration: An Important and Rare Urn by Frank Lloyd Wright." Available at http://www.wright20 .com/auctions/2015/11/design-masterworks/20.

Dickinson, Joy Wallace. "Roberts Brought Wright Style to Region's Landmark Buildings." *Orlando Sentinel*, 11 September 2011.

Dow, Arthur Wesley. *Composition: A Series of Exercises in Art Structure for the Use of Students and Teachers*, 9th ed. 1899; repr., Garden City, NY: Doubleday, Page, 1920.

Downs, Hugh, and The National Broadcasting Company. *Broadcast Wisdom: A Conversation with Frank Lloyd Wright*. Interview, 17 May 1953.

Drummond, William Eugene. *Our National Capitol: An Architect Proposes Minor Additions to Capitol and Extensive Changes within Its Environment Area*. Chicago: National Capitol, ca. 1946.

"Earl Groetzinger." Obituary. *Chilton Times*, 30 April 1936.

Eaton, Leonard. *Two Chicago Architects and Their Clients: Frank Lloyd Wright and Howard Van Doren Shaw*. Cambridge: MIT Press, 1969.

Fanning, Patricia J. *Artful Lives: The Francis Watts Lee Family and Their Times*. Amherst, MA: University of Massachusetts Press, 2016.

Farr, Finis. *Frank Lloyd Wright: A Biography*. New York: Scribner, 1961.

Fields, Jeanette S. "First Woman Minister Brought Wright to Village." *Wednesday Journal*, 27 May 1991.

———, ed. *A Guidebook to the Architecture of River Forest*. River Forest, IL: River Forest Community Center, 1981.

———. "Volunteers Renovate Wright in the Nick of Time." In "Three Decades of Renovating Wright," *Wednesday Journal*, special section, 21 March 2004, 38.

Fitzpatrick, F. W. "Chicago." *Inland Architect and News Record* 45 (June 1905): 47.

"For Sale at Oak Park: A Forest Avenue Property & A Chicago Avenue Property: Semi-Detached Dwelling for Sale Separately or Together, Partly Finished." Sales brochure. Copies in JLW-AAL and JLW-OPPL.

"Frank Lloyd Wright Chosen." *Oak Leaves*, 16 September 1905, 13.

Frank Lloyd Wright Home and Studio Foundation. *Frank Lloyd Wright Home and Studio Foundation Volunteer Manual*. 13th ed. Oak Park, IL: Frank Lloyd Wright Home and Studio Foundation, 1989.

———. *The Plan for Restoration and Adaptive Use of the Frank Lloyd Wright Home and Studio*. Chicago, IL: University of Chicago Press, 1978.

Friedman, Alice T. "Girl Talk: Feminism and Domestic Architecture at Frank Lloyd Wright's Oak Park Studio." In *Marion Mahony Reconsidered*, edited by David Van Zanten. Chicago: University of Chicago Press, 2011. 23–49.

Froebel, Friedrich. *Froebel's Chief Writings on Education Rendered into English*. Translated by Samuel Sigmund Fechheimer Fletcher and James Welton. London: Edward Arnold, 1912.

Furhoff, Robert A. "Frank Lloyd Wright Home and Studio Site Investigation." September 1985, FLWHSRC.

Futagawa, Yukio, ed. *Frank Lloyd Wright Monograph 1887–1901*. Vol. 1. Tokyo: A.D.A. Edita, 1986.

Gannett, William C. *The House Beautiful*. River Forest, IL: Auvergne, 1896–97.

Ganschinietz, Suzanne. "William Drummond: I. Talent and Sensitivity." *Prairie School Review* 6:1 (1969): 5–19.

Gebhard, David. *Purcell & Elmslie: Prairie Progressive Architects*. Salt Lake City: Gibbs Smith, 2006.

Gebhard, David, and Harriette Von Breton. *Lloyd Wright Architect: Twentieth Century Architecture in an Organic Exhibition*. Santa Barbara, CA: Standard Printing of Santa Barbara, 1971.

The GF News: Fifty Years of Progress. N.p.: General Fire-proofing, 1952.

Gill, Brendan. *Many Masks: A Life of Frank Lloyd Wright*. New York: G. P. Putnam's Sons, 1987.

Gorman, Carma R. "Fitting Rooms: The Dress Designs of Frank Lloyd Wright." *Winterthur Portfolio* 30:4 (Winter 1995): 259–77.

Goss, Peter L. "The Prairie School in Utah." *Prairie School Review* 12:1 (1975): 5–22.

———. "Taylor Woolley and the Wasmuth Folios." Recording, FLWHSF Lecture Series, Oak Park, IL, 24 October 1990, FLWHSRC.

Grainger, Alan. "Mr. Andrew Willatsen." Student Papers on the Architecture of Puget Sound: 1959–1970s, Architecture and Urban Planning Library, University of Washington Libraries, 1972. Available at http://cdm16786 .contentdm.oclc.org/cdm/ref/collection/archps/id/2744.

Granger, Alfred H. "An Architect's Studio." *House Beautiful* 7 (December 1899): 36–45.

The Greatest of the Expositions Completely Illustrated: Official Views of the Louisiana Purchase Exposition. NP: np, ca. 1904.

Griffin, Walter Burley. "A Eulogy of System." *City Club Bulletin* 7:6 (17 February 1914): 66.

Guarino, Jean. *Oak Park: A Pictorial History*. St. Louis: G. Bradley, 1988.

Hackl, Martin. *The Work of John S. Van Bergen, Architect*. 3rd ed. Oak Park, IL: Martin Hackl, 2001.

Hallmark, Donald. "Richard W. Bock, Sculptor, Part I: The Early Work." *Prairie School Review* 8:1 (1971): 5–18.

———. "Richard W. Bock, Sculptor, Part II: The Mature Collection." *Prairie School Review* 8:2 (1971): 5–29.

Hamilton, Mary Jane. "Albert Van den Berghen: An Elusive Figure in American Sculptural History." *Wright Angles: Newsletter of the Frank Lloyd Wright Home and Studio* 33 (May–July 2007): 3–7.

Hanks, David. *The Decorative Designs of Frank Lloyd Wright*. New York: E. P. Dutton, 1979.

Harrington, Elaine. "At Home in the Studio: H. H. Richardson and F. L. Wright." Abstract draft, August 1991. Copy in author's collection.

———. "Frank Lloyd Wright and the Art of Japan." *Frank Lloyd Wright Home and Studio Foundation Volunteer Newsletter,* March 1992, 9.

———. *Frank Lloyd Wright Home and Studio, Oak Park.* Stuttgart: Axel Menges, 1996.

"Harry Robinson." Obituary. *Chicago Tribune,* 19 August 1959.

Hasbrouck, Wilbert R. "The Architectural Firm of Guenzel and Drummond." *Prairie School Review* 1:2 (1964): 5–7.

———. *The Chicago Architectural Club: Prelude to the Modern.* New York: Monacelli, 2005.

———. "Influences on Frank Lloyd Wright: Blanche Ostertag and Marion Mahony." *Journal of Illinois History* 15 (Summer 2012): 70–88.

"Herbert W. Chamberlain, Obituary." In *Technology Review,* vol. 1. Cambridge, MA: Association of Alumni and Alumnae of MIT, 1899. 388–90.

Hildebrand, Grant. *The Wright Space: Pattern and Meaning in Frank Lloyd Wright's Houses.* Seattle: University of Washington Press, 1991.

Hines, Thomas C., Jr. "Frank Lloyd Wright—the Madison Years: Record versus Recollection." *Wisconsin Magazine of History* 50 (Winter 1967): 109–19.

History of the Louisiana Purchase Exposition. St. Louis: Universal Exposition Publishing, 1905.

Hitchcock, Henry-Russell. *In the Nature of Materials, 1887–1941: The Buildings of Frank Lloyd Wright.* New York: Duell, Sloan and Pearce, 1942.

Hoffmann, Donald. "Frank Lloyd Wright and Viollet-le-Duc." *JSAH* 28:3 (October 1969): 173–83.

———. *Frank Lloyd Wright's Dana House.* Mineola, NY: Dover, 1996.

———. *Frank Lloyd Wright's Robie House: The Illustrated Story of an Architectural Masterpiece.* New York: Dover, 1984.

Honor Bilt Modern Homes. Chicago: Sears, Roebuck, 1918.

Houston Architectural Survey. Houston: Southwest Center for Urban Research, 1980.

Hutt, Dana. "Paul F. P. Mueller." Research paper, University of Texas at Austin, 1993.

Illinois Office of Tourism. "Illinois Tourism Kicks Off National Travel & Tourism Week Announcing New Illinois Frank Lloyd Wright Trail." 7 May 2018. Available at https://media.enjoyillinois.com/press-releases/illinois-tourism-kicks-off-national-travel-and-tourism-week-announcing-new-frank-lloyd-wright-trail-in-illinois/.

Illsley, Charles E. "The Larkin Administration Building, Buffalo." *Inland Architect and News Record* 50 (July 1907): 4, illustrations.

Imperial Japanese Commission to the Louisiana Purchase Exposition. *The Exhibition of the Empire of Japan: Official Catalogue.* St. Louis: International Exposition, 1904.

"Insights from Preservation." Research Center Exhibit, October 1990, FLWHSRC.

Jameson, David. *Alfonso Iannelli: Modern by Design.* Oak Park, IL: Top Five Books, 2013.

Jayne, Leisa. "George Willis: A Brief Account of His Life and Works." 7 December 1981. Unpublished report in the George Willis reference file at the Alexander Architectural Archives, University of Texas at Austin.

Johnson, Donald Leslie. *The Architecture of Walter Burley Griffin.* Melbourne: Macmillan, 1977.

———. *On Frank Lloyd Wright's Concrete Adobe: Irving Gill, Rudolph Schindler and the American Southwest.* Surry, England: Ashgate, 2013.

Johonnot, Rodney F. *The New Edifice of Unity Church, Oak Park, Illinois, Frank Lloyd Wright, Architect.* Illustrated pamphlet. Oak Park, IL: Unitarian Universalist Church, Oak Park, 1906.

"June Weddings." *Oak Park Vindicator,* 29 June 1900, 1.

Kalec, Don. "The Frank Lloyd Wright Studio." Lecture, The Frank Lloyd Wright Home and Studio Foundation Volunteer Training Course, 10 February 1990.

Kamin, Blair. "The Mysterious 29: Frank Lloyd Wright Sleuths Are on the Trail of Who Designed Houses in River Forest and Other Chicago Suburbs." *Chicago Tribune,* 6 July 2008.

Key, Ellen. *The Morality of a Woman and Other Essays.* Translated by Namah [sic] Bouton Bothwick. Chicago: Ralph Fletcher Seymour, 1911.

Kipling, Rudyard. *From Sea to Sea: Letters of Travel.* Garden City, NY: Doubleday, Page, 1913.

Klinkow, Margaret. *The Wright Family Library.* Oak Park, IL: FLWHSRC, 1994.

Kothmann, Laytha Sue Haggard. "George Willis, Prairie School Architect in Texas." Master's thesis, University of Texas at Austin, 1988.

Kruty, Paul. "Chicago 1900: The Griffins Come of Age." In *Beyond Architecture: Marion Mahony and Walter Burley Griffin: America, Australia, India*, edited by Anne Watson. Sydney: Powerhouse, 1998. 10–25.

———. "Graphic Depictions: The Evolution of Marion Mahony's Architectural Renderings." In *Marion Mahony Reconsidered*, edited by David Van Zanten. Chicago: University of Chicago Press, 2011. 51–93.

———. "'A New Look at the Beginnings of the Illinois Architects' Licensing Law." *Illinois Historical Journal* 90 (Autumn 1997): 154–72.

———. "Walter Burley Griffin and the University of Illinois." *Reflections: The Journal of the School of Architecture* 9 (Spring 1993): 32–42.

———. "Walter Burley Griffin: An Architect of America's Middle West." In *Walter Burley Griffin in America*. Urbana: University of Illinois Press, 2001. 15–36.

Kruty, Paul, and Paul E. Sprague. *Marion Mahony and Millikin Place: Creating a Prairie School Masterpiece with the Help of Frank Lloyd Wright, Herman [sic] Von Holst, and Walter Burley Griffin*. St. Louis: Walter Burley Griffin Society of America, 2007.

Lakeside Annual Directory of the City of Chicago. Chicago: Chicago Directory, 1901.

Lakeside Annual Directory of the City of Chicago. Chicago: Chicago Directory, 1898.

Lamb, John M. "The Architecture of Punishment: Jeremy Bentham, Michael Foucault and the Construction of Stateville Penitentiary, Illinois." Typed manuscript. John M. Lamb Collection, Howard and Lois Adelmann Regional History Collection, Lewis University. Available at https://www.lewisu.edu/imcanal/JohnLamb/section_40.pdf.

"Leave Families; Elope to Europe: Architect Frank Lloyd Wright and Mrs. Edwin H. Cheney of Oak Park Startle Friends." *Chicago Tribune*, 7 November 1909.

LeCocq, Randall. *Frank Lloyd Wright in Montana: Darby, Stevensville, and Whitefish*. Helena, MT: Drumlummon Institute, 2013.

Legner, Linda. "John Van Bergen: The Wunderkind No One Noticed: Revelations of the Prairie School's Overlooked Genius." *Chicago Guide* 23 (April 1974): 126–30.

Leonard, John W., ed. "Arthur C. Tobin." In *The Book of Chicagoans: A Biographical Dictionary of Leading Men and Women of the City of Chicago*. Chicago: A.N. Marquis and Company, 1917. 678.

———, ed. "Charles Elmer White, Jr." In *The Book of Chicagoans: A Biographical Dictionary of Leading Men and Women of the City of Chicago*. Chicago: A.N. Marquis, 1911. 716.

———, ed. "Charles Erwin Barglebaugh." In *Who's Who in Engineering: A Biographical Dictionary of Contemporaries*. New York: John W. Leonard, 1925. 119.

Leroux, Charles. "Like Father, like Son, Lloyd Comes Home Making the Wright Impression." *Chicago Tribune*, 18 October 1976.

Lesniak, Jack. "Arthur B. Heurtley House, Oak Park." Unpublished training manual for the 2002 Wright Plus house walk. FLWHSRC.

Levine, Neil. *The Architecture of Frank Lloyd Wright*. Princeton, NJ: Princeton University Press, 1997.

———. "Frank Lloyd Wright's Diagonal Planning." In *In Search of Modern Architecture: A Tribute to Henry-Russell Hitchcock*, edited by Helen Searing. Cambridge, MA: MIT Press, 1982. 245–77.

———. "Frank Lloyd Wright's Own Houses and His Changing Concept of Representation." In *The Nature of Frank Lloyd Wright*, edited by Carol R. Bolon et al. Chicago: University of Chicago Press, 1988. 20–69.

———. *The Urbanism of Frank Lloyd Wright*. Princeton, NJ: Princeton University Press, 1916.

Love, Jeannine. "Blanche Ostertag: Another Wright Collaborator." *Frank Lloyd Wright Newsletter* 4:2 (1981): 11–16.

"A Lovely Wedding." *Oak Park Reporter*, 28 June 1900, 4.

Madlener House: Tradition and Innovation in Architecture. Chicago: Graham Foundation, 1988.

Mahoney, Patrick J. *Frank Lloyd Wright's Scholarly Clients: William and Mary Heath*. Buffalo: Buffalo State College, E.H. Butler Library, 2015.

———. *Frank Lloyd Wright's Walter V. Davidson House: An Examination of a Buffalo Home and Its Cousins from Coast to Coast*. Buffalo: Buffalo State College, E.H. Butler Library, 1911.

Mahony, Marion. "The House and Studio of a Painter." Bachelor's thesis, MIT, 1894.

Mahony Griffin, Marion. "The Magic of America." Draft versions at the Ryerson and Burnham Libraries of the Art Institute of Chicago and the New-York Historical Society.

Manson, Grant Carpenter. *Frank Lloyd Wright to 1910: The First Golden Age*. New York: Van Nostrand Reinhold, 1958.

———. "The Wonderful World of Taliesin: My Twenty Years on Its Fringes." *Wisconsin Magazine of History* 73 (August 1989): 35.

Marvel, Thomas S. *Antonin Nechodoma, Architect, 1877–1928: The Prairie School in the Caribbean.* Gainesville: University Press of Florida, 1984.

Matthews, Henry C. *Kirtland Cutter: Architect in the Land of Promise.* Seattle: University of Washington Press, 1998.

"McArthur, Albert Chase." In *National Cyclopedia of American Biography*, vol. 39. New York: James T. White and Company, 1954. 432.

McCarter, Robert. "Frank Lloyd Wright and the Nature of Concrete." *Ptah* 1 (2001): 3–19.

———. *Frank Lloyd Wright.* London: Phaidon, 1997.

McCrea, Ron. *Building Taliesin: Frank Lloyd Wright's Home of Love and Loss.* Madison: Wisconsin Historical Society Press, 2012.

McDonald, Bill. "'Frank Lloyd Wright Home and Studio." Unpublished training manual for the 2018 Wright Plus house walk. FLWHSRC.

McDougall, Isabel. "Blanche Ostertag, Artist." In *The Book Buyer.* New York: Charles Scribner's Sons, 1903. 25:309.

McGregor, Alasdair. *Grand Obsessions: The Life and Work of Walter Burley Griffin and Marion Mahony Griffin.* London: E-Penguin, 2014.

Meech, Julia. *Frank Lloyd Wright and the Art of Japan: The Architect's Other Passion.* New York: Harry N. Abrams, 2001.

Meehan, Patrick J. *Frank Lloyd Wright: Remembered.* Washington, DC: Preservation, 1991.

Michael, Vincent L. *The Architecture of Barry Byrne: Taking the Prairie School to Europe.* Urbana: University of Illinois Press, 2013.

"Miss Roberts, Bandshell Designer Dies." *Orlando Evening Star*, 28 December 1955, sec. 1: 1.

Molloy, Mary Alice. "Richardson's Web: A Client's Assessment of the Architect's Home and Studio." *JSAH*, 54:1 (March 1995), 8–23.

"Monographs on Architectural Renderers: X. The Work of Birch Burdette Long." *Brickbuilder* 23 (November 1914): 274–76.

Monroe, Harriet. "In the Galleries." *Chicago Examiner*, 13 April 1907.

Morgan, Donald, and John Altberg. *The Sutton House, McCook, Nebraska.* Hastings, NE: Cornhusker, 2008.

"Mosaics." *Inland Architect and News Record* 37 (March 1901): 16.

"Mr. and Mrs. Frank Lloyd Wright Left Last Week…." *Oak Leaves,* 25 February 1905, 22.

Muggenberg, James. "John Van Bergen: The Prairie Spirit into the Mid-Twentieth Century." *Prairie School Review* 13:1–4 (1976): 5–34.

———. "John Van Bergen: The Wunderkind No One Noticed: Revelations of the Prairie School's Overlooked Genius." *Chicago Guide* 23 (April 1974): 126–27, 131–33.

Nagelberg, Alvin. "Frank Lloyd Wright's Former Home at 951 Chicago Av. in Oak Park Up for Sale." *Chicago Tribune*, 5 October 1972.

"News of the Week: Chicago." *Construction News* (Chicago) 13 (8 February 1902): 88–89.

"News from the Class." *Technology Review* 2 (1900): 374.

"News from the Class." *Technology Review* 7 (1905): 253.

Nute, Kevin. *Frank Lloyd Wright and Japan: The Role of Traditional Japanese Art and Architecture in the Work of Frank Lloyd Wright.* New York: Van Nostrand Reinhold, 1993.

O'Gorman, James. "Henry Hobson Richardson and Frank Lloyd Wright." *Art Quarterly* 32 (August 1969): 292–315.

———. *Three American Architects: Richardson, Sullivan, and Wright, 1865–1915.* Chicago: University of Chicago Press, 1991.

Oak Leaves, 16 July 1904, 8.

"Oak Park Awaits Wright." *Chicago Tribune*, 24 September 1910, 9.

Oak Park Reporter, 8 January 1892, 4.

Orange County Department of Health, Orlando, Florida. Certificate of Death for Isabel Roberts, 1955.

"Our Illustrations." *Inland Architect and News Record* 52 (December 1908): 77.

Owens, Mazee Bush. *The Kansas City Art Institute and School of Design: A History of Community Achievement: 1885–1964.* Kansas City: n.p., 1965.

Peisch, Mark L. *The Chicago School of Architecture: Early Followers of Sullivan and Wright.* New York: Random House, 1964.

"Personal." *American Contractor* 34 (22 February 1913): 87.

Pfeiffer, Bruce Brooks. "Tre disegni inediti di Frank Lloyd Wright." *Domus* 713 (1990): 72–75.

———, ed. *Frank Lloyd Wright Complete Works.* Vol. 1, 1885–1916. Cologne: Taschen, 2011.

———, ed. *Letters to Clients: Frank Lloyd Wright.* Fresno: Press at California State University, 1986.

Pliny the Younger. *Letters.* Translated by William Melmoth, revised by F. C. T. Bosanquet. New York: P. F. Collier and Son, 1909–14.

"Portfolio of Current Architecture." *Architectural Record* 65 (May 1929): 435–66.

Purcell, William. *Parabiographies.* WGPP-NWAA.

Quinan, Jack. "Frank Lloyd Wright in 1893: The Chicago Context." In *Frank Lloyd Wright: In the Realm of Ideas,*

Carbondale: Southern Illinois University Press, 1988. 119–32.

———. *Frank Lloyd Wright's Buffalo Venture.* Petaluma, CA: Pomegranate Communications, 2012.

———. *Frank Lloyd Wright's Larkin Building: Myth and Fact.* Cambridge, MA: MIT Press for the Architectural History Foundation, 1989.

———. *Frank Lloyd Wright's Martin House: Architecture as Portraiture.* New York: Princeton Architectural Press, 2004.

———. "Frank Lloyd Wright, Photography and Architecture." *Frank Lloyd Wright Quarterly* 2:1 (Winter 1991): 4–7.

———. "Wright the Photographer." In *Frank Lloyd Wright's Fifty Views of Japan: The 1905 Photo Album,* edited by Melanie Birk. Rohnert Park, CA: Pomegranate Artbooks, 1996. 73–88.

"The Racine Sesquicentennial Committee and the Lincoln Fellowship of Wisconsin." Brochure, ca. 1998.

Ramsey, Ronald Lanier. "William Wells: Towers in Oklahoma." *Prairie School Review* 8:4 (1971): 5-13.

"Replica of the Original Fort Dearborn." *Chicago Tribune,* 5 March 1899, 1.

"Residence—$4,500." *Construction News* (Chicago) 35 (28 June 1913): 21.

"Residences, Flats, Etc." *Construction News* (Chicago) 12 (23 February 1901): 121–23.

Rhode Island Board of Agriculture. *Twentieth-Fifth Annual Report of the State Board of Agriculture Made to the General Assembly at Its January Session, 1910.* Providence, RI: E. L. Freeman, State Printers, 1910.

"The Richard W. Bock Sculpture Collection." Pamphlet. Greenville College, Greenville, Illinois.

Rieder, Joseph, and Wife [Justina]. To Anna Lloyd Wright, Warranty Deed. Vol. 30, 590, signed 10 April 1911, recorded 22 April 1911. Register of Deeds, County Court House, Iowa County, Dodgeville, Wisconsin.

"River Forest Women's Club." *Oak Leaves,* 10 February 1906.

Roberts, Isabel. Application for Membership, American Institute of Architects. 11 September 1921.

Robertson, Cheryl. *The Domestic Scene (1897–1927): George M. Niedecken, Interior Architect.* 2nd ed. Milwaukee: Milwaukee Art Museum, 2008.

———. *Frank Lloyd Wright and George Niedecken: Prairie School Collaborators.* Milwaukee: Milwaukee Art Museum, 1999.

———. "Mural Painting and the New Art." *Tiller* 1 (March–April 1983): 49.

Robinson, James Alexander. *The Life and Work of Harry Franklin Robinson, 1883–1959.* Hong Kong: Hilross Development, 1989.

Robinson, Sidney K. "Architectural Evolution of Unity Temple." Foreword to *The Noble Room: The Inspired Conception and Tumultuous Creation of Frank Lloyd Wright's Unity Temple,* by David M. Sokol. Oak Park, IL: Top Five Books, 2008.

Roseberry, C. J. *University of Illinois Directory for 1929.* Urbana-Champaign: University of Illinois, 1929.

Ruskin, John. *Seven Lamps of Architecture.* Sunnyside, Orpington, Kent: G. Allen, 1889.

Saint, Andrew. "Frank Lloyd Wright and Paul Mueller: The Architect and His Builder of Choice." *Architectural Research Quarterly* 7:2 (June 2003): 157–67.

Sanderson, Arlene. "Anniversary Recalls Significant Dates." *Wright Angles: Newsletter of the Frank Lloyd Wright Home and Studio* 14:4 (Fall 1988): n.p.

"Scholars' Conference: Summary of Adaptive Use and Restoration." 31 October 1977. FLWHSRC.

Schrenk, Lisa D. "The Frank Lloyd Wright Home and Studio Foundation Educational Programs: Number of People Reached Directly by Educational Programs." Ca. 1991. Copy at FLWHSRC.

———. Introduction to *Your Future Home.* Washington, DC: American Institute of Architects Press, 1992. v–xxiv.

Scott, Franklin W., ed. *The Semi-Centennial Alumni Record of the University of Illinois.* Chicago: R. R. Donnelly and Sons, 1918.

Scully, Vincent J., Jr. *The Shingle Style and The Stick Style: Architectural Theory and Design from Richardson to the Origins of Wright.* Rev. ed. New Haven, CT: Yale University Press, 1971.

Secrest, Meryle. *Frank Lloyd Wright: A Biography.* New York: Alfred A. Knopf, 1992.

"Selected Miscellany: In General." *Brickbuilder* 10 (January 1901): 17–21.

"Shepard, Clarence Erasmus." In *National Cyclopedia of American Biography,* vol. 40. New York: James T. White, 1955; repr., Ann Arbor, MI: University Microfilms, 1967.

Shimoda, Kikutaro. *"Ideal Architecture … Business Building … Barrack.…"* Tokyo: n.p., 1928.

Siry, Joseph M. "The Abraham Lincoln Center in Chicago." *JSAH* 50:3 (September 1991): 235–65.

———. "Frank Lloyd Wright's 'The Art and Craft of the Machine': Text and Context." In *The Education of the Architect,* edited by Martha Pollak. Cambridge, MA: MIT Press, 1997.

———. *Unity Temple: Frank Lloyd Wright and Architecture for a Liberal Religion.* New York: Cambridge University Press, 1996.

Sloan, Anne. "Homing In on the Heights: Residents and Developers Vie for the Heart of a Historic Houston Neighborhood." *American Bungalow* 68 (November 2010–February 2011): 68–81.

Smith, Nancy K. Morris, ed. "Letters, 1903–1906, by Charles E. White, Jr. from the Studio of Frank Lloyd Wright." *Journal of Architectural Education* 25 (Fall 1971): 104–12.

Sokol, David M. *The Noble Room: The Inspired Conception and Tumultuous Creation of Frank Lloyd Wright's Unity Temple.* Oak Park, IL: Top Five Books, 2008.

Spencer, Robert C., Jr. "The Work of Frank Lloyd Wright." *Architectural Review* (Boston) 7 (June 1900): 61–72.

"Spend Christmas Making 'Defense' of 'Sprit Hegira.'" *Chicago Tribune,* 26 December 1911, 1.

Sprague, Paul E. *Guide to Frank Lloyd Wright & Prairie School Architecture in Oak Park.* Chicago: Chicago Review Press, 1986.

Storrer, William A. *The Architecture of Frank Lloyd Wright: A Complete Catalogue.* 3rd ed. Chicago: University of Chicago Press, 2002.

———. *The Frank Lloyd Wright Companion.* Chicago: University of Chicago Press, 1993.

"Stoutly Defends Erring Husband." *Chicago Tribune,* 8 November 1909, sec. 1: 7.

Sturgis, Russell. "The Larkin Building in Buffalo." *Architectural Record* 23 (April 1908): 310–21.

"Successful Houses III." *House Beautiful* (15 February 1897): 64–69 plus plates.

Sullivan, Louis H. "What Is the Just Subordination, in Architecture Design, of Details to Mass?" Lecture presented 2 April 1887. In Louis H. Sullivan, *Kindergarten Chats and Other Writings* (New York: Dover Publications, 1968). 182–86.

———. "The Young Man and Architecture." *Inland Architect and News Record* 35 (June 1900): 38–40, 49. Reprinted in Louis H. Sullivan, *Kindergarten Chats and Other Writings,* 214–23. New York: Dover, 1968; and in *Louis Sullivan: The Public Papers,* edited by Robert Twombly. Chicago: University of Chicago Press, 1988. 131–144.

Summers, Maud. *First Reader.* New York: Frank D. Beattys, 1908.

"Synopsis of Building News." *Inland Architect and News Record* 23 (March 1894): 24.

Tafel, Edgar, ed. *About Wright: An Album of Recollections by Those Who Knew Frank Lloyd Wright.* New York: Wiley, 1993.

"Testimony of Paul P. Mueller, Testified in Court." In *Nine Commentaries of Frank Lloyd Wright,* edited by Edgar

Kaufmann Jr. Cambridge, MA: MIT Press for the Architectural History Foundation, 1989. 42–62.

Thorpe, John. "Wright Studies Outline: The Restoration and Adaptive Reuse of the Frank Lloyd Wright Home and Studio." 1990. FLWHSRC.

"Three Decades of Renovating Wright." *Wednesday Journal Special Section,* 31 March 2004.

"To Rent." Classified ad, *Oak Leaves,* 22 December 1938.

"Tobin, Arthur Collson." In *National Cyclopedia of American Biography,* vol. 33. New York: James T. White, 1947.

Tolles, Bryant Franklin, Jr. *Summer Cottages in the White Mountains: The Architecture of Leisure and Recreation, 1870 to 1930.* Hanover, NH: University Press of New England, 2000.

Trezevant, Bob. "Laying the Foundation for Historic Preservation: A Timeline, 1946–Present." *Wednesday Journal,* 25 November 2014, available at http://www.oakpark.com /News/Articles/11-25-2014/Laying-the-foundation-for -historic-preservation/.

"Trust Acquires Wright Home." *Preservation News* 15 (October 1975): 1–6.

Twombly, Robert C. *Frank Lloyd Wright: An Interpretive Biography.* New York: Harper and Row, 1973.

———. *Frank Lloyd Wright: His Life and His Architecture.* New York: John Wiley and Sons, 1979.

———. *Louis Sullivan: His Life and Work.* Chicago: University of Chicago Press, 1986.

———. *Louis Sullivan: The Public Papers.* Chicago: University of Chicago Press, 1988.

"Unity Club of Unity Church." *Oak Leaves,* 24 March 1906 12.

US Census Bureau. *1910 United States Federal Census.* 6 May 1910.

US Department of the Interior, National Park Service, Interagency Resources Division. "Guidelines for Evaluating and Documenting Traditional Cultural Properties," *National Register Bulletin* 38 (1985).

Van Rensselaer, Mariana Griswold. *Henry Hobson Richardson and His Work.* Boston: Houghton, Mifflin, 1888; repr., New York: Dover, 1969.

Van Zanten, David T. "The Early Work of Marion Mahony Griffin." *Prairie School Review* 3:2 (1966): 5–23.

———. "Frank Lloyd Wright's Kindergarten: Professional Practice and Sexual Roles." In *Architecture: A Place for Women,* edited by Ellen Perry Berkeley. Washington, DC: Smithsonian Institution Press, 1989. 55–61. Reprinted in *Not at Home: The Suppression of Domesticity in Modern Art and Architecture,* edited by Christopher Reed. London: Thames and Hudson, 1996. 92–97.

Vandewalker, Nina C. "Excerpt from the Kindergarten

in American Education, New York, 1908." In *Nine Commentaries of Frank Lloyd Wright*, edited by Edgar Kaufmann Jr. Cambridge, MA: MIT Press for the Architectural History Foundation, 1989. 7–18.

Venteicher, Wes. "Frank Lloyd Wright Home and Studio Celebrating 40 Years of Tours." *Oak Leaves*, 15 July 2014.

Vernon, Christopher. "Berlage in America: The Prairie School as 'The New American Architecture.'" In *The New Movement in the Netherlands, 1924–1936*, by Jan Molema. Rotterdam: 010 Publishers, 1996. 131–52.

———. "'Expressing Natural Conditions with Maximum Possibility': The American Landscape Art (1901–c.1912) of Walter Burley Griffin." *Journal of Garden History* 15:1 (1995): 19–47.

———. "Introduction to the Reprint Edition." In Wilhelm Miller, *The Prairie Spirit in Landscape Gardening* (1915), edited by Robin Karson. Amherst: University of Massachusetts Press / Library of American Landscape History, 2002. ix–xxx.

———. "John Blair, Landscape Gardening and the Prairie School." *Wright Angles: Newsletter of the Frank Lloyd Wright Home and Studio* 29:2 (2003): 3–7.

Village of Oak Park, Illinois, Permit Processing Department. Historical files (microfiche) for 951 Chicago Avenue, Oak Park, Illinois.

Von Holst, Hermann Valentin. *Modern American Homes*. Chicago: American Technical Society, 1912.

"Walter Burley Griffin." *Who's Who in America*. Chicago: A.N. Marquis, ca. 1917. 1003–4.

Weil, Zarine, ed. *Building a Legacy: The Restoration of Frank Lloyd Wright's Oak Park Home and Studio*. San Francisco: Pomegranate, 2001.

Weirick, James. "Marion Mahony at M.I.T." *Transition* 25 (Winter 1988): 48–54.

Wight, P.B. "H.H. Richardson." Obituary. *Inland Architect and Building News Record* 7 (May 1886): 59.

Williams, Charles. Interview by Norman Johnston and Hermann Pundt. Conversation #1, 7 August 1974. Architecture and Urban Planning Library, University of Washington Libraries.

Wilson, Richard Guy. "Chicago and the International Arts and Crafts Movements: Progressive and Conservative Tendencies." In *Chicago Architecture 1872–1922: Birth of a Metropolis*, edited by John Zukowsky. Munich: Prestel-Verlag, 1987. 209–27.

Wine, Lois. "Wright's Home Is Studio: Local Artists Make Over Frank Lloyd Wright Residence into Art Rendezvous." *Oak Leaves*, 6 January 1923.

Withey, Henry F., and Elsie R. Withey. *Biographical Dictionary of American Architects, Deceased*. Los Angeles: New Age, 1956.

"Wood in Architecture." *Progressive Architecture* 44 (June 1963): 110–15.

"Work of Frank Lloyd Wright—Its Influence." *Architectural Record* 18 (July 1905): 60–65.

"The Work of Guenzel and Drummond." *Western Architect* 21 (February 1915): 11–15, plates.

Wornall Homestead. "Our Homes." Available at http://www.wornallhomestead.org/our-homes/.

"Wright Divides Home to Protect His Soul." *Chicago Examiner*, 8 September 1911, 1.

Wright, Eric Lloyd. Foreword to *Building a Legacy: The Restoration of Frank Lloyd Wright's Oak Park Home and Studio*, edited by Zarine Weil. San Francisco: Pomegranate, 2001.

Wright, Frank Lloyd. *An American Architecture*. Edited by Edgar Kaufmann. New York: Horizon, 1955.

———. "Architecture and Music." *Saturday Review of Literature* 40 (28 September 1957): 72–73.

———. *Ausgeführte Bauten und Entwürfe von Frank Lloyd Wright*. Two folios. Berlin: Verlegt bei Ernst Wasmuth A.G., 1910; repr., Studies and Executed Buildings by Frank Lloyd Wright, New York: Rizzoli, 1986.

———. *An Autobiography*. 1st ed. London: Longmans, Green, 1932. Reprinted in *Frank Lloyd Wright Collected Writings*, vol. 2, *1930–32*, edited by Bruce Brooks Pfeiffer New York: Rizzoli, 1992. 102–382.

———. *An Autobiography*. 2nd ed. New York: Duell, Sloan and Pearce, 1943.

———. *An Autobiography*. 3rd ed. New York: Horizon Press, 1977.

———. Duplicate passport application. Issued 20 July 1910, American consulate, Rome. "United States, Passport Applications, 1795–1925." Images. FamilySearch, http://FamilySearch.org. National Archives and Records Administration, Washington, DC.

———. Frank Lloyd Wright: *Ausgeführte Bauten*. Berlin: Ernst Wasmuth A.-G., 1911.

———. *Frank Lloyd Wright Collected Writings*. 5 vols., edited by Bruce Brooks Pfeiffer. New York: Rizzoli, 1992.

———. *Hiroshige. An Exhibition of Colour Prints from the Collection of Frank Lloyd Wright*. Chicago: Art Institute of Chicago, 1906.

———. "In the Cause of Architecture." *Architectural Record* 23 (June 1908): 4, 155–221. Reprinted in *In the Cause of Architecture*, edited by Frederick Gutheim. New York: Architectural Record Books, 1975.

———. "In the Cause of Architecture, Second Paper: 'Style, Therefore, Will Be the Man, It Is His. Let His Forms Alone.'" *Architectural Record* 35 (May 1914): 405–413. Reprinted in *In the Cause of Architecture*, edited by Frederick Gutheim. New York: Architectural Record Books, 1975.

———. "In the Cause of Architecture, I: The Logic of the Plan." *Architectural Record* 63 (January 1928): 49–57. Reprinted in In the Cause of Architecture, edited by Frederick Gutheim. New York: Architectural Record Books, 1975.

———. Interview with Mike Wallace. *The Mike Wallace Interview Show*, CBS, 1 September 1957.

———. *The Japanese Print: An Interpretation*. Chicago: Ralph Fletcher Seymour, 1912. Rev. and enl. ed., New York: Horizon, 1967.

———. *The Natural House*. New York: Horizon Press, 1954.

———. *A Testament*. New York: Bramhall House, 1957.

———. *Two Lectures on Architecture*. Chicago: Art Institute of Chicago, 1931.

———. "The 'Village Bank' Series. V." *Brickbuilder* 10 (August 1901): 18–19.

"A Wright House on the Prairie." *Prairie School Review* 2:3 (1965): 5–19.

Wright, Lloyd. Radio broadcast. Bruce Radde's Radio Program, KPFA-FM (Berkeley, CA). In *Frank Lloyd Wright: Remembered*, edited by Patrick J. Meehan. Washington, DC: Preservation, 1991. 218–30.

Wright, John Lloyd. *My Father Who Is on Earth*. New York: G. P. Putnam's Sons, 1946.

Wright, Olgivanna. *The Shining Brow: Frank Lloyd Wright*. New York: Horizon, 1960.

"Wright Returns to Oak Park Wife." *Chicago Tribune*, 9 October 1910, 1.

Index